RACE AND ETHNICITY IN COMPARATIVE PERSPECTIVE

The National Political Science Review

Volume 7

THE NATIONAL POLITICAL SCIENCE REVIEW

EDITOR
Georgia A. Persons
Georgia Institute of Technology

ASSOCIATE EDITORS
Robert C. Smith
San Francisco State University
Cheryl M. Miller
University of Maryland-Baltimore County

BOOK REVIEW EDITOR
Paula D. McClain
University of Virginia

EDITORIAL BOARD

Nolan Jones
National Governors Association

William Daniels
Rochester Institute of Technology

Charles Hamilton
Columbia University

Lenneal Henderson
University of Baltimore

Mack Jones
Clark Atlanta University

Edmund Keller
University of California
Los Angeles

Mamie Locke
Hampton University

Susan MacManus
University of South Florida

Lois Moreland
Spelman College

William Nelson
Ohio State University College Park

David Covin
Sacramento State University

Charles E. Jones
Georgia State University

Michael Preston
University of Southern California

Wilbur Rich
Wellesley College

Joseph Stewart, Jr.
University of New Mexico

Linda Williams
University of Maryland

RACE AND ETHNICITY IN COMPARATIVE PERSPECTIVE

The National Political Science Review

Volume 7

Georgia A. Persons, Editor

Transaction Publishers
New Brunswick (U.S.A.) and London (U.K.)

Copyright © 1999 by Transaction Publishers, New Brunswick, New Jersey.

All rights reserved under International and Pan-American Copyright Conventions. No part of this book may be reproduced or transmitted in any form or by any means, electronic or mechanical, including photocopy, recording, or any information storage and retrieval system, without prior permission in writing from the publisher. All inquiries should be addressed to Transaction Publishers, Rutgers—The State University, 35 Berrue Circle, Piscataway, New Jersey 08854-8042.

This book is printed on acid-free paper that meets the American National Standard for Permanence of Paper for Printed Library Materials.

ISSN: 0896-629-X
ISBN: 0-7658-0435-2
Printed in the United States of America

Contents

Acknowledgments	ix
Editor's Introductory Note *Georgia A. Persons*	1

SYMPOSIUM: RACE AND ETHNICITY IN COMPARATIVE PERSPECTIVE

Politics and Social Change: The Demise of the African-American Ethnic Moment? *Georgia A. Persons*	3
African Immigrants in France: SOS Racisme vs. the National Front *Lorenzo Morris*	20
A Dream Deferred: The Abortive Efforts of the Parliamentary Black Caucus in Great Britain *Charles E. Jones*	37
Race, Class, Equal Opportunity Policies, and Local Government: The Case of Liverpool *William E. Nelson, Jr., and Gideon Ben-Tovim*	53
Racial Consciousness, Afro-Brazilian Electoral Strategies, and Regime Change in Brazil *Michael Mitchell*	64
Learning from Brazil's Unified Black Movement: Whither Goeth Black Nationalism? *David Covin*	84
Political Institutions, Agency, and Contingent Compromise: Understanding Democratic Consolidation and Reversal in Africa *Edmond J. Keller*	96

Pluralist Authoritarianism in Comparative Perspective:
White Supremacy, Male Supremacy, and Regime Classification 116
Ollie A. Johnson III

What is Ethnicity? A Comparative Analysis of Conflict
in Post-Communist Societies 137
Kathie Stromile Golden

AFRICAN-AMERICAN POLITICS IN CONSTANCY AND CHANGE

Thoreauvian Theater Impacting American Politics:
Martin Luther King's Media and His Leadership 154
Glenda Suber

The Recruitment of Blacks to State Courts of Last Resort 173
Nicholas O. Alozie

African-American Presidential Convention and Nomination
Politics: Alan Keyes in the 1996 Republican Presidential
Primaries and Convention 188
Hanes Walton, Jr., and Lester Spence

The Impact of Harold E. Ford, Sr.'s Endorsements
on Memphis Mayoral Elections, 1975–1991 210
Sharon D. Wright

American Civilization, Name Change, and
African-American Politics 221
S. N. Sangmpam

REFLECTIONS

Affirmative Action: What is the Question—Race or Oppression? 249
Mack H. Jones

BOOK FORUM

Review Essays

Politicians, Political Scientists, and Congressional Reform 259
William F. Connelly, Jr.

Conservatism, Extremism, and Ideology in a Post-Liberal Age 266
Euel Elliott

U. S. Foreign Policy in a Changing World:
Domestic Salience—Emerging Agenda 272
Karin Stanford

Book Reviews

Politics in Black and White: Race and Power in Los Angeles   281
reviewed by Ron Schmidt, Jr.

Real Choices/New Voices: The Case for Proportional
Representation Elections in the United States   283
reviewed by Kathleen Barber

Around the Cragged Hill: A Personal and Political Philosophy   286
reviewed by Sandra Gubin

The Presidency in a Separated System   288
reviewed by Randall Strahan

Abortion and American Politics   291
reviewed by Sharon D. Wright

Commodity Chains and Global Capitalism   293
reviewed by Herman Schwartz

Hemmed In: Responses to Africa's Economic Decline   295
reviewed by Margaret C. Lee

Making Common Sense of Japan   298
reviewed by Mayumi Itah

Mahatma Gandhi: Nonviolent Power in Action   301
reviewed by Sanjib Baruah

The Limits of Hobbesian Contractarianism   303
reviewed by Mark A. Graber

Values and Public Policy   306
reviewed by Steven Rhoads

When the Wall Came Down: Reactions to German Unification   308
reviewed by John S. Duffield

Invitation to the Scholarly Community   312

Acknowledgments

The Editor offers special thanks to Lenneal Henderson who, under an arrangement with the previous Editor, Matthew Holden, assisted in obtaining several of the manuscripts included in the symposium featured in this volume. Thanks also to Celia Grams, Georgia Institute of Technology for clerical and administrative support for this volume.

The Editor offers special thanks to Associate Editors Robert C. Smith and Cheryl M. Miller, and to numerous colleagues in the discipline who served as reviewers.

Editor's Introductory Note

In this issue of the National Political Science Review we engage the twin phenomena of race and ethnicity. In many parts of the world these two identity constructs are among the most powerful components of human and individual identity. Race and ethnicity frequently overlap with other major identity constructs such as religion and nationalism but generally surpass these constructs in influencing the social, economic, and political context of most societies and consequently structuring the life course of affected individuals. Although race and ethnicity are social constructs, they are frequently manifest in such pervasive and profound characteristics such that at times they appear to be immutably primordial. The articles in this volume engage the debates about the nature of ethnic identity and the dynamics that structure and alter its varied manifestations in different locales.

It is both analytically and practically useful to examine the issue of race and African-American identity within the context of comparative analyses of race and ethnicity. Doing so forces us to raise questions that are rarely if ever examined by scholars of African American politics, namely, whether African American racial/ethnic identity is ultimately a transitory phenomenon, and what are the consequences of its possible, or likely, transitory nature? These are the kinds of questions that emerge when we examine the African American experience in the United States as merely one variant of global ethno-racial conflicts A symposium focusing on race and ethnicity in comparative perspective is particularly timely given the approach of a new millennium which is universally defined as "the age of high technology and globalization." This appellation invokes varied images of advanced modernity, while ongoing experiences of racial and ethnic oppression and genocide stand in interesting juxtaposition. Globalization in its generic sense is not a new phenomenon. There have always been transnational explorations, trade and commerce, and migrations resulting in mixing and remixing of racial and ethnic demographics worldwide. What distinguishes the newer globalization is the cumulating impact of advanced technologies on this age old process, and the resulting gnawing intimacy of that which we now call the global village that is transforming and redefining the full range of human interactions. Underlying many of the articles in this volume are echoes of questions concerning the consequences of this new globalization for the identity constructs of race and ethnicity. It is hoped that questions provoked by this symposium will facilitate new paths of scholarly inquiry.

This volume also contains a collection of articles that add issues of race that are exclusive to the American context and the African American struggle for equality. Collectively, this set of articles reflects both the advances in the utility of racial identity as a political resource and the constraints imposed by race as a seemingly immutable discriminatory marker. It is hoped that this contradictory situation of constancy and change in regard to the African American predicament will also provoke new paths of scholarly inquiry.

Georgia A. Persons

Symposium: Race and Ethnicity in Comparative Perspective

Politics and Social Change: The Demise of the African-American Ethnic Moment?

Georgia A. Persons

Georgia Institute of Technology

This essay is driven by two sets of interwoven and interrelated concerns regarding both the theory and practice of that which we call black politics. The first set of concerns is best characterized by what one might euphemistically call "the malaise of black politics." This euphemism refers to the fact that both the study and practice of black politics in America has reached a state of seeming inertia. There is very little which is new in terms of theory building or engaging analyses on the part of scholars. In analyzing the practice of black politics, scholars are increasingly inclined to speak disparagingly and despairingly of a politics without meaning or strategic logic. We see a persistence and preponderance of studies which describe and analyze the racially tinged dynamics of electoral contests in which blacks figure prominently as candidates or as major voting blocs. Most of these studies are directed toward answering questions about the changing or unchanging tendencies of whites to, with a few exceptions, offer only limited support for black candidates or only limited support for black issues and concerns.

Some studies of electoral dynamics specifically focus on deracialization strategies, defined as the eschewing of issues and tactics that are explicitly designed to mobilize black voter support beyond expressions of racial solidarity based on the symbolism of black candidates in favor of an issue set and campaign tactics designed to appeal to white voters by embracing issues that tend towards neutrality in racial impact and which can be projected as embracing the greater interests of all voters independent of race. Such studies follow the same line of inquiry as the general set referred to above. Careful analysis of deracialization cases always return to questions of the issue set on which such campaigns are mounted and the relevance of these campaigns in supporting a purposive politics of black advancement.

In the main, studies limited to explicating racial dynamics in electoral contests have long ceased to inform, particularly in terms of theory building, and only offer the negligible contribution which keenly observant laypersons might assert without the benefit of presumably sophisticated analysis: that in spite of three decades of exposure to large numbers of black candidates, and in spite of adjustments in issues and tactics on the part of black candidates, that is, the adoption of strategies of deracialization, white voters, in the main, do not vote for black candidates in large numbers when there is a choice of a white candidate to support. This singular finding holds whether the unit of analysis is a mayoral race, a contest for governor, a campaign for Congress, the state legislature, city council, or school board. In the main, black electoral successes are by far disproportionately attributable to solid black voter support.

A major dimension of the malaise of black politics is evidenced by the fact that analysts of black politics, especially black analysts, endlessly lament what they see as the lack of purpose in black politics in actual practice. At the core of the lament is a recognition and assertion that black politics has lost its zeal and purpose, and yet the black predicament persists as one of social inequality for all blacks, significant economic disparities for most blacks, and economically dire straits for a disproportionate number of blacks. The once promising momentum provided by a highly charged socio-political movement and the expectations of a responsive environment in major policy-making bodies of the national government have eroded into memory and history. Indeed, the current lament is reinforced and made more poignant by analyses of the high tide of black politics, that is, the civil rights movement and its successor movement, the electoral-based "new black politics." Such analyses are nearly consistent in suggesting that the legacies of this extended mobilization are significantly disappointing and very much wanting. The most recent and noted analysis of this type is that by Robert C. Smith in his latest book which bears the very provocative title of *We Have No Leaders* (Smith, 1996).

Yet despite this lament and the recognition of a decided and seemingly irreversible change in the nature, thrust, and direction of black politics, analysts of black politics generally have not responded with a conceptual framework which takes account of this change. Yet major questions are raised by this situation. How do we understand this state of affairs? What does this situation convey about the limits of social and political change, and how might the lessons of this situation inform the practice of black politics in the future?

A second major set of concerns which drive the thrust of this essay has to do with how to merge effectively an informative and engaging discussion of the African-American predicament of race in the United States with considerations of ethnicity in comparative perspective. Any analytical or expository exploration of race and ethnicity in comparative perspective encounters both awkwardness and significant difficulties when considering the U.S. context and the situation of blacks in America. There is an almost universal tendency to say and think "race" when considering the situation of blacks in the United States. This is reasonable given the omnibus, though bogus, category of race that has been applied to peoples around the world and the continuing legacies of slavery that significantly define the black predicament in the United States. In the international context, when examining or explaining intergroup conflict, which appears to be defined by differences of basic group identity, analysts and lay persons alike are inclined to label such conflicts as ethnic-based conflicts, frequently so even when such conflicts also parallel demarcations along lines of skin color, or what we call race. In the United States one rarely hears use of the concept of ethnicity anymore though the concept was liberally applied to conflicts in the late 1800s and around the turn of the century. In the current period one sees liberal use of the concept of "minority group conflict" in reference to conflicts between blacks and other minorities, and use of the term racial conflict for conflicts between groups which are lumped together as blacks and whites. In the United States, the issue of race has, in the main, easily dwarfed issues of ethnicity for the past 100 years.

Yet from the perspective of scholarship and theory, important questions emerge in joint considerations of race and ethnicity. One compelling question that immediately arises is how does the situation of African Americans and the U.S. race problem fit within a comparative framework? How might the conceptual lens of ethnicity inform the African-American predicament? By predicament I refer to the persistent oppression of blacks as an identifiable group in American society and the persistent failure of varied strategic efforts to satisfactorily ameliorate or resolve that predicament. In terms of the practice of black politics, are there insights from the experiences and analyses of ethnicity as a social and political phenomenon which might inform the development of strategic considerations in the struggle for full social and political equality for African Americans?

The objectives of this essay are not to provide definitive answers to the questions raised to this point or other questions raised herein. Rather the objectives are more modest. A primary objective is to provoke reflection on the status and thrust of African-American politics by viewing them through the conceptual and analytical lens of ethnicity. Implicit, and sometimes explicit, in this discussion is the assertion that the conceptual framework of ethnicity elicits insights—especially those of a developmental perspective—which are not provided by the traditional analytical framework of race. A second objective of this essay is to provoke scholarly and practical discourse about African-American politics from a fresh, and perhaps controversial, perspective which might in turn lead to consideration of some of the issues raised and implied herein in a more structured research agenda. A considerable portion of this essay is devoted to the scholarly explication of the concept of identity, a discussion which is likely to be quite familiar to comparativists but less familiar to scholars of American politics. The focus then shifts to a discussion of the ethnic experience in America as a means of rounding out an analytical canvas against which to contemplate the evolving status of blacks in the United States and the state of black politics. In a sense the essay ends where it begins, by raising questions about what the current state of practical politics and scholarly considerations in African-American politics portend for the future of black America. In this regard the essay is admittedly incomplete, a condition imposed in part by the very nature of the questions raised herein.

How might we begin an analysis that facilitates consideration of the racial situation in the United States through the conceptual lens of ethnicity? First, we must consider that within the context of a global or comparative scanning of intergroup conflicts, which can be characterized as ethnic conflict or ethno-racial conflict, the African-American situation is merely one of a large set of ethnic-based conflicts that have been played out in varying degrees of hostility and abject inhumanity across space and over the span of history, and which persist to the present time. Indeed such conflicts are a constant, over time and across space. Although the specific groups involved vary from place to place and time to time, the phenomenon of ethnic or ethno-racial conflict appears a constant of the global human condition. In other words, that which we call a problem of race in America is but a variant of global, ethno-political conflict.

A crystallization of the argument which is posited here as evolving theory and which provides the context for considering the remainder of this essay may be stated as follows: Is there in effect an identifiable and relatively brief period in the socio-political history of an oppressed ethnic group when the group is able to utilize its ethnic identity as a primary resource to achieve optimum mobilization, reap maximum possible benefits from the host political system, after which the group experiences a phased demobilization when both the strengths and benefits of ethnic identity wane and eventually disappear? In other words, is there an "ethnic moment" in the life of oppressed ethnic groups when the group experiences some indeterminate level of successful political and social mobilization and empowerment after which the significance of ethnic identity in determining the political behavior of the group wanes and the strength of and attachment to the ethnic bond dissipates? The obvious follow-up questions are: Have we experienced the apogee of the African-American ethnic moment in the United States and might we now be well into experiencing the demise of the African-American ethnic moment? If so, what are the implications of this kind of socio-political life-cycle for the theory and practice of black politics?

Understanding the Ethnic Phenomenon

At any point in time there exists numerous open conflicts around the world which are fueled by ethnic differences. Death tolls mount in numbers which stagger and numb the mind. Like a migrating viral strain, the phenomenon of ethnic conflict occurs in what are seemingly random patterns in different settings across space, and appear endlessly over the span of time. As Harold Isaacs so poignantly described it, "Ishmael and Isaac clash and part in panic and retreat to their caves" (Isaacs, 1975: 3). From time to time analysts have calculated both the number of open ethnic conflicts and their accompanying death tolls. Some 7.5 million deaths have been attributed to ethnic conflicts between the end of World War II and 1968 in some two dozen conflicts (Isaacs, 1975: 3–4). More recently Ted Gurr identified some 233 groups worldwide who were, in 1990, experiencing either economic or political discrimination, or both, and who were potential candidates for open, warlike ethnic conflict or, who were already engaged in such conflicts. Other tallies have gone as high as 435 depending on the categorization scheme utilized and the time in which the tallies were taken (Gurr, 1993).

One might expect that a phenomenon of such universality and such serious consequences might be fully understood except that a review of the literature does not point to this conclusion. It is rather the case that the best scholarly explanations of the phenomenon of ethnicity are at once complementary, contradictory, and also confusing.

In regard to scholarship on ethnicity, analysts generally set forth two major explanations of its origins. The primordialist perspective views ethnicity as a basic group identity: "basic in that fundamental human attributes are passed down from one generation to another" (Isaacs, 1975). These "assumed givens of social existence" include blood and kinship connections, broadly shared ancestral ties, shared religion, language, historical experiences, common social mores, similar and distinguishing physical characteristics (Geertz, 1973; Isaacs, 1975).

According to this perspective, one is born into an identity which is not only significant but is frequently so intense as to appear immutable over time and across space. According to this view, ethnicity derives from a cultural interpretation of descent (Keyes, 1982) and though the strength of this bond varies widely from person to person and from society to society, these bonds are seen as emanating from an affinity that is more "natural and even spiritual" than other social bonds, such as social class, for example (Geertz, 1973; Stack, 1986). Ethnicity is seen as a basic individual and group identity which may wax and wane in intensity but yet remain as a persistent or permanent part of the individual attachment and group existence (Stack, 1986: 9).

The primordialist perspective embraces a strong socio-psychological dimension which bonds the individual to the group and which answers the profoundly fundamental question of "Who am I?" According to this view, ethnicity also serves as a basis for distinguishing the group at the level of "we" and differentiating the group from "the other." It is this latter manifestation of the meaning and significance of ethnicity as identity which forms the basis of irrational appeals and fuels the oppressive and genocidal tendencies ever present in human history.

While the primordialist perspective acknowledges changes in the relative intensity of ethnic identity over time and across space and different circumstances, it is the rigidity of the primordialist perspective in its focus on the persistence of ethnic identity which forms the basis of major challenges by the structuralist or instrumentalist perspective. In brief, the structuralist/instrumentalist perspective holds that ethnic identity is socially constructed without the necessity or prerequisite of deep cultural ties, and derives from objective intergroup differences in the distribution of economic resources and political authority. From this perspective, ethnicity is situational and is greatly influenced and determined by social contexts in which rights, opportunities, and the distribution of other resources are determined differentially by the rules of the game which prevail in a given social setting. Ethnicity then is one of many social identities such as social class upon which individuals may form bonds. Both ethnicity and social class, it is argued, are identities that are structurally determined, and thus are not only situational but also transitory. Ethnicity in this view is seen as a form of social identity which individuals adopt in the pursuit of self-interests and collective group interests and is defined in relation to distinct stimuli (Nagel and Olzak, 1982; Rothchild, 1981).

The structuralist/instrumentalist perspective holds that much of ethnic identity and resulting ethnic mobilizations stem from processes of modernization which bring different groups together in sustained, competitive interactions. In these situations, ethnicity emerges not as a natural tendency, but as a practical tendency which serves a particular social function directed towards advancing individual self-interest and collective group interests. Challengers argue that structuralist interpretations of ethnicity are embedded in the larger worldview of liberalism, which holds that "as mankind moved from a primitive, tribal stage of social organization to an advanced state of modernity undergirded by advanced industrialization, capitalist political economy, and the forces of globalization, such premodern and atavistic ties as ethnicity would recede in salience and even disappear" (Stack, 1986: 6; Smith, A., 1981). But as has been pointed out "the enlightenment project" has failed; postmodern society is not at all free of supposedly premodern and atavistic ties such as ethnicity.

The primordialist and structuralist perspectives stand at opposite ends of a continuum of explanations and analytical engagements of the phenomenon of ethnicity. What we might refer to here as some middle-ground perspectives help to account for the many questions that fertilize the analytical common ground between these two dominant perspectives. The merger of the two dominant perspectives appear in conceptualizations that focus more on the dimensions and manifestations of change in the strength of ethnic identity. These merger perspectives, referred to as ethnogenesis perspectives, hold that ethnicity is analogous to "a gyroscope which changes form, content, and boundaries over time, and which crystallizes in response to a range of political, social, economic, and cultural forces" (Keyes, 1982).

For the ethnogenesis perspectives, ethnicity in its many variants manifests a momentum which at times "veers toward assimilation and at other times leans toward more highly conscious differentiation," or stated another way, "swings from permeability and fluidity to intense ethnonationalism" (Smith, A., 1981; Stack, 1986). While these perspectives recognize the role and significance of external stimuli in generating and fueling ethnic identity and thus parallel structuralist perspectives, ethnogenesis perspectives also effectively assert the permanency of ethnicity as a more or less residual social formation that may be called forth to assume a forceful and salient position in individual identity and collective group behavior. Ethnogenesis perspectives parallel primordialist perspectives in arguing that it appears difficult, if not indeed wishful, to firmly assert that ethnicity as a significant factor in individual and group identity ever disappears in the sense that it becomes so irrelevant as to be essentially or effectively forgotten, or rendered largely impervious to effective appeals.

Part of the complexity of understanding ethnicity, particularly in some parts of the world, is its very close companionship with other forms of individual and group identity. For example, ethnicity in many settings is reinforced by other major formations of individual and or group identity, such as religion and nationalist identity. In some cases, ethnicity effectively exists coterminously with religion and/or nationalism such that the two are intertwined and effectively inseparable (Gellner, 1994; Smith, A., 1991; Ryan, 1990). While it is relatively easy to comprehend that religious identity is a social adaptation, it is much less readily comprehended that ethnic identity is similarly an adaptation, a mere social construction. Yet many analysts insist that ethnic identity like religious identity are both social constructs.

There are other conceptualizations of ethnicity that similarly constitute middle-range theories. For example, Ted Gurr somewhat sidesteps the primordialist versus structuralist dichotomy and debate by classifying all ethnic groups as communal groups. According to Gurr, communal groups are highly persistent, having antedated the emergence of the modern state system, and are destined to persist and re-emerge independent of the drawing and redrawing of nation-state boundaries. For Gurr, "communal groups are psychological communities: groups whose core members share a distinctive and enduring collective identity based on cultural traits and lifeways that matter to them and to others with whom they interact." Gurr identifies multiple bases for communal identity including shared historical experiences or myths, religious beliefs, language, ethnicity, region of residence, and sometimes customary occupations. We see significant elements of both the primordialist and structuralist perspectives within Gurr's conceptualization. Indeed, in his noted study of comparative communal groups, Gurr "assumes that all collective identities, whether centered on a communal group or a national state, are to a degree situational and transitory." Yet he does not totally embrace the extreme of this position, which regards all communal groups as merely one variation of transitory association created to pursue the material and political interests of the group members. However, Gurr does assert that the emergence of unity among ethnoclasses, such as Asian Americans, is the cumulative consequence of their treatment by dominant groups (Gurr, 1993).

Gurr is one of a few analysts who have included African Americans in globally comparative classification schemes of ethnic or communal groups. Gurr asserts a basic dichotomy between communal groups: national peoples and minority peoples. National peoples are defined as regionally concentrated groups that have lost their cultural and linguistic distinctiveness and want to protect or re-establish some degree of politically separate existence. In contrast, minority peoples are defined as having a defined socioeconomic or political status within a larger society—based on some combination of their ethnicity, immigrant origin, economic roles, and religion—and are concerned about protecting or improving that status. National peoples seek separation or autonomy from the states that rule them; minority peoples seek greater access or control (Gurr, 1993: 15). African Americans are further classified by Gurr as an example of an ethnoclass, distinct in their economic status within the broader society and persistent in their demands for more equitable treatment. The solidarity of ethnoclasses is presumed to be largely a function of their treatment by dominant groups. For Gurr, ethnoclasses differ sharply from other communal groups such as ethnonationalists who might be engaged in fighting a civil war or defending indigenous rights (Gurr, 1993).

Obviously the situation of African Americans somewhat straddles that of ethnonationalists in that they were once the subjects of a civil war, and for various brief moments in their political development, the urge for sectional, cultural, and political separation has been manifest at various levels of saliency. The key determinant of the current status and subsequent classification of African Americans among communal groups is the fact of major changes in the group's status which have been wrought via protest, public policy, and subsequent broad-based social change such that the level of oppression experienced by the group is frequently highly amorphous and generally less than egregious when compared with earlier experiences and conditions. Thus, within the context of theories of comparative communal groups, the status of African Americans as an ethnoclass in American society means that the strength of the ethnic bond between African Americans, while enduring, is not expected to have as firm a basis for persistent social and political mobilization as that of some other communal or ethnic groups.

In sum, how is it that we understand ethnicity? Ethnicity is a highly complex phenomenon and is manifest in myriad variations and complexities in different settings around the globe. Analysts seem to have arrived at general consensus on some major elements and characteristics of ethnicity:

1. Ethnicity emanates from within and among specific groups and has at its base an intentional inclusivity and deeply held sense of identity which has psychological, socio-cultural, and political dimensions.
2. Ethnicity is a form of basic human identity and is more enduring and more amenable to social and political manipulation than other social formations, such as social class.
3. Ethnicity at times appears to be primordial, or socially analogous to a genetically determined condition, however, it derives from a cultural interpretation of descent.
4. Ethnicity is a social construct that varies in its profundity under different circumstances. Ethnicity varies in intensity over time and thus is not fixed.
5. There is little support, theoretical or empirical, for the notion that ethnicity is a "pre-enlightenment" phenomenon that automatically disappears in the face of modernization.
6. Explanatory theories of how the demise of ethnic consciousness occurs are incomplete though various processes have been observed, and analysts agree that history is replete with evidence of the rise and fall of ethnic groups, and the complete demise of some ethnic groups.
7. Explanations of the demise of ethnic groups, through loss of ethnic consciousness or absence of identifiable physical presence include: (a) conquest and coerced assimilation; (b) immigration and eventual voluntary assimilation; (c) conquest and extinction; and (d) successful assimilation and extinction.

The American Ethnic Experience

If, comparatively speaking, African Americans comprise an ethnoclass as Gurr contends, then we might ask what has been the experience of other ethnoclass groups in the U.S. context and how might these patterns inform an assessment of the African American ethnoclass experience? There are, of course, some major differences between African Americans and other minority or ethnoclass groups in the United States. First, the intensity and level of oppression experienced by African Americans has no parallels among the experiences of other groups in the United States. Second, the enduring marker of skin color has not been a part of the ethnic experience of other groups. Both of these factors have at times been immutable obstacles that have at later times appeared to be at least marginally transcendent. The elusiveness of the menace of race needs no explanation here.

Despite the social and political preponderance of a racial divide in America, the nation has had an interestingly rich ethnic experience in which the place and status of multiple ethnic groups or ethnoclasses have evolved over time, and in which ethnic identity among different groups has waxed, waned, and seemingly dissipated as a salient factor in political behavior. In fact, in terms of political empowerment, one can readily identify an extended pattern of ethnoclass succession, of which blacks have been a part.

The main ethnic experience in America that has reached maturity has been that of the groups that are referred to collectively as white ethnics. Other groups have manifest a different and still evolving ethnic experience. For example, Asians have been present in the United States for an extended period of time and the diversity among this group has increased over time. However, their presence has only recently been translated into nascent political capital and we have not seen the use of the kind of ethno-racially based mobilization that has characterized black and Hispanic politics. In characterizing the Asian-American ethnic experience in the United States, one can reasonably argue that it is still evolving. One can make a similar argument about the still evolving Hispanic experience in the United States. Although Hispanics have increasingly utilized ethnic appeals in political mobilization (Kitano and Daniels, 1988).

The core of the American ethnic experience tracks back to: (1) the great wave of immigration that characterized the late 1800s and early 1900s; (2) the unfavorable treatment of these immigrants by the first settler group of white Anglo-Saxon Protestants; and (3) the emergence of majoritarian democracy in America. This specific time period was one of major social and political change. Structural changes expanded the franchise to all white males by elimination of the requirement of ownership of property as a requirement for voting. The adoption of the secret ballot led to the subsequent displacement of one social class group by other groups in the ranks of political leadership. The latter developments were facilitated by the emergence of ethnic voting in which individuals utilized ethnic group identity as the basis for political appeals and group mobilization. Ethnic voting quickly became a reliable mechanism for empowerment of immigrant groups, first by the Irish who also utilized a common religion as a reinforcing factor. The Irish Catholics were followed by Italians, Poles, Jews, and other groups. Robert Dahl characterized the phenomenon of ethnic-based appeals as such: "Any political leader who could help members of an ethnic group to overcome the handicaps and humiliations associated with their identity, who could increase the power, prestige, and income of an ethnic or religious outgroup, automatically had an effective strategy for earning support and loyalty" (Dahl, 1961: 33).

In the American ethnic experience, the expression of ethnicity in political form reflected the use of ethnicity as a practical mechanism for securing enhanced rewards from the political system. In terms of broad based sociopolitical change, a system of cumulative inequalities in which social status, education, wealth, and political influence were united in the same hands gave way to a system of dispersed inequalities in which different groups had access to different kinds of resources (Dahl, 1961). This confluence of structural changes, which made for a more egalitarian political environment, and social change, which made for a political climate that was generally more receptive to participation by out-groups, has been repeated over time in the United States. The result has been a succession of ethnic and racial groups including most recently African Americans and Hispanics who have taken their turn on the political stage. In the latter case, socio-political change and group succession have come as the result of social movement activity and protracted political struggle, which resulted in structural changes that facilitated political mobilization. However, the mobilizing political appeals have been racial and ethnic appeals, made easy by drawing on the stark contrasts in the social, economic, and political status between blacks and whites, with Hispanics having benefited from the policy advances extended to them in the aftermath of the civil rights movement.

Ethnic voting in America saw its apotheosis in the political machine that dominated big-city politics and heavily influenced national politics for decades. The political machine was undermined by the structural changes that were wrought by the Progressive Reform Movement of the early 1920s and that largely reflected a class-based backlash of middle-class WASPs (white Anglo-Saxon Protestants). However, also contributing to the demise of the political machine and the phenomenon of ethnic voting was the social and economic upward mobility of the white ethnic groups that formed the primary support base of these phenomena. In short, successful assimilation led to a diminished need for ethnic-based political support structures and a decline in ethnic political appeals and ethnic responses. While a total loss of ethnic identity in social and cultural dimensions has most likely not occurred, there does seem to have been a real demise in politically significant ethnic solidarity, which is operational on a sustained basis among white ethnic groups in America, with the possible exception of Jews. Jews in the United States form a primary support base for the struggle of Jews in Israel and, according to Gurr's definition, constitute a national people. Many American Jews are very closely identified with the Israeli struggle for a secure Jewish homeland and this is one factor that helps to reinforce their group identity. For other white ethnic groups who were merely "minority peoples" seeking to improve their social and economic status within the mainstream host society, the success of that struggle has resulted in a significant demise in ethnic identity and solidarity as a salient factor in political behavior.

Major analysts of the American ethnic experience in have always assumed that the significance of ethnic identity would wane over time, change forms, and largely persist as a residual effect on voting behavior. It was assumed that ethnic voting would evolve from its manifestation as a reflector of socioeconomic homogeneity within a given ethnic group to a later function as a means of achieving symbolic political representation in electing members of the group to political office by appealing to group members across all socioeconomic strata and to a final stage when the ethnic group became socioeconomically heterogeneous such that ethnic appeals alone would be insufficient to win votes (Dahl, 1961; Persons, 1991). One analyst states it in this way: "It seems likely that this will be the legacy of ethnic politics: when national origins are forgotten, the political allegiances formed in the days of ethnic salience will be reflected in the partisan choices of many totally assimilated descendants of the old immigrants" (Wolfinger, 1965).

What might we conclude about the American ethnic experience? We might easily make a compelling argument that "the ethnic moment" for white ethnic groups in the United States, with the possible exception of Jews, has flourished and passed largely because the external stimuli that buttressed such ethnic identity and solidarity have significantly waned. The U.S. ethnic experience has been one in which the place and status of multiple ethnic groups have evolved over time, in which ethnic identification among different groups has been strengthened as a response to hostile treatment by dominant groups, in which ethnic identity has been utilized as a political resource in exacting particularistic political and economic gains from the society, and in which, for many groups, ethnic identity has waxed, waned, and significantly dissipated if not disappeared.

In the main, the legacy of the ethnic experience in America has been a significant flavoring of the national culture and a significant though mainly temporary impact on the nation's politics. Ethnicity has not remained a persistent determinant of the nation's politics nor of the status of different groups. One might argue that the phenomenon of race has had a homogenizing effect on white ethnic identity in the United States, thereby weakening retention of politically connected ethnic identity. Or one might argue the structuralist perspective, that the need for ethnic-based mobilization among white ethnics no longer exists and therefore the level of ethnic identity has waned accordingly.

Incomplete Empowerment and the Issue of Effective Strategies

Clearly, the central question to which this essay points is whether the African-American ethnic moment has passed, or will pass in a manner similar to that of white ethnics in America and that of other ethnic groups around the world. Direct assessment of that question is beyond the objectives and scope of this essay. However, the question is powerfully suggestive of the need for exploring alternative explanatory paths in assessing the situation of post-civil rights black politics, and for contemplating the future state of black America. Much of the lament of post-civil rights black politics and thus the implicit and sometimes explicit explanation of the situation focuses on the issue of strategic failures in the sense of what are perceived as actually defective strategies or a failure to effectively achieve necessary strategy shifts. Indeed, it is worth noting that the focus on strategy has been central to both the scholarly analysis and actual practice of black politics. There has been a consistent focus on the benefits and limitations of identifiable and reasonably well developed strategies for political empowerment, and much of our understanding of black politics is built around an understanding of the significance and consequences of a given strategy in relation to others. Moreover, the significance of strategies, both for analysis and practice, is that they: demonstrate the operationalization of an ideological, philosophical, or strategic/tactical formation over time and its consequences; illumine the evolution and unfolding of specific forms of resource formation and mobilization and permit evaluation of the same; and permit assessment of the efficacy and limitations of specific strategies and attendant tactics.

Although analysts might disagree somewhat on the specifics and the order of the delineation below, there is general agreement that black politics after slavery has evolved along the following sequence of strategies:

1. Efforts on the part of "the race men" to effectively articulate the interests of the black race and thereby secure appreciation and respect for a viable course of sustainable economic and social pursuits for blacks as a separate race.
2. Efforts to establish and/or agree on an overarching political ideology that would anchor and direct the political, social, and economic development of the black race.
3. The convening of national conventions of black leaders over many decades in efforts to develop, agree on, and execute national strategies for the political uplift of the race.
4. Litigation-based efforts to secure basic citizenship and civil rights through the courts.
5. The civil rights movement and mass-based mobilization in protest actions to secure rights and public policy responses.
6. The new black electoral politics and the use of black voter mobilization to support black office holding and a desired institutionalization of black interests within the political system.
7. The leveraging and targeted delivery of black votes in presidential contests tied to demands for specific policy and programmatic benefits.
8. The pursuit of policy gains through a significant presence in policy-making institutions of national government.
9. A partial adoption of deracialization to expand black office holding beyond a constrained tether to black bloc voting in order to secure statewide office, and to increase the number of black elected officials.
10. An absence of strategy and an absence of effective organizational resources within the black community to deal with the black predicament.

The delineation of strategies is useful in that on reflection one observes that this series of strategies, though each might have been somewhat faulty in conceptualization and execution, promised and delivered some progress for the race, or at least a sense of forward movement in the struggle. Comprised of a seemingly reasonably ordered outlook and approach toward securing a better future for the race, this past stands in stark contrast to the major defining characteristics of the current period: a situation in which the notion of racial justice has lost its hold on the nation's consciousness; the absence of a compelling narrative of our future as a race, even at the rhyming, rhetorical level; and a sense that a long-standing embrace of the liberal-integrationist ideology now, in the face of persistent segregation in schools and residential patterns, looms large as a ghastly social chimera. Given this situation, is it reasonable to assume that "relief is just a strategy away"? If so, then what should be the next strategy; around what assumptions and goals should it be anchored?

In one of the most thorough and compelling analyses of black politics in the post-civil rights era, Robert C. Smith implicitly proffers that the civil rights movement was the quintessential effective strategy for black liberation. It is against this standard that Smith implicitly evaluates several lesser strategies—the leveraging of black votes in presidential elections and the pursuit of administrative appointments in the federal policy-making apparatus—which have been pursued in the wake of the civil rights movement. Smith reaches some strong conclusions in his analyses and I paraphrase them here: (1) black political organizations were not well suited to the demands of post-civil rights politics in America, not for pressing systemic responses and change, nor for sustaining an effective mobilization of the black community; (2) in regard to efforts to institutionalize an effective black presence and effective coalitional support for black interests in the institutions of government, such efforts in the post civil rights era have been woefully inadequate; (3) black political efforts have increasingly been caught up in a game between the Democratic and Republican parties, each of whom have sought to reap the benefits of black voter support without incurring the costs of courting that support; (4) that political, social, and economic gains in the post-civil rights era have been far less than satisfactory because the logic of civil rights legislation—upon which many such gains may have been supported—may well have run its course. Perhaps predictably, Smith calls for a return to effective strategy, for development of a mass mobilization for social change.

Perhaps because the past frequently looks more perfect than the present, in reflecting on past strategies one might conclude that the black political leadership has been reasonably astute in gauging the unfolding of change and circumstances such that they adapted reasonably well in engineering the shift from one strategy to another, that is, except for the current period. There is a general consensus among analysts and activists that black politics lost its anchor at the end of the civil rights movement, and there is a correspondingly implicit explanation that the cause was a defective strategy or defective strategy shift (Walters, 1980). Yet, there is no apparent recognition of how best to institute corrective action, nor any apparent sense of just what should be the thrust of the next strategy.

The contributions of the Robert Smith book are many, but its major contribution is the accomplishment of its stated purpose: providing an explication of how the American political system has processed black political demands in the post civil rights era. Smith refers to this as an assessment of the institutionalization of the civil rights movement. In engaging in this explication, Smith raises a critical question, indirectly and perhaps unwittingly, which continues to haunt this reader: whether by bringing the formal rules and procedures of political and social life into theoretical compliance with the dictates of racial justice, the American political system has reached the limits of its capacity for processing of the race problem beyond symbolic responses. If one gives serious consideration to this question, then the issue of effective strategies takes on a very different meaning.

The Long Pause: An Alternative Explanation

There are other scholarly conceptualizations that inform this discussion and one is particularly worth noting, work by Hanes Walton on what he terms the political context variable. Walton defines the political context in both macro-level and micro-level connotations. In its macro-level connotation, the political context encompasses the total political environment to include a particular time period and a particular place, and the convergence of political leadership dynamics, public sentiments on key issues, the nature of public discourse, and the kind of issues that dominate the public agenda. In its micro-level connotation, the political context may refer to a single key variable, such as race, which produces a contextual effect. Walton argues that the dynamic of race is co-directional in its contextual effect in that white behavior around race can influence black political behavior, and black presence in the physical environment as well as strong advocacy of black issue positions can have a strong effect on white voting behavior and political attitudes. In regard to the current period, Walton defines the changed political context as characterized by the revitalization of race as a wedge issue during the Reagan and Bush administrations and the resulting unfavorable change in the support, interpretation, and enforcement of public policies that had favored black equality and that were the legacies of the civil rights and Great Society eras of black political mobilization and Democratic party dominance (Walton, 1997).

The greater contribution of Walton's thinking to this discussion is his notion of serial contextual revolutions and corresponding counter-contextual revolutions. Walton sees contextual revolutions as total transformations of the socio-political environment in which politics occurs. He identifies two recent partisan driven contextual revolutions as having occurred during the Kennedy-Johnson years of 1960–1968, and that of the Reagan-Bush era that continues to define the current period. He identifies two counter-contextual revolutions that were launched by blacks as having occurred during the period 1800–1865 ensuing from actions at the state level to eliminate slavery and racial oppression, and during the 1950s and 1960s when the black struggle to end racial segregation ushered in social and legal support for desegregation. Walton concludes that blacks must continually seek to wage counter-contextual revolutions just to ensure and reestablish their constitutional and legal rights, and that blacks will continue to find novel responses to contextual transformation (Walton and Generett, 1997).

We can easily interpret Walton's argument to suggest that the current period is just another in a series of long pauses in which blacks must work towards a convergence of factors that will make for a political context, inevitable in its coming, which will be more favorable to black interests. The implications of this theory point to an implicit but strongly held assumption that underlies scholarship on black politics: that there will be continual progressive development in black political life leading to an ultimate goal of liberation. It should be pointed out that Walton's thoughts as presented and interpreted here are not part of an extended presentation of a theory of contextual revolutions and the scholarly community must await his full development of such a theory.

Politics and Social Change: After the Long Pause

Hanes Walton's analysis of contextual revolutions resonates with a consistent theme in American political history of a kind of periodicity or cyclical pattern in the formation of a temporally bound, but determinative socio-cultural ethos that forms the crucible out of which politics emerge and that shapes the bounds of that which is acceptable and possible within the political realm at any given time (Burnham, 1970; Huntington, 1981; Schlesinger, 1986). This phenomenon may also be subsumed under the conceptual rubric of social change. By social change I refer to broad-based change or evolution in public values, attitudes, and sentiments, which in turn have varying ramifications in all aspects of human existence, including changes in gender roles, family life, politics and culture, religion, civic life, scientific thinking, and more. Among the forces that spur broad-based social change are major technological developments; major economic change, especially changes in the nature of work; large-scale movements of human populations; natural and man-made disasters such as famine and war; and collective action such as social movements. Social change redefines expectations, values, and preferences, both individually and collectively, thereby transforming society. In reflecting on the evolution of the various strategies delineated earlier in this essay, one can discern some of the broad contours of social change that have undulated across time and altered the proximate contexts within which various strategies have been deployed. What may have appeared to be defective strategies may, on closer examination, yield insights into how strategies were overtaken or undermined by the forces of social change.

Analysts are much accustomed to focusing on how some dimensions of social change affect and alter the context of black life although one can easily argue that much more research in this vein is urgently needed. However, we have not focused much on how black life, in terms of behavioral manifestations, is shaped and altered by broad-based social change. Contemplation on a few questions will illumine this point. For example, it is easy to think of African-American identity as significantly primordially determined. However, to a non-negligible extent the identity of African Americans has been defined by the black-white racial bifurcation that has characterized American society. What will be the impact on black identity as that bifurcation breaks down? To state the question differently, how will a growing multicultural society affect African-American identity? We have recently seen that a gradual assimilation via interracial marriages has led to demands for non-racial or multi-racial identities on the U.S. Census by individuals who would have earlier accepted the heretofore inevitability of being labeled African-American (Cose, 1997).

What will be the long-term impact of a growing public discourse and much informal public policy that suggests an interchangeability of minority groups? Increasingly African Americans are being morphed into a generic category of minorities or people of color, suggestive of a kind of multicultural pacifism in which the disadvantaged status of blacks ceases to warrant a claim on national politics and public policy. We might contemplate the fact that African-American descendants of Generation X will have no links to the civil rights movement, neither in direct memory nor via direct connections of their parents to this defining moment in African-American life and identity.

The notion of the African-American ethno-racial moment in demise suggests that, due to major social change, the experience of blacks in America has reached a critical point of transition in which both the behavior of the larger political system towards blacks and the behavior of blacks as a group will manifest profound changes. There is inherent in the structuralist view of ethnic identity a co-directionality of behavior between the host political system and the ethnic group that is mutually re-enforcing. System behavior induces group behavior and group behavior induces system behavior, at least up to a certain point. The "certain point" is largely an unknown as analysts have little understanding of the life cycle of ethnic conflicts nor any meaningful cross-national understanding of the peaceful resolution of ethnic conflict. Peaceful resolution seems to occur within the context of ineluctable change with critical turning points and key variables being largely unidentifiable except as historical conjecture. Clearly one cannot argue with great confidence that we are indeed witnessing the demise of the African-American ethnic moment. We can only raise questions of whether there is something peculiarly different and extraordinarily meaningful about the nature of these times in regard to the future status of blacks in America, for African-American group identity, and for the theory and practice of black politics.

References

Burnham, Walter Dean. 1970. *Critical Elections and the Mainsprings of American Politics*. New York: Norton.
Cose, Ellis. 1997. "Census and the Complex Issue of Race." *Social Science and Modern Society*, 34, 6 (September/October): 9–13.
Dahl, Robert. 1961. *Who Governs? Democracy and Power in an American City*. New Haven: Yale University Press.
Geertz, Clifford, 1973. *The Interpretation of Cultures: Selected Essays*. New York: Basic Books.
Gellner, Ernest. 1994. *Encounters with Nationalism*. Cambridge, MA: Blackwell Publishers.
Gurr, Ted. 1993. *Minorities at Risk: A Global View of Ethnopolitical Conflicts*. Washington, DC: United States Institute of Peace.
Huntington, Samuel P. 1981. *American Politics: The Politics of Disharmony*. Cambridge, MA: Harvard University Press.
Isaacs, Harold. 1975. *Idols of the Tribe: Group Identity and Political Change*. New York: Harper and Row.
Keyes, Charles F. 1982. "The Dialectics of Ethnic Change." In *Ethnic Change*, ed. Charles F. Keyes. Seattle: University of Washington Press.
Kitano, Harry, and Roger Daniels. 1988. *Asian Americans: Emerging Minorities*. Englewood Cliffs, NJ: Prentice Hall.
Nagel, Joane, and Susan Olzak. 1982. "Ethnic Mobilization in New and Old States: An Extension of the Competition Model." *Social Problems*, 30, 2 (December): 122–37.
Persons, Georgia. 1991. "Politics and Changing Political Processes in Urban America." In *Contemporary Urban America*, ed. Marvel Lang. Lanham, MD: University Press of America.
Rothchild, Joseph. 1981. *Ethnopolitics: A Conceptual Framework*. New York: Columbia University Press.

Ryan, Stephen. 1990. *Ethnic Conflict and International Relations*. Brookfield, VT: Dartmouth Publishing Company.
Schlesinger, Arthur, Jr. 1986. *The Cycles of American History*. Boston: Houghton Mifflin.
Smith, Anthony. 1981. *The Ethnic Revival in the Modern World*. Cambridge: Cambridge University Press.
———. 1991. *National Identity*. Reno: University of Nevada Press.
Smith, Robert. 1996. *We Have No Leaders: African Americans in the Post-Civil Rights Era*. Albany: State University of New York Press.
Stack, John F., Jr. "Ethnic Mobilization in World Politics: The Primordial Challenge." In The Primordial Challenge: Ethnicity in the Contemporary World, ed. John F. Stack, Jr. Westport, CT: Greenwood, 1986.
Walters, Ronald. 1980. "The Challenge of Black Leadership: An Analysis of the Problem of Strategy Shift." *The Urban League Review*, 5 (Summer 1980): 77–88.
Walton, Hanes, Jr. "The Political Context Variable: The Transformation Politics of the Reagan, Bush, and Clinton Presidencies." In *African American Power and Politics*, ed. Hanes Walton, Jr., 9–32. New York: Columbia University Press, 1997.
Walton, Hanes, Jr., and William O. Generett, Jr. 1997. "African Americans, Political Context, and the Clinton Presidency: The Legacy of the Past in the Future." In *African American Power and Politics*, ed. Hanes Walton, Jr., 373–78.
Wolfinger, Raymond. "The Development and Persistence of Ethnic Voting." *American Political Science Review* 59 (1965): 896–908.

African Immigrants in France: SOS Racisme vs. the National Front

Lorenzo Morris

Howard University

At the close of a presidential election rally in the spring of 1995 a group of twenty or more demonstrators from the National Front of Jean-Marie Le Pen encountered a young Moroccan on the street. They beat him brutally, threw him in the Seine River and killed him. Why? Because he was not white and he looked North African. After more than a decade of heightened national attention to racism, one might have expected major political consequences, certainly immediate major national protests. While there were some protests, the election campaigns continued largely unaffected. Why is there so little chance that these protests will take on an institutionalized political form? And why, by contrast, is xenophobic politics so easily overlooked?

In fact, the National Front (FN for Front National) and Le Pen, having just won a historic electoral vote of 15 percent, emerged as the most strident of the political right next to the winning party of incoming president Jacques Chirac. It was politics as usual with xenophobia spreading below the surface. What happened to the pro-left leading protests, for which France is well-known, can best be understood by looking at the nontraditional forms of immigrant-related political debate.

In a 1986 anti-government protest in Paris, the only person to die was a North African college student. The student, an Algerian immigrant, gave his life on behalf of one or more of the many causes that thousands of high school and college students had distilled into a major public thrust against the forces of law and order defending the authority of the ministry of education. Yet, no one knew quite why that particular student had joined the protesters. He, like many others, might well have been inspired to join by SOS Racisme, a civil rights group of considerable influence in France. In contrast, however, that same year thousands of Algerian workers and long-term residents were threatened with deportation as a result of a new immigrant law. Although many protested the law, including the SOS Racisme (SOS-R) leadership, the organization as a whole never seemed able to mount the kind of intense public protest generated by the national education changes. Evidently, their leaders were willing to struggle over the deportation issue but incapable of making the issue a fundamental priority of the organization, much less one of the nation. If the right of African citizens of France to enjoy the full benefits of French society was to be fundamental, then the right of an African to remain in France was not. The first order of SOS-R's politics was to protect the African/Arab French. Any order of business relating to non-French people, though African or Arab, was therefore automatically second. A question remains for many observers as to whether assuming a place, however temporary, for Africans and Arabs in France does not conflict with that first priority. For the African French political leadership there is, therefore, a potential, if not immediate, conflict between the interests of African French citizens and the needs of Africans who merely reside in France.

"The right to be different," a vice president of SOS-R proclaims in the resonant tone of someone expounding a universal dictum, "leads to a difference of rights."[1] The affirmation through law or public policy of the distinctive cultures and customs of any racial ethnic group should be accordingly characterized as a latent threat to the rights and opportunities of all people who are different. The fact that he had in mind the African-Islamic contingent of second-generation French citizens places the statement at the center of a brewing political and ideological controversy. Because the leadership of his civil rights organization shares his views, it sets this, the largest of black African-Arab associations in France, at odds with several other pressure groups. This is unfortunate for SOS-R, which has been embattled from its beginnings with diverse interests and political parties. It is no longer just their primary opposition that they have annoyed. It is rather their presumed allies in the struggle for interracial equality and stability in France.

Yet, the primary opposition grows increasingly stronger in terms of policy influence, popularity, and local electoral office, specifically the National Front (FN for Front National) of Jean-Marie Le Pen. The Le Pen party not only opposes the legislative legitimation of cultural differences, it opposes the bulk of policy and legislative demands from people who are culturally different. The target of Le Pen's political crusade is the population of unambiguously African and Arab immigrants, even if his presumed nuances of xenophobia and racism have been subject to debate. By contrast, one might well expect similarly unambiguous preferences from SOS-R as it engages in a struggle for a firm place in the French ideological landscape. Instead, the opposite seems to have happened. In the face of the FN's extremism, the SOS-R has become more centrist and more compromising in its ideology and political goals. It would perhaps make political sense for SOS-R to soften its positions in search of the French political center of power. If its assimilation into an interest group structure of party politics were a certainty or even a possibility, a change of attitude would be quite logical. Yet, according to the claims of the leadership, that has not been happening; there are no party linkages and no partisan alliances.[2] Although there have apparently been some unannounced linkages with the Socialist party associates of François Mitterand, no major firm partisan base has been established. Thus, the explanation of the SOS-R behavior is more likely to reside in its own external struggle or in its own internal dilemmas.

The explanation for the centrist revolution of SOS-R, in contrast to that of other French anti-racist groups, it is hypothesized, emerges more from its internal weakness than from the pressures of its political or social environment. Specifically, ambiguities in its own ideological self-concepts, or what it means to be "different," have been tied to: (1) a retreat from African nationalism; (2) an emphasis on legalistic tactics and institutionalized forms of protest; and (3) a "francization" of the organization's structure and membership.

In what is often referred to as "the iron law of oligarchy," Robert Michels argues that organizations struggling with other groups tend toward hierarchy.[3] If that is generally true, as the acquired wisdom of political science suggests, it may not be true for unassimilated racial/ethnic interest groups. Rather, in the face of political assault from the xenophobic political right, some groups, such as SOS-R, respond by seeking to diversify their membership in terms of socioeconomic and political criteria. Thus, SOS-R has sought not only to expand its organization, it can be argued, but also to loosen the ideological and participatory constraints on its followers. It is perhaps consistent with Michels that the formal administrative procedures of SOS-R have tightened but still its political dimensions have opened up. At the same time (over more than a ten-year period since 1984), other African/Arab organizations have apparently become more "nationalistic" while SOS-R has become more French.

Nevertheless, SOS-R continues to struggle with its own ideological dilemma—one that it shares, in some sense, with civil rights groups in the United States, particularly the NAACP. To paraphrase the African-American expression of that dilemma, they might well ask themselves, as W. E. B. DuBois asked over a half-century ago: "Am I French, African, Arab or what? Must I cease to be one in order to survive? Or can I be both?"[4] In many ways his questions apply to French Africans today, although on the European side they are better understood as the answers, rather than the questions about assimilation. The primary political problems for French racial assimilation rests in the fact that appropriate questions have only begun to be articulated. Only recently have the French had to face the possibility that an enduring sense of racial and cultural consciousness might substantially impair the integration of Africans and Arabs into their once "homogenous" society. The real ideological ambiguity resides in their unsuccessful attempts to deny or reject the political forms of assimilation between the race-specific exclusion of an immigrant population and social integration.

Thesis and Antithesis: The Concomitant Growth of the National Front and SOS Racisme

Almost as striking as the concurrent emergence of the FN and SOS-R since 1984 are the differences in organizational structure and participation between the two. Although they both seek ultimately to appeal to the same centrist population with opposing ideological sentiments, their approaches and tactics are so different that they minimize direct political confrontation. This is not to say that violent "physical" confrontations have been minimal, but simply that they have not been systemic and structured.

Perhaps the most important structural difference is evident in the fact that the Le Pen organization emerged as a political party while SOS-R emerged as a social or protest movement. This difference is significant because it attenuates the image of Le Pen as an anomalous extremist in that the FN has adopted an institutionalized form and evolved through governmentally oriented channels. One might say that even when the FN is being unreasonable and xenophobic, the packaging of its arguments and the way they are presented generally adhere to quite reasonable traditions. SOS-R, on the other hand, has followed the untraditional path of a movement to an interest group without acquiring open partisan links. As a consequence, the methods SOS-R uses to present its positions are less traditional and more disturbing to the French electorate than the positions themselves. This suggests that the French political context was more disposed to Le Pen's appeals than early criticisms have suggested.

The Institutionalization of the National Front

In the decade since the FN's burst of electoral popularity in 1984 it has experienced some loss of popular appeal according to public opinion polls. At its lowest point, however, the joint popularity of Le Pen and his party never sunk below 15 percent of voters. Accordingly, *Le Monde* pollsters asked, "Are you in agreement with the ideas promoted by Le Pen and the National Front?" The affirmative answers reached as high as 30 percent in 1991.[5] Still, these proportions seemed to be well beyond the range of concrete electoral support, at least until the April 1995 presidential election.

The FN's acquisition of 11 percent of the total vote in the 1984 European Community elections suggests popular strength, but hardly electoral preponderance. Opinion polls, however, indicate a much greater sympathy for the party in the electorate on questions of immigration. A 1985 Le Figaro survey found, for example, that Le Pen was second only to François Mitterand in popular perceptions of his solutions to the immigration problem. Moreover, a near majority thought Le Pen expressed the latent sentiments of the French toward immigrants (effectively African-Arab immigrants):

The best solutions to the immigrant problem were proposed by:
  1. François Mitterand   20%
  2. Jean Marie Le Pen   15%
  3. Jacques Chirac   14%

As far as Jean Marie Le Pen and immigration issues are concerned, do you think:
  1. He says out loud what most of the French really believe 46%
  2. He takes positions which are unacceptable and which willfully make a caricature of the real situation 42%
  3. No opinion 12%

Source: *Le Figaro*, December 10, 1985 [6]

The latter responses also indicate a polarization of opinions on the FN on which SOS-R might be expected to capitalize. When SOS-R can seek out the electorate repelled by Le Pen, they cannot really draw on his weakness in part because of a second structured difference between the two organizations. The FN is structured like a mass-based political party with the potential for appeals to multiple interests, while SOS-R retains the structure of a protest organization varied only by its litigation and "educational" components. As a consequence, they cannot offer an electoral alternative nor support one.

Throughout the 1980s, the ideological center of French politics, though hard to define, was obviously somewhere just to the right of socialist François Mitterand and to the left of traditional liberal Jacques Chirac. That relegated SOS-R to the off-center left and Le Pen's National Front to the very off-center right. So far off-center was Le Pen from the beginning that the term "extremist" applied to him seemed more descriptive than depreciative. Yet, the applicability, and even the accuracy, of the term extremism depends on an ideological orientation that rejects fundamental compromise with the established political center. In this sense, Le Pen was more theoretically than substantively extremist. He not only courted the political center and its centrist politicians, he even moved toward an adaptation of their partisan styles. In retrospect, the FN looks more like a reluctant political movement that formed the cocoon of a nascent traditional political party.

Racial and immigration issues provided the basis for its extremist image and its movement flair. More important, however, race may have provided a deceptive disguise for rather standard partisan competition launched against an unimaginative partisan center. Racially sensitive and xenophobic politics thus gave a distinctive and defining ideological tenor to the FN's public image. Racial and nationalistic assertions effectively revitalized ideological debate in French politics (even though it may have narrowed the scope and depth of the debate).

Without the FN, Mitterand's Socialists, the RPR, and the UDF as well as other parties may have been ideologically less and less distinguishable. Also, the ideological tenor of the FN was essential protection against its dissolution into the backdrop of the multiparty system that defines the landscape of French politics. Unlike SOS-R with its inspiring leader and inspired following, the FN had a much more charismatic leader than one might have assumed given the nature of its following. It tended to attract an active partisan following from the other political parties, mostly but not exclusively, from the right. Without its leader's flair for audacity as well as faux pas, the FN would look like any other developing party. It was, of course, more hierarchically organized than most but perhaps less than others, for example George Marchais's Communist party.

The proof of FN's institutionalization in the French partisan spectrum resides in its electoral persistence, its increasing success, and its constituent diversity. Rather than fading into the ideologically decorative extremist backdrop of French Politics, Le Pen acquired 15 percent of the first round of the vote in the presidential elections of April 1995. That is just six points short of the first score of the eventual presidential winner Jacques Chirac. This strong showing has solid electoral roots.

The diversity of the FN electorate is hinted at by the surprising popularity it shares with Chirac's RPR party among the young voters in 1995. The FN's strongest support came from voters in the 25–34 age group. Its concentration of support among voters under 25 was exceeded only by the conservative RPR, which won 28 percent of their vote in the first round. In contrast, only 21 percent of this age group voted for the first round winner, Socialist Lionel Jospin.[7]

The fact is that Le Pen's party has expanded its appeal to some low-income sectors of the electorate to reinforce its stability. It won an impressive 35 percent of the vote among the unemployed.[8] It also continues to excel among industrialized area workers and, understandably, in areas experiencing high immigrant pressures. Effectively then, the party has become an integral part of the electoral mainstream in France while remaining ideologically extremist. In 1995, it found itself in a uniquely influential position to bring ideological pressures on the presidency of Jacques Chirac.

The Stabilization of the National Front vs. SOS Racisme

In other words, the FN started out with a radical ideological agenda constructed on a traditional political structure while SOS-R started with a radical political structure pushing an ideological agenda that had a strong rapport with the ideological center of the French party system. In fact, the relationship of SOS-R to the center of French politics reflects the logical rapport of party politics and civil rights claimants. Civil rights groups tend to undergo an ideological evolution toward the center while remaining structurally and behaviorally static.

The heightening or sharpening of ideological differences related to race among the party's constituents emerges from interviews with party leaders about racial and immigrant issues. In one of the interviews in which leaders of the major political parties responded to the same questions, the organizing role of ideology can be readily shown. The differences between party leaders are less significant in themselves than in the ways their audiences may transform them. Another major civil rights organization, France Plus, asked the six major presidential

candidates in 1988 the following questions: "Are the rights of citizenship and the rights of nationality the same? Do you make a distinction between being a French citizen and being a French national? If yes, which rights are different one from the other?"[9] To these questions François Mitterand summarily responded: "the immigrants in France who are legal residents can consider themselves at home, and they must be governed by the same rules as French workers. Equality of rights is very simply tied to equality of duties." In contrast, Jean Marie Le Pen responded to the same questions from a more partisan perspective. He said: "One of the high priority claims of the immigration lobby is to recognize 'residence' in France as effectively providing standing before the judicial system with the goal of institutionalizing a citizenship with rights...but without duties.... It is our consideration that there must be a perfect accord between citizenship and nationality."[10]

The primary issue raised in these questions concerns the privileges and protection of citizenship versus the more limiting privileges of legal residence and national identity. Both Mitterand and Le Pen seem to agree that citizenship can be earned by service to the nation and particularly by service to its economic interests. While Mitterand implies that French citizenship may become an obligation of the state to its long-term immigrant workers, Le Pen focuses on work and "duty" as prerequisites to citizenship. In practice and implementation, these differences would be more technical than ideological were the issues not forced into a broader context of interethnic and interracial party politics. Le Pen attacks the immigrant lobbies first, not so much because of their legislative or parliamentary influence, but rather because they are involved in party politics. He brings into question the legitimacy of any "foreign" representation in the French political process. More precisely, he assumes that any such immigrant participation will be deemed sociologically illegitimate by the electorate. He calls on the French voters' sense of their parliamentary traditions in which the cultural homogeneity of the interest group and lobby leadership was never in doubt. Although this argument clearly draws its strength from a xenophobic disposition, it is also clearly a call for traditional party legislative politics.

As a result, the primary question of immigrant status, including the regulation of residency and citizenship, was expanded into questions of both and race and partisan politics. Le Pen did not, and perhaps could not, allow his party to be drawn into a debate over policy implementation even when the questions were narrow. Rather, he exaggerated substantive disagreements through references to race/ethnicity while linking both to structural issues in party politics.

In contrast to the FN, SOS-R as an organization should be predisposed to ideological controversy because it was born as a protest group. Its membership base is presumably anti-establishment in origin. While its current composition will be discussed later, the starting point is important. Like the FN, SOS-R grew unevenly in terms of region. The FN emerged first in the industrial centers fearful of high levels of immigrant labor and in the South (and in some northern towns). SOS-R emerged first in Paris, and especially in its cultural and educational centers. The specific regional base is significant primarily because SOS-R, unlike the FN, had a singular regional appeal in the highly cosmopolitan areas like Paris and, to a lesser extent, Marseille. Perhaps more important, SOS-R grew largely around the upwardly mobile populations of students with some professional and skilled labor. In contrast, the FN, though originally based in the lower class, had a fairly broadly based socioeconomic constituency to start with. The failure of SOS-R to structure its tactics to encourage participation from less sophisticated segments of the population make it politically less competitive. In terms of moral and ideological appeals, however, SOS-R should certainly have the advantage in the land of "equality and fraternity."

Immigrant Issues and Policy Debates

"A hundred years ago, the idea of creating a statue of Liberty on French soil would never have occurred to anyone," observes population analyst Diane Pinto:

> The famous words of poetry by Emma Lazarus: "Give me your poor, your wretched" could only have applied to America which defined its essential self as a land of immigrants. France, by contrast, incarnated in its glorious and secular past as a nation-state has assimilated its numerous immigrants in silence as if it

were a peripheral and secondary phenomenon in relationship to the nation's real historic and cultural identity...an identity that was diligently codified and transmitted through the system of education.[11]

She may as well have added that the United States would never have had a Commission of Nationality propose a comprehensive "code" of nationality as happened in France. Not that the United States is less nationalistic than France, but rather that Americans are less disposed to opening their national identity to political or intellectual debates. Nor is the size of immigration an explanation because France has had a higher rate of immigration in many decades of the twentieth century than the United States.[12] Rather, the code of nationality debate was a symptom of the emerging racial and cultural conflict that SOS-R would confront in 1986 as its first major legislative issue.

The Code of Nationality Issue and the Fear of Immigrants

The code of nationality debate was a mobilizing crisis for SOS-R, according to its leaders.[13] As proposed in 1986, the code of nationality would impose several constraints on the acquisition of French citizenship. Of particular concern to SOS-R was the provision requiring all children (of immigrants) to have lived in France for five years in order to be eligible for citizenship. Criticizing a public commission report on the code, Harlem Desir, president of SOS-R, said "this was the hour of truth" for French integrity on race. He added, "all children born on French soil are French, unless they refused the option."[14] A member of that commission, the Commission des Sages, responded: "If we accept such a proposal, tomorrow chartered planes of pregnant women coming from the entire world will be arriving to deliver their babies at Orly airport."[15] This conflict was aggravated by the intrusion of the FN. In the spring of 1987, for example, the FN held a rally of 15,000 people under the theme "to be French has to be merited."[16] While the code may have been conceived as legal adjustment to a 1974 law closing off general immigration, it quickly took on racial and xenophobic overtones.

The Perceived Immigrant Threat

Accordingly, the debate over the legal definition of nationality opened more widely the door to legally sanctioned anti-immigrant government practices. Restricted access to public resources and services in France for immigrants was complemented by dramatic efforts to expel more non-permanent residents. At the same time, the number of school-age foreigners denied admission to public school increased from 51,000 rejections in 1986 to 71,000 in 1987. Similarly, the number of immigrants led across the French borders more than doubled in the two-year period between 1985 and 1987 from 7,000 expulsions to almost 16,000 expulsions.[17]

Those expulsions were a direct result of the Pasqua Law as well as a natural long-term consequence of the French preoccupation with codifying their sense of national belonging. The law eliminated the protection of immigrants by a judicial commission empowered under previous law (the Questiaux

Law, 1981) to pass judgment on proposed expulsions. As a consequence of the Pasqua Law, immigrants of less than three years residency whom the prefect deems a "threat to public order" can be summarily expelled without judicial recourse.[18] From a nationalist frame of mind, in which one seeks to identify and reassert the nation's self-defining characteristics of good French citizenship, unemployment and homelessness might well be considered by the police as evidence of a threat to the viability of French society. While most prosperous nations restrict entry on the basis of social order, the French concern for the manner and extent of assimilation into the larger, presumably homogeneous, society makes those restrictions more demanding.

The politically responsive softening of immigration law in 1989 through the Joxe Law nevertheless served to reinforce the emphasis on national identity. The Joxe law permits judicial recourse for those targeted for expulsion. There was a public image proliferated in the national media and carried in the international media of immigrants being uprooted and forced across the border into lives of economic uncertainty and renewed deprivation. A concern for human rights, or at least the media image of such concern, may well have necessitated a rewriting of the immigrant residency requirements. Humanitarian concerns notwithstanding the criteria for the successful recourse to judicial intervention still depend on the immigrant's level of economic and cultural integration. If the undocumented immigrant has not secured a place of employment in the French economy and does not fit in culturally, there is no effective recourse from expulsion. In effect, therefore, the law reinforced the intent of the code of nationality to define some forms of behavior or life styles as legitimately French and others as unacceptably non-French. The threat to French traditions was, therefore, a persistent factor in political arguments over immigration law.

Conveniently enough, those traditions have held well enough to permit the selection with popular support of Charles Pasqua, the author of the most restrictive immigration legislation in France, to head the ministry in charge of immigration. Ironically, he became a spokesperson for the rather moderate UDF presidential candidate in 1995. Pasqua's immigration politics had not evolved, but the ideological center of French politics had been pushed further to the right by Le Pen.

If immigration is economically useful, as it has been historically in France, then it follows that periods of economic retrenchment tend to breed hostility to it.[19] By 1974, the public apparently saw no continuing economic justification for it. Although legal barriers did not stop high levels of illegal immigration, the law clearly reduced employment possibilities for unskilled immigrant labor. In the 1980s resident immigrant labor declined by about two-thirds. Family immigration also declined sharply. Only the proportion of political refugees grew, as shown in Table 1.

The cultural, rather than racial, implications of anti-immigration policy in the 1970s and 1980s is indicated by the uneven impact of the restrictions on Algerian versus other immigrants. In 1973, Algerians were the largest group of immigrants and by 1985, they were clearly second to the Portuguese (see Table 2). Algerians have clearly been the object of special prejudice in France given their special historical access and greater numbers. In fact, a policy favoring the restriction of Algerian immigration and, in contrast, the en-

Table 1
Change in Immigrant Labor in France 1981–1986

Year	Permanent Labor	Family Immigration	Political Refugees
1981	33,433	41,560	7,000
1982	96,962	47,366	13,000
1983	18,483	45,731	14,000
1984	11,804	39,586	16,000
1985	10,959	32,512	21,000
1986	11,300	28,000	30,000

Source: La Croix (Jan. 9, 1988)

Table 2
Distribution of Selected Immigrant Groups in France

Country	1973	1981	1985
Western European	2,053,000	1,746,000	1,518,000
Moroccan	270,000	444,000	559,000
Polish	91,000	66,000	60,000
Portuguese	812,000	839,000	846,000
Tunisian	149,000	193,000	226,000
Turkish	45,000	118,000	154,000
Yugoslavian	79,000	68,000	66,000

Source: Le Quotidien (Jan. 8, 1988)

couragement of Moroccan, Portuguese, and Yugoslavian was publicly proposed in 1962.[20] As some studies of prejudice have suggested, proximity can breed contempt when the conditions of interaction for two groups involve substantial socioeconomic and cultural dissimilarities.

It is equally likely that the greater numbers and visibly slow assimilation of Algerian immigrants in France have generated a set of mutual cultural and political barriers against openness to new immigrants. Clearly, there is some hesitancy on the part of Algerians to pursue their own immersion into a French national identity. As evidence, Algerians are statistically much less inclined to formally request French citizenship than are long-term residents of other nationalities.

That their lack of assimilation is beyond their singular control and is, in part, subject to racial or cultural bias, is indicated by the generally low rates with which Muslim African residents acquire French citizenship. Of the ten immigrant groups shown in Table 2, Africans (Algerians, Moroccans, and Tunisians) constituted 44 percent in 1985. Yet their rate of citizenship acquisition was minuscule in comparison to their proportion. In 1982, only 12 percent of the newly nationalized French citizens were of African origin as against 80 percent of those of European descent.[21]

The significance of the cultural problem that SOS-R must face is expressed by the even greater imbalance among Africans acquiring citizenship. Less than 14 percent of the Africans nationalized in Paris, according to one study,

Table 3
Origins of Aliens in France by Nationality

Country of Origin	Acquired Citizenship		Non Citizen		Total	
	% down	% across	% down	% across	% down	% across
Algerian	5.5	13.5	21.9	86.5	15.5	100
Moroccan	5.1	47.2	3.9	52.8	4.5	100
Tunisian	12.6	60.6	5.2	39.4	8.0	100
Other African	3.3	75.2	1.3	24.8	1.7	100
Number	115,000		188,000		298,000	

Source: C. Bonvalet (1987) p. 236.

were Algerian (see Table 3), and yet they make up the majority of African immigrants.[22] The significance of this imbalance goes beyond discrimination inasmuch as Algerians are disproportionately inclined to reject citizenship after passing the ten-year residency threshold. This may well be because they, as a group, are more familiar than most with the difficulties of integrating into French society. In surveys, they explain that they only came to make money and return home, but they rarely do. They rarely make enough money. The more likely explanation is that they feel unwelcome.

Their discomfort has both a socioeconomic and cultural basis. Yet, their political organizations have difficulty addressing these problems. SOS-R has focused on socioeconomic inequality but as for cultural differences, it says, in effect, that no one can be guaranteed "the right to be different." Thus, SOS-R has done little to promote African immigration beyond opposition to the code.

An apparent justification for some reserve on the part of SOS-R in the encouragement of immigration comes from the composition of its active supporters. Not only are the clear majority of its supporters French by birth, the majority of its members of North African extraction are second- or third-generation French. As a result, the political orientation of its members is more likely to be directed toward the "ethnic" French than toward people with only a tenuous relationship to French identity. Among second-generation French Arabs, colloquially known as Beurs, there is considerable ambiguity about the traditions and values that immigrants reinforce. Beur girls in high school, for example, face critical personal conflicts in adapting to the fundamentally secular life styles required in French schools and yet abhorred by most of their fathers. The fact that they often excel over Beur boys in school is evidence that French culture has a "liberating" value for them.[23]

Still, at many levels the Beurs share a community of political interests with recent immigrants. On virtually all issues their politics are to the left of the French majority. One study found that about 47 percent voted Socialist and another 26 percent voted Communist or other extreme left party in 1988.[24] Not only do they share their left leanings with immigrants, they also share areas of concentration in terms of residence and some social economic conditions. For example, the city of Marseille in the south of France has one of the highest concentration of Beurs and immigrants in the country.

Socioeconomic Issues and Pressure Politics

In terms of socioeconomic factors, there is a strange kind of international rapport among western blacks in the diaspora. In living conditions, income, occupational status, education, and housing, blacks in the United States and France are similarly on the bottom. For example, the majority of the prison population in the United States is black, although blacks are an overwhelming minority of the total population. In several districts in France, ironically, blacks are also the majority of the prison population, though they are an even smaller minority.[25] For the majority of young immigrants, one study observes in a similar vein, "police and judges embody the racism and discrimination of [which African immigrants] feel they are the victims."[26]

Many, if not most, French politicians will say that there are very few ghettos in France and yet many districts on the outskirts of Paris and Marseille call to mind Harlem, New York. On the other hand, there has been a comparatively pronounced commitment to preventing ghettos in French politics since the 1950s. At most, only about 4 percent of the French population is of African or Arab origin, and yet their regional concentration frequently produces proportions of 15 percent or more. On the community levels, blacks are frequently the large plurality of residents. The public housing projects (called HLMs) are increasingly African and Arab. According to a government-sponsored study of discrimination, four times as many immigrants live in substandard housing as citizens.[27]

The French government has committed its agencies to preventing housing segregation with some success. One public agency, the Fund for Social Action (FAS), provided a variety of grants to local communities and immigrant groups for the express purpose of impending "cultural and social" isolation. After 1986, however, it indirectly subsidized the projects of the Office of International Migration, which has sent established African residents back to Africa.[28]

Ironically, the Fund subsidized several of the immigrant associations created since 1981. This kind of culturally sensitive government initiative apparently left SOS-R without a clear political agenda on housing. On the one hand, it made immigration a secondary interest. On the other hand, it could only attack housing policy at the risk of alienating a possible ally of immigrant associations as well as potential supporters of their own interests.

Employment discrimination is illegal in France as it is in the United States.[29] In other words, it is widespread. On direct racial or ethnic grounds, there may be less discrimination in France because of the prior economic disadvantage of first- and second-generation African-French. In this regard, public agencies helped French businesses recruit unskilled North African labor through the first half of the twentieth century.[30] Today, as always, immigrants belong to the most vulnerable category of workers. About 9 percent (1.6 million people) in the French job market are foreigners.[31]

In the early 1960s an Arab-French labor association, Movement des Travailleurs Arabes (MTA), led a hunger strike across France.[32] Given its modest impact, the hunger strike was probably ill-conceived, if not ill-considered, in terms of French culture. Just as a hunger strike hardly fits in French labor tradition, racial ethnic protest has not been very effective. In some part, protest may be weak because effective protest may require a substantial degree of social integration. In large part, however, African immigrants have been deprived of effective leadership because they include very few professionals. While data on this point is scant, North Africans in France have less than 1 percent of their number in the well-paid professions.[33] Perhaps more significant, politically, the second-generation blacks in France constitute nearly all the black professionals but they are less interested in immigration.

How SOS-R has addressed this issue is reflected through its concern with education. Specifically, it has focused its attention more on the preparation of future generations than on immediate employment inequality. Concern with the future is, of course, quite understandable for a group composed of youthful members but age is only a partial explanation. Other African-oriented pressure groups have placed a greater emphasis on employment discrimination, leaving SOS-R a competitive edge only in the more middle-class political terrain.

In French education, there are striking differences in attainment based on social class without regard to race. For example, 50 percent of the children of professionals had received high school diplomas at a "normal" age by 1984 as opposed to 11 percent of unskilled workers.[34] By this standard, blacks fared reasonably or very well, since black children of the upper classes succeed as well in school as white French according to a 1983 report of the Ministry of Education.[35] Still, no more than 10 percent fall into this category. The vast majority of Africans, however, succeed less well in school than their traditional French counterparts.

A politically significant reason for the inequality in education attainment beyond social class resides in culture, language, and religion. The 1989 protest of four Muslim French girls who insisted on wearing veils against school regulations is expressive of SOS-R political dilemma. Given France's secular tradition, the imposition of religious deference on public functions creates a disruption in itself. The presence of a "foreign" religion is still more disruptive. The response of SOS-R to this problem has been to call for unofficial and extracurricular acceptance of Moslem differences in school (interviews). It has, however, supported secularism. In addition, it calls for some recognition of and instruction in Arabic language, but it insists that French must be the language of education. How SOS-R arrives at these kinds of positions on social issues can be explored through a look at its membership structure.

The Structure of Membership in SOS Racisme

In terms of its membership, SOS-R had to be mobilized by the code on nationality debate because a substantial proportion of its claimed 17,000 membership is made of long-term non-citizen French residents. In particular, that includes African/Arab students born or raised in France. Similarly, it was virtually compelled to protest the 1986 Pasqua law which encouraged the voluntary deportation of immigrants. It was compelled first because of the implicit racism of the law that ran directly counter to the founding principles of SOS-R. Second, it was compelled to preserve its credibility as the primary representative of African residents of France, which the controversy put at risk. For as much as its interests were at stake, however, the protests of

SOS-R seem relatively mild when compared to its persistent objections to the code of nationality. Even when compared to the intensity of its concerns with French public schooling, one has to wonder where the heart of the organization lies. Is its primary ideological commitment to the protection of racial minorities in France and only coincidentally to anyone else? It may well be that undocumented workers and the unemployed African immigrants in France have become a political inconvenience, if not a political liability, for SOS-R. In this regard, it looks more like a traditional interest group and less like a protest organization.

In large part, the sociological composition of SOS-R's membership helps to explain its ideological anomalies. The increasing institutionalization of its constituency, in terms of schooling, public service dependence, and public sector employment, seems to correspond to a sense of distance from recent immigrants as well as a greater identification with French institutions, if not with the French themselves. Apparently, a large majority of the SOS-R membership can be considered middle-class and only a quarter of it described as lower-class.[36] In terms of residential and schooling patterns, therefore, SOS-R members and African immigrants may well occupy much of the same space, but their specific experiences and basic access to opportunities are likely to be quite different.

About 50 percent of SOS-R members are college or high school students. At least 60 percent come from middle-class families (interviews). Approximately 40 percent are attending or have attended a university. It is less surprising, therefore, that their leaders claim that racial discrimination is only a problem at the university level in education.

The organization's hesitancy to confront the immigration issue, per se, as one of its primary objectives is also reflected in its members, who are at most 10 percent immigrants. Approximately 30 percent are second-generation. The rest are a mixture of French ethnics and "français de souche" (indigenous French). Moreover, its local leadership seems to have aged faster than its membership. SOS-R continues to recruit effectively among high school students. Thus, the average age of the membership is 18 to 19 years old. The average age of the local committee chairs and the national council members, however, is much older ranging from 25 to 35 years old.[37] As a result, the leadership is more heavily socialized in French traditions than much of the African following. The youthful rank and file, on the other hand, is tied by multiple institutional constraints including school. These constraints would tend to encourage protest against the lack of institutional assimilation rather than toward greater separation. The militancy of SOS-R's protest against racism is, therefore, an indirect expression of the membership's sense of inclusion in French institutions.

On housing and community issues, there are comparable membership bases. About 30 percent are from Paris, where there is also a high immigrant concentration. A surprising 45 percent, however, are from small- and medium-sized towns where immigrant concentrations are low (interviews). The organization is composed of approximately three hundred local, quasi-independent committees spread across about a hundred towns.[38]

Similarly, for employment and educational issues, the composition of SOS-R presages its politics. At least 90 percent of immigrants are in semi-skilled and unskilled labor, while almost half of SOS-R members are skilled laborers, students, or professionals.

When SOS-R launched its influential anti-racism campaign with the slogan, "Don't Bother My Buddy" (Touche pas a mon pote), its leaders may not have given much thought to how relatively well off their friends were compared to others of African descent in France.

Conclusion

In an article on SOS-R, François Dubet raises an interesting question. He comments: "SOS Racisme, by its name alone, presents itself as a protest essentially defined by what it protests. But can SOS Racisme remain a pure and simple movement oriented toward public opinion? Doesn't it risk its own fairly rapid self dilution? Doesn't it stimulate too much ambiguity in its impact?"[39] When these questions were posed to an SOS-R vice president, he responded that "we pay the price of our own success." In part, that is probably true, but their success would be almost impossible to measure. Their ideological goals are essentially affirmations of what French society has long claimed to be, namely egalitarian. Their specific policy and goals, as with the code of nationality, have been conflictual but their methods have not. They leave the field of political articulation and implementation open to the political parties from which they structurally distance themselves. In effect, they succeed by a political persuasion and influence impossible to measure. At the same time, they concede an important part of the political field, electoral politics, to their hostile opposition. The National Front of Le Pen as well as the Club d'Horlage (an ideologically similar group) are thus structurally better suited to promote public policy.

Perhaps more significant, their real success may have preceded rather than followed their activism. Rather than organizational victories on the political field, one could say they have succeeded through the individual successes of their members and supporters. Specifically, the SOS-R adherents are enormously better off than the African/Arab community they seek to promote. On all socio-economic criteria, they are substantially more assimilated than the rest of their racial/ethnic groups. When they reject cultural differentiation, they are also rejecting that part of their own heritage from which they are more distant than other Africans/Arabs in France. Yet, a fundamental claim of the organization on public opinion and political leadership resides in these kinds of differences. They want to legitimate their cultural interests, almost ex post facto, and yet they do not seek to perpetuate them in law or in government structures. Here is their dilemma: they promote the status of people who are different but they reject the right to be different.

Notes

Unless otherwise indicated, all references to statements of SOS Racisme leaders are based on a series of interviews conducted at its Paris headquarters in July 1989. All English translations from French language sources are the author's own and, therefore, are subject to imperfection.

The author wishes to express his gratitude to the Center for Documentation of the Ecole Nationale d'Administration in Paris for its documentation assistance and to the Center for Urban Progress at Howard University for its support. He is also grateful to Clarence Lusane and Maurice Carney of Howard University for their research assistance.

1. I conducted interviews with a small number of SOS Racisme officers and members at the organization's national headquarters in the summer of 1989, originally in French.
2. Conclusion drawn directly from statements of SOS-R national officers.
3. Robert Michels, *Political Parties* (New York: Dover Publications, 1959), 42.
4. William E. B. DuBois, *The Souls of Black Folks* (New York: Fawcett Publications), 16–17.
5. *Le Monde* (February 4, 1994): 8.
6. "Immigration: un probleme clé," *Le Figaro* (December 1985): 7, based on opinion of SOFRES.
7. *L'Expres* (May 4, 1995): 12–15.
8. Ibid.
9. *Liberation* (April 22, 1988): 18–21.
10. Ibid.
11. Diane Pinto, "Immigration: l'ambiguité de la reference americaine," *Pouvoirs*, 47 (1988): 93.
12. Sophie Body-Gendrot, "Les Immigrants dans la vie politique aux Etats-Unis et en France," *Revue Europeene des Migrations Internationales*, 4, 3 (1988): 9.
13. Interview with a vice-president and founder of SOS-R.
14. *Ouest-france* (January 15, 1988). Commentary is by Pierre Kattenbach, a member of the Commission des Sages, with citations from Harlem Desir.
15. Ibid.
16. *Le Figaro* (April 6, 1987), a report on the National Front.
17. *Le Monde* (January 3, 1989): 14.
18. *Liberation* (July 6, 1989): 35–37.
19. See Gerard Noirel, *Le Creuset Français* (Paris: Editions du Seuil, 1988). See also Albano Cordeiro, *L'Immigration* (Paris: La Decouverte, 1983).
20. Patrick Weil, "La Politique française d'immigration," *Pouvoirs* (1988): 51.
21. *Le Quotidien* (January 8, 1988), report based on data from the Commission des Sages.
22. Catherine Bonvalet, "Les Parisiens dans leur maturité: origine, parcours, integration," *Population*, 42, 2 (March–April 1987): 236.
23. Rémy Leveau and Catherine Wihtol de Wenden, "La deuxième generation," *Pouvoirs* (December 1988): 61.
24. Fatiha Dazl and Rémy Leveau, "L'integration par la politique: le vote des Beurs," *Etudes*, 369, 3 (September 1988): 183.
25. *Le Nouvel Observateur* (March 22 to 28, 1988): 183.
26. Didier Lapeyronnie, "Assimilation, mobilisation et action collective chez les jeunes de la seconde generation de l'immigration Maghrébine," *Revue Francaise De Sociologie*, 28, 2 (April–June 1987).
27. Michel Hannoun, *L'Homme est l'Esperance de L'Homme: Rapport sur le racisme et les discriminations en France au secretaire d'Etat* (Paris: La Documentation Francaise, 1987), 129.
28. Catherine Wihtol de Wenden, "Politiques de l'immigration," *Hommes et Migrations*, 1119 (February 1989), 14.
29. M. Hannoun (1987), 63.
30. A. Cordiero (1984), 20–22.
31. Report of the Groupe de Travail, "Le Devoir d'insertion," *Hommes et Migrations*, 452–54 (March–May 1984): 1984.

32. Gilles Verbunt, "Immigrés et associations," *Les Temps Modernes*, 452–54 (March-May 1984): 2062.
33. G. Noiriel, appendix.
34. Serge Boulot and Danielle Boyson-Frandel, "L'Echec scolaire des enfants de travailleurs immigrés," *Les Temps Modernes*, 452–54 (March-May 1984): 1904.
35. D. Lapeyronnie, 294.
36. In interviews, SOS-R officers gave me their impressions and estimates but they said they had no precise income data on their membership.
37. Harlem Desir, "SOS Racisme, hier et demain..." *Hommes et Migrations*, 1118 (January 1989): 8.
38. Ibid., 3.
39. François Dubet, "SOS Racisme et la revalorisation des valeurs," *Hommes et Migrations*, 1109 (January 1988): 38.

A Dream Deferred: The Abortive Efforts of the Parliamentary Black Caucus in Great Britain

Charles E. Jones

Georgia State University

A record number of minority candidates were elected to the legislative assembly in Great Britain during the 1987 parliamentary elections. Four nonwhite members were placed in the House of Commons, while one black member entered the House of Lords. This nonwhite legislative contingent constitutes the largest minority delegation in the long and illustrious history of Parliament and represents the embryonic stage of black legislative participation in Great Britain.[1] Shortly after their arrival at Westminster, the black members formed the Parliamentary Black Caucus (PBC) to maximize their legislative influence. The adoption of the caucus mechanism by Britain's minority legislative delegation mirrors the prevailing mode of political action utilized by African-American legislators in the United States at both the national (Barnett, 1975; Smith, 1981; Jones, 1987a) and state (McGriggs, 1977; Bragg, 1979) levels.

Moreover, the selection of the caucus-based legislative strategy by the newly elected black members of Parliament reflects an electoral variant of the Pan Africanist political expression (Edmondson, 1968). Pan Africanism underscores the interdependence of people of African descent, which necessitates economic, cultural, and political unity of black people throughout the African diaspora. Political cooperation and linkage between the Parliamentary Black Caucus and its U.S. counterpart, the Congressional Black Caucus (CBC), constitute a concrete application of Pan African unity. Ronald Walters (1993: 190), in his excellent study *Pan Africanism in the African Diaspora*, writes that, "in spite of its [PBC] relatively small membership, it was able to command the support of a much larger body of fraternal legislators in show of concrete camaraderie."

Parallel social and political predicaments of African Americans and people of African descent in England have fostered a political kinship between the two groups. David Upshal (1989a: 15), a political reporter of England's leading black newspaper, notes, "[P]eople in Britain often talk about the need to follow the example of black American achievement if we are to advance towards equality. The launch of the Parliamentary Black Caucus represents a historic and crucial step in that direction." Notwithstanding the lofty aspirations of the nonwhite members of Parliament to emulate the pattern of African-American legislative participation, the formal coalescing of the black Parliamentary delegation into the PBC was a short-lived experiment. The Parliamentary Black Caucus, initially formed in 1988, officially disbanded after a mere three years (*The Voice*, 1991: 1).

This study examines the formation and organizational dynamics of the now defunct, international racial legislative subgroup. Furthermore, the analysis addresses both the impediments that undermined the viability of the Parliamentary Black Caucus and the potential for future black legislative empowerment in Great Britain. Informal group theory provides the analytical framework for this assessment of the embryonic stage of minority parliamentary participation in England. This study also draws on the experience gleaned from the evolution and institutionalization of the Congressional Black Caucus which enhances our insight of cross-national black legislative participation.

Black Legislative Caucus Politics: The Utility of Informal Group Theory

The formation of racially based caucuses by black legislators is a derivative of the black power political strategy in the United States. Smith (1981: 437) notes that "by the end of the 1960s black power had fostered two remarkable developments in black politics in the United States: It had contributed to the development of a black ethnic tradition and to the development of an emergent independent black organizational structure." The caucus device has been the primary vehicle of black participation in the legislative arenas of the United States (Miller, 1990). McGriggs (1977: 130–31) explains that "the existence of a black caucus represents the group coalition of black politicians formed for the purpose of attempting to translate the goals of blacks into public policy by bargaining with the power structure from a position of strength." At the national level black members of Congress formed the CBC in 1971 (Barnett, 1977), while at the state level black legislators in Missouri formally organized as early as 1966 (Perry, 1976).

To be sure, informal organizations have long been a part of the legislative landscape in the United States. In Congress, for example, state party delegations represented the earliest form of this entity (Truman, 1956). The Democratic Study Group (DSG) created in 1958 by liberal Democrats in the House of Representatives (Stevens, Miller, and Mann, 1974) and the Wednesday Group founded in 1963 by moderate Republicans to offset Democratic dominance in the lower chamber (Groennings, 1973) were both precursors to the proliferation of contemporary congressional informal organizations in the 1970s. However, both the external origin and explicit racial objective of African-American legislative subgroups differentiate the black legislative caucus from its conventional counterpart.

Informal group theory provides the conceptual framework for this analysis. This analytical framework was selected because of its underlying premise of collective political action. Ultimately, effective black legislative participation rests on coordinated rather than individual discrete action. Moreover, the functions performed by informal organizations also prove instructive in assessing the nature and character of black parliamentary participation in Great Britain. Outcomes of informal group functions serve to mitigate the political shortcomings of the typical black legislative delegation. Regardless of the political setting, black legislators often suffer from junior status, numerical disadvantage, and a hostile political environment. Such political liabilities are partially diminished via effectual informal group interaction.

Specifically, the unofficial group in the legislative process generates an "esprit de corps" among the members of the organization (Fiellin, 1962). Legislative caucuses "are a mechanism for the development of close rapport, confidence in one another's political judgment and mutual support" (Groennings, 1973: 75). This service has particular relevance for the black legislative members who frequently operate in an alien and often hostile environment. In addition, the development of a sense of "we-ness" within the black legislative delegation contributes to group solidarity—a critical political resource of legislative politics.

Promotion of group cohesion constitutes an important outcome of informal group participation (Fiellin, 1962; Deckard, 1973; Jones, 1987b). In a study of voting behavior in the House of Representatives from the 84th to the 91st Congress, Stevens, Miller, and Mann (1974: 67) found that the cohesion of liberal members increased as a result of the formation of the DSG. Group solidarity becomes a vital political asset because the ability to deliver a bloc of votes enhances one's bargaining leverage. This legislative capital partially compensates for the numerical disadvantage of black legislative delegations.

Of equal importance for black legislators is the function of constructive opposition (Groennings, 1973: 76–77). The informal organization serves as a permanent entity within the legislature not only to monitor policies of the executive branch, but also to scrutinize the actions of the two legislative parties. It provides a legislative mechanism for the articulation and protection of black group interest. Indeed, "in many ways the Parliamentary Black Caucus, like the CBC, was born out of a recognition that the problems confronting blacks required a strong and unified black political voice to serve as the conscience of the nation" (JCPS, 1989: 1).

Unofficial legislative groups also provide vital research services for legislators. Mark Ferber (1971: 266) found the members of the Democratic Study Group combined their resources and created a staff to provide liberal policy analyses that enhanced the liberal voice in the House of Representatives. Black legislators have a similar need for skillful and in-depth research from a black perspective in order to effectively represent the black community.

Finally, informal organizations contribute to the cultivation and formation of external interests (Stevens, Hammond, and Mulhollan, 1981). Informal groups create "advisory bodies drawn from outside interests to assist the group in shared policy goals" (Stevens, Hammond, and Mulhollan 1981: 18). Again, due to their small number, black representatives are in need of support mechanisms to maximize black legislative influence.

In sum, the perpetual minority status of black legislators underscores the importance of collective action via the caucus mechanism to ameliorate political liabilities and institutional biases. It was the benefits of the caucus mode of participation that the minority members of Parliament sought when they formally organized in 1988. Members of the Parliamentary Black Caucus explain that "the need for such a caucus in Britain derives from the fact that black representatives are in a minority and in a hostile environment which has never before had to confront the issues of race and race relations which the caucus has a duty and an obligation to raise" (PBC, 1989: 5).

Formation of the Parliamentary Black Caucus

The general election in 1987 was a landmark event in Great Britain. It resulted in the first black representation in the House of Commons during modern times. During this election five minority members were elected to Parliament. One lone member, Lord David Pitts, served in the upper chamber while the remaining four nonwhite legislators were members of the House of Commons. Since the historic 1987 election two additional minority members have entered Parliament (see Table 1). Britain's parliamentary delegation reflects the country's heterogeneous minority community. Three members have Afro-Caribbean ethnic origins while another three minority members of Parliament are of Asian descent. Paul Boateng is the only member of African origin and Diane Abbott remains the sole minority female to serve in Parliament. All but one of the nonwhite members are members of the Labour party (see Table 1).

Unlike the black congressional delegation in the United States, who first interacted informally through the Democratic Select Committee before forming the Congressional Black Caucus (Barnett, 1977: 3), the black members of

Table 1
Nonwhite Members in the Parliament of Great Britain, 1987–1993

Ethnic Member	District	Chamber	Ethnic Origin	Political Party
Diane Abbott	Hackney North and Stoke Newington	House of Commons	Afro-Caribbean	Labour
Paul Boateng	Brent South	House of Commons	African	Labour
Nirj Deva	Brentford and Isleworth	House of Commons	Asian	Conservative and Unionist
Bernard Grant	Totteham	House of Commons	Afro-Caribbean	Labour
Piara Khaba	Ealing Southall	House of Commons	Asian	Labour
David Pitts	Hampstead	House of Lords	Afro-Caribbean	Labour
Keith Vaz	Leicester	House of Commons	Asian	Labour

Source: Commission for Racial Equality, London, England.

Parliament organized formally from the outset. Their immediate efforts in 1988 to institutionalize black participation in Parliament can be attributed to the existence and success of the CBC. Black members of Parliament reminded the British political audience that "the concept of a Black Caucus at the level of national government is not a new one. In the United States of America, the Congressional Black Caucus has existed for nineteen years" (PBC, 1989: 5).

Formation of the PBC was publicly announced during its inaugural weekend program on March 31, 1989 (*Financial Times*, 1989: 4). A three-day affair that entailed lavish receptions, political seminars, and gala dinners including one held at the Palace of Westminster was modeled on the CBC's "Annual Legislative Weekend"(*The Voice*, 1989: 4). The yearly affair of the Congressional Black Caucus is a highly popular and successful African-American political event that consists of several fundraising activities, legislative workshops, and task force meetings (Jones, 1987a: 235).

A thirty-member delegation of the African-American politicos attended the inaugural weekend of the PBC. Among these were the presidents of the National Association of Black County Officials, the National Black Caucus of State Legislators, the National Black Caucus of Local Elected Officials, and the National Conference of Black Mayors (JCPS, 1989: 1). The CBC chair, and five other CBC members, as well as the president of the Joint Center for Political and Economic Studies and other black political operatives also attended this historic event (PBC, 1989: 23). African-American participation in the inaugural weekend of the Parliamentary Black Caucus reflected both the symbolic and the substantive linkages between the plight of people of African descent on either side of the Atlantic.

Lord Pitts of Hampstead (*The Voice*, 1989: 1) proclaimed that, "[T]his is a moment pregnant with symbolism and promise for our people on both sides of the Atlantic." This black transatlantic cooperation was further extended when members of the Parliamentary Black Caucus attended the CBC's nineteenth annual "Legislative Weekend." As Amelia Parker, the CBC's executive staff director, explained, "[T]he trip provided new avenues of communications. Our ability for collective resolutions through global cooperation has been greatly enhanced" (Solanki, 1989: 11).

Like the CBC, the Parliamentary Black Caucus operated on a bipartisan basis. At the time of the founding of the PBC all five minority members of Parliament belonged to the Labour Party. During its brief history, the PBC delegation never exceeded four members. Paul Boateng, one of the five minority candidates elected to Parliament in 1987, declined to join the PBC. Clearly, the small size of the PBC membership precluded the organization from exercising any meaningful bloc voting in the 650-seat House of Commons.

According to one PBC member, the organization provided the black members of Parliament with a vehicle "to work together on a common platform to address the issue of race within mainstream politics."[2] The goal of the PBC was "to raise issues of race and race relations in Parliament and through other channels open to members of Parliament, for example, directly with ministers and government institutions" (PBC, 1989: 5). This objective was consistent with that of the CBC: "to serve as legislative advocates in the U.S.

Congress to represent the interests of a national constituency [African-Americans], while addressing the concerns of our particular district" (Jones, 1987a: 221). Legislative priorities of the PBC included securing anti-discrimination legislation, improving the conditions of minority communities within the inner cities, and seeking an active role in shaping the country's foreign policy towards third world countries (PBC, 1989: 5).

Paradoxically, despite its limited membership base the nascent organization adopted an elaborate and formal leadership structure, which included a chairmanship occupied by Bernie Grant, and treasurer and secretary positions filled by Keith Vaz and Diane Abbot respectively. This saturation of leadership officers in the PBC underscores the importance of securing a "critical mass" membership base before formally coalescing. Adherence to this requisite "membership threshold" was apparent in the formation of the Congressional Black Caucus (Barnett, 1977), as well as in the formal development of the North Carolina Black State Legislative Caucus (Miller, 1990).

During the first year of its existence, PBC activities were supported by one paid staff member. The caucus administrator, the only full-time staff member of the organization, was assisted by a network of volunteers. Publication of *The Black Parliamentarian*, the organization's quarterly publication, was a central staff responsibility. According to the chair of the PBC, the magazine served "as a forum for discussion within the black communities" (Grant, 1989: 1). He further added that, "[N]o issue will be too controversial for this magazine, nothing affecting the black communities will be too hot or too cool for the magazine to handle" (Grant, 1989: 1). PBC's operations were funded by the Barrow Cadbury Fund, a British philanthropic organization, which awarded a four-year grant of approximately $25,000 per year to the parliamentary racial subgroup (PBC, 1989: 5).

While the formation of the Parliamentary Black Caucus represented a potential vehicle for maximizing black legislative influence, its viability was hampered by a host of individual and organizational problems. At the outset the PBC's viability was hampered by the refusal of Paul Boateng to unite with the other minority members in forming the racial legislative subgroup. Boateng's failure to join the PBC served to undermine the strategy of black self-determination in the nation's legislative arena. This disunity among the black members of Parliament weakened significantly the important symbol of racial solidarity. Boateng's decision to distance himself from the PBC was based on his aversion to racially based politics. Boateng proclaimed that, "caucuses based on skin color are not the way to proceed. You make progress by constructing alliances, not by walling yourself off" (Broder, 1989: A17). He further declared, "I am a politician who is black, not a black politician" (Broder, 1989: A17). Boateng's disdain for racial politics mirrors the deracialization outlook of some of the current generation of African-American politicians (McCormick and Jones, 1993).

In addition, the ongoing acrimony among the membership hindered the effectiveness of the organization. Clashes between various members of the PBC were of a personal rather than ideological nature. Ironically, the distinction of being the highest ranking black officials in the country appears to have inflated the membership's sense of self-importance. As a PBC member explained, "we are all mega stars in our communities." Unbridled adulation of the nation's minority community for the black parliamentary delegation partially accounts for the tendency of some PBC members to exhibit self-aggrandizing behavior. In the view of one political observer, the black members of the Parliament are "extremely arrogant and brash and have a distortion of their self-importance." One PBC member lamented that "we don't do anything in unison." Suffice it to say, the PBC never obtained the "sense of weness" that informal organizations provide.

Parliamentary Black Caucus operations were also beset with organizational problems. Chris Grant, the first caucus administrator, resigned after a two-month tenure because of a confrontation with PBC member Diane Abbott during the group's inaugural weekend activities. Grant and three volunteers announced their resignation as a result of what they contended was the outrageous behavior of Abbott (Upshal, 1989b). In a letter that was leaked to the press, the volunteers complained that they were "subjected to a humiliating tirade from Abbott" and "[of] witnessing further abuse against Grant" (Upshal, 1989b). Abbott's position as caucus secretary was jeopardized as a result of the controversy, which further reinforced the perception of egomaniacal behavior of the PBC's membership. Moreover, the incident adversely impacted the organization's capacity to provide much needed research services to the black members of Parliament.

Organizational effectiveness of the PBC was further hampered by the decision of the Barrow Cadbury Fund to change its funding format. Rather than making one allocation to the PBC as whole, the Barrow Cadbury Fund now allocated its monies equally among the individual members. This new funding policy impaired the PBC's efforts toward collective action since it gave individual black members of Parliament greater financial independence.

From the preceding analysis, it is clear that the PBC was constantly floundering and in a state of organizational limbo during its very brief history. A member of the Westminster press corps notes that the group was marred by "an inability to get their act together" and concludes that the "PBC has been quite a disappointment." During its formative years, the CBC also experienced a similar state of organizational limbo and underwent a process of self-evaluation and re-organization (Barnett, 1975). However, any attempts to revitalize the PBC must take into account structural factors in the British political landscape which are identified in the next section of the study.

Institutional and Environmental Impediments

Successful adoption of any strategy is invariably linked to the relevant political environment. Institutional imperatives, environmental dynamics, and political developments of a political arena may render some tactics ineffective. This political reality confronts the black members of Parliament. Its brief existence indicates that the formation of the PBC was not only hampered by intra-caucus obstacles but perhaps was equally undermined by an inhospitable institutional setting.

Contrary to the fragmented congressional arena in the United States, the consolidation of power characterizes the deliberative process in the Parliament of Great Britain. Executive dominance (King, 1976), programmatic and cohesive political parties (Epstein, 1956; Rose, 1983), and circumscribed policy entrepreneurial opportunities for individual members of Parliament (Mellors, 1978) produce a highly centralized British legislative arena.

Executive dominance is evident in the initiation of legislation, the staffing of government and the control of patronage resources. Philip Norton, a leading parliamentary authority, observes that "the executive dominates both the business program (deciding what will be debated and when) and the voting of Parliament" (1984: 260). The pervasive and encompassing role of the executive branch in the legislative affairs of the country renders the rank-and-file member of Parliament politically impotent. Needless to say, this institutional arrangement poses a formidable obstacle to independent black parliamentary participation.

Centralized authority in Parliament is further reinforced by the absence of a powerful committee structure. A primary source of decentralization in the congressional arena is the presence of permanent standing committees. Even in the era of congressional reform, these legislative entities remain an important source of power for individual members of Congress. Senator Daniel P. Moynihan's (New York) reign over the finance committee attests to the power and influence of contemporary congressional chairs.

In marked contrast, standing committees in the House of Commons tend to operate on an ad hoc basis, lack both the investigatory and veto authority of its U.S. counterparts, and are directed by chairs who are appointed and who are expected to be politically neutral (Norton, 1984: 265). In short, "[U]nlike United States congressional committees, standing committees are not a burial ground for bills. Rather, they serve as temporary transit points in their passage" (Norton, 1984: 265).

An emasculated committee system combined with the absence of a seniority system in the British Parliament precludes yet another basis of individualized power for the black parliamentary delegation. The congressional norm of seniority has been the single most crucial determinant of CBC's influence in the House of Representatives. During the 103rd Congress (1993–94), CBC members chaired three standing committees and eighteen subcommittees. Ironically, if it were not for the reform of the 1970s, CBC chairs would have even greater latitude to operate on behalf of African-American political interests.[3] Nonetheless, executive prerogative rather than continuous tenure in office remains the operative rule for filling influential positions in Parliament. Such authority, no doubt, circumvents the influence of the body's membership.

Prominent stature of political parties in the legislative process of England also differs dramatically from its U.S. counterparts. Compared to congressional political parties, the party organ in Parliament is a highly cohesive and disciplined legislative entity (Epstein, 1956; Rose, 1983). Davidson and Olezek (1990: 345) report that, "[U]nlike parliamentary systems the U.S. Congress rarely votes along straight party lines and never brings down the government in power (unless one counts impeachment of the president)." Schwarz and Shaw (1976: chapter 4) empirically documented the divergent levels of party cohesion in the two cross-national legislative bodies. Schwarz and Shaw investigated the level of party cohesion in the legislative bodies of four countries and found that both Conservative and Labour party members "maintained cohesion on 95 percent or more of the roll call votes" (Schwarz and Shaw, 1976: 119). Conversely, the two parties in Congress failed to vote along partisan lines on more than 70 percent of the roll call votes (Schwarz and Shaw, 1976: 119).

Party loyalty in the British Parliament reduces what Glenn Parker (1989: 4–7) describes as policy entrepreneur legislative behavior. The lack of policy independence on behalf of the members of Parliament impedes the effective articulation of minority political interest in Great Britain.

Parliamentary leadership possesses the requisite rewards and sanctions to ensure party unity. British party leaders control campaign resources, media access, and patronage powers which furnish the necessary leverage to command conformity among its membership. Consequently, there is little tolerance for party insubordination as is evident in the 1987 Nottingham controversy in which Labour leader Neil Kinnock removed Sharon Atkins, a black candidate, as the party nominee of a safe parliamentary seat (Lindsey, 1989: 151). Atkins incurred the displeasure of the party leadership when she criticized the Labour party for not addressing the policy interests of the British black community. Although Atkins (Monroe, 1988: 33) declared that "I don't want a parliamentary seat if I can't represent black people," her removal as the party nominee demonstrates the perils of maverick political behavior in Great Britain.

Indeed, many of the features of the parliamentary arena circumscribe policy entrepreneurial opportunities for Britain's national legislators. Parker (1989: 4) writes that in the United States, "members operate as individual policy entrepreneurs in a variety of ways: casting votes, drafting bills and amendments, sponsoring legislative measures, participating in floor and committee debate and engaging in committee and subcommittee deliberations (hearings, mark-ups, investigation, preparations of reports accompanying legislation)." These avenues are closed to the members of Parliament as a result of executive ascendancy and party domination. Individual policy pursuits in the British legislative arena are further minimized by the restricted use of private bills and weak staff support.

Norton (1984: 266) notes that, "[S]o limited is the time available and so great the number of members wishing to introduce bills that a ballot is held each parliamentary session (that is, each year). The 20 members coming to the top in the ballot have priority in introducing bills." Suffice it to say, the procedure for introducing private legislation in Parliament stifles individual legislative initiatives. Therefore, without the support of the party, the black Parliamentary delegation will find it difficult to sponsor legislation beneficial to the country's minority community.

Similarly, limited staff resources of parliamentary members deny an opportunity for policy entrepreneurial pursuits available to their U.S. counterparts. Personal staff of the typical member of Parliament pales in comparison to the average fifteen-member staff of legislators in the House of Representatives and to the average thirty-one-member staff of U.S. Senators (Davidson and Oleszek, 1990: 140). This disparity in staff resources "helps to explain a number of cross-national differences in constituency services practices" (Cain, Ferejohn, and Fiorina, 1981: 118).

Staff resources available to CBC members have been crucial in supplementing the activities of the organization, particularly prior to the 1982 adoption of new procedures regulating informal organizations in the House of Representatives. In addition to utilizing funds from office allowances to help finance caucus operation, CBC members also depend on their respective individual staffs to provide assistance in carrying out CBC task force activities. An independent base of resources remains elusive for the black members of Parliament. However, it should be noted that 1994 rule changes passed by the Newt Gingrich led Republican controlled House of Representatives have eliminated public funding of caucus operations. This reform will undoubtedly adversely affect future CBC effectiveness.

In short, the congressional caucuses of the United States appear incompatible with the legislative institutional setting of Britain. "Registered All Parliamentary Groups" are the closest approximate of congressional informal organizations in Parliament. These British legislative entities are "restricted to those groups including at least five members of the governing party and five from the opposition party" (Coleman, 1990: 23). "Registered All Parliamentary Groups" lack the formality and capacity to influence the policy process of its congressional counterparts. Coleman (1990: 23) explains that, "The practical limitations enforced on such groups by the strength of the party system and the weakness of individual MPs, help to illustrate the same restrictions that are applied to the PBC. Their legislative function can only be tenuous."

Convergence of the inimical institutional features of Parliament and the salient environmental factors of the larger political arena undermine the effective utilization of the caucus mode of political action in Great Britain. Specifically, the black Parliamentary delegation is beset by a numerical disadvantage. Minority members occupy a mere six of the 650 seats in the House of Commons. Clearly, such a stark numerical disparity makes it difficult for the black Parliamentary delegation to exercise any meaningful influence via racial bloc voting.

Moreover, the small percentage of the minority population in Britain makes the exponential growth in the size of the parliamentary black delegation highly unlikely. The nonwhite population currently constitutes 4.6 percent (2.6 million people) of the British citizenry (Anwar, 1990: 33). Political leverage of the minority community in England is further weakened by the lack of population dispersion throughout the country. Consequently, William Nelson (1991: 23) concludes that "the absence of significant Black numbers in Britain and of strategic concentration (with the exception of some London boroughs) means that the interests of the Black community can easily be marginalized and ignored by white politicians and political institutions."

Therefore, the goal of proportional representation by the minority population in the British Parliament (thirty-two seats), rather than the acquisition of the seats necessary to constitute a formidable voting bloc, appears to comport more with the country's environmental dynamics. Currently, there are only three parliamentary districts with a 40 percent or more minority population, while another thirteen districts are composed of a minority constituency ranging from 24 to 37 percent (see Table 2). These seats represent the greatest likelihood of increasing the number of minority parliamentary members.

Table 2
Parliamentary Districts with 15%+ Minority Population

District	%Minority Population
*Brent South	46%
*Southall	44%
Ladywood	42%
*Tottenham	37%
Small Heath	36%
Sparkbrook	36%
*Newham NE	33%
*Newham NW	33%
*Hacknewy N. & Stoke Newington	31%
*Brent E	30%
Bradford W	28%
*Leyton	27%
Leicester E	26%
Leicester S	26%
*Hackney S & Shoreditch	25%
*Vauxhall	27%
*Behnal Green & Stephney	24%
*Tooting	24%
*Brent N	23%
*Croydon NW	23%
*Deptford	23%
*Norwood	23%
*Battersea	22%
*Hornsey & Wood Green	21%
*Islington N	21%
*Peckham	21%
Slough	21%
Warley E	21%
Blackburn	20%
*Feltham & Heston	20%
*Ilford S	20%
*Streatham	20%
*Walthamstow	20%
Wolverhampton SW	20%
Huddersfield	19%
*Hammersmith	18%
Luton S	18%
*Southgate	18%
Stretford	18%
Wolverhampton SE	18%
Coventry NE	17%
*Dulwich	17%
*Edmonton	17%
*Harrow E	17%
*Finchley	16%
Perry Bar	16%
*Bow & Poplar	15%
Derby S	15%
*Hendon S	15%
Walsall S	15%
*Westminster N	15%

* = London Metropolitan Area
Source: Adapted from Marian Fitzgerald, "Black People and Party Politics in Britain" Runny Mede Research Report 1987, p. 4.

However, minority mobilization and representation is further complicated by the diversity of the nonwhite community in Great Britain (Nelson, 1991: 23–24; Goulbourne, 1990: 10–13). In England the various nonwhite groups—Afro-Caribbeans, Asians, and Africans—have organized around the political construct of "blackness." Goulbourne (1990: 10) explains that "blackness" retains its unity as a construction against whiteness and its attendant cultural and ideological hegemony, and against its economic and political domination." The problem lies in the heterogeneous nature of the groups falling under the political rubric of "blackness." These three diverse ethnic groups do not share a common culture or leadership, which increases the likelihood of disunity and inter-group competition.

Another characteristic of the British polity that contributed to the impotency of the short-lived Parliamentary Black Caucus has been the slow development of minority social and political organizations. One political observer contends that "black activism is in its nursery form." While Fitzgerald (1990: 27) argues that "it is important to note that—by contrast with the U.S.A. with which facile parallels are often drawn—Britain has no real tradition of ethnic politics." To be sure, this observation does not imply that blacks in Britain are without a legacy of protest and political activism against racial discrimination (Fryer, 1984). Black British urban rebellions date back as early as 1919 in the port city of Liverpool (Fryer, 1984: 298–316). This pattern of resistance continued to occur in the British political setting during the 1980s with the eruption of the Notting Hill carnival riots (Walters, 1993: 162–164).

Rather, the minority ethnic tradition in England suffers from weak pluralist organizational development. Multiplicity of interest groups which characterize African-American participation (Perry, 1991) has not yet materialized in the British minority community. In other words,

> a "major difference between the two countries lies in the fact that, over time, American blacks have been able to create their own institutions as a way of dealing with the many barriers to economic, social, and political equality. These include historically black colleges and universities, political and civil rights groups, fraternal organizations, and business and research institutions." (JCPS, 1989: 2)

Coleman (1990) suggests that the low level of formal minority interest aggregation in Great Britain was a favorable condition for the Parliamentary Black Caucus. He points out that, "Unlike the atmosphere of tense competition faced by the CBC (primarily from the NAACP) the PBC has no rival claiming national leadership."

Nevertheless, this line of reasoning overlooks a critical by-product of intra-group competition. Competition among the constellation of African-American political organizations provide an important mechanism of leadership accountability. Absence of this countervailing pressure in Britain's black political community permits the minority members of Parliament to advocate contradictory policies. Such was the case when the black members of Parliament supported Neil Kinnock's removal of Sharon Atkins from the party slate in 1987.

The preceding analysis of the failed efforts of the PBC clearly indicates that the black parliamentary delegation must navigate a course through formidable political obstacles. While the British political setting appears to be nonconducive to autonomous informal congressional organizations, there are, nonetheless, actions that can be undertaken to enhance black parliamentary representation. This study concludes with a discussion of suggestions for strengthening minority legislative participation in Great Britain.

Conclusion: Prescription for Effective Black Parliamentary Participation

Since the dissolution of the PBC, the minority parliamentary delegation has been in a state of flux. The interplay of organizational weaknesses, institutional impediments, and environmental barriers has rendered the caucus device politically ineffective. Nevertheless, opportunities for improving the legislative capabilities of the black members of Parliament which are independent of the institutional obstacles do exist.

For example, a precondition to future legislative effectiveness is the suppression of personal ego-laden clashes between the black members of Parliament. A shared commitment to work in unison with one another is not contingent upon the institutional features of Parliament. In order for the parliamentary black delegation to provide effective symbolic representation (Pitkin, 1967) for the country's minority community, a sense of "we-ness" among the members is critical. Furthermore, the acquisition of funding resources independent of philanthropic foundations does not require attention to the institutional arrangements of Parliament. Adequate funding not only provides the black members of Parliament with a degree of political autonomy, but will also offset the weak staff resources available to all backbenchers. Given the realities of the British political setting a more prudent approach for the black members of Parliament may, in fact, entail working on an ad hoc basis within the Campaign Group. This left-wing Labour party cleavage would provide ethnic minority members with a broader base of support.

Notes

This research was supported by an Old Dominion University summer faculty fellowship and a research award from the Institute for the Study of Minority Issues of Old Dominion University. Additional funding was provided by an African-American Research and Development Grant sponsored by the Provost office of Georgia State University.

1. The terms minority and black are used interchangeably in this essay which comports with the political construct of "blackness" in British minority politics (see Goulbourne 1990: 10–11).
2. All unattributed quotes appearing in this essay were derived from open-ended interviews with a member of the Parliamentary Black Caucus, members of the British Press, and Black British community activists. These interviews were conducted in London, England, by the author during the period of July 8 through July 15, 1990. Subsequent research was conducted in England in October.
3. During the 94th Congress (1975–76) the Democratic party members enacted a reform that conferred the Democratic caucus with the authority to elect committee chairs, which minimizes the seniority norm in Congress. See Leroy N.

Rieselback, ed., *Legislative Reform: The Policy Impact* (Lexington Mass: Lexington Books, 1978). Moreover, in 1993 the Democratic caucus granted a litany of rights and subcommittees under the "Subcommittee Bill of Rights." Example of these rights include established subcommittee jurisdictions; the authority to select subcommittee chairs; and a sufficient budget. See David Rhode, "Committee Reform in the House of Representatives and the Subcommittee Bill of Rights" *The Annals* 411 (January 1974): 39–47.

References

Anwar, Muhammad. 1990. "Ethnic Minorities and the Electoral Process: Some Recent Development." In *Black Politics in Britain*, ed. Harry Goulbourne, 33–47. Brookfield: Gower Publishing Company Limited.

Barnett, Marguerite R. 1975a. "The Congressional Black Caucus." *Annals of the American Academy of Political and Social Sciences*, 32: 34–50.

———. 1977. "A Historical Look At the CBC." *Focus*, 5: 3–4.

Bragg, Richard L. 1979. *The Maryland Black Caucus as a Racial Group in the Maryland General Assembly: Legislative Communities and Caucus Influence on Public Policy*. Unpublished dissertation, Howard University.

Broder, David S. 1989. "British Blacks Grow Restless." *The Washington Post* (July 4): 17.

Cain, Bruce, John Ferejohn, and Morris Fiorina. 1981. "Constituency Service in the United States and Great Britain." In *Congress Reconsidered*, ed. Lawrence C. Dodd and Bruce Oppenheimer, 109–30. Washington, DC: Congressional Quarterly Inc.

Coleman, Jeremy D. 1990. "What Policy Lessons Can Be Learned By the Parliamentary Black Caucus from the Experience of the Congressional Black Caucus?: A Comparative Analysis of Two Pressure Groups Within the U.S. and British Legislative Bodies." Politics and Parliamentary Studies, Leeds University, England, senior thesis.

Davidson, Roger H., and Walter J. Oleszed. 1990. *Congress and Its Members*. Washington, DC: Congressional Quarterly Press.

Deckard, Barbara. 1973. "State Party Delegations in the U.S. House of Representatives: An Analysis of Group Action." *Polity*, 5: 311–334.

Edmondson, Locksley. 1968. "The Internationalization of Black Power: Historical and Contemporary Perspectives." *Mawaza*, 1: 16–27.

Epstein, Leon. 1956. "Cohesion of British Parliamentary Parties." *American Political Science Review*, 50: 46–59.

Ferber, Mark F. 1971. "The Formation of the Democratic Study Group." In *Congressional Behavior*, ed. Nelson W. Polsby, 249–69. New York: Random House.

Fiellin, Alan. 1962. "The Functions of Informal Groups in Legislative Institutions." *Journal of Politics*, 24: 72–91.

Financial Times. 1989. "MPS Launch Black Caucus in Parliament." (April): 4. London, England.

Fitzgerald, Marian. 1990. "The Emergence of Black Councillors and MPS in Britain: Some Underlying Questions." In *Black Politics in Britain*, ed. Harry Goulbourne Brookfield: Gower Publishing Company Limited.

Fryer, Peter. 1984. *Staying Power: The History of Black People in Britain*. London, Pluto Press.

Goulbourne, Harry, ed. 1990. *Black Politics in Britain*. Brookfield, Gower Publishing Company.

Grant, Bernie. 1989. "The Dawning of a New Era." *The Black Parliamentarian: Magazine of the Parliamentary Black Caucus*, Vol. 1, 1.

Groennings, Sven. 1973. "The Clubs in Congress: The House Wednesday Group."

In *To Be a Congressman and the Promise of Power*, ed. Sven Groennings and Jonathan P. Hawley, 73–98. Washington, DC: Acropolis Books.

JCPS (Joint Center for Political Studies). 1989. "American Delegation Attends Inauguration of Parliamentary Black Caucus." *Political Trend Letter in Focus*, 174: 1–4.

Jones, Charles E. 1987a. "An Overview of the Congressional Black Caucus 1970–1985." In *Readings in American Political Issues*, eds. Franklin D. Jones and Michael O. Adams, 219–40. Dubuque, IA: Kendal Hunt.

———. 1987b. "United We Stand, Divided We Fall: An Analysis of the Congressional Black Caucus' Voting Behavior, 1975–1980." *Phylon*, 48: 26–37.

Kavanagh, Dennis. 1989. *British Politics: Continues and Change*. Nottingham University: Oxford University Press.

King, Anthony. 1976. "Modes of Executive-Legislative Relations: Great Britain, France, and West Germany." *Legislative Studies Quarterly*, 1: 11–35.

Lindsey, Lydia. 1989. "An Historical Overview of the Political Status of Blacks in England, Since 1945." *The Western Journal of Black Studies*, 13: 146–55.

McCormick, Joseph, and Charles E. Jones. 1993. "The Conceptualization of Deracialization: Thinking Through the Dilemma." In *Black Politics: Issues of Leadership and Strategy*, ed. Georgia A. Persons, 66–84. New York: HarperCollins College Publishers, 66–84.

McGriggs, Lee A. 1977. *Black Legislative Politics in Illinois*. Washington, DC: University Press of America.

Miller, Cheryl M. 1990. "Agenda-Setting by State Legislative Black Caucuses: Policy Priorities and Factors of Success." *Policy Studies Review*, 9: 339–54.

Mellors, Colin. 1978. *The British MP*. London: Saxon House.

Monroe, Sylvester. 1988. "Blacks in Britain: Grim Lives, Grimmer Prospects." *Newsweek Magazine* (January 4): 32–33.

Nelson, William E., Jr. 1991. "Constraints on Black Political Emergence in Britain: Lessons from Liverpool." Paper Presented at the Annual Meeting of the American Political Science Association, August 29–September 1.

Norton, Phillip. 1984. *The British Polity*. New York and London: Longman Inc.

Parker, Glenn R. 1989. *Characteristics of Congress: Patterns in Congressional Behavior*. Englewood Cliffs, NJ: Prentice Hall.

Parliamentary Black Caucus. 1989. "Why Set Up a Parliamentary Black Caucus?" *The Black Parliamentarian: The Magazine of the Parliamentary Black Caucus*, 11, 5.

Perry, Huey L. 1991. "Pluralist Theory and National Black Politics in the United States." *Polity*, 32: 549–65.

Perry, Robert T. 1976. *Black Legislators*. San Francisco: Rand Research Associates.

Pitkin, Hanna. 1967. *The Concept of Representation*. Berkeley University of California Press.

Rose, Richard. 1983. "Still the Era of the Party Government." *Parliamentary Affairs*, 36: 282–99.

Schwarz, John E., and L. Earl Shaw. 1976. *The United States Congress in Comparative Perspectives*. Hinsdale, IL: The Dryden Press.

Smith, Robert C. 1981. "Black Power and the Transformation from Protest to Politics." *Political Science Quarterly*, 96: 431–43.

Solanki, Paresh. 1989. "Westminster Caucus Spreads Its Wings." *The Voice* (October 3): 11. London, England.

Stevens, Arthur G., Susan W. Hammond, and Daniel P. Mulhollan. 1981. "Changes in Decision-making Networks in the Congressional System: An Examination of the Role of Informal Groups." Paper presented at the Annual Meeting of Western Political Science Association, Denver, March.

Stevens, Arthur G., Arthur H. Miller, and Thomas E. Mann. 1974. "Mobilization of

Liberal Strength in the House, 1955–1970: The Democratic Study Group." *American Political Science Review*, 68: 667–81.

Truman, David B. 1956. "The State Party Delegation and the Structure of Party Voting in the U.S. House of Representatives." *American Political Science Review* 50 (December): 1023–45.

Upshal, David. 1989a. "A Step in the Right Direction." *The Voice* (November 8): 15. London, England.

———. 1989b. "Angry Abbot Sees Red Over *Voice* Story." *The Voice* (April 25): 3. London, England.

The Voice. 1989. "U.S. Thumbs Up to Black Caucus." (April 4): 1. London, England.

———. 1991. "Black Caucus Scrapped." (April 2): 1. London, England.

Walters, Ronald W. 1993. *Pan Africanism in the African Diaspora: An Analysis of Modern Afrocentric Political Movements*. Detroit: Wayne State University Press.

Race, Class, Equal Opportunity Policies, and Local Government: The Case of Liverpool

William E. Nelson, Jr.
Gideon Ben-Tovim

Ohio State University
University of Liverpool

The Case of Liverpool

The large-scale settlement of hundreds of thousands of individuals from the New Commonwealth countries into Britain since World War II has brought into sharp relief issues of race, class, and equal opportunity in the United Kingdom. Significant research on racism and social change in Britain has emerged over the past two decades (see Solomos, 1989; Braham, Rattansi, and Skellington, 1992; Gilroy, 1987; Rex and Tomlinson, 1979; Sivanandan, 1982; Goulbourne, 1990). Much of this research has focused on the changing racial character of British immigration policy, the impact of the black vote on the fate of the Labour party in national elections, and the election of black members to parliament from predominantly black boroughs in London. Only recently has serious attention been given to the local politics of race in Britain outside the London metropolitan area (see Ben-Tovim, Gabriel, Law, and Stredder, 1986; Goulbourne, 1990).

This paper seeks to contribute to the analysis of issues of race, class, and urban policy in Britain by focusing on a major city located in northern England, Liverpool. Why should we consider Liverpool as a case study centering around issues of race, class, and urban policy in Britain? Liverpool is a uniquely important focus of such analysis because it is the home of Britain's oldest black community, stretching back a number of generations until at least the eighteenth century (see Law and Menfrey, 1981). The permanent settlement of black seamen in Liverpool beginning in the eighteenth century led to the formation of a substantial locally born black community with formal British citizenship and without the significant linguistic, cultural, or religious differences from the local population that has characterized patterns of minority settlement in other British cities. The black community in Liverpool is not primarily an immigrant community. Long before the potato famine that brought the Irish to Liverpool in massive numbers, blacks were a significant part of the Liverpool population (Fryer, 1984: 33–44).

The experiences of the black community in Liverpool also deserve intensive examination because these experiences provide crucial insight into the meaning of formal citizenship for the black population in Britain. Our study of Liverpool illuminates the limits on the access to full citizenship rights by black British citizens imposed by the problems of racism at structural, institutional, and individual levels in British society. The argument we advance here is that the pattern of discrimination faced by blacks in Liverpool differs in intensity, extent, and nature from the barriers to full citizenship rights faced by the white working class (for confirmation, see Gifford, Brown, and Bundey, 1989: 63–85). Blacks in Liverpool experience a unique form of racism that robs black citizens of many of the benefits normally accorded to members of the working class. Liverpool is therefore a valuable case study in which many of the issues in the race/class debate can be illuminated.

Liverpool also represents a valuable case study of the politics of race in Britain. Much of value can be learned from the lengthy involvement of the black community in Liverpool in the struggle against racism and for racial equality. What are the limits and possibilities of black political mobilization within a political process that is not substantially open to black political participation? How do white controlled institutions respond to black demands for justice and equal opportunities in Britain? An examination of issues of race, class, and equal opportunity in Liverpool should shed penetrating light on these questions.

Political Demand and Government Response

Urban rebellions staged by blacks in Liverpool in 1919, 1948, and 1981 have compelled both the national and local governments to place issues of race equality in Liverpool on the public agenda. In the wake of the 1981 events, a number of new policy initiatives were developed, including the appointment of a minister for Merseyside, the creation of a local government corporation, and the establishment of two urban task forces. These measures were not sufficient to thwart the emergence of bitter confrontations between the black community and the Labour controlled city council. Conflict between the black community and the city council was especially strong during the years 1983–1987 when the council was under the control of Labour militants dogmatically opposed to the implementation of anti-racist policies (Liverpool Black Caucus, 1986: 85–120).

In recent years a key area of black political demand and mainstream institutional response has been around the terrain of equal opportunity policies and practices, including the development of forms of "positive action." At the national level there has been considerable local government action, particularly by Labour councils, as well as considerable central government resistance. This paper will provide an assessment of the initiatives that have been demanded, opposed, and adopted within this framework in Liverpool. The findings of this study should be of international significance, since the moves towards greater European integration will inevitably require the adoption of effective equal opportunity policies as a crucial part of the European Social Charter for the 1990s.

Blacks in Liverpool: Political Dilemmas

The black community in Liverpool has experienced a system of racial oppression unparalleled in the United Kingdom. Discriminatory housing policies have confined black residency principally to an urban community known as Liverpool 8 or the Toxteth/Granby area. This community is characterized by weak housing stock and a lower level of public services. Blacks seeking to escape the ghetto and move to better-off communities have been prevented from doing so by discrimination in the allocation of housing by the city council, as well as private housing associations (Commission for Racial Equality, 1984). Blacks who have managed to move away have suffered from harassment and abuse by their neighbors; these situations have frequently become so untenable that blacks have had no choice but to move back into Liverpool 8 after striving for many years to move out.

Blacks experience unusual discrimination in areas of employment, education, and health (Gifford, Brown, and Bundey 1989; Torkington, 1983). There is no professional class in the black community because blacks have been systematically denied opportunities for higher education and professional training (Gifford, Brown, and Bundey, 1989: 115–34). Unemployment in the black community is stupendous. One study placed black teenage unemployment at 70 percent (Connolly and Torkington, 1990). A survey of black youth between 17 and 19 found that only 17 out of 134 (12.7%) young blacks interviewed were engaged in full-time employment (Connolly and Torkington, 1990: 7). Most of these black youth had been involved in extensive government-financed youth training schemes (YTS); rarely did these experiences lead to employment.

Blacks are almost totally excluded from jobs in the private sector. There are few blacks employed in jobs in the downtown city center. One company, Littlewoods, has strongly embraced policies of equal employment opportunity. The greatest discriminator in employment is the city council, with blacks holding less than 1 percent of some 30,000 jobs under the control of the council.

In a variety of key social areas, progress for the black community in Liverpool has been extremely slow. The Gifford Report documents continuous harassment of black youngsters in school, racism by teachers, and a pattern of black educational underachievement (Gifford, Brown, and Bundey, 1989). Blacks are systematically cut off from health services by public and private health delivery agencies and suffer immensely from the consequences of poor health care. The most salient and emotional area of social discrimination is in the area of criminal justice and police enforcement. Liverpool police are among the most brutal in Britain. The black community is heavily patrolled; black citizens are frequently harassed and criminalized (Gifford, Brown, and Bundey, 1989: 159–97). Police behavior has been a flash point of continuing conflict between the black community and Liverpool city government.

The system of racial oppression in Liverpool has insulated the black community from important arenas of political activity and suppressed the development of effective black political resources. Political mobilization in the black community has been stifled by the absence of effective middle-class leadership, and the prevalence of a low sense of political efficacy that results, among other things, in low election turnout and campaign participation.

As an electoral force, blacks in Liverpool are placed at a substantial disadvantage by their relatively small numbers. Present estimates place the size of the black community, including Liverpool-born blacks, African Caribbeans, and Asians at 8 percent. Geographically, blacks are physically concentrated in the Granby-Toxteth area. This means that they only theoretically play a role in selecting 3 of 99 city councillors. Presently one black person serves on the city council; three councillors represent the Granby Ward where blacks make up 40 percent of the total population.

The black community is very ethnically diverse. Liverpool-born blacks make up the largest proportion of the black community. This fact is extremely important since blacks in Liverpool have a decidedly different perspective on the political system, based on their experience with racism dating back over 200 years, than the members of immigrant communities. Since the early 1940s, Liverpool has drawn an increasing number of its black residents from the Caribbean and South Asia. These multiple social groupings have presented strong challenges to the task of mobilizing cohesive black strength in the political process. The problem of group solidarity is compounded by the prominent role played by the Commission for Racial Equality (CRE) and Community Relations Commissions (CRC) in the articulation of black interests. While the CRC in Liverpool has tended to be more radical and community-oriented than in other British cities, its position as a government institution charged with the responsibility of mediating community demands has had the principal effect of stifling the growth of independent politics and creating strong competition by community groups for government-based resources.

This pattern of black interest group articulation has not produced black political quiescence. Blacks in Liverpool have a history of resistance and political activism that dates back several centuries. Many blacks in Liverpool were involved in the international movement to abolish slavery. Black resistance and protest began to take on a formal organizational presence in Liverpool in 1937 with the founding of the Liverpool Association for the Welfare of Colored People. In the 1940s the fight for black freedom in Liverpool was lead by The League of Colored People, The International Race Relations Committee, The Colonial Defense Committee, and The Colonial People's Defense Association. In the 1950s The Merseyside West Indians Association emerged as a separate political caucus focusing on the special interests of West Indians. Black activism in Liverpool flourished in the 1960s, taking the form of mass demonstrations and the formation of black nationalist groups such as the Young Panthers. In the 1970s a multiracial coalition called the Merseyside Anti-racist Alliance (MARA) launched a vigorous campaign to stamp out right-wing extremism by white nationalist groups such as the National Front. The work of this group was complemented by the activities of an autonomous black group called The Liverpool Black Organization. Out of this movement a number of key community institutions were formed, including the Charles Wootton Center for further education, South Liverpool Personnel Employment Center, the Caribbean Center, and the Pakistan Center. The early years of the 1980s witnessed the explosion of urban riots in Liverpool's black community. Law enforcement officials from across Britain were dispatched to Liverpool to quell the disturbances. In the aftermath of the riots, a number of new black political organizations were formed, including the Liverpool Defense Committee, and the Liverpool Black Caucus. During the 1980s the Black Caucus played a highly visible role in community politics. Operating as an auxiliary unit of the CRC, the Black Caucus functioned for a time as an advisory unit to the city council. In this capacity, it lobbied vigorously for the creation of positive action programs that would expand employment and social service benefits for the black community. City elections in 1987 resulted in the election of the first black representative to the city council as well as the emergence of two independent black candidates for the council running under the banner of the Federation of Black Liverpool Organizations.

Equal Opportunity Policies and Local Government

Despite the commitment of Liverpool black citizens to the ideals of representative government and democratic participation, the black community remains largely an underclass excluded from the normal fruits of citizenship that the working class as a whole enjoys, such as access to council employment, access to council housing, access to old people's homes, access to home helps, and land access to adoption and fostering opportunities. Community politics in Liverpool in recent years has centered around the struggle to place race equality policies on the public agenda and redistribute resources to combat poverty and social instability in black neighborhoods. Liverpool's experience in this crucial area helps to illuminate the potential for progress, as well as the potential for blockage, extant within the British political system.

The politics of race equality in Britain has not been static. Strong resistance to the hoary pattern of racial inequality by black activists and their allies in the anti-racist lobby effectively produced an alteration in race relations policies in the 1970s and 1980s. During these years a new model of race equality policy-making at the local level was institutionalized. Key elements of this new model included: comprehensive equal opportunity statements (frequently encompassing issues of gender and disability as well as race); overhaul of employment procedures, including opening up posts to external advertisement; training staff in nonracist practices and procedures; ethnic monitoring, and the setting of racial equality employment targets; positive action training schemes and access courses to insure more black staff appointments at a range of occupational levels; and financial, advisory, and practical support for local black businesses, community projects, and ethnic centers.

In the field of service delivery, a key theme has been the commitment to equality of treatment and outcome, not just of opportunity. Thus, policies have been reviewed in housing, social service, and education to remove sources of indirect as well as direct discrimination and disadvantage embedded in "normal" department procedures and practices. Practical measures have been implemented to recruit and train black staff, to support ethnic minority cultures, and to provide ethnically or racially specific services. To insure an ongoing corporate policy commitment on race issues and regular involvement of local black communities in decision-making, race equality units, and committee structures have been established within the formal institutional apparatus of the local authority (Ben-Tovim, 1983: 158–66). These positive local government developments, pushed with particular energy where black people have taken an active role in the leadership or management of local councils, have been paralleled by occasional initiatives by employers, public bodies, and specific positive action agencies. The outcome of such initiatives has been a shift in the employment and service-delivery profile of some of the institutions involved to a more equitable racial distribution. But these still exceptional in-roads into patterns of racial equality have been counter-balanced by trends and forces that have inhibited, subverted or counteracted progressive race equality initiatives.

During the mid-1980s the Thatcher government took determined efforts to inhibit the spending patterns and independent strength of the urban local authorities, including the tightening of fiscal restraint and the abolition of a whole tier of government. Those local authorities that had been taking the most radical forms of anti-racist action (e.g., the Greater London Council and the Inner London Education Authority) were the most heavily punished by central government; and, indeed, it was precisely the anti-racism of many of the left-wing authorities that became a key ideological undercurrent of the growing attack on the role of inner city local authorities that was the keynote of Thatcher's third election victory in 1987. Thus, a crude "anti-anti-racism" emerged in the mid-1980s, through an alliance of the intellectual right and the Thatcherite popular press, which portrayed individuals or authorities taking firm anti-racist action as mentally deranged, disloyal, and part of the loony left. Attacks on the reform campaign of the anti-racist alliance were enhanced by the mark failure by left-wing municipal authorities to build a solid base of public understanding and support for the new approaches to race equality policy-making they adopted.

What British society experienced in the 1980s was the convergence of a number of forces that undermined progress on racial issues. First there was the traditional strand of British conservatism, liberalism, and socialism that has found it ideologically difficult to really accept the need for racially specific forms of social intervention or for black self-help organizations (Gilroy, 1987). This reluctance is reflected in the ambiguity of Britain's race relations legislation and the Labour party's official opposition to black sections. Second, there was the racial tension that flared up around the issue of third world immigration to England. Anti-immigration policies have given many Britons the notion that it is whites rather than blacks that should be the focus of governmental protective action (Solomos, 1989: 48–67). Third, the outbreak of community riots in British cities gave political advantage to conservative law and order forces seeking to suppress the aims and aspirations of minority groups pushing for fundamental social and economic change in British society (Sivanandan, 1982: 23–46). Liverpool provides a clear example of what happens when these kind of negative attitudes are translated into public policy. The response of the Liverpool city council to the 1981 riots was an urban regeneration policy that focused on high profile policies such as the renovation of the Royal Albert Dock that benefited white business interests while by-passing the local black community. Black leaders complained bitterly that no blacks were employed at the Albert Dock renovation site, but their criticisms had no effect.

Liverpool: The Case for Positive Action

The Liverpool experience also confirms that the policy thrust around equal opportunities and positive action still remains an essential component of the struggle towards racial equality. Liverpool has been the site of "urban regeneration" interventions from the perspective of the right and the left, which have both failed to build in a specific anti-racist dimension and have equally failed to diminish the problem of racial inequality outlined above. Thus, in response to the disturbances of 1981, the government developed its vision of urban alliance between the central government and the private sector. This policy response has increasingly strengthened the power and authority of private business interests at the expense of the powers of local city councils; policy initiatives by local councils are being replaced by policy mandates exercised by non-elected local government institutions such as the Merseyside Development Corporation, the Task Forces, and the City Action Teams (Ben-Tovim, 1988: 144–54). These new institutions have tended to by-pass local black community organizations as well as local authorities. Lacking mechanisms to target and monitor black community needs and to work collaboratively with black organizations or local councils, their normal mode of operation has been to support relatively minor or marginal one-off schemes or businesses geared toward the launching of highly visible, prestigious projects, such as The Garden Festival, The Albert Dock, and The Tate Gallery. These projects have produced no employment or training gain for the local minority population (Ben Tovim, 1988: 146–48). A key central government failure, then, has been its property-led emphasis on the physical regeneration of inner city areas rather than the prioritizing of social objectives, such as the systematic targeting of employment and training opportunities for specific groups of disadvantaged residents. At the same time, the general withdrawal of funds from inner-city areas, together with the new social policies for social security, taxation, and housing have exacerbated still further the discriminatory impact of mainstream policies on depressed inner-city neighborhoods. The period of militant control of the Liverpool City Council from 1983 to 1987 was the mirror image of the government's reduction of race to general economic policies. Thus, on the one hand the government assumed that black economic progress would come from benign and color-blind generalized revitalization public investment and local private sector initiatives, and on the other hand, the former militant leadership assumed that its own version of urban regeneration (a generalized strategy of house building, environmental improvement, and job protection) would be to the benefit of the working class as a whole, and that to promote black interests explicitly would be illegitimate and divisive.

In Liverpool strong socialist class action without a specific anti-racist perspective has left the economic inequality facing the city's black citizens intact. Because of the lack of employment targeting and contract compliance actions there has been no increase in black employment, either within the council or by private contractors working in Liverpool on house-building. Similarly, the lack of ethnic monitoring and targeting has enabled new housing opportunities to fundamentally by-pass the black community.

Hence, the Liverpool case study provides clear confirmation of the growing recognition in Britain, as in the United States, that a general rise in local economic activity does not necessarily result in a "trickle-down" of employment benefits to specific disadvantaged or underprivileged groups, such as inner-city black populations. On the contrary, Liverpool demonstrates that there can be no substantial economic development to benefit the black community as a whole unless specific race equality policies, safeguards, and measures are built into a broad range of progressive economic and social strategies.

Liverpool: The Current Race Equality Agenda

With the advent of a new Labour administration in 1987, containing former critics of the previous aggressively color-blind militant administration, an attempt has been made to reconstruct the city's urban regeneration policy within a context that provides for the explicit targeting of black community needs, adopts clear positive action initiatives, and explicitly cooperates with rather than confronts black community organizations.

The need for cooperation with the new local units of central government and with the local private sector is acknowledged, with the emphasis being on the development, by all agencies involved, of mechanisms that quite explicitly target employment training, educational, and business opportunities toward the black population. Thus, a substantial positive action scheme to provide training leading to council employment for 600 local black people has been set up by the city council. Considerable support is being given to a range of local black organizations, including housing associations, training agencies, and voluntary groups. The council has established interpreting and immigration units as well as a Mental Health Center. There is increased provision for black access to higher education initiatives. Agreements on equal opportunities and local labor are being sought with major contractors, investors, and local employers. Council housing opportunities are now monitored to ensure that racial bias is not influencing the allocation process. Many long-standing discriminatory recruitment practices, including trade union nomination rights have been stopped.

Such local initiatives, of course, can have only a relatively limited impact. To be fully effective, these measures require the leverage of meaningful and nationally established legal pressures and strong economic sanctions and rewards with respect to targets and timetables for minority training and employment. These employment measures also need to be complemented by a comprehensive range of interventions in economic, housing, social welfare, and legal institutions to offset the racially discriminatory effects of current government policies.

The need for concerted and radical national action on broad social and economic policy fronts, as well as improved national anti-racist policy development and legislation, should not have a disabling effect with respect to local initiatives to advance race equality and promote racial justice. The sort of equal opportunity and positive action initiatives that Liverpool is now developing are still a necessary part of the local race equality agenda—though it must be acknowledged that in Liverpool there still exist rather underdeveloped resources, mechanisms, and structures for policy development, monitoring, community involvement, and community accountability as the Gifford Report points out.

Equal opportunity and positive action policies, then, are essential in that they can bring about immediate benefits by opening up more employment, training, and business opportunities and by making council services more accessible and accountable to minority communities. Such initiatives can also help open up space for increasing political power for minorities, for forging alliances with progressive political forces, and for the development of more extensive social, economic, and political changes. But as we have stressed, such initiatives can be easily marginalized; elected members and senior managers of local authorities are easily satisfied by cosmetic gestures that leave intact the existing distribution of economic, political, and administrative power. Race equality policies can be counter-productive if introduced without adequate understanding support and alliances both within and outside of the local authority. Like other aspects of local government, access to the levers of power can be used to benefit the individual rather than the community, so that openness, monitoring and accountability, and the maintenance of proper professional standards are essential in the implementation of equal opportunity policies.

Conclusion

The positive action initiatives adopted and implemented by the Liverpool City Council, while important, represent only modest first steps. Much work needs to be done to bring social justice to Liverpool's exploited black community. As we have stressed, initiatives from the local authority must be undergirded by innovations, pressures, and sanctions from the central government. The American experience clearly demonstrates that intervention by the national government is an absolutely essential prerequisite for the effective implementation of affirmative action policies in local communities. When the national government indicates that it is unwilling to cut off funds to institutions that discriminate, the interests of minorities suffer. Positive action requires collective effort. It is the responsibility of government at all levels to make discrimination against minorities not only illegal but unprofitable. Cosmetic gestures and rhetorical proclamations are not sufficient to do the job. Private sector employers must come to know that equal opportunity for minorities is good business; they must also anticipate that when they fail to follow equal employment practices they will receive a swift, punitive response from appropriate government monitoring agencies.

There remain a multitude of troubling racial problems in Liverpool. Police enforcement is a source of major tension; the drug problem is becoming a critical factor in the health and educational profile of the black teenage population; the black community remains almost completely underrepresented in the political process with one black councillor (out of 99 councillors) and no blacks in key positions in the Labour party.[1]

The Liverpool example provides a definitive demonstration of the inadequacies and dangers of a narrow color-blind class approach to the problem of racism. It suggests firmly and poignantly that what is required is cooperative action at all levels of government and in the private sector to reduce racist thinking, raise the level of self-esteem for minorities, provide targeted, race-specific opportunities for social, economic, and cultural advancement, and facilitate the establishment of bases of meaningful political power so that minorities can become effectively involved in the process of government in their own behalf.

Note

1. Currently, the single black councillor is Petrona Lashley. Moving up in the leadership ranks of the Labour party, Ms. Lashley has advanced to the position of deputy lord mayor. Recently, her aspirations to become the first black lord mayor of Liverpool has been thwarted by newspaper revelations that she was arrested and fined for prostitution three times in the 1970s.

References

Ben-Tovim, Gideon, ed. 1983. *Equal Opportunities and the Employment of Black People and Ethnic Minorities on Merseyside*. Liverpool: Merseyside Association for Racial Equality in Employment and Merseyside Area Profile Group.

———. 1988. "Race, Politics and Urban Regeneration: Lessons from Liverpool." In *Regenerating the Cities: The UK and Experience*, ed. Michael Parkinson, Bernard Foley, and Dennis Judd. Manchester: Manchester University Press.

Ben-Tovim, Gideon, John Gabriel, Ian Law, and Kathleen Stredder, eds. 1986. *The Local Politics of Race*. London: MacMillan Education, LTD.

Braham, Peter, Ali Rattansi, and Richard Skellington, eds. 1992. *Racism and Antiracism: Inequalities, Opportunities, and Politics*. London: Sage Publishers, LTD.

Commission for Racial Equality. 1984. *Race and Housing in Liverpool: A Research Report*. London: Commission for Racial Equality.

Connolly, Michelle, and N.P.K. Torkington. 1990. "Black Youth and Politics in Liverpool." In Occasional Paper Series, Department of Sociology, University of Liverpool.

Fryer, Peter. 1984. *Staying Power: The History of Black People in Britain*. London: Pluto Press.

Gifford, Lord, Wally Brown, and Ruth Bundey. 1989. *Loosen the Shackles*. London: Karia Press.

Gilroy, Paul. 1987. *There Ain't No Black in the Union Jack: The Cultural Politics of Race and Nation*. London: Hutchingson Press.

Goulbourne, Harry, ed. 1990. *Black Politics in Britain*. Aldershot, England: Avebury Press.

Law, Ian, and June Menfrey, eds. 1981. *A History of Race and Racism in Liverpool, 1660–1950*. Liverpool: Merseyside Community Relations Council.

Liverpool Black Caucus. 1986. *The Racial Politics of Militant in Liverpool*. London: Runnymeade Trust.

Rex, John, and Sally Tomlinson. 1979. *Colonial Immigrants in a British City*. London: Routledge and Kegan Paul.

Sivanandan, A. 1982. *A Different Hunger: Writings on Black Resistance.* London: Pluto Press.
Solomos, John. 1989. *Race and Racism in Contemporary Britain.* London: MacMillan Education, LTD.
Torkington, N.P.K. 1983. *The Racial Politics of Health—A Liverpool Profile.* Liverpool: Merseyside Area Profile Group.

Racial Consciousness, Afro-Brazilian Electoral Strategies, and Regime Change in Brazil

Michael Mitchell

Arizona State University

Introduction

The consolidation of democracy marks a new chapter in Brazil's political history. Brazilians generally have enjoyed the fruits of a sustained evolution from authoritarian rule to a more open and competitive political process. And specifically, since 1986, Afro-Brazilians, as well as women, workers, Brazil's indigenous peoples, and other traditionally excluded political groups, have been able to press their collective claims for political inclusion without the threat of reprisals that would have been expected from the previous authoritarian regime (Della Cava, 1989; Mainwaring, 1989; Keck, 1989; McRea, 1992; Cardoso, 1992). Nevertheless, nestled within this consolidation process is a set of historical and institutional constraints that effectively narrow the range of political action of these groups. This is especially the case with regard to the incorporation of Afro-Brazilians into the electoral arena during the consolidation process. Afro-Brazilians have had to confront the question of whether they can effectively utilize the resource of racial or group consciousness in the circumstances of a democratic consolidation.

The thesis proposed in this article is that while racial consciousness represents a genuine political resource for Afro-Brazilians its use is conditioned by the particular circumstances of the Brazilian democratic consolidation. Even though Afro-Brazilians have rallied to racial consciousness as the inspiration for creating social movements (Nascimento, 1992; Gonzalez, 1985), its utility remains limited in the electoral arena, more so than has been the case for Afro-North Americans. The article argues further that the *continuismo* in the consolidation process, that is, the persistence of old patterns and practices of previous regimes to be found in the present one, account for enduring limitations on the politics of racial identity in Brazil.

The analysis here draws on the insights taken from a current perspective in the study of comparative politics known as the "new institutionalism" (March and Olsen, 1989; Steinmo, Thelen, and Longstreth, 1992). The insights gleaned from this approach in general terms suggest the following. The institutional features of a political arena determine the outcome of political conflicts. In other words, political outcomes are defined by both formal institutional settings as well as the procedures, practices, and norms that give substance to formal institutions. In this regard James March and Johan Olsen (1989) have developed the following reasoning. Political behavior, according to March and Olsen, cannot always be analyzed in the abstract context of absolute certainty and perfect information. In most situations political actors fashion their behaviors and decisions from cues taken from pre-established rules of conduct, codes, norms, and conventions that reduce the uncertainty of their political environments.

Norms and rules, however, need not be completely rational. As such culture, history, tradition, and values assume a heightened importance in understanding political behavior. Moreover, certain rules or codes have a staying power that gives shape to the predictability of political outcomes. Rules may be invoked, in fact, in a manner that excludes the interests of some segments of society. In the case of Afro-Brazilian political action there occurs a "mobilization of bias" (in Shaatschneiderian terms) against the use of racial consciousness as the principal vehicle of electoral success.

Since the inception of mass politics in Brazil, launched by the Revolution of 1930, Afro-Brazilians have tried to secure a foot hold in the electoral process. Despite these efforts Afro-Brazilians have been unable to gain the kind of prominence in the electoral arena equal to that of, say, Afro-North Americans in their own national context. Afro-Brazilians have had to confront a series of recurring political patterns that have effectively blunted the ability of Afro-Brazilians to enter the electoral arena with any sustained force. And, without a solid base in the electoral arena, Afro-Brazilians have had to devise strategies of electoral competition that diminish the prospects of using racial consciousness as a political resource. The "new institutionalism" therefore suggests posing questions about the ways in which interests are ruled out of the political arena, and the ways in which the bias of a particular institutional framework conditions the decisions, strategies, and behavior of the actors affected by that bias.

The second of the insights derived from the "new institutionalism" suggests that the evolution of political conflicts are set in "path dependent" directions. These directions become fixed in a nation's history and produce recurring patterns of political competition, conflict, and control. The analysis here focuses on Afro-Brazilian responses to the historical institutional determinants that underlie the Brazilian democratic consolidation.

Salient Features of Brazilian Democratic Consolidation

An observation that reads to the effect that the Brazilian democratic consolidation is still haunted by an atmosphere of uncertainty runs the risk of appearing to be somewhat exaggerated. Nonetheless, however much of the memory of authoritarian rule recedes in the Brazilian collective memory and however unlikely the possibility of a political crisis emerging that triggers the reestablishment of an authoritarian regime, the outcome of consolidation continues to travel toward some still undefined point of closure. Brazilian politics still carries within it a set of unresolved tensions that distinguish it from advanced liberal democracies.

Kurt Von Mettenheim (1995) has captured these tensions in his description of Brazilian politics as a dichotomous electoral universe that is shaped by the dialectical tendencies of direct democracy and state-sponsored representation. In Von Mettenheim's view Brazil's electoral system allows for, and, in fact, is structured by, voters' expectations of democratic performance on the one hand and patronage-based political parties on the other. In other words, the electoral system operates on the basis of citizens' normative or ethical evaluations of government performance which are then channeled into party preferences through the delivery of political patronage. The pattern that Von Mettenheim paints with this description is of a politics beset by a profound duality.

In light of Von Mettenheim's perceptions, the current democratic consolidation can be described in the following terms. In one sense the consolidation represents a genuine break with the past. Eliminated from Brazil's institutional life, for example, are the corporatist restraints that had hindered the development of autonomous working-class political movements (Keck, 1992; Coelho and Nantes de Oliveira, 1989: 69–71). And, as José Álvaro Moisés (1993) has pointed out, dramatic socio-demographic changes have taken place over the past decades that have introduced new factors into Brazilian politics. For example, the electoral universe has expanded significantly. From 1964 to 1989 it experienced a two-fold increase in the number of eligible voters (from 29 to 56 percent of the population). In addition, 70 percent of the voters casting ballots in the 1989 presidential elections were doing so for the first time (Moisés, 1993: 578–80). In other words the consolidation process has been more than a reconstitution of democratic institutions suppressed by an authoritarian regime. It has also turned out to be a completely new experience for entire generations of Brazilians. The democratic consolidation has also fostered an environment that has allowed for the resurgence of black social movements. In the wake of the erosion of authoritarian controls there emerged within Brazilian civil society black social movements of considerable regard (Hanchard, 1994; Andrews, 1991), the most renowned of which has been Movimento Unificado Negro (the MNU), the largest and most sustained of black Brazilian protest movements of this century.

Nevertheless, contained within this democratic consolidation are older and more settled ways of conducting the business of politics. Astute observers (Souza, 1989; Hagopian, 1992; Fleischer, 1990; Graham, 1990) have made note of the pattern in which remnants of the old regime survive in uneasy coexistence with the new democratic order. Some of the observations regarding this pattern are:

1. Political relationships based on clientelist controls held in place through the distribution of governmental patronage.
2. A weak political party system that frequently reflects the ambitions of strong personalities rather than the programs and ideologies of distinct cleavages and constituencies.

3. The resilience of authoritarian elites in repositioning themselves favorably in the newly created political party system of the democratic regime.

These are, in fact, political patterns that have beset Brazilian politics for most of the twentieth century. Clientelism, for example, is a legacy of the First Republic (1889–1930) in which rural oligarches, often appropriating the title of *coronel* for themselves, dominated local and national politics to the exclusion of the more modern-oriented urban middle classes and the rural and urban masses (Flynn, 1978: 13–17; see also Leal, 1975). Clientelism resurfaced in the populist democratic regime of the late 1940s and 1950s, and was regarded as the major source of power of Getúlio Vargas, the leading political figure of the era. Clientelism developed to such proportions during this time that it contributed forcefully to weakening the very credibility of the populist regime of 1946–1964 (Flynn, 1978: 200–203, 267–72; Ianni, 1968). It survived through the authoritarian regime, and even received that regime's grudging acknowledgment of its significance and power in Brazilian politics (Diniz, 1982).

Political parties have rarely functioned as organizations that coherently organize the vast array of interests in Brazilian society. The populist regime (1945–1964) was particularly susceptible to this weakness. And even into the democratic consolidation after 1985 they have continued to operate as vehicles for the ambitions of strong-willed personalities. Two personalities who come readily to mind in this regard are Leonel Brizola, former governor of Rio de Janeiro, who represents a leftist personalism, and Paulo Maluf, former mayor of São Paulo, who embodies a right-wing variant of populism. As such they have served neither as conduits for strictly rational or negotiated policy-making nor as agents of well-defined constituencies (Mainwaring, 1988).

Authoritarian elites have displayed a remarkable capacity to survive regime change. Perhaps the most dramatic illustration of this is Getúlio Vargas's extraordinary comeback in the democratic regime of the 1940s and 1950s after the toppling of his authoritarian regime in 1945. And more recently, authoritarian elites have weathered the democratic transition as well, as former president José Sarney has shown in his climb to leadership in the party (the PMDB) that had opposed the authoritarian regime which he supported during the 1970s.

These patterns have had a direct bearing on the capacity of Afro-Brazilians to use their political resources. Afro-Brazilians have been particularly vulnerable to populist and clientelist politics. The politics of clientelism has situated Afro-Brazilians in power relationships in which their support for strong leaders has more often than not served to enhance the electoral power of leaders whose loyalty to and sympathies for Afro-Brazilians would easily give way to other concerns and constituencies. As previous research has shown, both the overt and subtle appeals to Afro-Brazilians have led blacks to embrace the politics of populism behind which lay clientelist forms of political control (Souza, 1971; Soares, 1985; Castro, 1993). Moreover, the survival of the authoritarian elites of the old regime into the new democratic order have made it all the more difficult for blacks to independently promote non-elite agendas in the electoral arena.

This sketch of some of the characteristics of Brazilian democratic consolidation suggests some of the options that Afro-Brazilians might contemplate as they calculate the extent of their involvement in the electoral arena. Among these strategies are the following (also see Andrews, 1991: 195–96):

1. To form alliances within the existing party system and to attempt to make the best of clientelist arrangements.
2. To outflank clientelism by building alliances with parties that have shunned clientelist arrangements with their constituencies.
3. To avoid the dangers of clientelism altogether by striking out on an independent course and developing strategies that would provide them relative autonomy in the electoral arena such as establishing independent political parties based on appeals to racial consciousness.
4. To withdraw completely from the electoral arena and rely solely on the efforts of social movements and nongovernmental organizations to advance the cause of blacks.

In this respect Afro-Brazilians face a situation somewhat different from Afro-North Americans. Even though the politics of racial consciousness of Afro-North Americans suffers from serious constraints, the nature of those constraints differs substantially from the nature of those encountered in Brazil. In the United States the insertion of racial consciousness into electoral politics has become a commonly recognized and widely accepted feature of black North American politics. In fact, much of the discussion of black American politics in the United States assumes that its core rests in the dynamic of racial consciousness. In the North American context the extent of racial consciousness is so pervasive that it is further assumed to have predictable effects in black political life (Dawson, 1994; Chong, 1991; Henderson, 1987; Barker, 1987; Preston, 1987; McCormack and Smith, 1989; Gurin et al., 1989; Pinderhughes, 1990; Shingles, 1981). In this sense, and notwithstanding current Supreme Court rulings on majority-minority voting districts, the institutional arrangements of American politics lend themselves more readily to the insertion of racial consciousness, or a "black utility heuristic," to use Michael Dawson's terms (Dawson, 1994), into electoral politics in the United States. In the Brazilian case black aspirants to elective office must deal more profoundly with the shadows of their own national past. These, in effect, channel the use of racial consciousness into the particular contours of Brazilian politics.

What follows is a discussion arranged historically, and covering a period from 1930 to 1996. The thrust of this discussion is to outline the several strategies which Afro-Brazilians have contemplated and adopted in dealing with some of the long-standing institutional patterns in Brazilian politics. The general argument proposed is that black electoral strategies have been predicated on the institutional constraints specific to Brazilian political development. The discussion is divided into four sections corresponding to the cycles of regime change in which Afro-Brazilian electoral politics has emerged. Illustrations of these strategies are drawn mainly from the experience of blacks in São Paulo, although reference is made to other experiences as well.

Electoral Politics from the Revolution of 1930 to the Democratization of 1945–1964

One of the earliest manifestations of Afro-Brazilian electoral politics surfaced in the aftermath of the Revolution of 1930. The revolution, led by Getúlio Vargas, effectively ended the total dominance exercised by Brazil's rural oligarches over national politics (Skidmore, 1967: 3–21; Flynn, 1978: 59–84). It also created an opening, however narrow, for non-elite groups to press their demands for inclusion into Brazilian politics. The Revolution of 1930 had far reaching consequences on Brazilian political life that lasted well beyond its demise. Initially, it promised to open Brazilian politics to the modernizing and non-elite groups whom the rural oligarches of the previous regime had suppressed. It even briefly experimented with procedures for widening political participation and guaranteeing economic and social rights for the largely disenfranchised masses. Nevertheless, it eventually adopted the corporatist controls on mass politics that would remain in place for the next fifty years.

In the circumstances of the 1930 revolution, the Black Brazilian Front (*Frente Negra Brasileira*) entered the political scene as the first major Afro-Brazilian social movement of this century (Fernandes, 1965, vol. 2: 12–13). In these surroundings the leadership of the Front debated the merits of entering the electoral arena. Several of the leaders argued that Afro-Brazilians should establish at least some symbolic black presence in the politics of the new era.

In the municipal elections of 1933 the Front actively promoted the candidacy of its president, Arlindo Veiga dos Santos, to the City Council of São Paulo. Santos was somewhat of an ill-suited candidate for office. His longstanding monarchist views as well as his contacts with the Brazilian Fascist movement placed him at ideological odds with the democratic republic which the revolution claimed to be reconstructing.

Veiga dos Santos's candidacy aroused considerable opposition among those who then held power for reasons other than his monarchist views. The pretext that brought this opposition to light was the Front's decision to register itself as an independent black political party (Fernandes, 1965, vol. 2: 36–37). At first a challenge was lodged against the Front's efforts on the arguable grounds that Brazil's electoral laws prohibited the creation of a political party based exclusively on a racial constituency. Eventually, however, the Front's attempt to enter the electoral arena would be caught in the events that led to the end of the 1930 revolution. Faced with armed insurgencies from the left and the right Getúlio Vargas suppressed his opposition, shut down democratic institutions, and established an authoritarian regime known as the *Estado Novo*. With his creation of the *Estado Novo* in 1937 Getúlio Vargas declared all political parties to be in permanent recess, a measure that affected the Front fatally (Fernandes, 1965, vol. 2: 47; Mitchell, 1977:133). The Front's entry into electoral politics fell victim to authoritarian repression.

The ironic result of the Revolution of 1930, which rose to challenge the grip that Brazil's rural oligarches held over national politics, was to further entrench the patterns of political control that served as pillars of the discredited First Republic. Under the *Estado Novo* Getúlio Vargas had converted these controls into explicitly corporatist features of a transformed Brazilian state. Vargas went on to reinforce these patterns during the democratic restoration of the 1940s and 1950s after his dramatic return to national politics in the late 1940s. Under the democratic regime, constitutionally established in 1946, Vargas deftly used the political party system through patronage and clientelist relationships to co-opt both rural oligarches and the emerging urban working class in order to strike a delicate balance between antagonistic forces that rapid modernization was pushing to hostile extremes. Vargas skillfully manipulated the reach of the state as well as the party system to subordinate the interests of civil society to the ends of the state that he embodied. And, after his death in 1954, his protégés and regional political bosses would continue to employ these structures of political control. In the political universe that Vargas had created few in the democratic restoration of the 1940s and 1950s could escape the reach of clientelist politics.

The restoration of Brazilian democracy in 1945–1946 once again posed questions for Afro-Brazilians regarding the tangible and symbolic benefits of engaging in electoral politics. Not the least important of these questions was the extent to which blacks could muster any advantage when faced with the subtle constraints of populist and clientelist politics under a new democratic regime. José Correia Leite, one of the most respected black leaders in São Paulo at the time, anticipated this problem. Correia Leite was not convinced that the reestablishment of party politics would redound to the complete benefit of the Afro-Brazilian community. In Correia Leite's view any black standing before the more powerful interests in Brazil's political parties could only be a junior partner at best, serving more at the behest of party elites than as defender of black interests. Correia Leite consistently held the position that blacks ought to maintain a respectful distance from all partisan politics. While a committed democrat he remained weary of Brazil's democratic institutions, and specifically of its political parties (Correia Leite, 1992: 130–31, 210–11, 223–34). And, despite Correia Leite's cautions, Afro-Brazilians invested their efforts in electoral politics with little or no tangible success (Andrews, 1991: 182–88, 320; Fernandes, 1965, vol. 2: 56–57).

Electoral Politics During the Authoritarian Regime: 1964–1982

The leaders of the military coup of 1964 declared that their intent was to revamp the Brazilian state according to a blueprint that detailed the reorganization of Brazil's economic and political life. At the start, the regime set out to restructure rather than destroy the political institutions of the past. In fact the regime gained substantial civilian support premised on the claim that civilian political institutions would continue to function even if in a curtailed fashion. However, the military never fully satisfied its conservative supporters in this regard and as a consequence turned original supporters into ardent critics (Reale, 1977).

Nevertheless, in 1966 General Humberto Castello Branco, head of the military government, issued Institutional Act #2, which restructured Brazil's party system. The multiparty system of the past was replaced by an arbitrarily drawn two-party system. One party, ARENA, was to represent the regime; the other, MDB, became a catch-all opposition composed of politicians whom the regime wished to consign to a political limbo (Skidmore, 1988: 45–47, 64–65). While operating in an extremely restricted fashion, especially under the threat of cancellation of electoral mandates and suspension of citizenship rights, political parties retained some conventional functions such as organizing blocks within legislatures, nominating candidates for elective office, and offering limited resources for candidates' electoral campaigns.

Anyone with political ambitions had to learn quickly how to maneuver within this restricted party system. One Afro-Brazilian who grasped the new rules of the game was Adalberto Camargo, elected to congress for the first time in 1966 under the party banner of the MDB. Camargo shrewdly calculated the advantages of a situation in which few at the time could have seen much prospect. It was a situation well suited for an outsider to enter. Neither Camargo's race nor his modest background would count against him in running for an office that conveyed little real power or that contained dubious symbolic value.

If Camargo never tried to hide the fact of his racial identity he neither made any militant expression of it. Nor was he a particularly charismatic figure. Camargo's diligence and attention to detail, however, allowed him to build a credible political machine (Fontaine, 1985: 62–63). By the time of his second congressional campaign he had become one of the five top vote getters in his party. Moreover, he worked to promote the careers of other black candidates such as Theodosina Ribeiro in the São Paulo state legislature, and Paulo Ruy in the São Paulo city council.

Camargo's own political program rested squarely in business. In fact politics had become his second career after achieving success at building a lucrative car dealership. His political program reflected this background. His legislative initiatives and his constituency work focused on furthering business ties between Brazil and the countries of Western Africa. Camargo established the Afro-Brazilian Chamber of Commerce with this end in mind (Costa, 1982: 60–66; Hanchard, 1994: 85–86). Camargo maintained constituent contacts on this level as well. He was a regular and prominent member of the São Paulo's Clube Aristocrata, which served as a point of contact for São Paulo's black business elite. As can be imagined, Camargo took an essentially conservative stand in racial politics. His guiding assumptions were that the racial integration of Brazilian society was an end in itself and that this could be achieved by working within established institutions, and, not coincidentally, within those created by the authoritarian regime.

Camargo's own career was undone by the redemocratization process. His crisis came shortly after the regime's second party reorganization in 1979. Under the regime's new plan, parties were permitted to form more open and natural constituencies than was the case under the rigid and artificial two-party system created by Castello Branco in 1966. The situation of party reorganization posed a problem for Camargo and his protégés. Which of the newly created parties would they join? Camargo's political acumen failed him on this occasion. He, Ribeiro, and Ruy opted to join the PDS, the party still loyal to the regime. In effect Camargo had moved to the right at a time when the ideological momentum within the party system was shifting to the left. This proved to be a fatal miscalculation. Camargo, as well as Ribeiro and Ruy were all defeated in their respective races in the elections of 1982 (Fontaine, 1985: 63; Valente, 1986: 78).

Another prominent black politician of the era was less a victim of democratization than a casualty of the willful force of authoritarian rule. This was Esmeraldo Tarquínio whose electoral victory in the mayoral race in the city of Santos in 1968 was annulled by the authoritarian regime. Tarquínio was somewhat of a contrast to Adalberto Camargo. His career began with his involvement in the labor movement. In the 1950s he served as a São Paulo state legislator whose primary constituency was made up of the stevedores of Santos. Tarquínio, moreover, was a charismatic figure who enjoyed widespread popularity, particularly among the dock workers of Santos. Tarquínio's ties to the black community, however, were a secondary concern. Nevertheless, he attempted to maintain links to both the stevedores and the black community of São Paulo (Correia Leite, 1992: 170). Some, in fact, criticized him for keeping the two constituencies separate, and of pitching different appeals to either (Valente, 1986: 61–62). Operating from his position of strength within the labor movement Tarquínio acted confidently and independently of the authoritarian regime. This independence had limits, however. Tarquínio was quite open in declaring his suspicions about the cancellation of his electoral mandate. He attributed it to the traditional elites of Santos, who, Tarquínio has asserted, appealed to the generals of the regime to prevent a black, and particularly a left-leaning militant one, from assuming the city's most prestigious office (author's interview with Tarquínio, July 14, 1970). Such was the nature of the arbitrariness of authoritarian rule.

The preceding sketch of these two figures serves to highlight the uneven impact that the authoritarian regime had on black electoral politics. The regime would allow an expressly black presence in politics but only to a certain point. On the one hand the regime acted with little hesitation in eliminating what it perceived as a beyond the bounds of acceptable racial protocol. Esmeraldo Tarquínio was the victim of this perception. On the other hand the regime extended a certain tolerance towards Adalberto Camargo, whose ideological sympathies lay closer to the regime's than Camargo's party affiliation indicated. In the end both figures illustrated the precarious nature of black electoral politics under authoritarian rule. Camargo, for his part, would not survive the transition to democracy and would fall into political obscurity. Tarquínio, on the other hand, would die prematurely while in the process of making substantial headway in rebuilding his own career during the early stage of the democratic transition (Valente, 1986: 62).

Electoral Politics: From Transition to Consolidation, 1982–1994

In 1982 the transition to democracy had reached a critical point. By then sufficient pressures for reform had mounted to force the regime into making significant concessions to democratic insurgents (Skidmore, 1988: 233–36). The most important of these concessions was the decision to allow the forthcoming gubernatorial elections to be held in an open and direct manner rather than through the indirect method instituted by the authoritarian regime. The direct elections of 1982, which also included elections for congress, state legislatures, and city councils, broadened the range of offices to be disputed openly. Free party competition thus became a fresh component in Brazilian politics and in the process, nudged the regime further along the path toward democratization.

The political parties rushed into the breach to capture ground denied them during the period of authoritarian controls. One untapped resource of electoral support was the potential for racial consciousness to attract votes (Andrews, 1991: 195). In São Paulo each of the five major parties (the PDS, the PTB, the PDT, PMDB, and PT), in fact, fielded a sizable number of black candidates. In all, fifty-four black candidates stood for elective office in São Paulo in 1982 (Valente, 1986: 54, 73–76). Blacks spread their candidacies almost evenly across the major parties.

Particularly in the state of São Paulo, the elections of 1982 released a pent-up store of opportunities for blacks entering the electoral arena. The 1982 elections would allow them to test the depth of public sentiment for race conscious politics. Black candidates incorporated appeals to racial consciousness to varying degrees in their campaigns. Some ran campaigns that relied almost exclusively on the premise that racial consciousness would galvanize a large number of black voters, while others strenuously avoided making race consciousness appeals. Still others chose a moderate course in which they pitched limited race consciousness appeals, so as not to affect their standing among other nonblack constituencies (Valente, 1986: 54–65).

The highest offices for which blacks ran in these elections were the several congressional seats in the state's delegation. Three candidates stood out in these races as the most visible and significant. The three, Adalberto Camargo, Milton Barbosa, and Hélio Santos, represented different approaches to the use of racial consciousness. Camargo, as discussed previously, couched racial matters in a conservative, business-oriented way. Milton Barbosa took the opposite tack. Barbosa was one of the founders of the Movimento Negro Unificado. He was looking to make a successful move from protest activist to elected official. Barbosa chose the PT party from which to run since it most comfortably accommodated the members of Brazil's new social movements into its organization. Hélio Santos occupied the center between Camargo on the right, and Barbosa on the left. Santos opted to run on the PMDB ticket, which constituted the largest, and the most moderate of the opposition to authoritarian rule. While Santos made racial appeals in his campaign he insisted that his candidacy was one to represent multiple constituencies (Valente, 1986: 54–65).

The extent to which racial identification figured into actually attracting votes was disappointing. None of the three most noted black candidates competing for congressional seats won their races. In fact both Camargo and Barbosa fared rather poorly. Neither Camargo nor Barbosa managed to gain more than approximately 7,000 votes respectively out of a total of 90,743 cast for all black congressional candidates (Valente, 1986: 73–76). These results were particularly telling for Camargo whose experience and organization could not produce significantly more votes than Barbosa, a relative neophyte, who lacked Camargo's connections and resources. Nevertheless, all things being equal, the reasonable conclusions to be drawn were that voters were slow to embrace Barbosa's somewhat militant projection of racial consciousness and unwilling to show continued satisfaction with Camargo's conservative, pro-regime positions.

Hélio Santos did rather well by comparison. He received 30 percent (27,462 of 90,743 votes) of all votes cast for black congressional candidates who comprised a field of eleven prospects (Valente, 1986: 73–76). Santos held one advantage over Barbosa and Camargo. This was his calculation of the drift in the partisan preferences among the voters. Santos ran on the PMDB ticket, the party that overall scored the greatest success in these elections. Moreover, he struck a course between Barbosa's social movement militancy and Camargo's establishment conservatism. While identifying himself as a black candidate, he also made a point of broadening his appeal to constituencies beyond the black community. And on the whole Santos's showing suggested that racial consciousness could have an impact on electoral results, but only in limited circumstances.

The direct elections of 1982 revealed something further. The regime's signaling of a genuine democratic opening may have raised expectations beyond which a black electorate was willing to go. What is remarkable about these elections is the disillusioning result in the face of the large number of black candidates who entered the race. The 1982 elections indicated that, at least, the pace of democratization and the cultivation of racial consciousness within a black electorate were at this point dissymmetric phenomena.

The congressional elections of 1986 marked another important juncture in the democratization process. These elections would culminate in the formation of a constituent assembly that would take the first steps toward dismantling the institutional apparatus of the disintegrating authoritarian regime.

Rio de Janeiro produced two new figures in black politics, who would seize the opportunities offered by these circumstances. One of these personalities was Carlos Alberto Oliveira dos Santos, known as Caó. The other was Benedita de Souza da Silva, popularly know as Benedita. Both served as strong advocates for Afro-Brazilian causes in the constituent assembly. They sponsored one provision that gave constitutional weight to new sanctions against racial discrimination, thus abrogating the rather innocuous Affonso Arinos anti-discrimination law of 1950. In addition they were instrumental in establishing constitutional protection over the site of the insurrectionary slave republic of Palmares, a protection that gave the Palmares site the designation of a National Patrimony.

On the surface Caó's and Benedita's different choices of party affiliation suggest that they had distinct approaches to the long-standing questions regarding blacks' entry into the electoral arena. Caó chose the PDT, while Benedita opted for the PT. The PDT could not completely shake its image as being the party controlled by a regional boss, Leonel Brizola, who was then governor of the state of Rio de Janeiro. Brizola was closely associated with the populism of the 1950s, having served as a lieutenant in the PTB, the party created by Getúlio Vargas to mobilize his working-class base of support. Brizola was steeped in the clientelist politics of the populist regime, and rightly or otherwise lived with the suspicion that he had formed the PDT to bring back the old populist style of political leadership as well as to promote his own presidential ambitions.

Benedita, on the other hand, joined a party with no trace of populism or clientelism in its past. The PT, in fact, was a creature of the democratic transition. Its beginnings lay in a series of strikes launched in the late 1970s by workers in São Paulo. The offshoot of these protests was the founding of the Partido dos Trabalhadores, or the PT, expressly for the purpose of establishing a political organization that would be completely independent of the state and a party system dominated by clientelist politics (Keck, 1992: 61–85). As it grew the PT would extend its range of interests and would attempt to attract elements of the so-called new social movements into its ranks.

The contrast between the PTD and the PT lay in their different conceptions of the relationship between state, party, and civil society. The former followed in the tradition of parties dominated by a strong leader and patronage politics; the latter attempted to chart a new course in Brazilian politics of establishing the autonomy of the party and civil society in relation to the state. A choice between these two would imply the manner in which an aspiring black politician would opt to enter into the political arena.

Nevertheless, there were similarities between Caó and Benedita that went beyond party affiliation. They both fashioned strategies of electoral appeal and representation that relied on racial consciousness and identity as just one among several ways of establishing their links to Brazilian voters. In fact the careers of Caó and Benedita closely resemble that of a figure of a previous era, Esmeraldo Tarquínio. Both Caó and Benedita, as with Tarquínio, built parallel bases of support which linked the black community to other nonblack constituencies. Their own personal backgrounds would reinforce this style of leadership.

Caó's leadership was formed in the student milieu of his native Bahia. In Rio he went on to assume leadership in several journalist associations from which he began building his public reputation (Costa, 1982: 144–49; Câmara Dos Deputados, 1987: 160). In 1982 he was named to the post of minister of labor in the cabinet of Governor Leonel Brizola (Hanchard, 1994: 134).

Benedita is best known by the campaign description: *mulher, favelada, e negra* (woman, from the *favelas*, and black). This description encapsules the multiple identities that define her public life. Benedita's background is rooted in the *favelas* of Rio de Janeiro (Mendoça and Benjamin, 1997). It is from this base that she rose to political prominence. Initially, she assumed leadership in *favela* associations and quickly acquired a reputation as an effective spokesperson for the *favela* communities. Her university degree in social work was solid training in this regard. In any event Benedita entered electoral politics on the strength of her leadership in this area, and won her first election in 1982 to the city council of Rio (Câmara Dos Deputados, 1987: 143; Mendoça and Benjamin, 1997).

Benedita's career hit rocky shoals in 1992, when she was defeated in a run-off election for mayor. Running for a citywide office exposed Benedita to some of the harsher aspects of the electoral politics entering its phase of consolidation. The tinder that sparked the opposition which would assume racist proportions was the campaign slogan she adopted. She promised to paint Rio with a "new face" by representing the heretofore invisible figures of Rio's dispossessed. Her opponent turned this campaign image on its head. Cesar Maia of the PMDB developed a strategy to appeal to Rio's affluent citizens. Maia subtly raised the question of whether Rio with its own image to protect could tolerate being governed by a black, a woman, and someone who openly avowed her sympathies with Rio's poor (Brazil Network, 1992).

Openly, however, Maia used the issue of integrity against Benedita. During the final stages of the campaign, stories began appearing prominently in Rio's media of Benedita's son having gained a municipal position allegedly by fraudulent means. Maia even attempted to taint Benedita with the authoritarian past by pointing to a position she occupied in the 1970s in the city's Transit Department. Maia alleged that Benedita could have obtained such a position only with the endorsement of the then reigning political boss, Carlos Chagas Freitas. Maia raised enough doubts about Benedita's probity to have the national leadership of the PT distance itself from her campaign. Ultimately, Maia's strategy paid off, and Benedita was defeated. As democratization progressed into the stage of consolidation racism would seep into open electoral competition. Benedita, nevertheless, would make a dramatic comeback in 1994 by winning election to the national senate.

The Consolidation Phase: The Municipal Elections of 1996

On November 15, 1996, a black economist and native of Rio de Janeiro, Celso Pitta, was elected Mayor of São Paulo. As a consequence of his election Pitta would preside over a city of 11 million people, and the most highly industrialized urban center in Latin America. In his first bid for elective office Pitta won decisively over his opponent, Luiza Erundina dos Santos, a former mayor of São Paulo. Celso Pitta's success could be interpreted in several ways. In one not wholly inaccurate reading it could be taken as a sign that Afro-Brazilians were finally entering the mainstream of Brazilian life. Pitta's inauguration would reflect a general feeling that a black person could posses sufficient competence to merit the confidence of a cosmopolitan, world-class Brazilian city. Pitta had broken through Brazil's color barrier.

As reflected in coverage by the Brazilian local news weeklies *Veja* and *Trovão*, racial consciousness played a significant part in this campaign, although in complex and not always straight forward ways. Pitta had not been a figure with any ties to black social movements, nor did he consider his candidacy, initially, to have any racial significance. Throughout most of the campaign Pitta insisted that his candidacy not be looked on as a "black" one. Pitta's patron, outgoing mayor Paulo Maluf, also made efforts to dispel the notion that Pitta's victory had any racial significance (*Veja*, November 20, 1996: 32). Nevertheless, Pitta's campaign aroused considerable black interest. Some segments of the black community urged voting for Pitta as a matter of racial pride (*Trovão*, July, 1996). Pitta's victory was no doubt an occasion of pride for São Paulo's Black community. The news weekly *Veja* (November 20, 1996: 32), for example, reported that blacks throughout the city had made visible and celebratory displays of Pitta's campaign signs just prior to the election.

In other terms, however, Pitta's victory was part of a complex dynamic in the politics of democratic consolidation in which Pitta's candidacy served as a chess piece in a larger contest among more powerful rivals who vied with each other over position in the next presidential elections. In one important sense Pitta's victory was as much a show of strength for his benefactor, Maluf, as an achievement in Pitta's own right.

Pitta's entry into the political limelight was sudden and unexpected. He was a last minute surrogate for Maluf whom Maluf had chosen when an attempted approximation with his rival, President Fernando Henrique Cardoso, had fallen through. And, according to one account, Maluf's team of advisers took the news of Pitta's selection in the atmosphere of a wake. Uppermost in Maluf's advisers' minds was the question of Pitta's race. One is quoted to have declared that, "São Paulo would never elect a Black" (*Veja*, September 4, 1996: 20). In fact there was little in Pitta's background to suggest that Maluf had chosen a person with any tested political skills. Pitta can best be described as a technocrat. He received his university degree in economics from the University of Leeds, and studied public administration at Harvard University. His first association with Maluf was as an accountant in Maluf's sprawling business empire. There Pitta formed a close association with Maluf and rose through the ranks, gaining Maluf's increasing confidence. From Maluf's business enterprises Pitta moved on to Maluf's municipal administration. He served as secretary of finances in Maluf's administration prior to being chosen for the race.

Few would deny that Pitta is anything but Maluf's own political creation. Maluf threw all of the resources at his command into Pitta's campaign. This included highly priced marketing consultants, and hefty campaign contributions from Maluf's allies in the private sector. Maluf's involvement in Pitta's campaign ran to such an extent that it was actually considered a referendum on Maluf's own administration (*Veja*, September 18, 1996: 32–35).

Maluf, in fact, was leaving office with unusually high approval ratings (*Veja*, October 9, 1996: 32). Maluf owed his popularity to an old habit in Brazilian politics, devoting expenditures to large public works. Among his major accomplishments was an ambitious low-cost public housing program, known as Project Singapore, which transformed several of the city's *favelas* into permanent housing structures. These projects allowed Maluf to cultivate the image of a mayor of action, an image that had appeal to a wide cross-section of São Paulo's electorate (*Veja*, October 9, 1996: 33).

Since his first appearance in Brazilian politics in the 1970s during the height of authoritarian rule Maluf had aimed his political ambitions farther than municipal administration. In fact he acquired the reputation of being something of an opportunist even within authoritarian political circles. He went to great lengths to advance his career in these circles. Ironically, Maluf played an unwitting part in the democratization process when, in 1985, he made a bid for the nomination from the authoritarian regime's party, the PDS, in the presidential elections scheduled for that year. Taken aback by Maluf's audacity, members of the PDS, whose support Maluf needed, turned against him and instead defected to the candidate of the opposition, thus allowing Tancredo Neves, the opposition candidate, to win the election under the rules laid down by the regime itself. In any case Maluf has proven himself to be both unquenchable in his ambition and resilient in his ability to survive the regime transition. He is one of many of the supporters of the former authoritarian regime who has successfully weathered the transition from authoritarian rule.

The style of Pitta's campaign and the forces behind it signaled the reemergence of an older pattern in the electoral arena regarding blacks in Brazil. This was the pattern of the politics of clientelist populism, which was especially pronounced in the 1950s. What the Pitta campaign signified was the resurgence of this brand of clientelist politics, but now of a right-wing inspired populism represented by Paulo Maluf. The contemporary brand of clientelism would have the effect, as did the populism of the past, of compromising the capacity of race-conscious politics to operate as a resource of independent black political action.

Conclusion

The benefits that Afro-Brazilians derive from a democratic regime are normative and strategic. In the first instance, since democratic regimes operate on the ethical premises of guarantees protecting life and limb, Afro-Brazilians can, in fact, organize political action in ways that call attention to the disparity between the moral precepts of equality and actual practice. Afro-North Americans recognize this situation as the "American Dilemma," coined by Gunnar Myrdal over fifty years ago. Democratic regimes also affirm the principle of accountability, which defines the permissible limits of state power. Unquestionably, in this normative sense, democratic consolidation has brought gains for blacks. Even though one cornerstone of this consolidation, human rights, remains vulnerable to abuse, extra-judicial violations of these rights have seeped into the national debate as the target of reforms. If Brazilian elites have been slow to offer correctives to these abuses, in any case they have extended an official recognition, even if in simply symbolic terms, of the corrosive impact of these abuses on Brazilian society (Brasil. Presidência, 1996).

In a strategic sense, however, the consolidation of Brazilian democracy possesses serious limitations which undermine the ability of Brazilian society to achieve the normative goals of creating a more just society. On a strategic plane, where Afro-Brazilians must compete for political power within a certain institutional framework, their efforts at pursuing policies of change run up against institutional biases. The perspective of the "new institutionalism" offers clues to identifying some of these drawbacks. The "new institutionalism" calls attention to the manner in which historical continuities in the institutional design of politics shape the decisions and options open to political actors in a particular political arena. When Afro-Brazilians enter the electoral arena they do so under the conditions determined by Brazilian institutional history. A glance at the struggle for electoral presence during the cycles of regime change suggests the kind of impact that electoral institutions have had on black politics in Brazil.

The reinvention of the party system through cycles of regime change have, in fact, allowed for the persistence of chronic weaknesses in the electoral system. Political parties are defined more as simple structures of power and opposition in which little incentive develops to delineate ideological differences, or to build party support based on stable constituencies. As Olavo Brasil de Lima (1990) and others have pointed out, these are the characteristics that, historically, have distinguished the Brazilian party system from those of Western Europe and the United States. In these circumstances parties employ whatever means at their disposal to incorporate similarly sought after constituencies into their domains. As a result, parties compete for black constituencies by using an amorphous kind of racial consciousness that dilutes its power as a cue for determining party preferences. And, as a consequence, political parties offer little in the way of opportunities for allowing racial consciousness to mature as a political resource, or for formulating coherent programs for the advancement of Afro-Brazilian interests.

Relationships of political dominance and control have a way of adapting to the more formal institutional change that have developed over the course of Brazilian history. Variants of *coronelismo* and dependent populism are already apparent in Brazil's new democracy. Afro-Brazilians fall into these patterns at the risk, at the very least, of being consigned to a junior partnership with little effective power or influence to wield. Various re-inventions of the party system and the persistence of clientelist relationships are the institutional patterns that condition the use of racial consciousness by Afro-Brazilians in Brazil's electoral politics.

Also, one cannot overlook the pervasive and direct effects of racism on Brazilian politics. Challenges to black candidates in the electoral arena can be couched in ways that delegitimize their candidacies as something un-Brazilian. Benedita da Silva succumbed to this kind of treatment in her race against Cesar Maia in 1992 for the mayoralty of Rio de Janeiro. Alceu Collares, an Afro-Brazilian and former governor of the state of Rio Grande do Sul, as well, has made mention of the veiled allusions to racial stereotyping that confronted him while in office (*Veja*, November 20, 1996: 34–35).

Because of these institutional constraints the electoral strategies that blacks pursue deliver at best moderate, but no permanent success. The goal of autonomy in the electoral arena, for example, cannot be fully achieved in this institutional environment. As a consequence, blacks fall back on the strategy of either cultivating multiple constituencies, or of striking bargains under arrangements dictated by clientelist politics. In both instances racial consciousness as a political resource is compromised to one degree or another.

The strategy of combining multiple constituencies points up an important difference between the United States and Brazil. In the United States institutional arrangements lend themselves to using racial consciousness as a political resource and of making appeals primarily if not exclusively to black constituencies. The two-party, single-member district system tends to create structural incentives which promote this. In Brazil the multiparty, proportional representation system, along with the other informal institutional constraints, discourages this. Curiously, however, institutional changes in the United States may require a closer examination of the Brazilian case. The two recent U.S. Supreme Court decisions limiting the drawing of "majority-minority" election districts (*Shaw v. Reno*, 1993; *Miller v. Johnson*, 1995) will have the effect of compelling black candidates in the United States to build alliances among multiple constituencies if they are to be successful in the electoral arena.

In any case the puzzle confronting black electoral politics in Brazil is in determining just how to transpose the openings offered by democratic consolidation from the terrain of normative democracy into the electoral sphere where the task of competing for political power makes it necessary to calculate ways of winning elections and representing black constituencies. A brief second look at the democratic consolidation process provides some clues. What is important to emphasize about the process is that, as it has evolved, it has institutionalized, simultaneously, *both* the features of past regimes as well as new elements that emerged during the transition phase of democratization. One of these new elements is the broadened significance of elections in the minds of Brazilian voters. During the transition from authoritarian rule elections assumed a plebiscitary character, in which voters registered their appraisals of the continuing legitimacy of the authoritarian regime (Von Mettenheim, 1995). In successive elections, from 1974 to 1982, the several defeats suffered by regime candidates signaled the erosion and eventual collapse of authoritarian rule. At issue during this process was the global normative debate over the expediency of authoritarian rule versus the higher ethical imperatives of reestablishing a democratic regime and the rule of law.

According to Kurt Von Mettenheim the electoral arena as presently composed has in fact institutionalized the normative inspirations of democratization originating in the period of transition. Contemporary elections do, in fact, involve debates over grand issues such as the distribution of wealth, the extent of state control over the economy and the regulation of its capitalist forces, and the very desirability of democracy itself. And evidence suggests that this plebiscitary feature of institutional democracy has found its way in ongoing public debate. For example, political attitudes display a certain antagonism toward the Brazilian establishment. The respected news weekly *Veja* has reported on the growing sentiment about entrenched economic and political elites, against whom public opinion has shown increasing hostility. Anti-elite feeling has intensified to the point, according to *Veja*, that much of Brazilian political discourse from left to rights is now dominated by an anti-elite rhetoric (*Veja*, June 26, 1996).

Nevertheless, the electoral arena also encompasses those structures that mediate voters' response to the regime. These mediating structures, political parties, as this analysis has argued, retain weaknesses that have traditionally plagued Brazilian democracy. It is in this latter arena where blacks operate at a disadvantage. If blacks are to secure genuine representation in the electoral arena a proper balance must be struck between the structural level, that of political parties, and to a greater extent the plebiscitary level of politics. In other words a link must be established between the core ethical elements of Brazilian democracy and the structural requirements of electoral politics. One strategy for striking this balance would consist of articulating issues in broad ethical terms, such as regarding the universal issue of human rights. Raising black concerns to the plebiscitary level of politics would strengthen their position in the electoral arena.

One specific proposal that illustrates how this strategy would be put into practice would be to convert policy statements on human rights issues, such as the recently announced *National Program on Human Rights* (Brasil. Presidência, 1996) into the plebiscitary arena of electoral politics. Such a maneuver would present to voters an issue that has a direct impact on black constituencies, since blacks are one of the likeliest victims of human rights abuses. It would also do so in a manner in which Brazilian voters have grown accustomed through the transformation of electoral politics into a plebiscitary terrain. And, just as issues such as constitutional reform, preference for the presidential or parliamentary system, and the extent of privatization have reflected plebiscitary or normative dimensions of Brazilian democracy, so too can black issues succeed in acquiring this plebiscitary character. In this regard the work of nongovernmental organizations which promote such issues become less than bystanders to electoral activity, or completely independent of it, rather than actual and necessary links for true black electoral success. In any event the success for Afro-Brazilians in the electoral arena of Brazil's consolidated democracy will start first from the framing of black issues in terms that draw them closer to actually testing the ever-expanding bounds of Brazil's still evolving democracy.

References

Andrews, George Reid. 1991. *Blacks and Whites in São Paulo: 1888–1988*. Madison: University of Wisconsin Press.
Barker, Lucius. 1987. "Ronald Reagan, Jesse Jackson, and the 1984 Presidential Election: The Continuing American Dilemma of Race." In *The New Black Politics*, ed. Michael Preston, Lenneal Henderson, and Paul Puryear, 29–44. New York: Longmans.
Brasil. Presidência. 1996. *Programa Nacional de Direitos Humanos*. Brasília: Presidência da República, Secretaria de Comunicação Social, Ministério da Justiça.
Brazil Network. 1992. *Contato*, 5: 7/8 (November 30).
Câmara Dos Deputados, República Federativa Do Brasil. 1987. *Assembléia Nacional Constituinte—1987: Reportório Biográfico*. Brasília: Câmara Dos Deputados.
Cardoso, Ruth Correa Leite. 1992. "Popular Movements in the Context of the Consolidation of Democracy in Brazil." In *The Making of Social Movements in Latin America*, ed. Arturo Escobar and Sonia E. Alvarez. Boulder, CO: Westview, 291–302.
Castro, Monica Mata Machado de. 1993. "Raça e Comportamento Político," *Dados*, 39 (3): 469–91
Chong, Dennis. 1991. *Collective Action and the Civil Rights Movement*. Chicago: University of Chicago Press.
Coelho, João G.L., and Antonio Carlos Nantes e Oliveira. 1989. *A Nova Constituição*. Rio de Janeiro: Revan.
Correia Leite, José. 1992. *E Disse O Velho Militante José Correia Leite*. São Paulo: Secretaria Municipal de Cultura.
Costa, Haroldo, ed. 1982. *Fala, Crioulo*. Rio de Janeiro: Editôra Record.
Dawson, Michael C. 1994. *Behind The Mule: Race and Class in African-American Politics*. Princeton: Princeton University Press.
Della Cava, Ralph. 1989. "The 'People's Church,' the Vatican, and *Abertura*." In *Democratizing Brazil*, ed. Alfred Stepan, 143–67. New York: Oxford.
Diniz, Eli. 1982. *Voto e Maquina Política*. Rio de Janeiro: Paz e Terra.
Fernandes, Florestan. 1965. *A Integração do Negro na Sociedade de Classes*, 2 vols. São Paulo: Dominus.
Fleischer, David. 1990. "The Constituent Assembly and the Transformation Strategy: Attempts to Shift Political Power in Brazil from the Presidency to Congress." In *The Political Economy of Brazil*, ed. Richard Graham and Robert H. Wilson. Austin: University of Texas Press.
Flynn, Peter. 1978. *Brazil: A Political Analysis*. Boulder, CO: Westview Press.

Fontaine, Pierre-Michel. 1985. "Blacks and the Search for Power in Brazil." In *Race, Class, and Power in Brazil*, ed. by Pierre-Michel Fontaine, 56–72. Los Angeles: University of California, Los Angeles, Center for Afro-American Studies.

Gonzalez, Lelia. 1985. "The Unified Black Movement: A New Stage in Black Political Mobilization." In *Race Class, and Power in Brazil*, ed. Pierre-Michel Fontaine. Los Angeles: University of California, Center for Afro-American Studies.

Graham, Richard. 1990. "Dilemmas for Democracy in Brazil." In *The Political Economy of Brazil*, ed. Lawrence Graham and Robert Wilson, 7–25. Austin: University of Texas Press.

Gurin, Patricia, Shirley Hatchett, and James S. Jackson. 1989. *Hope and Independence: Black Response to Electoral and Party Politics*. New York: Russell Sage.

Hagopian, Frances. 1992. "The Compromised Consolidation: The Political Class in the Brazilian Transition." In *Issues in Democratic Consolidation*, ed. Scott Mainwaring, Guillermo O'Donnell, and J. Samuel Valenzuela, 243–93. Notre Dame, IN: University of Notre Dame Press.

Hanchard, Michael. 1994. *Orpheus and Power*. Princeton: Princeton University Press.

Henderson, Lenneal. 1987. "Black Politics and American Presidential Elections." In *The New Black Politics*, ed. by Michael Preston, Lenneal Henderson, and Paul Puryear, 3–28. New York: Longmans.

Ianni, Octavio. 1968. *O Colapso do Populismo no Brasil*. Rio de Janeiro: Civilização Brasileira.

Keck, Margaret. 1989. "The New Unionism and the Brazilian Transition." In *Democratizing Brazil*, ed. Alfred Stepan, 252–96. New York: Oxford.

———. 1992. *The Workers Party and Democratization in Brazil*. New Haven: Yale University Press.

Leal, Victor Nunes. 1975. *Coronelismo, Enxada e Voto*, 2d. ed. São Paulo: Alfa-Omega.

Lima, Olavo Brasil de, Jr. 1990. "A Experiência Brasileira Com Partidos e Eleições." In *O Balanço do Poder*, ed. Olavo Brasil de Lima, Jr., 9–13. Rio de Janeiro: IUPRJ.

Mainwaring, Scott. 1988. "Political Parties and Democratization in Brazil and the Souther Cone." *Comparative Politics*, 21: 91–120.

———. 1989. "Grassroots Popular Movements and the Struggle for Democracy: Nova Iguaçu." In *Democratizing Brazil*, ed. Alfred Stepan, 168–204. New York: Oxford.

March, James G., and Johan Olsen. 1989. *Rediscovering Institutions: The Organizational Basis of Politics*. New York: The Free Press.

McCormack, Joseph P, II, and Robert C. Smith. 1989. "Through the Prism of Afro-American Culture: An Interpretation of the Jackson Campaign Style." In *Jesse Jackson's Presidential Campaign*, ed. Lucius Barker and Ronald Walters. Urbana: University of Illinois Press.

McRea, Edward. 1992. "Homosexual Identities in Transitional Brazilian Politics." In *The Making Of Social Movements in Latin America: Identity, Strategy, and Democracy*, ed. Arturo Escobar and Sonia E. Alvarez, 185–203. Boulder, CO: Westview.

Mendoça, Maisa, and Medea Benjamin. 1997. *Benedita*. Rio de Janeiro: Maud.

Mitchell, Michael. 1977. "Racial Consciousness and the Political Attitudes and Behavior of Blacks in São Paulo, Brazil." Ph.D. Dissertation, Indiana University.

Moisés, José Álvaro. 1993. "Elections, Political Parties and Political Culture in Brazil: Changes and Continuities." *Journal of Latin American Studies*, 24 (October): 575–611.

Nascimento, Abdias do. 1992. *Africans in Brazil*. Trenton, NJ: Africa World Press.

Pinderhughes, Dianne. 1990. "The Articulation of Black Interests by Civil Rights, Professional, and Religious Organizations." In *The Social and Political Implications of the 1984 Jesse Jackson Campaign*, ed. Lorenzo Morris, 125–34. New York: Praeger.

Preston, Michael. 1987. "The Election of Harold Washington: An Examination of the SES Model in the 1983 Chicago Mayoral Election." In *The New Black Politics*,

ed. Michael Preston, Lenneal Henderson, and Paul Puryear, 139–71. New York: Longmans.
Reale, Miguel. 1977. *Da Revolução à Democracia*, 2d. ed. São Paulo: Convívio.
Shingles, Richard. 1981. "Black Consciousness and Political Participation: The Missing Link." *American Political Science Review*, 75: 76–91.
Skidmore, Thomas. 1967. *Politics in Brazil: 1930–1964*. London: Oxford University Press.
———. 1988. *The Politics of Military Rule in Brazil*. New York: Oxford University Press.
Soares, Glaucio, and Nelson do Vale Silva. 1985. "O Charme Discreto do Socialismo Moreno," *Dados*, 28 (2).
Souza, Amaury. 1971. "Raça e Política no Brasil Urbano." *Revista de Administração de Empresas*, 11 (4).
Souza, Maria do Carmo Campello. 1989. "The Brazilian 'New Republic': Under the Sword of Damocles." In *Democratizing Brazil*, ed. Alfred Stepan, 351–94. New York: Oxford.
Steinmo, Sven, Kathleen Thelen, and Frank Longstreth. 1992. *Structuring Politics: Historical Institutionalism in Comparative Analysis*. Cambridge: Cambridge University Press.
Valente, Ana Lúcia. 1986. *Política e Relações Raciais: Os Negros e as Eleições Paulistas*. São Paulo: FFLCH/USP
Von Mettenheim, Kurt. 1995. *The Brazilian Voter: Mass Politics in Democratic Transition, 1974–1986*. Pittsburgh: University of Pittsburgh Press.

Learning from Brazil's Unified Black Movement: Whither Goeth Black Nationalism?

David Covin

Sacramento State University

Introduction

In the United States there is a long train of black nationalist thought, orientation, and activity.[1] It has had social, cultural, religious, and economic manifestations. It has produced some of the most systematic and probing thought arising from black people in this country. It has produced vital and long-standing institutions.[2]

But for the most part it has been an approach that has been scattered—both geographically and temporally. And, with a few, significant exceptions, it has had no mass base. Certainly, in the contemporary era—since the end of the Universal Negro Improvement Association (UNIA)—there has been no national, mass-based black nationalist organization that has had a clear and consistent political agenda with a meaningful national impact. The Nation of Islam has come closer than any organization to achieving such a standing, but it has only *come closer*. It has not achieved such a result.

In fact, aside from the Garvey movement, the only black political movement in this country's history that had a mass base was the civil rights movement. There the mass base was afforded by the unpredictable phenomenon of a mass movement. But if there is to be a predictable, sustained mass presence in a black political agenda, it cannot rest on anything as elusive and ephemeral as a mass movement. It must have an institutional base. How is that to be done? The mechanism long proffered by Harold Cruse has been a political party. Without going into the discussions that arose in the National Black Assembly and National Black Independent Party (NBIPP) regarding the character of a black political party in the United States, we may certainly assert that no mass, black political party of any kind has ever been built in the United States. But this conundrum—of how to link black consciousness and a black nationalist leadership cadre to a mass base—is not unique to the United States. It is present throughout the diaspora. It may be instructive to see what is being done along these lines in other places. By examining what people do elsewhere we may be able to develop some comparative insights.

In this paper I endeavor to find such comparative illuminations. Specifically, I examine how a black consciousness organization in Brazil, the Unified Black Movement (MNU), addressed the question of black consciousness and politics, particularly during 1992 and 1993. My consideration is limited to the MNU in Bahia state. Most of these considerations apply in a general sense to the MNU nationally because the MNU is a national organization and develops national policies. The particulars and implementations of the national policies, however, can vary quite considerably from region to region as the contexts are considerably different. I hypothesize that the central difficulty faced by the MNU is the same one found here in the United States: how to link a black consciousness political organization to a mass base.

To determine MNU political practice, particularly during 1992–93, I have examined MNU publications, statements by MNU leaders and members, MNU activities, and assessments of people critical of the MNU. It is important to establish that the MNU policies of 1992–1993 did not arise out of a vacuum, but out of a rich organizational and contextual history. The MNU starting point was not 1992–93; hence, what we witness in that period rests on a specific and complex legacy.

I am not going to chart that history here. Much of that has been done elsewhere.[3] One point I will establish, however, is that in 1991 at its national conference, the MNU made a decision that became a departure of sorts from its past and that directly influenced the political line of 1992–93. That decision was to actively involve itself in the 1992 municipal elections and to do that from the standpoint of a black organization following a specific, black agenda.[4]

During the 1992–93 period I have identified an MNU political line with sixteen key components. In the following sections I will consider these components *ad seriatum*. In the section on culture I describe the MNU's particular interpretation of the intersecting roles of politics and culture. Next I look at seven components of the MNU line that I label core beliefs. Following that, I state four elements of the MNU line oriented toward Brazilian regime practices. Finally, I chart three components of the line related to what I call agenda projects. By that I mean projects that derive from the black agenda established by the core beliefs. These projects are intended to counter regime practices. In the last part of the paper I make some reflections on my hypothesis regarding the MNU—that its central difficulty is the same one faced by black nationalist organizations in the United States, building a mass base—and I also undertake some reflections on the comparative implications of the considerations developed in this paper.

Culture

Culture is integral to all the other elements of the MNU political line and is inseparable from them. I am nevertheless going to discuss it as a separate topic. It is important to identify it and to treat the MNU's conception of it because it has a significant impact on the whole MNU political line. To the MNU, politics and culture are inseparable. That means that a cultural line is political, and also that a political line has cultural dimensions.[5]

The MNU line, however, takes this train of thought one step further to assert that the MNU's political line must be rooted in the culture of the Afro-Brazilian community.[6] This, one might note, is an Afro-centric perception of politics. To implement this latter conception of its line, the MNU has chosen to work with and in specific Afro-Brazilian cultural organizations, including encouraging its members to join specific Afro-Brazilian organizations as individuals.[7] It is also important to recognize in light of my central hypothesis that many of these cultural organizations have mass bases.

Core Beliefs

The Importance of Black Consciousness

The MNU political line establishes the importance of black consciousness. It is important to recognize that this is a radical stance in Brazil. Twenty years ago it was illegal. Today it is regarded as racist. Michael Mitchell comments on the consternation caused by Brazilian users of the Internet simply because of the appearance of the term, "Afro-Brazilian."[8] In Brazil "black consciousness" is the assertion of a distinction between Afro-Brazilians and other Brazilians. This is a condition of which the official ideology of "racial democracy" does not admit.[9] Nevertheless, the MNU specifically asserts that black people in Brazil are discriminated against because of their race. It declares that racial democracy in Brazil is a myth.[10]

While Brazilians cannot deny that whites dominate the upper strata of politics, economics, and the social structure in the country, and that black people proliferate in the lower reaches, popular culture and official ideology maintain that these conditions are the result of the "residue" of slavery combined with people's innate abilities. The MNU says no. The terrible lives of most Afro-Brazilians result not only from slavery, but also from current, racist practices.[11] Brazil, today, declares the MNU, is structured as a racial hierarchy.[12] In that hierarchy black women are exploited sexually.[13]

The Majority of the Brazilian Population is Black

Brazil has many terms for classifying people by race. Most of these terms apply to people with African ancestry. The most frequently used such terms are: *Negro, Pardo,* and *Mulato*. There are many variations, such as *mulata-morena* or *mulata-loira,* but the three former terms are the primary classifiers. The MNU rejects them all. According to the MNU, *Negros, Pardos,* and *Mulatos* are meaningless distinctions. They are terms that all identify people of African descent. All people of African descent constitute "one race, one unique people."[14] MNU members are fond of saying, "Yes, we are the majority of the Brazilian population—but we don't know it!"[15]

This condition, that the MNU perceives the majority of the Brazilian population as black, has profound consequences for the MNU political line, particularly as it is distinct from a black nationalist line in the United States. In the United States, a black nationalist line must operate in a context where the black population is considerably in the minority. This has all kinds of implications for the directions and possibilities of such a line. With Brazil's black population, the nationalist line has the possibility of directing the politics of the entire country. It has the possibility of being the dominant line. That condition has important implications for both the content and the ambition of the nationalist line. This point is seen directly in the next component of the MNU's line.

The Necessity to Construct a Political Project from the Point-of-View of Black People

This is the heart of the MNU change of direction first taken in 1991. It is a call for a specific, national black agenda. In the 1993 national conference this resolution, sponsored by the delegation from Bahia, was the conference's central agenda item, and was supported by the national conference.[16] But it had also been emphasized by the organization much earlier.[17]

In addition to the general idea of a national black agenda, it also included specific elements of that agenda. One is that black people are responsible for reconstructing their own history and lives.[18] In order to do this they must organize themselves as black people.[19] This is something that Afro-Brazilians do not consciously do on a large scale. There are many organizations in Brazil that are primarily black. This is not, however, primarily a result of conscious decisions, but is a result of the conditions in which Afro-Brazilians live and work. They live with each other. Therefore, they organize samba schools, *capoeira* schools, *Candomble' terreiros*, which almost always are predominantly black and often entirely black. But they do not choose to do this. The MNU says that in the future these organizations—as black organizations—must be formed as a matter of conscious choice. The MNU declares that black people must be independent as a racial group.[20] The point is that they must not only organize as a racial group, but also that those organizations must be independent. That departs from the traditional practice that black Brazilians—however they are organized, or even when they are not organized at all—tend to be dominated—if not controlled—by white Brazilians.

In keeping with that principle, the MNU says that in the current system, race determines the place that groups occupy in the structure of power and wealth in the society.[21] The national myth is that such places are determined by ability. To accept that position—as most Brazilians do, black, white, and otherwise—means that one accepts that black Brazilians are endowed with pitiful capacities.

The MNU rejects that vision. It is a vision that proclaims that Euro-Brazilians are the "natural" leaders of political parties, labor unions, business enterprises, the military, the church, social life, any settings in which large numbers of Euro-Brazilians and Afro-Brazilians interact. This means, in part, that the racial question is only secondary to other questions of social meaning—secondary to questions of class, ownership of wealth, gender, the environment. Certainly, so the line goes, black people are discriminated against, but it is because they are poor. Yes, black women constitute the bulk of domestic servants and mulatas are exploited as sex symbols, but in both cases that is because they are women. Certainly, black people live amidst cesspools and filth, but that is because the plutocrats have no respect for any environment except their own. They are intent on making money, not on the color of the people they exploit.

The MNU rejects these interpretations in its declaration that the racial question is not secondary.[22] On the contrary, the MNU position is that the racial question must be established as the national question.[23] This means, in part, that Brazilian society must be transformed. But it is not to be transformed willy-nilly. It is to be transformed from the point of view of black people.

This particular emphasis of the MNU line—that the racial question must become the national question and that Brazilian society must be transformed from the point of view of black people—is made possible because of the MNU position that most people in Brazil are black. It follows, therefore, that black people from a black perspective should direct the destinies of the country. Brazil, as many people, both white and black, are fond of saying, is in many ways an African country. The MNU says, since this is so, the country should act like it. It should be led by black people from a black perspective.

This cannot be done easily because the place of one race in society cannot be changed without affecting the place of others.[24] Therefore, to effect such change Afro-Brazilians will have to fight for political representation that identifies with the aspirations of black people.[25] They will have to participate directly in their communities' struggles and thereby raise their level of consciousness.[26] The MNU has already pointed out the potential of such a strategy by participating in municipal elections—as black people—with some degree of success.[27]

It is Necessary to Transform the Reality in Which Black People Live

This, of course, is the point of a black agenda. The MNU identifies some of the characteristics it would envision in such a transformed society. Because the effort would have to begin from a point-of-view which is African-centered, there would have to be means to introduce an African-centered worldview at the core of Brazilian perceptions. One means of contributing to that aim would be to revise textbooks in schools to introduce the history of Africa and of Africans in Brazil to the children of Brazil.[28] Introducing that point of view would also mean turning back to learn from the heritage of Zumbi and Palmares, letting them serve as models of how black people can organize a society.[29] (Zumbi was the leader of the seventeenth-century free African community of Palmares in what is now the Alagoas state of northeastern Brazil.) This reconstructed society, like that of Palmares, must be based on a respect for the differences among peoples. The necessity of transforming black people's reality means building a society without racism and without exploitation.[30] This is what it means to have an African-centered point of view and to build a society rooted in that vision.

Most Black People Internalize the Ideologies of Oppression

Constructing such a society, however, is difficult because most Afro-Brazilians are conditioned by the dominant myths and popular culture of Brazil. This means, for example, that Afro-Brazilians—like almost all other Brazilians—accept the sexual exploitation of black women as normal.[31] They see nothing to resist in that practice. Most Afro-Brazilians have a low level of racial and public consciousness.[32]

*Black People in Brazil Never Simply Accepted
Their Situation of Oppression and Exploitation*

This means that the sorry state of black consciousness is not irredeemable, because the Afro-Brazilian population, in addition to a legacy of internalizing their oppressors' ideology, also has a heritage of resistance. Official history hides from them the truth that the abolition of slavery in Brazil resulted from African resistance, including the *quilombos* (the free communities, like Palmares, formed by Africans who escaped from slavery and fought and agitated for the liberation of their fellows still in captivity).[33]

*The MNU is a National Political Organization
that is Democratic and Autonomous*

The MNU itself can serve as a base for the whole new direction that it envisions for Afro-Brazilians. It has, first of all, the well-being of Afro-Brazilians as its central mission. The basic purpose of the MNU is the defense of black people in every respect—political, economic, social, and cultural.[34]

Moreover, the MNU is in many respects representative of the Afro-Brazilian population. It is today a mosaic of political positions.[35] There's nothing wrong with that because Afro-Brazilians at large are not monolithic or unified on any questions.[36] Afro-Brazilians at large constitute a mosaic of political positions.

Adding to its ecumenical character, the MNU publicizes on a regular basis the activities of other black organizations.[37] It is through this recognition of the necessity for unity through diversity and acting it out in practice that it will be possible to build a democratic and autonomous base which can begin to transform the lives of Afro-Brazilians.

Regime Practices

*The Regime Practices Official Violence Against
Black People in a Number of Ways*

The context in which Afro-Brazilians live is determined by the regime. The mythology and practices of the regime are those that have to be overcome. Interlocking as a powerful and extensive web, they constitute a considerable obstacle. According to the MNU, many of the regime features of oppression operate at the crudest and, at the same time, the most effective level. They include multifarious ways of practicing official violence.

The official ideology and popular mythology in Brazil bemoan the culture of violence. By this they mean primarily the violence of street children, of hooligans and thugs from the favelas who prey on tourists and on the good, law-abiding folk of Brazil. The children, hooligans, and thugs they have in mind are mainly Afro-Brazilians. The MNU has another take on violence. To the MNU the worst violence in Brazil is the official police violence and the murder of black people. Indeed, the MNU says police violence against black people is increasing in intensity and spreading in geographical presence.[38] Certainly, if we want examples both of the practice itself and of the trend of its proliferation, we need not look far. The murders of children on the streets of Brazilian cities have repeatedly claimed headlines all over the world. These were not, however, a cross-section of Brazilian children. Even during the military dictatorship, according to the MNU, when there were international protests against the treatment of political prisoners, the majority of those killed by institutionalized, armed violence during the 1970s were of African descent.[39] The fact is, says the MNU, that black prisoners are always beaten, and almost always either tortured or murdered as well.[40] The regime has the most brutal means at its disposal to keep black people in their place because the police are the dominant class's instrument of violence against black people.[41]

Birth Control has Negative Implications for Black People

The regime practices sterilization and birth control as forms of racial violence.[42] This is part of the regime's strategy to whiten Brazil. But it is also a way of blaming the victims, of identifying false sources as the causes of problems. The MNU says that the Brazilian government would rather attempt to eliminate the black population than to address the true source of the problems.[43]

Education in Brazil is Racist

For all practical purposes there is no truthful teaching concerning Afro-Brazilians in the nation's schools. The educational system does not consider the role of Afro-Brazilians in building the country. Books and schools omit and distort their role in building the country and its culture.[44] By the same token, the country's educational system perpetuates a myth that there was no condition from which Afro-Brazilians had to be liberated and against which they had to struggle for their own liberation.[45] Books and schools omit and distort the Afro-Brazilian struggle for liberation.

*Clientism is a Method that the White Society
in Brazil Uses to Oppress Black People*

Euro-Brazilians use a paternalistic system of clientism in which they place Afro-Brazilian individuals and institutions under their group or individual protection.[46] This keeps Afro-Brazilians from being autonomous. They are always dependent on their white protectors or benefactors. The *patron* intercedes for the benefit of the client—who remains eternally grateful. Whether this is the maid, the chauffeur, the promising child of the gardener, the *candomblé terreiro*, the *afoxé*, the *capoeira* school, or the political candidate, the relationship remains the same. The African is subordinate to and dependent on the superior and dominant white.

Racism is International

The MNU's position is that it is important for Afro-Brazilians not to believe that the condition of racial oppression and exploitation is limited to Brazil. It is worldwide. What this means, most basically, is that the struggle against racial oppression is not a national struggle. It is an international struggle.[47] It is for this reason that the MNU is identified with the aspirations of Nelson Mandela and the black people of South Africa.[48] It is for this reason that the MNU declares that it is important to struggle against racism everywhere in the world and that the Brazilian struggle against racism must continue as long as there is racism anywhere in the world.[49]

Agenda Projects

The National Day of Black Consciousness, November 20, is Important

November 20 marks the anniversary of Zumbi's death. Since at least 1978, black consciousness militants in Brazil have identified that date as the most important one on the Afro-Brazilian calendar. This is in deliberate contrast with May 13, the anniversary of the official abolition of slavery, which the regime has established as the official recognition day for Afro-Brazilians.

For the MNU, establishing an African-centered national agenda means changing holidays from those designated by a Euro-Brazilian attitude to those designated by an Afro-Brazilian perspective. November 20, as the national day of black consciousness—a concept which is itself heretical—is therefore a critical part of an action agenda. It is a double rejection of Euro-Brazilian values and a double assertion of Afro-Brazilian ones: the rejection of Euro-Brazilian attitudes and of the Euro-Brazilian holiday; and the assertion of Afro-Brazilian attitudes and the Afro-Brazilian holiday.

The necessity to develop black consciousness in Brazil is perhaps the MNU's most enduring orientation. The possibility of all its other agendas hinges on its realization. The MNU states the crux of the matter this way, "How can you have a struggle against racism in Brazil, because how can you have a struggle against something that doesn't exist?"[50]

Black People have a Right to the Lands that They have Settled as Quilombos

All over Brazil, but particularly in the hinterlands, there are settlements of Afro-Brazilians founded by people who had escaped from the slave regime in Brazil. In densely populated areas many of these settlements (*quilombos*) have been incorporated into metropolitan areas. But in the hinterlands many of them exist today much as they have existed for over 100 years.

Africans have occupied and settled these lands for generations. Indeed, the new constitution recognizes their rights to them. But there is also a Brazilian law against racial discrimination and a Brazilian law against murder. Many of these *quilombos* are coveted by wealthy landlords and big companies. They do not hesitate to use the most underhanded and vicious means to oust the ancestral *quilombo* residents from their lands. Among other methods, they hire thugs to beat, burn, and kill the black people, to drive them off the lands. The MNU says these practices are unconscionable and must be stopped.[51] The black agenda demands that they be resisted.

It is Important to Recognize Discrimination Against Other Groups, Such as Women and Homosexuals

Because the African-centered perspective is intolerant of any kind of oppression and exploitation, and rests on a respect for the differences among peoples, an action agenda must be cognizant of and address the circumstances of other people. In that respect the MNU recognizes that the great majority of black women and black homosexuals experience a triple oppression. They must not only face oppression from classism and racism as other black people do, but also from sexism and homophobia, respectively.[52] In the business of alliances, however, the MNU position is that while such alliances with other groups are important, they must not diminish the autonomy of black people.[53]

Assessment

The MNU political line reveals components both of a philosophy and of an action program. Neither the philosophy nor the action program, however, explicitly addresses the need for a mass base for the MNU as a specific organization. But that concern is implicit in both the philosophy and the action program. It is implicit for both the black consciousness movement, overall, and for the MNU, specifically.

The MNU addresses the question of the mass base in three ways:

1. It is the motivating factor behind the necessity to construct a political project from the point of view of black people. That is an implicit recognition of the *necessity* for a mass base.
2. By joining cultural organizations which do have mass bases. The MNU seeks to hook onto the mass base. This is another implicit recognition of the necessity for a mass base.
3. By participating as black people in municipal elections. This is a way of engaging the mass base and of attempting to get them to be explicitly political. These are all ways— not mutually exclusive—of addressing the mass base question.

It is important, however, to recognize that these are all ways of implicitly addressing the mass base question. The MNU has not developed a line that addresses it directly, as a specific and individual question.

We do not know whether these approaches will work. But there is one clear weakness in the latter two (both of which are in some respects means of implementing the former one). That weakness is that in neither case is the mass base joined completely and specifically to an independent, autonomous, black political effort. This may be a shortcoming of the failure to address the mass base question explicitly. Mass-based cultural organizations are just that—mass-based *cultural* organizations. Even when the cultural organizations have important political dimensions—as do both Olodum and Ilé Aiyé, in both of which the MNU in Bahia participates—they still remain cultural organizations that are not designed or organized to implement political purposes. At best they foster political consciousness. But one has no handle on the respects in which that consciousness is actually germinated among members and supporters. Their primary allegiance may remain to the music and costumes and dance steps. Moreover, while the MNU may participate in the organizations, the allegiance of the mass participants is to the cultural organizations, not the MNU. As a matter of practice, the MNU does attract members and supporters from such cultural organizations, but not mass membership or even mass supporters. Indeed, the MNU is not a mass membership organization, nor has it made any arrangements for becoming one or for forming adjuncts that might be mass political organizations. This harkens back to the MNU's not having addressed the question of a mass base and its relationship to the MNU explicitly.

In the matter of the election campaigns, while the MNU did support—as a black organization—black candidates, those candidates ran on the PT (Workers' Party) ticket. Hence, the electoral base—if one may consider that as a mass base—was for the PT and not the MNU. This smacks of the clientism of which the MNU itself is critical.

Be that as it may, the MNU, though indirectly, has addressed the mass base question. It has not addressed it explicitly, and it certainly has not solved it. But in a comparative assessment it is evident that the MNU has gone further in addressing this question than SNCC, US, or the Black Panthers ever did in the heyday of black nationalism in the United States. They have gone further than the National Black Assembly or NBIPP ever did, and certainly further than any black nationalist organization currently on the national scene in the United States.

Harold Cruse recommends a national black political party—which does not address the question of how to make it a mass-based party. NBIPP may have been the only truly national effort to build such a party, but it was not at all mass-based. In the United States black people have not tackled the problem of how to build a mass-based political party, or a mass-based nationalist organization of any kind. The MNU has not done it in Brazil, either, but they have come two steps closer than Africans in the United States have.

Notes

This research was made possible by grants from the American Philosophical Society, the National Science Foundation, and the CSU Sacramento Awards Committee for Research and Creative Activity.

1. See Robert Smith, "Ideology as the Enduring Dilemma of Black Politics," in *Dilemmas of Black Politics*, ed. Georgia Persons (New York: HarperCollins, 1993), 211–24, for a particularly informed, deep, and astute consideration of this question. Smith explores the subject even more fully in *We Have No Leaders* (Albany: State University of New York Press, 1996).
2. This includes some representations of the traditional black church; some representations of traditional black businesses, including some elements of the black

press; and some specifically and self-conscious nationalist manifestations such as the Church of the Black Madonna, the Pan African Institute, and the Third World Press.
3. See, especially, Leila Gonzalez, "O Movimento Negro na ultima decada," in *Lugar de Negro*, ed. L. Gonzalez and Carlos Hasenbalg (Rio de Janeiro: Editora Marco Zero, 1982); and Leila Gonzalez, "The Unified Black Movement: A New Stage in Black Political Mobilization," in *Race, Class, and Power in Brazil*, ed. P. M. Fontaine (Los Angeles: UCLA Center for Afro-American Studies, 1986); David Covin, "Ten Years of a Brazilian Black Consciousness Movement: The MNU, 1978–1980," *The Journal of Third World Studies* (Fall 1990); *1978–1988 10 Anos de Luta Contra o Racismo* (MNU, 1988). See also the excellent discussion in Dunn, "Afro-Bahian Carnival: A Stage for Protest," in *Afro-Hispanic Review* 11, 1–3: 11–20.
4. Interviews with MNU members, Bahia, Brazil, July 1992.
5. I discuss this question at length in the article, "The Role of Culture in Brazil's Unified Black Movement: Bahia, in 1992," *The Journal of Black Studies* 27, 1 (September 1996).
6. Jonatas Conceicao da Silva, "Historia de Lutas Negras: Memorias do Surgimento do Movimento Negro na Bahia," *1978–1988 10 Anos de Luta Contra o Racismo* (MNU, 1988): 15–16.
7. Interview with Jonatas Conceicao da Silva, in Salvador, Bahia, July 14, 1992. Also the *MNU Jornal*, 22 (August-October 1993): 7, "To be more effective politically, we have to be existentially more cultural. To live Black, to think Black." This quote is also from Jonatas Conceicao da Silva.
8. Telephone conversation with Michael Mitchell, December 20, 1993.
9. I discuss this condition at length in David Covin, "Black Consciousness in the White Media: The Case of Brazil," *The Western Journal of Black Studies*, 15, 2: especially 99–101.
10. *Carta de Principios do MNU.*
11. "Por Uma Autentica Democracia Racial," *1978–1988 10 Anos de Luta Contra o Racismo* (MNU, 1988): 23.
12. Ibid., 24.
13. *Carta de Principios do MNU.*
14. "Por Uma Autentica Democracia Racial" (1988): 23.
15. Conversations with MNU members, Bahia, July 1992.
16. *MNU Jornal* (August-October 1993): 1.
17. *MNU Jornal*, 16 (June-August 1989): 1.
18. Poster, "O Dia Nacional Da Consciencia Negra."
19. *MNU Jornal*, 18 (January-March, 1991): 3.
20. *Movimento Negro Unificado: Contribuicoes ao 1o EVEN Sao Paulo, 14 a 17/11/91*, 3.
21. *MNU Jornal*, 22 (August-October 1993): 6.
22. *Movimento Negro Unificado: Contribuicoes ao 1o EVEN Sao Paulo, 14 a 17/11/91.*
23. *MNU Jornal*, 16 (June-August 1989): 1.
24. *MNU Jornal*, 22 (August-October 1993): 6.
25. Poster of 10th National Congress, April 8–11, 1993, Goias.
26. "Congresso do MNU Tese: Sexismo & Racismo," *1978–1988 10 Anos de Luta Contra o Racismo* (1988): 29.
27. Poster, "O Dia Nacional Da Consciencia Negra."
28. Ana Celia da Silva, "Estudos Africanos Nos Curriculos Escolares," in *1978–1988 10 Anos de Luta Contra o Racismo* (1988): 49.
29. Poster, "O Dia Nacional Da Consciencia Negra."
30. *Nego* (November 27, 1987): 15.
31. "Congresso do MNU Tese: Sexismo & Racismo," 1988.

32. "Movimento Negro Unificado—Brasil Documentado Apresentado No Simposio Em Apoio A Luta Pela Auto-Determinacao E Independencia Do Povo Namibio Sao Jose, Costa Rica," *1978–1988 10 Anos de Luta Contra o Racismo* (1988): 41.
33. *Nego*, 1987.
34. Jonatas Conceicao da Silva, "Historia de Lutas Negras: Memorias do Surgimento do Movimento Negro Na Bahia," (1988): 17.
35. *Movimento Negro Unificado: Contribuicoes ao 1o EVEN Sao Paulo, 14 a 17/11/91*, 3.
36. Ibid., 3.
37. This practice is readily observable in the reading of any issue of the *MNU Jornal* or its predecessor, *Nego*.
38. *Nego* (November 27, 1987): 15.
39. *MNU Jornal*, 16 (June-August 1989): 10.
40. Ibid., 1989, 10.
41. Ibid., 1989, 10.
42. *Movimento Negro Unificado: Contribuicoes ao 1o EVEN Sao Paulo, 14 a 17/11/91*, 2.
43. *MNU Jornal*, 16 (June-August 1989): 1. See also this interpretation from the *MNU Jornal*, 19 (May-July 1991): 3, "Letting cholera enter the country is the perfect solution in a fuller strategy for the extermination of Black people. The deaths seem natural...."
44. *1978–1988 10 Anos de Luta Contra o Racismo* (1988): 6.
45. Ibid., 6.
46. Jonatas Conceicao da Silva (1988): 9.
47. Poster of the 10th National Congress.
48. Ibid.
49. Jonatas Conceicao da Silva (1988): 15.
50. *MNU Jornal*, 16 (June-August): 1989, 10.
51. Poster, "O Dia Naciaonal da Consciencia Negra," and Poster, the Tenth National Congress.
52. "Congresso Do Movimento Negro Unificado Tese: Sexismo E Racismo," *1978–1988 10 Anos de Luta Contra o Racismo* (1988): 27.
53. *Movimento Negro Unificado: Contribuicoes ao 1o EVEN Sao Paulo, 14 a 17/11/91*, 5.

Political Institutions, Agency, and Contingent Compromise: Understanding Democratic Consolidation and Reversal in Africa

Edmond J. Keller

University of California, Los Angeles

We are far from the stage of a revolution in the democratic process in Africa, and yet democracy is the option which the governed prefer and which is easily denied them by government.
—Olusegun Obasanjo, 1991

In Africa...democracy is everywhere under construction; and yet, it is everywhere in doubt.
—Richard Sklar, 1986

Democracies become consolidated when people learn that democracy is a solution to the problem of tyranny, but not necessarily to anything else.
—Samuel P. Huntington, 1993

As the decade of the 1980s ended the world was in the midst of what many observers hailed as a worldwide democratic revolution. Samuel Huntington has described this period as the "Third Wave of Democratization" (1993), involving mostly the countries of Eastern and Southern Europe and South America. What was most significant about this process was not only that it signaled the collapse of Soviet-style communism, but also, through the miracle of satellite communications technology, these dramatic events were on a daily basis beamed into the homes of people in even the most remote corners of the earth. The world watched as the Berlin Wall came crashing to the ground; as the Romanian dictator Nicolai Ceaucescu fell victim to a popular uprising; as Czechoslovakia executed its *velvet revolution*; and as South Africa dismantled *apartheid* and replaced it with an all-race, multiparty democracy. Such events seemed to have a contagious effect, awakening democratic sentiments in societies long characterized by authoritarian rule. Nowhere was this truer than in Africa. Although Africa lagged behind in the Third Wave of Democratization, by the early 1990s all but a handful of authoritarian regimes on the continent had embarked on political liberalization programs leaning in the direction of multiparty democracy.

At this time, there was widespread agreement in the scholarly community that the significance of these changes was profound, and that serious attention should be devoted to studying these transformations. The moment was early, and some cautioned about forming too hasty and wrong-headed conclusions. While some scholars celebrated "the triumph of Western values," the demise of communism, and, indeed, Africa's second independence, others urged caution. Africa had had a false start with democracy before and there was no evidence that this episode would be any different. The question of the depth and durability of these political transitions in Africa begged for answers. However, the initial efforts to provide answers seemed based more on normative biases in favor of liberal democracy, and fervent hopes, than upon empirical evidence. Trying to do empirical research on this subject proved extremely difficult. In describing the field research problem as it related to Eastern Europe at the beginning of the Third Wave, Sidney Tarrow suggested that trying to come up with meaningful, testable hypotheses was like "trying to paint a moving train," or "trying to hit a moving target" (Tarrow, 1991: 12). Africanist researchers faced similar dilemmas. Nevertheless, they forged ahead.

What has been the record thus far? To what extent is there evidence that meaningful democratic breakthroughs have occurred? Even though it may still be too soon to tell very much, it would seem fruitful to engage in an interim assessment of democratic consolidation in Africa. We are now entering into a period of what are commonly viewed as "second elections," the elections following the ones that initially ushered in this latest round of experimentation with democracy. In some places, there were some initial limited democratic gains, but they were manifested only in some procedural minimums. Indeed there are some observers who will concede nothing more than that there has been some political liberalization in Africa, and not clear evidence of democratic consolidation. In a number of places, autocratic rulers simply allowed for multiparty elections while continuing to maintain a firm grip on politics and power. In other cases opposition forces, with the aid of civil society were able to topple the old order, and to promise a new day for democracy. However, from this point on matters were out of the hands of civil society and in the hands of traditional politicians.

Despite this mixed record, it seems reasonable to begin to raise questions about the extent to which democracy is being consolidated in various African countries and about the factors that might be contributing to this trend. In places where democratic consolidation seems not to be taking root, the question is why? What obstacles seem to be standing in the way?

The purpose of this essay is to critically assess the factors (structural as well as human agency) that seem to have facilitated or inhibited democratic breakthroughs and the consolidation process in Africa between 1990 and 1996. The remainder of the discussion is divided into two main sections. The first section considers theoretical perspectives on democratic consolidation, and sketches the outlines of an analytical framework that guides the second section. Particular attention is paid to the roles of institution building and human agency in democratic consolidation. The second section, based on empirical evidence, focuses on selecte d trends in the democratization process in Africa over the past several years. Examples are drawn from several countries. In the final section, I consider prospects for the future of democratic consolidation in Africa.

The primary thesis of this essay is that in order to assess trends toward democratic consolidation in Africa one must evaluate the efforts of state leaders in terms of their institutional choices and their statecraft. More progress toward democratic consolidation is made in places where leaders are willing to engage in contingent compromises,[1] thereby building trust in their chosen constitutional approaches to democracy, and through calculated statecraft, to make clear, credible commitments and promises that support this process. Groups that feel that their citizenship rights are protected and that incumbent regimes are committed to good governance as well as to democracy, even in times of economic hardship, will most likely not exercise their "exit option" or to engage in extra-constitution activities to make their voices heard (Haggard and Kaufman, 1995: 325–28).

Consolidating Democracies: Theoretical Perspectives

How do We Know Democratic Consolidation When We See It?

In contrast to early scholarship (Lipset, 1959; Moore, 1966; Rustow, 1970; Binder et al., 1971), which attempted to identify the preconditions for democratic consolidation, more recent work seeks to answer the question: "What conditions seem most conducive to the development of viable democracies?" (Przeworski, 1995). There is now general agreement that a cultural predisposition toward democratic institutions and practices considerably enhances the prospects for democratic consolidation. Horowitz (1991), Diamond (1997), Huntington (1993), Shin (1994), and others lay considerable emphasis on the formation of a democratic culture and the habits of democratic practice. This can only occur if democratic institutions are put into place, and allowed to function freely. Linz (1990: 158) argues that, "a consolidated democracy is one in which none of the major political actors, parties or organizations, interests, forces, or institutions consider that there is not any alternative to the democratic process to gain power, and that no political institutions or group has a claim to veto the actions of democratically elected decision makers."

While some scholars suggest that institutional design critically shapes the development of a democratic culture, others emphasize the role of governing elites in the creation and promotion of democratic institutions and practice. Przeworski, for example, suggests that without an effective state, democracy will not be sustained. Moreover, "the effect of democratization on political and economic conditions is contingent on the institutional viability and effectiveness of state institutions" (Przeworski, 1995: 4).

Although democratic institutions can be imposed on a society, and over time they could come to achieve widespread legitimacy, the general tendency is for the process of democratic consolidation to be a gradual and even halting process. Huntington (1993a: 172) notes that the first attempts to establish democracy in a society with no or only limited experience with this form of governance frequently fails. But, second efforts generally succeed. Even allowing for this, Huntington (1993b: 13) holds out little hope for sustainable democratic breakthroughs for countries such as those found in Africa. He suggests that this is largely due to their abject poverty and propensity toward political violence, and that fundamental social and economic structural changes must take place before democracy is to have a chance in most of Africa.

Larry Diamond (1997: 5) is less sanguine about the prospects for democratic consolidation in Africa. He argues that, more than anything else, African societies simply need *time,* time to build democratic institutions appropriate to their particular cultural and political circumstances, and to learn democratic habits.

Not only is democratization usually a gradual process, it is also usually uneven. Richard Sklar (1987: 691) has suggested that it is a mistake to look for "whole cloth democracy" in developing countries. Instead, he suggests, democracy comes in fragments and pieces. Leaders in contemporary Africa, for example, while yielding to pressures for political liberalization, have often stopped short of a full commitment to liberal democracy. There might be more press freedom without there being *absolute* press freedom; multiparty competition might be allowed without credible commitments on the part of incumbent politicians to absolutely free and fair elections. Huntington has noted, "A general tendency seems to exist for *Third Wave* democracies to become something other than fully democratic" (Huntington, 1996: 10). In the short run, democratic forces will often have to settle for partial victories such as the adherence of mainstream politicians to some procedural minimums of liberal democracy, such as multipartyism, regular elections, associational recognition, limited freedom of the press, and a respect for individual and group political rights (O'Donnell and Schmitter, 1989: 8). This is not to say that they should be content with limited democracy, but only that progress toward full-fledged liberal democracy is likely to be gradual and halting.

Bearing all of this in mind, it seems reasonable to suggest that in the near term, rather than being able to talk in any meaningful sense about democratic consolidation in Africa, we are likely only to be able to evaluate tendencies in that direction. In any case, toward this end, the commitment of politicians to some form of democratic compact and to the building and utilization of democratic institutions to achieve political ends is crucial.

Institutions and Consolidation

In order for democratic consolidation to have a chance of succeeding, political institutions that are acceptable to the major stakeholders in society must be agreed upon by political elites, and they in turn must be able to count on the support of their followers (Przeworski, 1991). Social conditions may be favorable for democracy, but without attention being paid to the design of democratic institutions, consolidation is likely not to occur. While there is general scholarly agreement on this proposition, there continues to be considerable debate about the desirability of institutional engineering, particularly in deeply divided societies. There are those who suggest that getting the institutions right far outweighs other factors contributing to democratic consolidation. Ottaway (1997) argues that it was just this type of thinking that seemed to guide Britain and France during the process of decolonization in Africa. They assumed that democratic institutions could be effectively grafted onto African states. However, this proved not to be the case. Social and political conditions existing in most African countries led to a rejection of nominally democratic institutions, in favor of various forms of authoritarianism. Similarly, consociational formulae have proved to be impossible to implement wholesale in Africa. Instead, the pattern has been intense negotiations, with leaders engaging in strategic interactions and making contingent compromises that lead to "rules of the game" that, while falling short of being optimal for all actors, allow progress toward democracy to be made. The process is helped along by the realization on the part of political elites that progress can only be made through bargaining and compromise (Sisk, 1995).

Constitutions are important because they formalize agreed upon political institutions and procedures (Murphy, 1993; Przeworski, 1991: 79-88). This is particularly the case in deeply divided societies. Institutions addressed in constitutions might include a presidential, a parliamentary, or a mixed form of government; types of electoral systems (e.g., proportional representation; majoritarianism; a single transferable vote system); party systems; judicial systems; and so forth. The exact institutions or mix of institutions generally tends to be determined during the course of negotiation. What is clear, however, is that institutions matter in democratic consolidation, and how institutions are chosen matters. At the same time it must be acknowledged that factors such as an incumbent regime that is uncommitted to true democracy, an unfavorable political culture, or exogenous factors, such as international economic crisis, could render ineffective otherwise appropriately designed political institutions.

Przeworski (1995: 5) notes that all societies involved in the process of building democracy face three common challenges: deciding upon substance versus procedure, agreement versus competition, and majoritarianism versus constitutionalism. In the course of deciding upon interim as well as permanent social contracts, elite negotiators must agree on the place of substance versus procedures. Since substance often carries moral overtones, it is unlikely that most social contracts in societies characterized by an extremely diverse citizenry will dwell much on substance. In the modern world, elites representing various communities in multiethnic or multiracial societies might agree that they are committed to multiracialism, but are unlikely to agree that one religion is the state religion. They are more likely to agree on a certain set of democratic procedures such as proportional representation, or majority rule/minority rights, or federalism, or term limits for elected leaders. Those negotiating the new social contract also must decide which issues are sacrosanct and which ones are open to competition. In order to contribute toward the consolidation of democracy, the resulting agreements must at the very least offer frameworks that are open-ended, and capable of processing a multiplicity of claims, interests, and values (Przeworski, 1995:

42). In other words, they must be organic constitutions that codify the rights of citizens of today as well as those of generations to come.

Human Agency and Consolidation

Institutions do not create themselves. They are the products of decisions made by elites. Under conditions of democracy, in the course of making institutional choices, these elites must engage in strategic interactions resulting in contingent compromises with one another. In order for democracy to have a chance to consolidate, elites must make the right institutional choices, choices that limit the incentives for elites and their constituents to revert to nondemocratic forms of politics. In other words, key elites must demonstrate a commitment to democracy. It is this kind of commitment that makes it possible for democratic institutions to take root and to become legitimized (Mainwaring, 1992; Shapiro, 1995). Elites committed to democracy can even help fledgling democracies survive crises that would ordinarily spell trouble for a regime not clearly committed to democracy. In the course of attempting to build democracy elites who constitute the state class as well as those representing diverse constituencies face a serious strategic problem: Deciding how to make credible commitments in the form of threats and promises (Przeworski, 1995: 25).

Not only must state elite demonstrate that they are determined to use their authority to effectively govern, but also that they are committed to democracy and social justice that go beyond the procedural minimum. In the process they build legitimacy in the general population, and not just in certain segments of society. Each individual and group must be convinced that they have rights as citizens within the particular polity, and that those rights are protected by constitutional writ (Kymlicka, 1995). A persistent problem in the consolidation of democracy is the need for a commitment on the part of leaders to the procedural minimums of democracy such as competitive elections, rule of law and judicial independence, but at the same time large segments of the polity feel as though their citizenship rights are not being respected. Diamond (1994) notes that: "democratic development and stability...in Africa require that each significant ethnic and regional group feels some identification with and stake in the political system. This requires that, even if they have no share in power at the center, they at least have control over their own more local affairs and the capacity to utilize these resources."

A primary indicator that democracy is being consolidated is the existence of effective citizenship rights for all. Without this it is impossible to speak of "democracy" in any meaningful sense. When citizens view the political system under which they live as fair, they are most often willing to work through any differences they might have with other groups in society. Under such conditions, elites would likely accept electoral defeat, if they believed the cards were not permanently stacked against them because of their ethnicity, religion, gender or region, and that they might have a chance of winning in some future election. At the same time, ethnic minorities might accept the failure of one of their own to secure a university placement or a bank loan, if they are convinced that they were not discriminated against because of their ethnicity.

Whatever political system obtains can be considered democratic only when citizenship rights are protected. In some cases this democracy can be pursued through undemocratic means such as political pact formation (Karl, 1990; O'Donnell and Schmitter, 1989). Political pacts are the result of deals negotiated among a number of elites representing distinct groups that constitute society. These can be ethnic, racial, religious, regional, or gender-based groups. This method is usually chosen because it tends to reduce open conflict and divisive competition. Pact negotiators are responsible to their constituents, but are generally free to negotiate on their behalf, and to enter into grand coalitions. Negotiators set the agenda, and through a process of contingent compromise they narrow the issues of disagreement and agreement. Each group's representative has a potential veto power during the course of negotiating the rules of the game (Hartzell and Rothchild, 1997). Some pacts are more inclusive than others. Inclusive pacts attempt to involve all groups of significance, but exclusive pacts might leave out fringe groups (Hartzell and Rothchild, 1997: 155). Stable democracy is promoted when all groups that count are part of the negotiations leading up to a new social contract.

In addition to elites, another dimension of human agency in the process of democratization is represented in what is commonly referred to as *civil society*. This term is often used to refer to autonomous organized groups bent on challenging authoritarian regimes to open up the political system and to respect their citizenship rights. In a seminal article on this subject, Jean-François Bayart defined civil society as the political space between the household and the state (Bayart, 1986). It is outside the formal political arena, but it can be drawn in when there exists a political crisis.

Civil society is not society writ large, but only a subset of it. What defines civil society is its agenda. It is created when autonomous associations adopt and act upon a civic agenda. In that sense the manifestation of civil society tends to be situational and intermittent. These groups may not have been born as civic organizations, but they are moved by circumstances to engage in politics. They might demand constitutional reform, governmental accountability, their human and political rights, and an end to official corruption. The groups that comprise civil society are usually intellectuals, artists, professionals such as lawyers and doctors, organized labor, church associations, women's and student associations.

Crawford Young (1994: 38) suggests that, based upon the vitality of autonomous associations concerned with political matters, the nationalist period in Africa could be considered to have been the "golden age" in the evolution of civil society. However, after independence, autonomous civic associations were either co-opted by mainstream political organizations or repressed by autocratic regimes, and forced to bide their time, waiting for openings in the political opportunity structure.

The first signs of a resurgent civil society began to appear in Africa at about the time of the overthrow of the Jaffar Nimeiri regime in Sudan in a popular uprising in 1985, but it was not until about 1988 that there were clear manifestations of a genuine political force that we could roughly classify as *civil society*. Since then, African civil society has not only grown; it has also changed, become emboldened, and focused on the spoils of national politics. In many cases, it has been the decisive catalyst in regime change

(Bratton, 1994: 51). However, the effectiveness of civil society in bringing about regime change is highly contingent, conditioned by other factors such as the relative strength of the incumbent regime, the role of external actors, the relative coherence of formal opposition groups, internal and external political and economic factors. Moreover, even when it is crucial in bringing about regime change, civil society's role is eclipsed in the aftermath. Because of its inchoate nature it is unable to play a direct role in policy formation, and only indirectly contributes to democratic consolidation.

In its most recent African manifestations, rarely has civil society been a coherent and cohesive mass movement with a clear sense of its identity and whose members share a common sense of their objectives. Instead, it has most often been comprised of a lose collection of groups with a vaguely defined common objective that often amounts to no more than a desire to oust corrupt or incompetent political regimes. In addition, and related to this, is that the civil society of today's Africa has tended to be ephemeral. It emerged in response to political crises, and co-opted by more institutionalized political forces such as formal opposition groups (Keller, 1996). The pattern has consistently been for civil society to retreat into hiding once victory has been secured or when defeat is certain, only coming out again when another crisis occurs that seems unmanageable through normal political institutions. At the same time, civil society might as well choose the "exit option," disengaging in frustration from politics.

Toward Democratic Consolidation in Africa?

Beginning with the founding elections in many countries in sub-Saharan Africa in the early 1990s there was a proliferation of political parties and multiparty systems. By mid-1996, the African Governance Program of the Carter Center was estimating that at least thirty out of forty-seven sub-Saharan countries were either fully or moderately democratic. These polities were said to be characterized by periodic and predictable competitive elections; generalized respect for human and political rights; freedom of association and expression; and respect for the rule of law. However, the question that must be asked and answered is: How deep and durable is democracy in these countries? The evidence clearly indicates that in most cases the jury is still out. While procedural democracy can be found in many places in Africa, full-fledged liberal democracy rarely exists.

Larry Diamond (1997: 3) distinguishes between *electoral democracy* and *liberal democracy*. Electoral democracy exists where there are regular, competitive, multiparty elections that can be considered at least somewhat free and fair. This is a form of procedural democracy and nothing more. However, the standard of liberal democracy is much higher. It requires that those who are elected be committed to good governance, political transparency, responsiveness, and responsibleness, respectful of human and political rights as well as the rule of law. According to *Freedom House*, at the beginning of 1996 something approaching this form of democracy existed in only seven African countries. A more common pattern is for there to be what Diamond (1997: 3–4) calls a form of *pseudo-democracy*.[2] In such cases, incumbent parties in a hegemonic fashion tend to keep a tight grip on politics. They utilize their offices to manipulate constitutions and other political institutions to their advantage and the disadvantage of actual or would-be opponents (Huntington, 1993b: 182–87). They use various means to keep from negotiating a new social contract with the formal opposition as well as with civil society.

Even in places where a political party has displaced an old autocrat by riding the crest of a multiparty democratic wave, in order to protect their newly won power it is common for new administrations to violate the very principles that they claim to hold so dearly. They come to see democracy as fraught with uncertainties and too confining; as a result, they themselves drift toward autocracy, and are quick to turn to institutional manipulation. Some even go so far as to completely renege on their commitments to democracy.

In 1996 in Zambia, for example, as the first elections following the return to multipartyism began, the regime of Fredrick Chiluba reformed the constitution to head off a possible serious challenge from former president Kenneth Kaunda and his United National Independence party (UNIP). Among other things, the revised constitution forbade any individual whose parents were not born in Zambia from running for the presidency. Kaunda's parents were alleged by Chiluba's Movement for Multi-party Democracy (MMD) to have been born in Malawi, thus making him ineligible to run for the presidency. At first Kaunda attempted to challenge this new law in the courts, but when that failed he urged his followers to boycott the fall elections. However, Kaunda's support base was extremely narrow, being confined mainly to Eastern Province, and it is not clear that his exhortations influenced voter turnout. Whereas external pressures five years earlier had been effective in bolstering civil society against the Kaunda regime, in 1996 civil society was in disarray and external pressures on Chiluba proved to be ineffective.

Further evidence of Chiluba's propensity to manipulate political institutions in favor of the MMD could be seen in how he utilized electoral rules; parliamentary procedures and government bureaucrats to frustrate and intimidate his opponents (Bratton and Posner, 1997; Simutanyi, 1997). The voter registration exercise leading up to Zambia's 1996 elections began in December of the previous year, and were controversial from the start. Opposition parties charged that the Israeli firm that had been hired to carry out the exercise had not been chosen in a transparent manner. However, the government rejected these charges and forged ahead. The resulting process was fraught with numerous irregularities. For example, thousands of people were left off of the voting register; several thousand young people below the voting age were registered; and there existed several thousand ghost voters on the books. In the end, UNIP, along with several other parties, boycotted the elections. Of the 2.3 million people said to have been validly registered to vote, 1.3 million actually voted. However, this must be considered in light of a total eligible population of 4.6 million. Because of the fact that the MMD used its incumbency to structure politics in its favor, its organizational strength, and the boycott of the election by major opposition parties, the MMD was able to capture 131 of 150 seats in parliament (*Economist Intelligence Unit*, 1997d: 9).

In other places such as Gabon and Kenya, autocrats have attempted to ward off proponents of democracy and good governance by institutional manipulation, fraud, and intimidation. They might allow for multiparty elections, but this amounts to no more than what Diamond refers to as electoral democracy, and falls well short of the liberal democratic ideal. Political liberalization occurs when new forms of political manipulation and obfuscation come into play.

In Gabon, President Omar Bongo has over the years been able to use the resources of his neo-patrimonial regime to co-opt potential opponents. Those who refused to be co-opted risked state repression (Gardinier, 1997: 147). On a number of occasions since 1968 Bongo got his supporters in the National Assembly to amend the constitution so as to enhance his own executive authority, and to institutionalize the role of his *Parti Democratique Gabonais*. In effect the party became the state and the state was the party. But by late 1994, with the endorsement of France, opposition forces were clamoring for political liberalization. Several of these groups meeting in Paris in November of that year signed an agreement calling upon Bongo to establish an independent electoral council to prepare the way for democratic elections. Rather than caving in, Bongo offered a counter-proposal: a referendum on what came to be known as the Paris Accords. This referendum took place in July 1995, and resulted in the popular endorsement of a full implementation of the Paris Accords. The Accords, among other things, called for a drastic reduction in the executive authority of the president, and for the country to be governed according to the rule of law. However, Bongo continues to manipulate institutions at his disposal to circumvent the full implementation of these new democratic procedures.

In Kenya, although President Daniel arap Moi agreed to allow for a multiparty system just prior to the national election in 1992, he used his presidential prerogative of calling a "snap election" at very short notice, thus adding to the confusion in the ranks of his opponents. The ruling party, the Kenya African National Union (KANU), was able to win just over 30 percent of the vote. However, this was sufficient to return Moi to office. Civil society had been vibrant, but the formal opposition parties proved not to be able to coalesce in a united front against KANU.

While multiple parties were allowed after 1992, other aspects of the legal codes and constitution enabled Moi *de facto* to continue his autocratic rule. As the opposition saw it, the problem was the constitution. It allowed for too many discretionary powers for the chief executive. In late 1994, elements of civil society led by Law Society of Kenya, the Kenya Human Rights Commission, and the International Commission of Jurists (Kenya Section) drafted what they called *The Model Constitution* (Proposal for a Model Constitution, 1994). Moi, however, dismissed the draft as well as its proponents as not representative of the Kenyan people. In his New Year's Eve address in 1994, the president agreed that the constitution should be reformed, but only by parliament. In the subsequent two years the government did nothing to follow through on Moi's pledge.

In the meantime, civil society resurfaced emboldened and more determined than ever to force constitutional reforms. In April 1997, elements of civil society and opposition parties met at Lamuru in Central Province to reconsider the notion of having a constitutional convention (*Finance*, 1997: 6–8). This convocation was called the National Convention Planning Committee and later constituted as the National Convention Assembly (NCA).

At the end of the meeting a manifesto was issued calling for minimum constitutional and administrative reforms prior to national elections.

At the conclusion of the Lemuru meeting, the assembly formed and empowered the National Convention Executive Council (NCEC) to organize a series of mass actions in an effort to force Moi to accede to these demands for minimum reform. Moi countered by claiming that constitutional reforms should be contemplated only after the impending national elections in 1997.

The primary objectives of the NCA included pre-election reforms that would require the winner of the presidency to secure at least 50 percent of the popular vote or face a runoff. The assembly also called for reforms to make it easier to register political parties, for the removal of restrictions on freedom of assembly, and for expanded press freedom.

Over the next three months following the Lemuru Manifesto, the NCEC publicly challenged the state. The most dramatic confrontation occurred on July 7, the date that commemorates the rebirth of multiparty democracy in Kenya in 1991. A rally in the center of Nairobi resulted in a police riot in which at least seven people were killed and many more badly injured. General Services Unit troops even went so far in hot pursuit of demonstrators as to storm parts of the University of Nairobi and to violate the sanctuary of a cathedral in the heart of town. By allowing these excesses, Moi was attempting to demonstrate to his opponents that he was not committed to wholesale liberal democracy, and that he would use whatever means he deemed necessary to suppress opposition. It appeared that he was committed more to authoritarian retrenchment than to reform.

Nevertheless, in August 1997, amidst growing pressures from civil society, as well as the international community over his regime's gross violation of human rights, Moi began to moderate his stance. Despite this, the IMF, citing Kenya's widespread government corruption and other financial scandals, suspended a $220 million loan to Kenya (Simmons, 1997). Shortly afterwards the World Bank followed suit and suspended a $71.6 million structural adjustment credit to Kenya until several conditions relating to good governance and corruption were met (All Africa Press Service, 1997).

Apparently sensing its newfound strength and buoyed by crucial external pressures, the NCA escalated its protest against the Moi regime. On August 8 it called a general strike that shut down commercial activities, especially in urban areas. It was clear by then that Kenya society had become so deeply divided that the only way to return to political comity would be through bargaining and compromise. However, Moi continued to view such an option as unnecessary. Grindle (1996: 155) has noted that the Moi regime's failure to acknowledge the role of governmental accountability, responsiveness, and responsibility to the polity undermines not only democracy but also economic development.

Even in places where newly elected regimes have reneged on democracy and are drifting toward autocracy or where old autocratic regimes have yielded to procedural democracy while maintaining hegemonic control over politics, it is fair to expect that some democratic gains have been made. Fragments of democracy enhance the possibility that other fragments will be added over time. Take Zambia for example. Even as the Chiluba regime was attempting to structure the 1996 elections to insure an MMD victory, it was promulgating a law creating a permanent human rights commission. This was hailed by the international community as a step in the right direction and a demonstration of Chiluba's commitment to good governance and democracy. At the same time, however, Chiluba's rubber-stamp parliament was considering a media bill that would require that a commission headed by a High Court judge license journalists (*Economist Intelligence Unit*, 1997e: 10). It also stipulated that journalists should have at least a B.A. in journalism or mass communications before being allowed to practice. The government, obviously feeling threatened by an increasingly free and critical independent print media, was seeking ways of controlling that segment of its opposition. The justification for the bill was that it created standards in the journalistic profession. Public objections to the bill led to its suspension in April.

Significantly, opposition politicians have not resorted to extra-constitutional measures to challenge the Chiluba regime. In fact, they have regularly taken their cases to the Supreme Court. For example, they have challenged in court the results of particular elections, the constitutional amendment relating to the eligibility to stand for president, and MMD corruption. This is clear evidence that some strides have been made in Zambia toward democratic consolidation, while elements of autocracy have persisted.

Another example of persistent autocratic tendencies, even in places that have accepted procedural democracy, can be found in Ethiopia where over the past five years there has emerged a vocal human rights lobby and a vibrant array of independent print media. As is the case with the MMD in Zambia, the Ethiopian People's Revolutionary Democratic Front (EPRDF) regime can on the one hand be lauded for many of its political and economic reforms; but, on the other, it must be criticized for significant failings. For example, although the judiciary has shown signs of independence, it is weak and overburdened. In addition, as a consequence of the implementation of the federal constitution, considerable powers have been devolved to the regions. The constitution clearly spells out that citizens have the same constitutional rights no matter when they live or travel in the country (*Proclamation of the Constitution of the Federal Republic of Ethiopia*, 1995: 9–16). However, in a 1996 human rights report the U.S. State Department found that violations of human and political rights were rampant on the part of some state and local governments. Although it proclaims its commitment to protecting these rights, the central government is not able to do so. In the Oromo Region, for example, members of the security forces and local governments for political reasons regularly violated the rights of citizens (e.g., detention without trial, extra-judicial killing). At the same time, the report goes on to note that the average Ethiopian community has much more control over its affairs than at any other time in modern history (*Economist Intelligence Unit*, 1997a: 14).

In places such as Burundi, Gambia, Niger, and Sierra Leone, military coups have reversed democratic breakthroughs, but it is remarkable how rare this has been. Some students of democracy have consistently argued that the critical test for democratic consolidation is the national elections immediately following the return to multiparty democracy. This is what Huntington (1993b: 266–7) has called the "two turnover test," and is characterized by a party that took power in an initial election losing power in a subsequent election. Success is proclaimed when defeat in the second election is magnanimously accepted. Such peaceful turnovers demonstrate a commitment to democracy on the part of both political leaders and the electorate. Recent elections in Benin and Madagascar seem to show that this might be happening in some places.

In March 1995 Nicephore Soglo was defeated in a return bid for the presidency by former dictator Mathieu Kerekou. More than 80 percent of the electorate turned out to vote. The Soglo regime had failed to significantly improve Benin's economic situation, and many viewed him as a worse autocrat than Kerekou had been. In addition, corruption continued unabated. All of this seems to have led many to consider giving Kerekou a second chance. Soglo had been ahead of Kerekou by two percentage points in the open elections, but in the run-off minority parties threw their support to Kerekou. Soglo charged voting fraud, but lost several appeals to the constitutional court. Only grudgingly did he accept the verdict of the people, before he went into several months of self-imposed exile in the United States. Just prior to his return to Benin in August 1995, Soglo was a more magnanimous loser, stating that the peaceful transfer of power to Kerekou was proof that democracy was being consolidated in Benin. He further stated, "Although we may not like the result, we should recognize that the elections took place, and that the transfer of power was non-violent" (*Economist Intelligence Unit*, 1996a: 33). Moreover, Soglo pointed to the endurance of freedom of the press, freedom of expression, an independent judiciary, and an electoral commission all as clear examples that democracy was taking hold in Benin (*Economist Intelligence Unit*, 1996b: 32)

Poor governance and corruption also led to the demise of the regime of Albert Zafy in Madagascar (*Economist Intelligence Unit*, 1997c). In August 1996 Zafy was impeached by parliament and forced to resign. Among other things, Zafy was never able to come to terms with the Bretton Woods institutions on macroeconomic reforms and this resulted in his being criticized both at home and abroad for inept governance.

A new round of national elections was organized for November 1996. Among the candidates for the presidency were Zafy and the man he had successfully deposed several years earlier, Didier Ratsiraka. Although the electorate had not forgotten the brutal dictatorship of Ratsiraka, it seems that the majority of the electorate could not forgive Zafy's managerial ineffectiveness. The vote seemed to be more anti-Zafy than pro-Ratsiraka. Even Ratsiraka himself admitted this, stating, "My victory is due more to the disillusionment of the Malagasy people toward the old regime than to their enthusiasm for me" (*Economist Intelligence Unit*, 1997c: 20).

Indeed Ratsiraka's victory hardly amounted to a mandate. He secured only 38 percent of the ballots in the initial voting, and only 50.7 percent in the run-off. Many voters did not feel that there was much of a choice between the two top vote getters, some describing it as being "like a choice between the plague and cholera."

All parties concerned accepted the results of Madagascar's "second elections," and there was clear evidence that democratic attitudes had begun to take hold among elites as well as in the mass public. To this extent it seems safe to say that despite the return of a former dictator, progress is being made toward democratic consolidation in that country. Moreover, early indications are that Ratsiraka was chastened by having lost in the first election, and committed now to attempting to satisfy international donors as well as domestic constituents.

Some "second elections" that do not result in the turnover of the incumbent regime can still manifest tendencies toward democratic consolidation. Such was the case in Ghana's 1996 presidential elections. In his first term since the re-introduction of multiparty politics, President Jerry Rawlings continued to lead his country's economic recovery, thereby being able to rely on both strong international and domestic support. In his bid for re-election, Rawlings scored a decisive victory, securing 58 percent of the vote. What was equally as significant was the high rate of voter turnout (75 percent). This figure was well above the 48 percent turnout four years earlier. Although opposition parties were able to organize themselves better than in the first election, they were only able to secure 66 of 200 parliamentary seats.

Rawlings clearly demonstrated that he had forsaken the autocratic ways that had characterized his rule prior to 1992, and his commitment to democracy, by the way in which he and his party, the National Democratic Congress (NDC), approached the elections. In contrast to the "second election" in Zambia, the electoral register in Ghana was not a subject of intense debate. It was built from scratch, and voters were freely allowed to register at the polling places where they would ultimately cast their votes. The transparency of this process seems to have served to engender trust among the electorate (Lyons, 1997: 6–7). At the same time, it was clear that incumbency had its advantages. The Rawlings regime was able to use the extensive and effective organization of the NDC as well as government resources to facilitate the NDC campaign. Rawlings, through effective statecraft, has developed the NDC into the only party with a national support base. By contrast, opposition parties tended to have very narrow, mostly ethno-regional support bases (*Economist Intelligence Unit*, 1997b).

Despite the return of the NDC to power, the opposition demonstrated support for the democratic rules of the game by accepting the verdict of the electorate as generally free and fair. This is not to say that there were not some alleged as well as real electoral irregularities, but it is generally agreed that the elections were on balance properly conducted. However, the real test for Ghana's fledgling democracy will come at the end of Rawling's second term. He is forbidden by law from standing again, and at the moment no one stands out as his peer in terms of charismatic appeal.

Societies that are deeply divided along ethnic, racial, or religious lines pose particular challenges to democratic consolidation. The first and most formidable challenge is the choice of institutions that facilitate the development of mutual trust among groups and enable them to construct a mutually acceptable social contract to frame group political relations. This requires that elites from all politically significant groups be willing and able to make credible commitments to the democratic process. Leaders under such circumstances demonstrate that they are willing to engage in contingent compromises in order to advance the causes of social equity and democracy.

South Africa and Ethiopia represent two of Africa's most deeply divided societies that have chosen the path of constitutionalism in an effort to consolidate democracy. On the one hand, South Africa's divisions are based both on race and ethnicity; and on the other, Ethiopia's divisions are largely ethnically based. The current regimes of each of these countries are the products of contingent compromises made during the course of devising a formula for democracy by compact.

Ten years ago few observers believed that *apartheid* in South Africa would soon end. The Afrikaner-dominated National party seemed firmly entrenched and strongly committed to maintaining white domination. However, beginning in the mid-1980s cracks began to emerge beneath the edifice of the apartheid regime. White businessmen began secret negotiations with the leadership of the African National Congress (ANC) in exile, and this was followed by similar initiatives by the white regimes. The late 1980s in South Africa were characterized by widespread violence, especially in black townships; sanctions had begun to hurt the country; and all of this was bad for business. In large measure this created an opening for soft-liners within the NP government, and with the replacement of President P. W. Botha by the more moderate F. W. de Klerk in 1989, the stage was set for the negotiating process leading up to the ending of apartheid and the introduction of all-race multiparty democracy (Sisk, 1995).

Whereas apartheid had enshrined white supremacy and a racial hierarchy by law, it was clear that the framers of the new social contract in South Africa would have to begin to look at the protection of group rights as the cornerstone of a new constitution. Group rights, then, translated into the guarantee of certain inalienable citizenship rights. Leadership on all sides would have to compromise in order to move the process of democratization along. For right-wing Afrikaners and Zulu nationalists this meant nothing short of their right to national self-determination up to and including separation from the state as it then existed. The interim constitution agreed to in late 1993 avoided dealing directly with the group rights issue, but it would not go away (Ottaway, 1994).

The negotiations over the interim constitution were the quintessential representation of pact making through contingent compromise. Discussion began with the NP dismissing the notion of majority rule as undemocratic. The ANC position was diametrically the opposite. The NP favored at the very least some sort of power-sharing arrangement. Over time each side was forced to compromise. In the end more than twenty organizations would participate in the negotiation process. At the extremes were the South African Communist party and the Concerned South Africans Group or Freedom Alliance, a marriage of convenience involving the Zulu nationalist Inkatha Freedom party, several militantly nationalistic Afrikaner organizations and the leadership of two homelands, Bophutatswana and Ciskei. The Alliance members were united only in their opposition to either a unitary South African state or a federal system that required a significant compromise of their sovereignty.

The Alliance proved not to be effective, but last minute concessions were made that kept Inkatha and several Afrikaner groups from rejecting the pact altogether. There developed among centrists who dominated the negotiations (NP, ANC, and the Democratic party) a consensus on the possible character of the post-apartheid democracy as well as the institutions that would support it (Sisk, 1995: 198–99).

The negotiations were thrown into crisis in early 1994 by a revolt against the government of Lucas Mangope in Bophutatswana by elements of the homeland civil service and other groups, and Mangope's response. Mangope moved to crack down on the revolt, and got support from armed Afrikaners who came to assist him. This "invasion" served to drive Mangope supporters and opponents together and to take measures to repel the offensive. From this point on homeland opposition to incorporation into South Africa was eliminated. However, the ANC and NP alliance was forced to make some limited concessions in order to keep the right-wing fringe groups committed to the elections of May 1994 that would usher in the transitional government, and lay the groundwork for the election of a constituent assembly to thrash out a permanent constitution.

South Africa represents a situation where contingent compromises among relatively strong parties forced the process to be open and transparent. This served to build trust in the process itself. Moreover, leaders representing the different groups were forced to behave in a manner supportive of the democratic process, thereby building even further trust.

The case of the EPRDF in Ethiopia is representative of a disingenuous attempt at pact making and contingent compromise. A major challenge facing the leadership of the EPRDF when it took over in 1991 was to address Ethiopia's historic problems relating to ethno-regional nationalism. Eritrea had finally won its independence after thirty years of protracted war against Ethiopia, and other nationality groups, such as the Ogaden Somalis and the Oromo, asserted their right to self-determination.

The EPRDF began as an umbrella organization of liberation movements that in the late 1980s formed a united front against the Marxist regime of Mengistu Haile Mariam. In May of 1991, this organization succeeded in routing the Ethiopian army, and gaining control of the reins of government. Rather than avoid dealing with the claims of ethnic groups to self-determination, as had been the case with previous regimes, the new government decided to tackle the issue head-on. The apparent hope was that by granting ethnic groups a measure of regional autonomy, what was left of Ethiopia could be held in tact. The EPRDF moved quickly after its victory to establish a transitional government. A national conference for this purpose was convened in July 1991 in an attempt on the part of the EPRDF to secure widespread acceptance among the general population. It resulted in the signing of a charter by the representative of some thirty-one political groups, the creation of an eighty-seven-seat Council of Representatives, and the establishment of the Transitional Government of Ethiopia (TGE). The largest number of seats was reserved for the EPRDF itself, and the Oromo Liberation Front (OLF) was second with twelve seats. Significantly, no political organization that predominately represented the formerly politically dominant ethnic group, the Amharas, was a signatory to the charter or represented in the council. In other words, the pact was exclusive rather than being inclusive.

Since Tigreans make up only about 10 percent of the Ethiopian population, the EPRDF could not hope to rule without forming a coalition government. It is the most organized among the political parties, and indeed, it is the only one with a national following. Politics is organized along ethnic line, and opposition parties are mostly based on ethnic affinities. The EPRDF has a Tigre and Amhara core, and it has created or co-opted other political groups comprised of other ethnicities. The OLF, arguably the most popular party among the Oromo, was not a part of the EPRDF, but initially it expressed a willingness to cooperate with the new regime as long as it agreed to power-sharing, and demonstrated that it was respectful of equal citizenship rights for all, especially the Oromo.

The OLF, like other ethnically based parties, was initially allowed into the Council of Representatives and the TGE, but it was not long before the OLF leadership came to doubt the commitment of the EPRDF to upholding Oromo citizenship rights. In 1992, just prior to local and regional elections, the OLF withdrew from the electoral process, and has been banned from Ethiopian politics ever since. Moreover, between 1992 and 1995, the pact that made up the TGE became ever more narrow. EPRDF members and the supporters of affiliated groups heavily dominated the constituent assembly, which drafted the permanent constitution. Therefore, it is clear that Ethiopia's experiment in pact making led much more to procedural or electoral democracy than it did to a more substantive, liberal democracy. Armed opposition from Oromo, Somali, and Islamic fundamentalist groups who feel that their citizenship rights are not protected under the new regime plagues the country.

Marina Ottaway (1994; 1997) has argued that basing regions on the predominant ethnic affinities of their inhabitants exacerbates rather than ameliorates ethnic conflict. However, there is no reason to believe that if regions had been organized on another basis that ethnic conflict would not occur. Rather than the ethnic basis of regions being the obstacle to democratic consolidation it seems more plausible that the new regime has yet to sufficiently assure large segments of certain nationality groups that their citizenship rights will be protected, and that it is committed in a credible way to democracy. In such cases, getting institutions right does not lead automatically in the direction of democratic consolidation. Instead, the trend seems more toward pseudo-democracy or limited democracy.

Conclusion

Despite some false steps and setbacks democracy seems to be reestablishing roots in many parts of Africa. It is too soon in most places to talk about the consolidation of sustainable democracy. In fact, in most places we can only speak of fragments of democracy. However, if there is the political will among contending political elites to maintain the democratic course, over time fragmentary gains will tend to cumulate, enhancing the possibilities that democratic culture and habits will become common place. To be sure there are places where we can only speak of procedural democracy or pseudo-democracy, but what is significant is that in recent years, the forces of democracy have undermined the autocratic project of integral states.

In large measure consolidating democracy depends upon choosing the right institutions; but this will only happen if there are elites willing to effectively implement democratic procedures. Leaders have to demonstrate not only a commitment to good governance, but also to civic tolerance and to enshrining in a constitution guaranteed citizenship rights and their equal application. In order to do this democracy must be negotiated. In some cases it might be negotiated through a national conference or convention; in others it might be the result of political pact making among elites. In either case, individuals and/or groups must be willing to make contingent compromises that, while perhaps not being optimal for any one party, are at least acceptable to all parties.

Despite a commitment toward effective statecraft and a willingness among political adversaries to engage in contingent compromise, democratic consolidation might be, and often is, slowed or derailed by unfavorable conditions in the international or domestic politico-economic environment. For example, pre-existing group conflicts that remain unmanageable; international economic crisis; war; or a governmentally weak state, might either singularly or collectively inhibit progress toward democratic consolidation. In the short term, in most places in Africa democratic consolidation is most likely to be slow, halting, and uneven. Yet, it seems reasonable that the overall trend will be in the positive direction.

Notes

I am grateful for the comments and suggestions on this paper provided by Donald Rothchild, Sandra Joireman, David Simon, and Mark Billera.

1. Terry Lynn Karl (1990) notes that the notion of contingent compromise involves contending social classes and political groups accepting some set of formal rules or informal understandings that determine "who gets what, where and how from politics." Contingency, then, means that outcomes depend less on objective conditions than on subjective rules surrounding strategic choices.
2. There is a good deal of terminological confusion as to how to describe what is happening with regard to the democratization process not only in Africa but elsewhere as well. There is a plethora of different subtypes of democracy that are advanced (e.g., semi-democracy, proto-democracy, guided democracy). I do not wish to contribute further to this confusion. However, I want to make it clear that what we are witnessing in most of Africa today is well short of liberal democracy, and may be most closely akin to Diamond's electoral democracy. See David Collier and Steven Levitsky, "Democracy with Adjectives: Conceptual Innovation in Comparative Research," *World Politics*, 49 (April 1997): 430–51.

References

All Africa Press Service. 1997. "Kenya's Democratization Process Enters Critical Phase." (August 18).
Bayart, Jean-François. 1986. "Civil Society in Africa." In *Political Domination in Africa*, ed. Patrick Chabal, 109–25. Cambridge: Cambridge University Press.
Binder, Leonard, et al., eds. 1971. *Crises and Sequences of Political Development*. Princeton, NJ: Princeton University Press.
Bratton, Michael. 1994. "Civil Society and Political Transitions in Africa." In *Civil Society and the State in Africa*, ed. John W. Harbeson, Donald Rothchild and Naomi Chazan, 51–82. Boulder, CO: Lynne Rienner, 51–82.
Bratton, Michael, and Daniel Posner. 1997. "A First Look at Second Elections in Africa, with Illustrations from Zambia," unpublished paper.
Collier, David, and Steven Levitsky. 1997. "Democracy with Adjectives: Conceptual Innovation in Comparative Research," *World Politics*, 49 (April): 430–51.

Diamond, Larry. 1994. "Rethinking Civil Society: Toward Democratic Consolidation." *Journal of Democracy*, 5, 3 (July): 4–17.
———. 1997. "Prospects for Democratic Development in Africa." *Hoover Institution Essays in Public Policy No. 74.* Stanford University: Hoover Institution.
Economist Intelligence Unit. 1996a. *Benin: Country Report*, 3d Quarter.
———. 1996b. *Benin: Country Report*, 4th Quarter.
———. 1997a. *Ethiopia: Country Report*, 1st Quarter.
———. 1997b. *Ghana: Country Report*, 1st Quarter.
———. 1997c. *Madagascar: Country Report.* 1st Quarter.
———. 1997d. *Zambia: Country Report*, 1st Quarter.
———. 1997e. *Zambia: Country Report*, 2d Quarter.
Finance. 1997. "Rebellion in Kenya: 'Moi's days Are Numbered'—The Underlying Factor." (July 22-August 4): 6–8.
Gardinier, David E. 1997. "Gabon: Limited Reform and Regime Survival." In *Political Reform in Francophone Africa*, ed. Clark and Gardinier, chapter 9.
Grindle, Merilee S. 1996. *Challenging the State: Crisis and Innovation in Latin America and Africa.* London: Cambridge University Press.
Haggard, Stephan, and Robert R. Kaufman. 1995. *The Political Economy of Democratic Transitions.* Princeton, NJ: Princeton University Press.
Hartzell, Caroline, and Donald Rothchild. 1997. "Political Pacts as Negotiated Agreement: Comparing Ethnic and Non-Ethnic Cases." *International Negotiation*, 2: 147–71.
Huntington, Samuel P. 1993a. "Political Development in Ethiopia: Peasant-based Dominant-Party Democracy?" Report to USAID/Ethiopia (May 17).
———. 1993b. *The Third Wave: Democratization in the Late Twentieth Century.* Norman: University of Oklahoma Press.
———. 1996. "Democracy for the Long Haul." *Journal of Democracy*, 7, 2 (April): 3–13.
Karl, Terry Lynn. 1990. "Dilemmas of Democratization in Latin America." *Comparative Politics*, 23, 1.
Keller, Edmond J. 1996. "Structure, Agency and Political Liberalization in Africa." *Journal of African Political Science*, 1, 2 (December): 202–16.
Kymlicka, Will. 1995. *Multicultural Citizenship.* Oxford: Clarendon Press.
Linz, Juan. 1990. "Transitions to Democracy," *Washington Monthly* (Summer).
Lipset, Seymour Martin. 1959, "Some Social Requisites of Democracy." *American Political Science Review*, 53: 69–105.
Lyons, Terrence. 1997. "The December 1996 Elections in Ghana," unpublished paper.
Mainwaring, Scott. 1992. "Transitions to Democracy and Democratic Consolidation: Theoretical and Comparative Issues." In *Issues in Democratic Consolidation*, ed. Scott Mainwaring, Guillermo O'Donnell, and J. Samuel Valenzuela. Notre Dame, IN: University of Notre Dame Press.
Moore, Jr., Barrington. 1966. *The Social Origins of Dictatorship and Democracy.* Boston: Beacon Press.
Murphy, Walter F. 1993. "Constitutions, Constitutionalism, and Democracy." In *Constitutionalism and Democracy*, ed. D. Greenberg et al., 3–25. New York: Oxford.
Obasanjo, Olusegun. 1989. "Remarks to the Conference on the Democratic Revolution." *Proceedings of a Conference Sponsored by the National Endowment for Democracy.* Washington, DC (May 1–2).
O'Donnell, Guillermo, and Phillipe Schmitter. 1989. *Transitions from Authoritarian Rule: Tentative Conclusions About Uncertain Democracies.* Baltimore, MD: The Johns Hopkins University Press.
Ottaway, Marina. 1994. *Democratization and Ethnic Nationalism: African and East European Experiences.* Washington, DC: Overseas Development Council.

———. 1997. "African Democratization and the Leninist Option." The *Journal of Modern African Studies*, 35, 1: 1–15.

Proclamation of the Constitution of the Federal Republic of Ethiopia. 1995. Addis Ababa: Federal Nagerait Gazeta of the Federal Democratic Republic of Ethiopia (21 August).

Proposal for a Model Constitution. 1994. *Kenya Tuitakayo (The Kenya We Want)*. Nairobi.

Przeworski, Adam. 1991. *Democracy and the Market: Political and Economic Reforms in Eastern Europe and Latin America*. Cambridge: Cambridge University Press.

———. 1995. *Sustainable Democracy*. New York: Cambridge University Press.

Rustow, Dankwart. 1970. "Transitions to Democracy: Toward and Dynamic Model." *Comparative Politics*, 2, 3 (April): 337–63.

Shapiro, Ian. 1995. "South Africa's Negotiated Transition: Democracy, Opposition and the New Constitutional Order." *Politics and Society*, 23, 3 (September): 269–308.

Shin, Doh Chull. 1994. "On the Third Wave of Democratization: A Synthesis and Evaluation of Recent Theory and Research." *World Politics*, 47 (October): 135–70.

Simmons, Ann M. 1997. "After 19 Years, Kenya's Moi Hears Doors Slamming at Home and Abroad." *Los Angeles Times* (August 9): A4.

Simutanyi, Neo. 1997. "Democracy on Trial: Political Opposition and the 1996 Zambian Elections," unpublished paper.

Sisk, Timothy D. 1995. *Democratization in South Africa: The Elusive Social Contract*. Princeton, NJ: Princeton University Press.

Sklar, Richard. 1986. "Democracy in Africa." In *Political Domination in Africa*, ed. Patrick Chabal. Cambridge: Cambridge University Press.

———. 1987. "Developmental Democracy." *Comparative Studies in Society and History*, 29, 4 (October): 686–714.

Tarrow, Sidney. 1991. "Aiming at a Moving Target: Social Science and Recent Rebellions in Eastern Europe." *PS: Political Science and Politics*, 24, 1 (March): 12–19.

Young, Crawford. 1994. "In Search of Civil Society." In *Civil Society and the State in Africa*, ed. Harbeson et. al., 33–50.

Pluralist Authoritarianism in Comparative Perspective: White Supremacy, Male Supremacy, and Regime Classification

Ollie A. Johnson III

University of Maryland

The problem of classifying political systems dates back to the Greek thinkers Aristotle and Plato, the more recent European theorists Marx, Weber, and Michels, and has continued in the work of American scholars Robert A. Dahl, Seymour Martin Lipset, and Samuel P. Huntington. These writers offered frameworks and theories that advanced our understanding of regime change. At the same time, they did not take the subordinate status of women and people of color fully into account when classifying political regimes and systems.[1] As a result, the vast literature on regime change has generally misclassified certain political regimes with both authoritarian and democratic features as basically democratic regimes. Regime misclassification has been perpetuated by scholars working in diverse intellectual traditions and using both qualitative and quantitative methods. This misclassification of national political regimes is a major intellectual problem and has contributed to questionable hypotheses and theories. The concept of pluralist authoritarianism (PA), a specific regime type, attempts to address this situation and provide a stronger analytical foundation for comparative regime analysis. Pluralist authoritarianism highlights white supremacy and male supremacy as manifestations of authoritarianism that have been ignored or minimized. The problem of regime misclassification and the concept of PA require a rethinking of comparative regime analysis.

This essay examines regime misclassification and its important consequences for social science research and scholarship. The first section highlights the problem as it relates to the basic typological distinction between democracy and authoritarianism. This section also illustrates how scholars working in various intellectual traditions have used conflicting conceptual and operational definitions resulting in widespread regime misidentification and descriptive distortion of numerous national political regimes. The second section offers pluralist authoritarianism as a solution to the problem of regime misclassification. The third part shows how white supremacy and male supremacy can be forms of pluralist authoritarianism. In the fourth section, the applicability of PA is demonstrated in a brief comparative historical analysis of three important cases of national regime evolution: the United States, Switzerland, and South Africa. The fifth section outlines how PA forces us to rethink regime classification and comparative regime theory. The conclusion summarizes the overall potential contribution of PA.

Authoritarianism and Democracy in Comparative Perspective: The Problem of Regime Classification

In recent writing on comparative politics and regime change, most scholars distinguish broadly between two types of national political regimes: democracy and authoritarianism. Whether a regime is classified as the former or the latter usually depends on how one scores or rates a set of defining elements of a national political regime: for example, competition, participation, and political rights/civil liberties (Mainwaring, 1992: 297–98) or public contestation and participation (Dahl, 1971: 6–9). Rueschemeyer, Stephens, and Stephens give the following definition of democracy: "It entails, first, regular, free and fair elections of representatives with universal and equal suffrage, second, responsibility of the state apparatus to the elected parliament (possibly complemented by direct election of the head of the executive), and third, the freedoms of expression and association as well as the protection of individual rights against arbitrary state action" (1992: 43).[2] Rueschemeyer et al. define an authoritarian regime as one lacking the first two elements (44). Many scholars recognize that regimes are rarely purely democratic or authoritarian, but usually have features of both types. Depending on the combination, scholars have developed additional regime types and subtypes. For example, Rueschemeyer et al. also identify totalitarian regimes, constitutional or liberal oligarchies, and restricted democracies (44).

Some scholars approach regime analysis in quantitative terms. These scholars treat a regime as a continuous variable based on a numerical index combining various indicators or measures that correspond to a regime's defining conceptual characteristics. In this way, a country's political system is ranked somewhere on a scale from no democracy to full democracy or no authoritarianism to full authoritarianism. Democracy and authoritarianism are seen as matters of degree or level rather than type. Both dichotomous and continuous approaches to regime classification have contributed to our understanding of regimes and regime change.

However, scholars using both approaches have tended to misclassify certain pluralist authoritarian regimes as democratic ones. Three examples will illustrate the widespread nature of the problem. In an important recent work, Huntington (1991) argues that there have been three waves of global democratization. The waves represent Huntington's qualitative classification of democratic regimes. Leading the first wave, which lasts from 1828 to 1926, is the United States. According to the author, the United States became democratic in 1828 when more than half of the adult white males voted in the presidential election. Gurr, Jaggers, and Moore (1990) use a quantitative classification scheme to trace the evolution of democracy and autocracy over time in Western Europe, North America, and Latin America. Using 10-point democracy and autocracy scales, the authors only classify two countries as 10 (most democratic) on the democracy scale in both 1878 and 1978. These countries are the United States and Switzerland (86). Finally, Rueschemeyer et al. also traced the development of democracy in Western Europe, North America, and Latin America using a sophisticated comparative historical analysis. They came to similar conclusions. The United States and Switzerland were among the world's earliest democracies. They classify the United States as a restricted democracy because of the oppression of blacks in the American South and argue that the authoritarian South coexisted with the democratic North and West until the South became democratic in the 1960s (1992: 85, 132).

These scholars misclassify the United States, Switzerland, and other countries as early democracies when they would be more accurately classified as authoritarian regimes according to the authors' own general conceptual definitions and criteria. For example, these scholars recognize that they classify regimes as democratic (full or restricted) in which 50 percent or more of the adult population are prevented from participating in politics. How do these authors reconcile this apparent contradiction? They develop operational definitions and indicators of democracy which enable them to include these countries as democracies. Because the gap between the conceptual and operational definitions is obvious, the authors generally defend their typologies/classifications explicitly by invoking three factors: *democratic subtypes, historical context*, and *group exceptionalism*. First, some scholars solve the problem of classification by creating an intermediate subtype of democracy such as restricted democracy, semi-democracy, or exclusionary democracy (Rueschemeyer et al., 1992; Diamond et al., 1990; Remmer, 1985). However, this solution still does not deal adequately with the individuals excluded from participation, competition, and political rights and the resulting contradiction for the concept of democracy. Second, other social scientists argue that we should not use twentieth-century standards to define regimes in the nineteenth century. In this way, they lower the classification criteria for the so-called early democratic regimes or "the first wave" countries in Huntington's terms (1991: 16). Third, some comparativists have advocated ignoring an oppressed group's experience altogether because of its exceptional nature or irrelevance to the country's alleged central democratic institutions. In this way, Rueschemeyer et al. explicitly defend excluding women and gender issues from their analysis of the emergence of democracy in Europe and the Americas (1992: 48, 301). Unfortunately, the use of democratic subtype, historical context, and group exceptionalism to apply different operational definitions of a single concept to different cases creates theoretical confusion and empirical distortion.

Scholars should use consistent operational definitions and indicators of a regime that correspond reasonably to conceptual definitions. This commitment to one standard will better enable us to determine whether a country is democratic and to observe and measure the progress of countries in attaining democracy. The full and free ability of all adults to participate in politics should be the basic minimal criterion of a democracy. Since voting is often seen as the basic act of democratic participation, universal adult suffrage should be a key indicator of a democratic political regime (Pateman, 1994: 331–33; Dahl, 1991: 6, 72–74).[3] Anything less than full inclusion compromises the meaning of democracy and preempts a series of questions about possible steps toward democratization.

This perspective would affirm that regime classification is always a question of type and a question of degree. Therefore, the fact that a country has more democratic features than all other countries should not be the only basis for its classification as a democratic regime. That classification should be based primarily on how the country's salient political features (i.e., defining regime elements) correspond to an explicit definition of democracy. Consider a hypothetical example. If 20 percent of country A's adults can vote and 10 percent of country B's adults have the franchise, then country A is (at least on the voting indicator) clearly more democratic than country B. However, country A is not a democracy because 80 percent of the people cannot vote. For the purposes of this essay, the conceptual definition of democracy given by Rueschemeyer et al. is adequate, but their operational definition, which includes 60 percent adult male suffrage, is not (1992: 303). In a democracy, all adults have the right under law to organize politically, elect representatives to run the government, and enjoy basic civil liberties and political rights. These liberties and rights include the right to vote, to speak freely, and to participate in politics without government harassment. These indicators are consistent with the general definitions in the literature.[4]

According to the above formulation, many countries normally classified as democracies should be reclassified as pluralist authoritarian regimes. The most dramatic example is the United States. In the United States, the vast majority of the people did not participate in the process establishing the country's political regime (Collier, 1990: 20, 26; Williamson, 1960; Dye and Zeigler, 1990: 22–50). Leading scholars of American and comparative politics have persisted in misidentifying the United States as an early democratic country (Lipset, 1981; Wood, 1991). As a result, the regime change literature has not fully compared the United States to other countries in which the real struggles of women and other excluded groups to gain the right to vote and exercise full political rights often lasted many decades and even centuries. Why have comparativists not recognized the early United States as a pluralist authoritarian country? As has been noted earlier, the invocation of democratic subtypes, historical context, and group exceptionalism has enabled scholars to classify the United States and several European countries as the world's first democracies. However, as a consequence in many instances, these writers have refused to take women and people of color seriously as human beings relevant to the system of governance. The nonparticipation of these groups in establishing the fundamental political rules of the game has long been a nonissue for political scientists. Pluralist authoritarianism will help us bring these excluded groups back into comparative regime analysis.

Pluralist Authoritarianism

Juan J. Linz defines authoritarian regimes as "political systems with limited, not responsible, political pluralism, without elaborate and guiding ideology, but with distinctive mentalities, without extensive nor intensive political mobilization, except at some points in their development, and in which a leader or occasionally a small group exercises power within formally ill-defined limits but actually quite predictable ones" (Linz, 1975: 264). More specifically, authoritarianism refers to a political regime in which the government restricts the people's ability to organize politically, denies free and fair elections, and violates basic civil liberties and human rights.[5] Extreme types of authoritarianism are totalitarian regimes in which masses of people are oppressed and even murdered for political and nonpolitical reasons. A classic case is Nazi Germany where six million Jews and millions of other human beings were killed. PA regimes are on the other end of the authoritarianism spectrum. Although PA goes counter to most writing in the field, PA does not stretch the concept of authoritarianism beyond recognition. In fact, many scholars have stretched the concept of democracy to include regimes in which more than 50 percent of the adult population cannot vote and even racial slavery is practiced.[6]

Pluralist authoritarianism (PA) attempts to address the problem of regime misclassification by providing a distinct category for national political regimes with both authoritarian and democratic elements. Pluralist authoritarian regimes deny part of the adult population the ability to participate and compete freely in formal institutional politics. Moreover, these nonparticipants often suffer formal and informal discrimination, violations of basic civil liberties, and human rights abuses. At the same time, PA regimes have limited participation, competition, and political rights/civil liberties. Operationally, these regimes are pluralist because they have at least two relevant political parties, formal suffrage granted to a portion of the population, and regular competitive elections for selecting government leaders.

The concept of pluralist authoritarianism highlights white supremacy and male supremacy as regime features that have been ignored or minimized.[7] The United States, Switzerland, and South Africa at various points in their histories serve as case studies of PA based on white supremacy and male supremacy. The United States and Switzerland are generally considered among the first modern political democracies. In fact, these countries are examples of late pluralist authoritarian regimes. They are similar in many respects to South Africa, a more widely recognized former authoritarian regime. These three countries share a political history of excluding important segments of their populations based on sex and race. In many instances, these exclusionary factors have led to most adults being unable to participate in founding the political regime, voting in key elections, and influencing relevant public policy.

While some PA regimes have been misclassified as democracies, others have been identified as authoritarian regimes. For example, Linz defines racial and ethnic democracies as "regimes in which the political process among those belonging to a racially defined group, particularly a minority of the population, satisfies our definition of democracy but permanently excludes another racial group (or groups), legally or by de facto coercive means. That exclusion does not allow us to fit such regimes into our definition of democracy" (1975: 321). Linz goes on to cite the Republic of South Africa as an example of this type of authoritarianism. Other authors have used the term *herrenvolk democracy* to describe this type of regime (Winant, 1994: xi, 5–6). However, for unknown reasons, Linz does not include other countries with similar exclusionary policies such as voting restrictions and widespread civil rights violations in his otherwise thorough analysis of nondemocratic regimes (1975: 264–65). The United States, Switzerland, South Africa, and other countries have been PA regimes for extended periods of their histories.

Some scholars of authoritarianism have allowed the presence of limited political participation and electoral competition to obscure their vision of the people excluded from PA systems. In this way, political scientists in particular have avoided the intellectual responsibility to account for these people. As a result, people marginalized within and excluded from participating in actually existing pluralist authoritarian regimes have also been excluded from scholarly analyses of these political systems. Feminist scholars have highlighted this problem around the world and especially in Latin America by comparing how authoritarian governments caused opponents and innocents in the 1960s and 1970s to disappear and how traditional social scientists caused women to disappear from any significant roles in history and politics (Miller, 1991; Carroll and Zerilli, 1993). The PA concept will enable us to help discover and recover important political actors.

PA assumes a "contamination" perspective on authoritarianism. Basically, a small or limited amount of authoritarianism can and usually does "infect" an entire political regime. For example, in the United States even after white women achieved the right to vote and participate in politics, the authoritarian structures and policies visited upon approximately 10 percent of the population contaminated the entire political system through the direct and indirect linkages between the oppressed African-American minority and the national polity via elections for federal representatives, senators, and the president. These elected officials had influence not only in the national legislative and executive arenas but obviously in the administrative and judicial arenas as well. Again, influence in these areas directly affected the disenfranchised African-American population and the formally enfranchised nonblack population (Key, 1949).

Obviously, "democracy" also contaminates, but in a different way. Opportunities for one group to participate in politics tend to lead to demands from other groups. However, complete and objective analysis should be the basis for classifying regimes, not exclusive focus on relatively privileged population groups. Thus, until all adults have equal political opportunities, rights, and protections, the political system is not democratic. In partial agreement with this view, Dahl preferred the more neutral term, polyarchy, rather than democracy to describe "relatively (but incompletely) democratized regimes" (1971: 8). While a sincere attempt to advance the comparative regime change debate, Dahl's use of polyarchy suffers from similar problems of regime misclassification (1971; 1989).

White Supremacy and Male Supremacy as Pluralist Authoritarianism

Following Fredrickson's definition, "white supremacy refers to the attitudes, ideologies, and policies associated with the rise of blatant forms of white or European dominance over 'nonwhite' populations. In other words, it involves making invidious distinctions of a socially crucial kind that are based primarily, if not exclusively, on physical characteristics and ancestry" (1981: xi). Similarly, male supremacy refers to the attitudes, ideologies, and policies associated with blatant forms of male dominance over female populations. It should be clear that white supremacy is a specific form of racial and ethnic supremacy. Theoretically, black, brown, and other racial/ethnic supremacies are possible.

White supremacy and male supremacy are central features of authoritarianism to the extent that they deny people the ability to participate in politics on free and equal terms. The historical record of the spread of capitalism, colonialism, and imperialism (intertwined with racism and sexism) in the eighteenth, nineteenth, and twentieth centuries confirms the broad scope of the problem (Rodney, 1974; Conniff and Davis, 1994; Millet, 1970). Historically, in country after country women generally received the franchise after men. Daley and Nolan emphasize the following point: "Nowhere did women's suffrage precede male suffrage" (1994: 9). Moreover, women were prevented from running for and serving in public office until after men gained this right. Women have also been denied the other basic rights and privileges of citizenship that their male peers have enjoyed. Legal systems dominated by men have considered women incapable of handling their personal, financial, and legal affairs. Women have traditionally suffered from various forms of active male discrimination and violence. Rape, domestic violence, sexual harassment, and financial dependence were all aspects of historical and international female subordination. In sum, women have been and in some countries, continue to be, specific victims of authoritarianism (French, 1992; Jonasdottir, 1994).

Most writers on comparative regime change have not acknowledged male supremacy as a form of authoritarianism. For example, in his discussion of the growth of democracy, Robert Dahl refers to "male polyarchies" without probing the fundamental contradiction regarding the exclusion of a large group of people, such as women, from the benefits of polyarchy. In this manner, Dahl's "male polyarchies" correspond analytically to the other democratic regime subtypes mentioned earlier such as restricted democracies, semi-democracies, and exclusionary democracies. Again, these subtypes are essentially mixed regimes with some authoritarian, pluralist, and competitive features. However, Dahl should be commended for pointing out that women only gained the right to vote internationally in the twentieth century (1989, 235). Consequently, before this century, nearly all political regimes were at best pluralist authoritarian regimes. If women could not vote and run for office, they could not participate and compete for formal political power. Conceptually and empirically, this state of affairs would be an example of pluralist authoritarianism even if all men enjoyed perfect political freedom and equality.

With the rise of European expansion and colonialism after the fifteenth century, white supremacy has been almost as widespread internationally as male supremacy. The results have been similar. Before and into the twentieth century, people of color have been systematically denied the basic civil liberties, political rights, and human rights that many whites have received.

For example, when most countries in the Americas gained their national independence in the early nineteenth century, the enslavement of Africans was widespread (Davis, 1975; Klein, 1986). Slavery, including racial slavery, is by definition an authoritarian system and, according to this article's framework, incompatible with democracy.[8]

After racial slavery was abolished, new forms of white racism usually emerged to perpetuate the subordination of black people in the Americas. In the United States, this oppression and authoritarianism took the form of the legal apparatus of racial segregation and institutionalized racial inequality (Woodward, 1974; Marable, 1991; Smith, 1995). In Latin America, blacks were subordinated by racist policies often without the explicit legal codification of white supremacy. European immigration was one way for white elites in Brazil and other countries to lighten their national populations and deny blacks jobs and opportunities for economic advancement (Skidmore, 1974; Rout, 1976; Minority Rights Group, 1995).

A Comparative Analysis of Pluralist Authoritarian Regimes: United States, Switzerland, and South Africa

In this section, the concept of pluralist authoritarianism is applied to three key cases: the United States, Switzerland, and South Africa. These cases were selected to illustrate empirically the usefulness of the concept, but also to demonstrate the integrity of the concept across time. Through a comparison of these cases, the applicability of PA (especially in its white supremacy and male supremacy forms) will hopefully convince scholars that the alleged first modern democracies, the United States and Switzerland, are analytically equivalent in many respects to one of the world's most notorious former pluralist authoritarian regimes, South Africa.

This section classifies these three national political regimes as PA regimes based on a general overview of competition, participation, and political rights/civil liberties in these countries. Since a comprehensive analysis of the political histories of these countries is beyond this essay's scope, the focus will be on the basic right to vote in fair elections at the national level. The assumption will be that if a population group cannot vote in elections, that group is being denied the ability to participate and compete in the political process as well as suffering violations of its basic political rights/civil liberties.

The United States is often referred to as the first modern democracy. The application of PA to American political history demonstrates that the United States was a latecomer to democracy. Switzerland is a country that comparativists usually identify as democratic despite the lateness with which women received the vote. Again, this case highlights that women were formally excluded from national politics until the 1970s. Finally, South Africa is a country that is generally acknowledged as being authoritarian until 1994 whether referred to as a racial "democracy" or oligarchy. The formal, legal, and racist exclusion of the black majority of the national population from South African politics while giving a small white group a range of citizenship rights and privileges parallels and clarifies the less formal, legal, and racist exclusion of people by other PA regimes. In sum, these cases illustrate the applicability of PA.

United States

The fundamental and incontrovertible point is that the vast majority of the American people were excluded from the early political process. From 1790 until 1965, the United States had a pluralist authoritarian regime that became increasingly less authoritarian. The United States did not have a personal dictatorship, a military authoritarian regime, or a totalitarian regime. Rather, the United States developed a pluralist authoritarian regime with elitist, white supremacist, and male-dominant features. As has been well documented, only propertied, white Christian adult males enjoyed the full rights of participation in the pre-Civil War period. Even if the U.S. regime had the broadest worldwide franchise of the early 1800s, that fact does not a democratic regime make. The international political context of slavery, colonialism, and imperialism meant that most of the world's population lived under brutal authoritarian conditions. Over time, these excluded groups were eventually incorporated into the American political system in different ways (Rogers, 1990). Native Americans forged legal agreements with the government that gave them a semi-autonomous status as "nations" on separate lands or reservations. White women were incorporated politically through the Nineteenth Amendment to the U.S. Constitution. This gave them the national right to vote in 1920. Most African Americans, on the other hand, only gained the right to vote in the mid-1960s with the passage of the Civil Rights Act of 1964 and the Voting Rights Act of 1965.

The following sections examine the evolving American pluralist authoritarian regime in three periods, 1790–1865, 1865–1920, and 1920–1965. The first period in American history is the most controversial and misunderstood. The United States was born in revolution against British colonialism. While the revolutionary war engulfed much of the new nation, the creation of the American republic and the first elections were the preserve of privileged white men. Women, as was the custom internationally, could neither vote nor run for office. They were not considered equal to men and did not enjoy the rights and liberties of founding fathers such as George Washington, John Adams, and Thomas Jefferson. African Americans were seen by many whites as less than fully human, somewhere on the evolutionary ladder between wild animals and humans (Jordan, 1968). In fact, in recognition of this slave status, they were defined by the constitution as three-fifths of normal white men for purposes of their slave masters' taxation and representation. Even poor white men, during this period between the founding and the Civil War, were initially restricted in their ability to vote and participate in politics. Finally, Native Americans, who had already suffered what some scholars describe as a "holocaust" between 1500 and 1800, continued to endure diseases, wars, removals, and general oppression by white settlers and the white national government (Thornton, 1987: 91–133). Despite the general oppression of the period, the latter half of the period had some pluralist and democratic features because the franchise was extended to a numerical minority of the population, most white men. These men did have a choice between political parties and enjoyed basic civil liberties and political rights.

In reflecting upon this first period of American political history, we must avoid the mistake that Alexis de Tocqueville (1945) made in *Democracy in*

America of analyzing a political system based largely on the behavior of people who enjoyed basic rights and privileges while minimizing the political situation of the vast majority of the excluded people. In this way, de Tocqueville's lucid analysis of blacks and Indians is not fully integrated into his description of the general political system. Another example of this type of analysis is Roche's characterization of the constitutional convention as a democratic reform caucus (1961). It can only be considered as such if no attention is given to the excluded majority who were to be governed and administered by decisions reached in the convention.

The second period (1865–1920) of American political history was also a period of pluralist authoritarianism. The period experienced expansion, contraction, and re-expansion of the franchise. The Civil War from 1861 to 1865 was the greatest and most violent domestic conflict in American history. In the end, the North defeated the South and promptly occupied the defeated region with federal troops. The war signaled the formal defeat of slavery and resulted in the Thirteenth, Fourteenth, and Fifteenth Amendments, which outlawed slavery and gave black men formal citizenship rights, including the right to vote. As a result, the 1870s and 1880s witnessed the election of black men to numerous local, state, and national offices in the South. This was the period of Republican Reconstruction (DuBois, 1992; Foner, 1990). Even in the 1880s, Frederick Douglass protested the emergence of post-slavery authoritarian practices against the black population:

> Flagrant as have been the outrages committed upon colored citizens in respect to their civil rights, more flagrant, shocking, and scandalous still have been the outrages committed upon our political rights by means of bull-dozing and Kukluxing, Mississippi plans, fraudulent counts, tissue ballots, and the like devices. Three States in which the colored people outnumber the white population are without colored representation and their political voice suppressed. The colored citizens in those States are virtually disfranchised, the Constitution held in utter contempt and its provisions nullified. (Fishel, Jr., and Quarles, 1967: 304–305)

By the 1890s, white elites had regained control of state power and disenfranchised black men. Federal troops no longer occupied the South and the Republicans agreed to the reimposition of white authoritarian rule that would endure until the 1960s.

Following the Civil War, white women continued to be denied the basic right to participate and compete in elections. They organized locally, regionally, and nationally for the right to vote. However, in a classic example of how elites can divide the oppressed, some male and female abolitionists (and supporters of women suffrage) decided to support the immediate right to vote for black men while advocating a delay for the enfranchisement of women as the only feasible political option. In response, some white women suffrage leaders protested in racist language the enfranchisement of black men. These leaders were outraged that "inferior" blacks would gain the right to vote before white women (Banaszak, 1996; Kerr, 1995; Terborg-Penn, 1995). Nonetheless, women persevered in the struggle for female suffrage and made limited progress in the West and North at the state level. Following World War I, women intensified the struggle. In August 1920, their pressure culminated in the passage of the Nineteenth Amendment to the Constitution. White women had finally gained the right to vote (Wheeler, 1995).

From 1920 to 1965, the third phase of American pluralist authoritarianism centered on the disenfranchisement and general oppression of African Americans. Most blacks still lived in the South under what one scholar has described as a "tripartite system of domination." According to Morris, "In the cities and rural areas of the South, blacks were controlled economically, politically, and personally" (1984: 1). White Southern elites had constructed a formal and informal system of white supremacy that perpetuated their power even in local districts in which blacks were the numerical majority. In addition to traditional authoritarian methods of physical violence and terror, whites developed new legal means of excluding blacks from the political process. These included literacy tests, poll taxes, and white primary elections (Key, 1949).

Beginning formally in the 1950s, African Americans initiated a new civil rights movement against the authoritarian structures pervasive in the South. This movement, led by African Americans and their organizations, was dedicated to among other things the right to vote in free and fair elections. The Rev. Dr. Martin Luther King, Jr., became the movement's greatest leader and spokesman (Garrow, 1986). Black political, religious, and student organizations worked in a nonviolent manner to persuade whites to support their rights as articulated in the U.S. Constitution and Declaration of Independence. Some whites and people of color joined in this struggle for freedom. At the same time, many white Southern leaders resisted the protesters' call for democratization. This refusal led to numerous violent clashes, beatings, jailings, and murders by conservative whites. Eventually, President Lyndon B. Johnson, a southerner from Texas, decided to put the weight of the federal government behind the efforts at progressive change. This culminated in the Civil Rights Act of 1964 and the Voting Rights Act of 1965, which gave the national government additional authority to protect blacks from the tyranny of the white southern majority. It is only with this protection that we can classify the United States as a democracy in a minimalist procedural sense.

Switzerland

Like the United States, Switzerland is often identified as an early democratic regime (Vanhanen, 1984; Huntington, 1991). More accurately, from 1848 until 1971, Switzerland had a pluralist authoritarian regime. Although the historical origins of the Swiss confederation can be traced to 1291 when three forest cantons pledged themselves to mutual support and defense, the modern Swiss nation can be considered to begin with the Constitution of 1848 (Rueschemeyer et al., 1992: 85–86). From the approval of this constitution until 1971, Swiss women were denied suffrage. Swiss women only gained the right to vote in national elections in 1971. In a few cantons, Swiss women were denied suffrage until the late 1980s and early 1990s (Banaszak, 1996; Bendix, 1992). Therefore, the myth of early Swiss democracy should be discarded and the reality of Swiss pluralist authoritarianism explored.

Historically, the Swiss pluralist authoritarian regime's defining feature was male supremacy. Because Swiss women could not vote, they could not run for office. Since they could not run for office, they clearly could not occupy any elective public office. Consequently, the Swiss case illustrates how male domination denied women the right to participate in and compete for formal political power. Opportunities for political involvement were denied to women at all levels: communal, cantonal, and federal. As a result, all the important institutions and organizations of Swiss politics were practically forbidden to women. In parallel fashion, until 1971 all major political decisions and policies were made essentially without the participation of women. Women were not considered Swiss citizens with equal rights, privileges, and responsibilities (Inglehart, 1983).

Switzerland should be identified as pluralist because men, in contrast to women, enjoyed an early suffrage, competitive party politics, and broad civil liberties. Swiss men created a political system that served them well over the years. This regime has been characterized as consocional (Lijphart, 1977; Steiner and Dorff, 1980). In this type of system, deep ethnic, linguistic, and/or religious group differences are recognized and respected by the major political leaders. Power is shared institutionally by elites representative of these groups. Moreover, regional and cultural autonomy is generally granted to ensure political stability. For example, in Switzerland, cantons are sovereign and exercise rights in all areas not delegated by the federal constitution to the federal government. However, in a way similar to the United States, Swiss women played no role in writing the Swiss constitution that gave institutional form to the polity. Nor did Swiss women participate in any of the leadership positions of the consociational regime because they were barred from politics.

Some male Swiss elites have defended the exclusion of women from national politics. One writer presented the following argument:

> The foreign readers of this pamphlet will no doubt wonder why the women's vote has not been introduced into Switzerland. Many parts of our country still hold to the view, probably based on old Germanic custom, that women's true place is the home and not public life. The women's part is to carry out her duties as a wife and mother in exemplary fashion. She has, it is argued, ways and means enough of influencing men indirectly for good in the fulfillment of their civic duties. As has already been pointed out, the suffrage went hand in hand with the bearing of arms. It is the militiaman who has to decide upon the welfare of the country. Finally, the majority of Swiss women have themselves felt no great desire for the suffrage. (Huber, 1946: 21)

Contrary to Huber's view, Swiss women wanted to participate in politics and campaigned many years for suffrage. In 1868, Swiss feminist Marie Goegg founded the Association Internationale des Femmes and later other organizations to fight for women's rights. Banaszak (1996) has identified several factors (strategies and tactics, political opportunities, and values and beliefs held by women suffrage activists) for why the American movement for women's suffrage was successful much earlier than the Swiss movement. She noted that, "It was only in the late 1910s that voting rights for women reached the public agenda and the fledgling woman suffrage movement took root in Switzerland" (14). Before and after World War II, Swiss women attempted to gain civil rights and suffrage. On many occasions, the proposals to enfranchise women were defeated by all male political bodies (Inglehart, 1983: 138–41).

Given their prominent position in the Swiss institutional structure, the cantons were the arenas in which many women suffrage activists struggled for the right to vote. "In 1959, Vaud and Neuchatel became the first two cantons to adopt full woman suffrage. In 1960, the canton of Geneve followed suit, and in 1966 voters in Basel-stadt enfranchised women in all elections" (Banaszak, 1996: 17). However, at the national level, women still had not gained enfranchisement. The new women's liberation movement of the late 1960s increased the protests, demands, and sense of urgency of female activists. Swiss male elites also received pressure from external sources. The Swiss government wanted to sign the European Human Rights Convention, but it contained sections granting political rights to women. In response, the government sponsored a referendum on woman suffrage which was approved on February 7, 1971, by 66 percent of the male electorate (18–19).

As might be expected, when women were denied the right to vote, they were also subordinated in other areas of politics and society.[9] Women could not run for office, earn equal wages for equal work, or have equal legal standing with men (Inglehart, 1983). If women were included in regime classification, Switzerland would shift from being an early democracy to a late pluralist authoritarian regime.

South Africa

From 1910 until the early 1990s, the country of South Africa had a pluralist authoritarian regime. The vast majority of the population was denied the right to participate in politics and had its civil liberties and human rights consistently violated. At the same time, a racial minority of the population was able to vote in relatively competitive elections and enjoyed some basic civil and political rights. Like Switzerland, South Africa for most of this century had a pluralist authoritarian regime.

Whites from the Netherlands and Great Britain entered the southern Africa region from 1600 to 1900 during which time they fought against each other, colonized the area, and enslaved the indigenous African population. In a defining historical moment, the British won the Boer War (1899–1902), but reached an understanding with the defeated Afrikaners (Dutch descendants) on a form of semi-sovereign rule within the framework of the British commonwealth. As a result, the four provinces (former colonies) of Transvaal, the Cape, Natal, and the Orange Free State formed the Union of South Africa in 1910 (Thompson, 1990).

From 1910 to 1994, the central feature of South African pluralist authoritarianism was white supremacy. During this period, blacks who represented over 67 percent of the population were not allowed to vote or run for office.[10] Asians and coloreds who represented together less than 13 percent of the population had their already limited voting rights abolished or reduced to irrelevance. White women gained the right to vote in 1930. Despite the political participation of white women, white men generally occupied the official positions of political and economic power. Throughout this century, the white community has been divided between Afrikaners and English speakers.

Blacks struggled for democracy throughout the period. In response, white elites developed various formal and informal mechanisms to maintain their power (Price and Rosberg, 1980). This process intensified in the post-World War II period. The National party, representing the Afrikaner hard-line position against racial equality, gained political power in 1948. From the 1950s through the 1980s, the National Party implemented its policy of "apartheid." This policy required strict racial separation and black subordination. Therefore, a huge legal apparatus, surpassing the racist laws of the United States, was created to consolidate and perpetuate white supremacy. These laws included the Population Registration Act, the Prohibition of Mixed Marriages Act, the Immorality Act, the Bantu Authorities Act, the Group Areas Act, the Internal Security Act, and the Terrorism Act (Fredrickson, 1981: 239–85; Adam and Giliomee, 1979).

These various acts oppressed blacks, but did not end their efforts to create a democratic regime. On many occasions, the South African police and authorities turned to terror to intimidate blacks, which lead to numerous violent conflicts, such as the Sharpeville massacre of 1960 and the Soweto uprising of 1976. The South African government also implemented various reforms to avoid democratization. In 1983, the government proposed a new tricameral national legislature to represent not only whites but also Indians and coloreds. Both moderate and radical black leaders condemned this initiative. The government's attempt to isolate the black community motivated the recently formed United Democratic Front to intensify its opposition to the regime's white supremacy. The struggle for democracy was rebuffed until the early 1990s when Prime Minister F. W. de Klerk concluded that maintaining the pluralist authoritarian apartheid regime was untenable. He released leading political prisoners, including African National Congress leader Nelson Mandela, from jail and began negotiating a political transition to democracy (Price, 1991). So far, the transition has been successful. In 1994, inclusive national elections were held; a new parliament was formed, Nelson Mandela was elected president, and a new constitution was approved.

Rethinking Regime Classification and Theories of Comparative Regime Change

The preceding comparative analysis of regime evolution in the United States, Switzerland, and South Africa attempted to make several fundamental points. First, each country denied at least half of its adult population the ability to participate and compete in national politics for decades. Second, when a portion of the national population cannot vote because of white supremacy or male supremacy, the regime should not be considered democratic. Third, pluralist authoritarianism more accurately describes regimes with mixed authoritarian and democratic features because it considers the entire relevant population, not only individuals and groups who enjoy democratic rights. Finally, PA forces us to reconsider existing regime classifications and theories.

The implications of the earlier conceptual and empirical analysis go beyond the three cases. There is a general need for regime reclassification. The United States and Switzerland are not the only cases in which important segments of the adult populations have been ignored while scholars have classified regimes as democratic or authoritarian or identified their levels of democracy or authoritarianism. Women, in particular, have been regularly ignored in regime typologies and analyses. As a result, the most prominent theories of comparative regime change have been based on regime misclassification.

Most comparative research on regime change is still guided by Lipset's classic formulation: "Perhaps the most common generalization linking political systems to other aspects of society has been that democracy is related to the state of economic development. The more well-to-do a nation, the greater the chances that it will sustain democracy" (1981: 31). Lipset argued that economic development creates the modern and moderate values, attitudes, behavior patterns, and organizations that are supportive of democracy. These organizations include political parties, labor unions, and schools. However, if one accepts the argument that many pluralist authoritarian regimes have been misclassified as democracies, then we must rethink Lipset's hypothesis and related theories in the field. Two of Lipset's stable democracies are the United States and Switzerland. Using the concept of PA to reclassify these and other wealthy countries would at the least delay by years the transition of some wealthy countries to democracy.[11] As a result, India, a poor third world country, achieved independence and democratic status in the immediate post-World War II period and before the United States and Switzerland.

Although there have been many quantitative studies on the relationship between economic development and regime type, these studies have perpetuated the error of identifying certain pluralist authoritarian regimes as democracies. This pattern has led to major contradictions in important qualitative and quantitative studies. Two recent and influential works by Rueschemeyer et al. and Huntington have this problem. Rueschemeyer et al. (1992) agree with Lipset's hypothesis of a relationship between economic development and democracy, but not his explanation of the correlation. They posit instead that democracy emerges specifically when economic development weakens or eliminates the most anti-democratic class, large rural landowners, while empowering the most democratic class, the urban working class. They revise Barrington Moore's "No bourgeois, no democracy" view of regime change to emphasize labor's central role in the democratization process (1966: 418). However, their argument is based on the alleged correlation between economic development and democracy. In this way, they can state that, "We are convinced that the main finding of the cross-national statistical work—a positive, though not perfect, correlation between capitalist development and democracy—must stand as an accepted result. There is no way of explaining this robust finding, replicated in many studies of different design, as the spurious effect of flawed methods. Any theory of democracy must come to terms with it" (1992: 4). This finding is the result of an inconsistency between conceptualization and operationalization. For example, Rueschemeyer et al. base their qualification of American democracy on the oppression of black men. If they had included women, the qualification would have become a reclassification of the United States as a pluralist authoritarian regime. Furthermore, if the authors had identified the exclusion of women as an authoritarian feature, they would have had to reclassify Switzerland and other European countries as pluralist authoritarian regimes. It would have forced the authors to review the general statistical correlation between economic development and democracy.

In another recent major study, Huntington (1991) also confirms Lipset's initial correlation. He argues that there have been three waves of democratization since the 1800s and that economic development has consistently been the most important structural factor promoting democracy. At the same time, Huntington argues that political leadership often determines whether the general conditions for democracy will be realized. Thus, economic development is a necessary but not sufficient condition for the emergence of democracy. The major flaw in his theoretical framework is again the misclassification of regimes. Huntington identifies the United States as the world's first modern democracy in 1828 without realizing that as a result he is guided away from analyzing the struggles of American women and blacks for democracy.

As a result of his misidentification of the early American political system and general misclassification of PA regimes, Huntington draws incorrect and partial lessons from each wave. First of all, the confirmation of the Lipset hypothesis is premature. If the United States, Switzerland, and other "first wave" countries were really pluralist authoritarian regimes and other poor countries became democracies before or closer in time to many wealthy ones, then these developments represent a clear challenge to theories that posit a link between economic development and democratization. The United States should be classified with other pluralist authoritarian regimes like the apartheid regime of South Africa. This reformulation would call attention to the treatment received by democratic opponents of PA regimes.

Conclusion

Scholars should review and reformulate current theories of regime change because the comparative regime change literature has systematically misclassified some pluralist authoritarian regimes as democratic regimes. If white supremacy and male supremacy are taken seriously, many of the "first wave" countries can correctly be seen as pluralist authoritarian regimes. Can a regime that legalizes slavery be a democracy? Can a regime that denies women the right to vote be a democracy? This article has argued that these types of regimes are not democratic. Some countries in Huntington's "second and third waves" would also have to be reclassified.

The concept of pluralist authoritarianism should help in creating new regime typologies and developing new hypotheses and explanations. The three case studies of the United States, Switzerland, and South Africa demonstrated that PA captures the complexity of certain political regimes in a way that accounts for all adults. Nonetheless, more research is needed to understand the political situation of excluded and oppressed populations, especially women and people of color. If we continue to ignore and minimize groups based on gender and race, we will perpetuate an incomplete and distorted picture of political change. The struggles of these excluded groups for democracy are central to the traditions of revolutionary and reformist regime change. In comparative regime studies, scholars should investigate the relationship between these groups and their national political systems.

This essay's main purpose has been to reopen debate on one of the oldest and most important topics in social science. Too many scholars have been inaccurate and inconsistent in the basic functions of describing, explaining, and predicting national political regimes and regime change. Logically, many conclusions of the comparative regime change literature must be considered unreliable. If pluralist authoritarianism does accurately describe a specific type of regime, new questions must be asked. What are the causes of PA? What are the consequences of PA? How are PA regimes related to authoritarian regimes? How are PA regimes related to democratic regimes? We do not have full answers to these questions, but they are worth pursuing.

Notes

1. I treat political regimes and political systems as similar in this analysis. Collier and Collier define a regime as,

   The formal and informal structure of state and governmental roles and processes. The regime includes the method of selection of the government and of representative assemblies (election, coup, decision within the military, etc.), formal and informal mechanisms of representation, and patterns of repression. The regime is typically distinguished from the particular incumbents who occupy state and governmental roles, the political coalition that supports these incumbents, and the public policies they adopt (except of course policies that define or transform the regime itself). (1991: 789)

2. This definition refers to what the comparative politics literature calls liberal, representative, or political democracy. Some scholars criticize these regimes as bourgeois or pseudo-democracy because of their emphasis on political procedures rather than the social and economic dimensions of politics. For informed discussion of these issues, see Green (1985), Held (1987;1995), and Robinson (1995).
3. Dahl (1991) gives seven characteristics of polyarchies, his preferred term for actually existing democratic regimes, including as number three: "Virtually all adults have the right to vote" (73). There will always be debate over the most appropriate definition and indicators of democracy. Future scholars should welcome this argument and attempt to build upon earlier efforts. For example, social scientists will likely integrate children into their future discussions of democracy and comparative regime change.
4. For other definitions, see Huntington (1991: 7) and Lipset (1981: 28). In his important work on citizenship, Marshall highlighted how civil, political, and social rights were only gained gradually over more than two centuries of political struggle and conflict in England (1964). Scholars should not equate the initial extension of civil and political rights to a numerical minority and the establishment of democracy.
5. See Linz (1964, 1975) and Collier (1979) for definitions and extensive discussions of authoritarianism. In a perceptive essay, Linz noted that authoritarian rule, in contrast to democratic and totalitarian rule, presented specific kinds of legitimacy and mobilization problems. For this reason, Linz described military rule in Brazil in the late 1960s and early 1970s as an authoritarian situation rather than an institutionalized authoritarian regime (Linz, 1973).
6. See Sartori (1970) and Collier and Mahon (1993) for good analyses of conceptual stretching and related methodological issues.
7. This article focuses on race and sex as key characteristics used to prevent some human beings from participating fully in politics. For a comprehensive analy-

sis, other characteristics such as class, age, religion, ethnicity, and so forth would have to be considered. According to PA, there are no analytical differences among characteristics that have been used historically and more recently to disenfranchise certain population groups. We focus on race and sex as two of the most important and neglected of these variables.
8. As Patterson notes, "slavery is the permanent, violent domination of natally alienated and generally dishonored persons" (1982: 13).
9. Thompson notes that,

> Because 60% of all voters in a 1981 referendum agreed to amend the constitution in order to give women and men equal rights, it was inevitable that women would ultimately get to vote at every level. In 1990 the Federal Tribunal ruled that Article 4 granting equal rights overrides Article 74 giving cantons the power to decide their own voting rules. Thus, in 1991 the last hold-out, Appenzell-Inner Rhodes, counted women's votes in its open-air assembly. The trend toward full equality for women was continued in a 1985 referendum which granted them equal marriage rights. The husband will no longer be the legal head of the household who could decide where to live, to what schools the children should go or whether the wife could open a bank account or take a job. (1995: 127)

10. There were minor exceptions. In the Cape, for example, black men had a restricted franchise which was revoked in 1936.
11. Diamond (1992) provides an excellent review and defense of the Lipset hypothesis. I disagree with Diamond's analysis, however, because it accepts the general misclassification of regimes that is widespread in the quantitative and qualitative literature.

References

Adam, Heribert, and Hermann Giliomee. 1979. *Ethnic Power Mobilized: Can South Africa Change?* New Haven: Yale University Press.

Banaszak, Lee Ann. 1996. *Why Movements Succeed or Fail: Opportunities, Culture, and the Struggle for Woman Suffrage.* Princeton, NJ: Princeton University Press.

Bendix, John. 1992. "Women's Suffrage and Political Culture: A Modern Swiss Case." *Women & Politics*, 12, 3: 27–56.

Carroll, Susan J., and Linda M. G. Zerilli. 1993. "Feminist Challenges to Political Science." In *Political Science: The State of the Discipline II*, ed. Ada W. Finifter. Washington, DC: The American Political Science Association.

Chehabi, H. E., and Alfred Stepan, eds. 1995. *Politics, Society, and Democracy: Comparative Studies (Essays in Honor of Juan J. Linz).* Boulder: Westview Press.

Collier, Christopher. 1990. "The American People as Christian White Men of Property: Suffrage and Elections in Colonial and Early National America." In *Voting and the Spirit of American Democracy: Essays on the History of Voting and Voting Rights in America*, ed. Donald W. Rogers. Urbana: University of Illinois Press.

Collier, David, ed. 1979. *The New Authoritarianism in Latin America.* Princeton, NJ: Princeton University Press.

Collier, David, and James E. Mahon. 1993. "Conceptual 'Stretching' Revisited: Adapting Categories in Comparative Analysis." *American Political Science Review*, 87 (December): 845–55.

Collier, Ruth, and David Collier. 1991. *Shaping the Political Arena: Critical Junctures, the Labor Movement, and Regime Dynamics in Latin America.* Princeton, NJ: Princeton University Press.

Conniff, Michael, and Thomas Davis. 1994. *Africans in the Americas: A History of the Black Diaspora.* New York: St. Martin's Press.

Dahl, Robert A. 1971. *Polyarchy: Participation and Opposition*. New Haven: Yale University Press.
———. 1989. *Democracy and Its Critics*. New Haven: Yale University Press.
———. 1991. *Modern Political Analysis*. Englewood Cliffs, NJ: Prentice-Hall.
Daley, Caroline, and Melanie Nolan, eds. 1994. *Suffrage and Beyond: International Feminist Perspectives*. New York: New York University Press.
Davis, David Brion. 1975. *The Problem of Slavery in the Age of Revolution, 1770–1823*. Ithaca and London: Cornell University Press.
Diamond, Larry. 1992. "Economic Development and Democracy Reconsidered." In *Reexamining Democracy: Essays in Honor of Seymour Martin Lipset*, ed. Gary Marks and Larry Diamond. Newbury Park: Sage Publications.
Diamond, Larry, Juan J. Linz, and Seymour Martin Lipset. 1990. "Introduction: Comparing Experiences with Democracy." In *Politics in Developing Countries: Comparing Experiences with Democracy*, ed. Larry Diamond, Juan J. Linz, and Seymour Martin Lipset. Boulder, CO: Lynne Rienner Publishers.
DuBois, W. E. B. 1992. *Black Reconstruction in America*. New York: Atheneum.
Dye, Thomas R., and Harmon Zeigler. 1990. *The Irony of Democracy: An Uncommon Introduction to American Politics*. Pacific Grove, CA: Brooks/Cole Publishing Company.
Fishel, Jr., Leslie H., and Benjamin Quarles, eds. 1967. *The Negro American: A Documentary History*. Glenview, IL: Scott, Foresman and Company.
Foner, Eric. 1990. "From Slavery to Citizenship: Blacks and the Right to Vote." In *Voting and the Spirit of American Democracy: Essays on the History of Voting and Voting Rights in America*, ed. Donald W. Rogers. Urbana: University of Illinois Press.
Fredrickson, George M. 1981. *White Supremacy: A Comparative Study in American and South African History*. Oxford: Oxford University Press.
French, Marilyn. 1992. *The War Against Women*. New York: Summit Books.
Garrow, David J. 1986. *Bearing the Cross: Martin Luther King, Jr. and the Southern Christian Leadership Conference*. New York: Random House.
Green, Philip. 1985. *Retrieving Democracy: In Search of Civic Equality*. Totowa, NJ: Rowman & Allanheld.
Gurr, Ted Robert, Keith Jaggers, and Will H. Moore. 1990. "The Transformation of the Western State: The Growth of Democracy, Autocracy, and State Power Since 1800." *Studies in Comparative International Development*, 25, 1 (Spring): 73–108.
Held, David. 1987. *Models of Democracy*. Cambridge, UK: Polity Press.
———. 1995. *Democracy and the Global Order: From the Modern State to Cosmopolitan Governance*. Stanford: Stanford University Press.
Huber, Hans. 1946. *How Switzerland is Governed*. Zurich: Schweizer Spiegel Verlag.
Huntington, Samuel P. 1991. *The Third Wave: Democratization in the Late Twentieth Century*. Norman and London: University of Oklahoma Press.
Inglehart, Margaret. 1983. "Sex Role, Historical Heritage, and Political Participation in Switzerland." In *Switzerland at the Polls: The National Elections of 1979*, ed. Howard R. Penniman. Washington, DC: American Enterprise Institute for Public Policy Research.
Jonasdottir, Anna G. 1994. *Why Women Are Oppressed*. Philadelphia: Temple University Press.
Jordan, Winthrop D. 1968. *White over Black: American Attitudes toward the Negro, 1550–1812*. New York: W.W. Norton & Company.
Kerr, Andrea Moore. 1995. "White Women's Rights, Black Men's Wrongs, Free Love, Blackmail, and the Formation of the American Women Suffrage Association." In *One Woman, One Vote: Rediscovering the Woman Suffrage Movement*, ed. Marjorie Spruill Wheeler. Troutdale, OR: NewSage Press.

Key, Jr., V. O. 1949. *Southern Politics in State and Nation*. Knoxville: The University of Tennessee Press.
Klein, Herbert S. 1986. *African Slavery in Latin America and the Caribbean*. Oxford: Oxford University Press.
Lijphart, Arend. 1977. *Democracy in Plural Societies: A Comparative Exploration*. New Haven: Yale University Press.
Linz, Juan J. 1964. "An Authoritarian Regime: Spain." In *Cleavages, Ideologies and Party Systems: Contributions to Comparative Political Sociology*, ed. Erik Allardt and Yrjo Littunen. Helsinki: The Academic Bookstore.
———. 1973. "The Future of an Authoritarian Situation or the Institutionalization of an Authoritarian Regime: The Case of Brazil." In *Authoritarian Brazil: Origins, Policies, and Future*, ed. Alfred Stepan. New Haven: Yale University Press.
———. 1975. "Totalitarianism and Authoritarian Regimes." In *Handbook of Political Science, Volume 3, Macropolitical Theory*, ed. Fred I. Greenstein and Nelson W. Polsby. Reading, MA: Addison-Wesley.
Lipset, Seymour Martin. 1981. *Political Man: The Social Bases of Politics*, expanded edition. Baltimore, MD: The Johns Hopkins University Press.
Mainwaring, Scott. 1992 "Transitions to Democracy and Democratic Consolidation: Theoretical and Comparative Issues." In *Issues in Democratic Consolidation: The New South American Democracies in Comparative Perspective*, ed. Scott Mainwaring, Guillermo O'Donnell, and J. Samuel Valenzuela. South Bend, IN: University of Notre Dame Press.
Marable, Manning. 1991. *Race, Reform, and Rebellion: The Second Reconstruction in Black America, 1945–1990*. Jackson: University Press of Mississippi.
Marks, Gary, and Larry Diamond, eds. 1992. *Reexamining Democracy: Essays in Honor of Seymour Martin Lipset*. Newbury Park: Sage Publications.
Marshall, T. H. 1964. *Class, Citizenship, and Social Development*. Garden City, NY: Doubleday.
Miller, Francesca. 1991. *Latin American Women and the Struggle for Social Justice*. Hanover, NH: University Press of New England.
Millet, Kate. 1970. *Sexual Politics*. Garden City, NY: Doubleday.
Minority Rights Group, eds. 1995. *No Longer Invisible: Afro-Latin Americans Today*. London: Minority Rights Publications.
Moore, Barrington. 1966. *Social Origins of Dictatorship and Democracy: Lord and Peasant in the Making of the Modern World*. Boston: Beacon Press.
Morris, Aldon D. 1984. *The Origins of the Civil Rights Movement: Black Communities Organizing for Change*. New York: The Free Press.
Pateman, Carol. 1994. "Three Questions About Womanhood Suffrage." In *Suffrage and Beyond: International Feminist Perspectives*, ed. Caroline Daley and Melanie Nolan. New York: New York University Press.
Patterson, Orlando. 1982. *Slavery and Social Death: A Comparative Study*. Cambridge: Harvard University Press.
Penniman, Howard R. 1983. *Switzerland at the Polls: The National Elections of 1979*. Washington, DC: American Enterprise Institute for Public Policy Research.
Price, Robert M. 1991. *The Apartheid State in Crisis: Political Transformation in South Africa, 1975–1990*. Oxford: Oxford University Press.
Price, Robert M., and Carl G. Rosberg. 1980. *The Apartheid Regime: Political Power and Racial Domination*. Berkeley: Institute of International Studies, University of California.
Remmer, Karen. 1985–86. "Exclusionary Democracy." *Studies in Comparative International Development*, 20, 4 (Winter): 64–85.
Robinson, Cedric. 1995. "Slavery and the Platonic Origins of Anti-Democracy." *National Political Science Review*, 5: 18–35.

Roche, John P. 1961. "The Founding Fathers: A Reform Caucus in Action." *American Political Science Review*, 55 (December): 799–816.
Rodney, Walter. 1974. *How Europe Underdeveloped Africa*. Washington, DC: Howard University Press.
Rogers, Donald W, ed. 1990. *Voting and the Spirit of American Democracy: Essays on the History of Voting and Voting Rights in America*. Urbana: University of Illinois Press.
Rout, Jr., Leslie B. 1976. *The African Experience in Spanish America: 1502 to the Present Day*. Cambridge: Cambridge University Press.
Rueschemeyer, Dietrich, Evelyne Huber Stephens, and John D. Stephens. 1992. *Capitalist Development and Democracy*. Chicago: University of Chicago Press.
Sartori, Giovanni. 1970. "Concept Misformation in Comparative Politics." *American Political Science Review*, 64: 1033–53.
Skidmore, Thomas. 1974. *Black into White: Race and Nationality in Brazilian Thought*. New York: Oxford University Press.
Smith, Robert C. 1995. *Racism in the Post-Civil Rights Era: Now You See It, Now You Don't*. Albany: State University of New York Press.
Steiner, Jurg, and Robert H. Dorff. 1980. *A Theory of Political Decision Modes: Intraparty Decision Making in Switzerland*. Chapel Hill: The University of North Carolina Press.
Terborg-Penn, Rosalyn. 1995. "African American Women and the Woman Suffrage Movement." In *One Woman, One Vote: Rediscovering the Woman Suffrage Movement*, ed. Marjorie Spruill Wheeler. Troudale, OR: NewSage Press.
Thompson, Leonard. 1990. *A History of South Africa*. New Haven: Yale University Press.
Thompson, Wayne. 1995. *Western Europe 1995*. Harpers Ferry, WV: Stryker-Post Publications.
Thornton, Russell. 1987. *American Indian Holocaust and Survival: A Population History since 1492*. Norman: The University of Oklahoma Press.
Tocqueville, Alexis de. 1945. *Democracy in America*. New York: Vintage Books.
Vanhanen, Tatu. 1984. *The Emergence of Democracy: A Comparative Study of 119 States, 1850–1979*. Helsinki: The Finnish Society of Sciences and Letters.
Wheeler, Marjorie Sprull, ed. 1995. *One Woman, One Vote: Rediscovering the Woman Suffrage Movement*. Troutdale, OR: NewSage Press.
Williamson, Chilton. 1960. *American Suffrage: From Property to Democracy 1790–1860*. Princeton, NJ: Princeton University Press.
Winant, Howard. 1994. *Racial Conditions: Politics, Theory, Comparisons*. Minneapolis: University of Minneapolis Press.
Wood, Gordon S. 1991. *The Radicalism of the American Revolution*. New York: Vintage Books.
Woodward, C. Vann. 1974. *The Strange Career of Jim Crow*. Oxford: Oxford University Press.

What is Ethnicity?
A Comparative Analysis of Conflict in Post-Communist Societies

Kathie Stromile Golden

Morris Brown College

Introduction

There is little doubt that the end of the cold war era has ushered in a "world order" that is much more chaotic and potentially more threatening to the established international political and economic alignments than was the bipolar system wherein the United States and Soviet Union sought to maintain a balance of power. During the 1990s a wave of ethnic conflicts, some more enduring than others, spanned the global system. For example, Carment and James (1997) contend that by 1993, there were at least 48 existing or potentially violent ethnic conflicts in progress around the globe, while Gurr (1993: 1) identified 114 ethnic based conflicts. However, by 1996, the total number of conflicts with 1,000 or more battlefield causalities had decreased to pre-cold war levels. And, although such conflicts have always permeated the international community, it was not until the collapse of the Soviet system that they became globally salient. That is, such conflicts are viewed as fault lines that, if left unchecked, can rupture existing levels of global security.

A compelling example of the significance of ethnic conflicts for global security is provided by the case of Rwanda. The ethnic conflict in Rwanda, which has spillover effects for Zaire and Burundi, threatened all of Central Africa and the Great Lakes regions. The genocidal conflict in Rwanda also demonstrates the interconnectedness between African conflicts and the global agenda. Specifically, conflict in Rwanda, as well as in other African countries, has regional and international ramifications, which are evident in refugee flows and environmental damage. Moreover, similar ethnic conflicts have resulted in African states losing control of territory, the ability to maintain transportation infrastructure, and the ability to provide basic services to their people (U.S. Institute of Peace, 1997). Each of these factors, in turn, impacts economic and social development, as well as democratization efforts.

A second, and equally poignant, situation that can be viewed as a threat to both regional and global security involves the Iraqi Kurds, who live on the borders of eastern Turkey, western Iran, and Soviet Armenia. Due to their geographical location, Kurds have been used as pawns in conflicts involving Iraq and its neighbors. For example, during the 1970s, the anti-Iraqi Kurds were armed and financed by the Shah of Iran (Weatherby, 1994: 226). In more recent years, there have been low-intensity conflicts between Kurds and authorities in Turkey, Iran, and Iraq. These conflicts revolved around the Kurds' quest for the creation of a Kurdish state, which would encompass portions of Syria, Iran, Iraq, and the northern tier of Turkey. Since 1991, Kurdish leaders have sought the creation of an autonomous Kurdish region in Iraq. Thus, there have been attacks on the Kurdish population by the Iraqi government.

The most recent conflict between the Kurds and the Iraqi government has multiple internal and external actors. Internally, there have been clashes between the Kurds and the government as well as disagreements among different factions of the Kurdish population. Externally, the conflict has, at various points, resulted in tensions between the Iraqi government, Syria, Iran, and Turkey. Additionally, there is some indication that Israel has become an indirect party to the conflict through its military alliance with Turkey (Tashin, 1997: 1). It should also be noted that the U.S. support of the Kurdish population serves to heightened tensions between the Kurds and the government. Obviously, the Kurdish situation is one among multiple flash points in the Middle East. However, the complexity of the problem and the involvement of external actors suggest that the potential for unrest in this region represents an ever-present danger that can destabilize the northern tier and subsequently have global significance.

Given recent incidences of ethnic hostilities, scholars and journalists now seem to attribute greater urgency to ethnic conflicts and seem inclined to more fully ponder the global consequences of protracted ethnic hostilities. A perusal of the *Washington Post, New York Times, Wall Street Journal*, and *Congressional Record*, from 1991 to 1993, makes clear the attention, and thus seeming urgency, given to ethnic conflicts since the collapse of communist regimes in Eastern Europe and the Soviet Union. In fact, an examination of the U.S. House of Representative's and the Senate's floor debates during a three-year span (1991–1993), reveals that both chambers engaged in almost daily discussions of ethnic conflicts in the Balkan region, Soviet successor states, and, albeit significantly less, Africa and Asia (Golden, 1994).

Ethnicity and all that it connotes has gained prominence in research focusing on post-communist struggles. In fact, the renewed attention given ethnicity suggests that the pervasiveness of communist rule had blinded both scholars and policymakers to the likely consequences of a "world order" less defined by superpower competition. Moreover, ethnic conflicts that surfaced immediately following the end of the cold war routinely were viewed by many as the natural playing out of centuries-old antagonisms that had been suppressed under the communist systems of Eastern Europe and the Soviet Union. Similar conflicts which developed in other parts of the world were sometimes viewed as stemming from the actions of those who were emboldened by the absence of superpower competition, which ended with the collapse of the Soviet regime. Such perceptions about ethnic conflicts throughout the former Soviet bloc soon were seriously challenged as the savagery of conflicts in the former Yugoslav Republic, Chechnya, and less bloody conflicts in other parts of the former Soviet Union and Eastern Europe continued to become increasingly visible and protracted. Scholars, policymakers, and journalists came to realize that some of these conflicts were much more than the releasing of centuries-old hostilities.

Ethnic conflicts, sometimes imbued with a nationalist slant, throughout Africa and other third world regions prior to the 1990s provide evidence that there were many missed opportunities for the development of greater insights into ethnic-based hostilities and strategies for creating viable solutions (Esman, 1994: 11; Diamond, 1994: xvi; McGarry and O'Leary, 1993: 1–2; Jentleson, 1996: 9–10). Policymakers and researchers were more apt to view conflicts in the third world as merely struggles for power and control over resources rather than primarily ethnic conflicts. Had they assigned greater importance and attention to these conflicts, they might have been in a better position to offer policy initiatives that would have averted some of the devastation and carnage associated with ethnic conflicts that have swept across parts of Eastern Europe, the former Soviet Union, and Africa during the 1990s (Jinadu, 1994: 163). The failure to give adequate attention to the role of ethnicity in third world conflicts is evident in the manner in which the superpowers involved themselves in such conflicts. Historically, external intervention, particularly by the superpowers, took the form of massive infusions of war-related materials and military training for both government troops and rebels rather than serious attempts at negotiated settlements. Moreover, one might question the extent to which the superpowers and/or their allies sought to discern the underlying causes of what appeared on the surface to be ethnic/ethno-religious, or nationalist conflicts (Rapoport, 1996: 12).

While an examination of third world conflicts prior to the 1990s would provide an interesting backdrop against which to analyze conflicts in postcommunist societies, the objective of this discourse is to draw upon scholarly discussions, journalistic accounts, and historical facts to provide a broad categorization of select conflicts throughout Eastern Europe and the former Soviet state. Personal conversations with Russian, Polish, and Hungarian citizens will be drawn upon to augment journalistic and scholarly discussions. Specifically, the analyses are directed at distinguishing between those conflicts in which appeals to ethnicity appear to be a primary tool utilized by political entrepreneurs to manipulate ethnic groupings, thereby exacerbating ethnic tensions, and those in which the intersection of other factors, such as personal economics, religious beliefs, and political aspirations of the citizenry fuel hostilities.

Cross-Cutting Theoretical Explanations

Although much scholarly disagreement surrounds the conceptualization of ethnicity, there appears to be a consensus about its importance as an explanatory variable in research focusing on post-communist conflicts. According to Lake and Rothchild (1996: 6) ethnic conflict is caused by collective fears of the future (see also Esman, 1994: 2; Rapoport, 1996: 12). Fears about physical safety and assimilation into a dominant culture or hegemonic state can lead to intergroup violence (Lake and Rothchild, 1996: 8–9). While arguments focusing on ethnic groups' concerns about survival have always had prominence in scholarly discourse, there remains a need to engage in research that further explores the role of fear and other dimensions and expressions of ethnicity. Thus, we must seek explanations for ethnic conflict that will enable us to predict and distinguish between situations that are purely driven by ethnic differences and those in which ethnicity is a ruse, used to leverage the resources of political leaders. This type of explanation is made compelling by conflictual situations that have involved a combination of widespread violence, state failure, and spillover into neighboring states.

Two approaches—primordialist and instrumentalist—dominated the literature for much of the cold war era. And, although each posits plausible explanations for ethnic conflict, the robustness of those explanations are compromised by theoretical and methodological weaknesses. Nonetheless, a brief overview of each is important for establishing theoretical underpinnings for this discussion.

The primordialist approach views ethnicity as a collective identity deeply rooted in historical experience (Esman, 1994: 10) or biological traits (Lake and Rothchild, 1996; Isaacs, 1975: 38). According to this school of thought, ethnic divisions and schisms are "natural" but violent conflict is not necessarily perpetual. Conflict is, however, embedded in ethnicity.

Critics of the primordialist approach take issue with the primacy given ethnicity in the examination of intergroup warfare. Lake and Rothchild (1996) contend that the "Most frequent criticism of the primordialist approach is its assumption of fixed identities and its failure to account for variations in the level of conflict over time and place." It does not account for extended periods wherein ethnicity is not a salient political characteristic or situations in which ethnic groups peacefully coexist (Radcliff, 1994: 7). Explanatory weaknesses such as these raise important questions for research focusing on post-communist ethnic conflicts. For example, what accounts for variations in the level and intensity of ethnic conflict throughout Eastern Europe and Soviet successor states? Why was the dissolution of the Czechoslovakian state relatively more amicable than that of the Yugoslav Republic and the former Soviet Union?

Somewhat less reliant on the primacy of ethnicity, is the instrumentalist approach. Instrumentalists do not view ethnicity as static, but rather as a dynamic political tool that can be manipulated somewhat at will (Lake and Rothchild, 1996: 7; Horowitz, 1985). Further, the fluidity of ethnicity makes possible the taking on of ethnic identifications perceived to offer the greatest economic, political, or social advantages to the individual. Esman (1994: 11) notes that for instrumentalists ethnicity is either an ideology that elites construct and deconstruct for opportunistic reasons or a set of myths calculated to mobilize mass support for the economic or political goals of ambitious minorities. This approach, then, suggests that individuals can take on and jettison ethnic identifications somewhat at will. It assumes that a critical mass of citizens will, based on self-interest, support the goals of manipulative elites. This assumption fails to consider that individuals will likely have a need to be relatively certain about material gains that will accrue because of their support for the elites' agendas.

In fact, the instrumentalist approach has come under criticism for its view that ethnicity is something that can be decided upon by individuals somewhat at will and for the notion that it is a social construction that is embedded within and controlled by the larger society (Lake and Rothchild, 1996: 7). Critics of this approach argue for a relational framework that provides, in their view, a greater understanding of ethnicity. For example, Esman (1994: 13) argues that, "As a collective identity ethnicity is shaped by self-identification as well as by internal differences and external constraints."

A third and increasingly popular approach is constructivist. Constructivists attempt to bridge primordialist and instrumentalist explanations. And, as such, constructivists seek to provide the relational framework called for by critics of the instrumentalist approach (Gurr, 1993: 141). According to Esman (1994) this approach allows for the variability of ethnic solidarities, past as well as present, and regards ethnicity as one of several identities. This school of thought contends that although ethnicity is subject to change, it is not completely open, and is constructed from a massive collection of social interactions. In short, ethnicity is viewed as a social phenomenon. Conflicts are viewed as outgrowths of certain types of social systems (Lake and Rothchild, 1996: 7–8). Criticism of the constructivist approach hinges on its inability to explain class and other materialist based conflicts.

Although each approach offers a useful basis for analyzing the intersection of ethnicity and conflict, neither provides a groundbreaking conceptualization of ethnic conflict. It appears that any conflict in which there are identifiable cultural, "tribal," clan, or racial differences can be labeled an ethnic conflict. Arguably, intergroup differences might have significance for the intensity and duration of hostilities but such differences might actually serve to obscure the underlying causes of conflict. Thus, it is tempting to use ethnicity as a sort of "catch-all" label for internal conflicts. And, it must be recognized, conflicts may readily dissolve in ethnic-based struggles. In such instances, ethnicity has relevance for the outcome but is not necessarily a primary factor in terms of the onset of hostilities.

The voluminous body of work that has materialized since the collapse of the Soviet bloc includes research on conflicts that have been labeled as ethnonationalist (Walker, 1993; Dreyer, 1993; Smith, 1993; Connor, 1994), ethno-religious (Harff, 1993; Rapoport, 1996; Little, 1996), or just ethnic. Interestingly, this genre of research rarely, if ever, provides precise conceptualizations for the variants of ethnic conflict. For example, Rapoport (1996: 3) notes that ethno-religious conflicts tend to be among the more violent conflicts, but we are never informed of what constitutes an ethno-religious conflict. To the extent that conceptual rigor is lacking, it is virtually impossible to identify with a high degree of precision the primary cause(s) or underlying nature of conflict.

The difficulty of establishing causality stems in part from the fact that key players and their objectives are not always identifiable. Instigators rarely articulate the exact reasons and motives that propel them to specific courses of actions. Additionally, there often can be multiple, not clearly identifiable factors impacting the process. Given that the establishment of causality is, at best, difficult, we must not engage in conceptual stretching. Nonetheless, it is possible, even useful, to categorize conflicts. Categorization helps to systematize the search for underlying causes of conflicts and aids in the search for appropriate explanations for delimited cases under specified conditions (Schermerhorn, 1970: 237).

One of the most ambitious attempts to classify conflicts and/or potentially conflictual situations is represented by the work of Ted Gurr (1993), which has as its focus minorities at risk. Although Gurr's work provides interesting and useful insights for distinguishing between conflicts and their underlying causes, he primarily categorizes conflicts as nonviolent protest, violent protest, and rebellion. Each category is viewed as a form of what Gurr refers to as ethno-political conflict. Moreover, the discussion suggests that a number of the conflicts are nationalist endeavors. Thus, Gurr's classificatory system might be used to assess the level of violence attending different conflict.

Seymore (1994) classifies conflicts in terms of the following five forms of nationalism:

> *Classical Nationalism*—the movement of minorities in pursuit of independence as a nation-state or autonomy within an existing state. It tends to be inclusionary and participatory until its goals are achieved.
>
> *Irredentist Nationalism*—efforts to join co-ethnics in other sovereign states or to acquire former territories. Such efforts necessitate the support of relevant foreign states.
>
> *Unexpected Nationalism*—the use of ethnic mobilization by governments of countries that emerged from empires not so much as a result of their own efforts but because of the collapse of central authority.
>
> *Retrenchment Nationalism*—efforts of a formally dominant nationality to cope with the loss of territory or status. It can affect countries where public participation has fallen or where the dominant community feels it has had to concede too much to rising minority populations.
>
> *Xenophobic Nationalism*—a response to a perceived decline in status at home to immigrant or other minority populations. It often entails violence directed at the hated group. (5–6)

The problem with Seymore's categorization lies in the fact that it does not account for conflict revolving around religion per se and, although each has an ethnic component, ethnicity is not given primacy in any of the forms. In spite of shortcomings, these two classification systems can be used to provide a backdrop against which to examine Eastern European and Soviet successor state conflicts.

I propose that two additional forms—ethnonationalism and religious nationalism—to those posited by Seymore. The following conceptualizations are offered:

> *Ethnonationalism*—discourse that emphasizes priority and preeminence of one particular ethnic and cultural community over others. This is what Max Weber (1968) terms movement away from legal-rational norms toward an ethnically discriminatory and preferential political and legal system.

Religious Nationalism—discourse that emphasizes the predominance of one set of religious tenets/beliefs over others in the life on the nation. It might advocate the development of a state religion, and in some instances runs parallel to and supports nationalist or ethnic struggles. Religious nationalism can be used as a tool in the pursuit of ulterior ethnic or nationalist motives.

As is evident from these seven descriptions, nationalism can be applied to a variety of situations and the categories are not mutually exclusive. And, though there are those who would argue that it is more feasible to view post-communist conflicts strictly within the context of intergroup differences, it behooves us to exercise caution in utilizing ethnicity as a primary explanatory variable for all cases. Moreover, depending on the demographics and history of the nation-states under study, it might be more appropriate to engage in research that focuses on providing a more comprehensive analysis of the intersection of ethnicity and nationalism. Arguably, the concept of nationalism, which can be linked to the idea of a powerful community of people who share a common language, or religion, or culture, or political experience, is more amenable to this type of analysis. And, though it might not be entirely possible to establish causality, we can began to identify correlational patterns, which necessitate an analysis of the circumstances surrounding conflicts.

Categorizing Post-Communist Conflicts

The artificial boundaries established after the dissolution of empires in Eastern Europe and in conjunction with Russian and Soviet expansionism intermingled groups of people separated previously by ethnic, religious, and national boundaries. These differentiated populations were forced by the communist regimes to suppress their previous identities, and to forfeit their property (real estate, land, and capital) rights to the communist state. Post-communist conflict, then, might be viewed as ethnic group competition for control of economic resources and political institutions that had been confiscated and taken over by the communist regimes. Lines have been drawn on the landscape and the competitors have more or less differentiated themselves along pre-communist ethnic, religious, and nationalist identities. They seek to modify or revert to some variant of old national identities, which were more or less grounded in ethnicity. The discussion that follows represents an attempt to identify the primary factors impacting post-communist conflicts by examining the conditions and events surrounding the conflicts, identifying key players, key issues, and citizens' and governmental actions.

The selection of conflicts to be examined and categorized was determined by their significance for global and regional stability, prominence in American foreign policy discussions, causalities, duration, and historical context. Theoretical considerations necessitated the inclusion of conflicts characterized as having low significance for global stability, comparatively few causalities, and relatively short durations. Eight conflicts—three from Eastern Europe and five from Russia and Soviet successor states—are examined.

Tajikistan

The conflict in Tajikistan represents a battle for power between two groups—Kulyabis and Khojandis—who populate different regions of the country. The conflict resulted in more than 20,000 casualties (Erlanger, 1993: A2). Although there is a religious (Islam) aspect and an ethnic factor, the conflict is more about the distribution of political power. Presently the Kulyabis dominate the government and are resisting efforts geared toward greater power sharing. It should also be noted that the two groups were allies under the leadership of the old guard (communists). Thus, it appears that neither ethnic group differences nor the creation of national identity is at the heart of the conflict. It is more a conflict that revolves around the creation of a more representative government.

Bosnia-Herzegovina

Since 1991 news reports have bombarded us with the unfolding of events in the former Yugoslav Republic, with a significant portion of these reports focusing on Bosnia-Herzegovina. Of the eight conflicts, this one has received the greatest amount of international attention. The war in Bosnia-Herzegovina began in April 1992. However, long before the official start of the conflict leaders of the three ethnic-based national parties had heightened the sense of fear and mistrust among the different ethnic groups by blaming the others for their own history of oppression and misery (Pajic, 1995: 155). The conflicting parties—Croats, led by Croatian President Franjo Tudjman; Muslims, led by Bosnian President Alija Izetbegovic; and Serbs, led by President Slobodan Milosevic—are Bosnia's three main ethnic groups. The three groups seek to control the territory each seized in combat and to create a new Bosnian government made up of three ethnically based states. The government seeks to maintain Bosnia as a multiethnic state.

Bosnia has a mix of Catholic Croatians, Orthodox Serbs, and Muslim Bosnians. Throughout the conflict Muslims and Croatians have been pitted against each other, while both groups have been fighting the Serbs. For example, Muslims and Croats fought a bitter ten-month war in 1993–94, while the main Muslim-Serb conflict raged on (Reuters, 1996). Within one-and-a-half years of the conflict, more than 140,000 persons lost their lives, 300,000 were injured, and millions were displaced ("Informe Sobre," 1993). Ethnic cleansing (genocide), the bombing of places of worship, and various war crimes committed by all parties to the conflict have created a climate that both conditions and reinforces interethnic group intolerance. Such a climate compels individuals to take on specific ethnic identities or completely disengage themselves. Generally, it appears that members of each ethnic group are seeking security and protection, albeit fragile, offered by collective identity. Certainly, the leaders of each ethnic group have exhibited low, if any, tolerance for each other. Some of them, such as Slobodan Milosevic, have even managed to whip their people into a frenzy, which does not contribute to resolution of the conflict.

North Ossetia

North Ossetia, a republic in southern Russia, is populated by Ossetians (53 percent), Russians (30 percent), Ingush (8 percent), and others (9 percent)

(Seymore, 1994: 60). Ossetians and Ingushetians are primary parties to the conflict, which is recognized as the first large-scale ethnic war in the reconstituted Russian Federation. Essentially, returning Ingush refugees are attempting to regain territory and property confiscated when they were deported from the Republic during the Stalinist era. The territory is now inhabited by North Ossetians who are resistant to giving up control of the area and property.

The Ingushetians are making property claims in the Prigordny region. It is important to note that the Ingushetians view themselves as victims of an Ossetian conspiracy (Kasaev, 1996). They justify their rights to reclaim the area by invoking the Russian Statute on Rehabilitation of Repressed People," which was adopted in April 1991. The statute allows for the return of communal control over ethnic homelands of peoples who had been subject to mass repression and deportation under Stalin. The statute, however, failed to include important details about the rights of people presently inhabiting the land. Kasaev (1996: 5) notes that the dismemberment of the Checheno-Ingush Republic also contributed to the breakdown in Ossetian-Ingushetian relations. These events coupled with the fact that Ingushetia was not among the Russian regions that signed the Union Treaty, which provided the legal basis for the coexistence of regions and the republic of the Russian Federation, effectively left the Ingushetian without a homeland. Meanwhile, there was organized harassment against the Ingushetians. And even though Russia is a party to the conflict, hostilities result more from the breakdown in relations between the Ossetians and Ingushetians.

The Ingushetians' attempt to reclaim their "historical homeland" might be viewed as an ethnic conflict similar to that of the Palestinians, while the Ossetians, like the Israeli, are seeking to guard their homeland. Clearly this is a conflict about space, which is undergirded partially by appeals to a collective identity. Moreover, it is not clear that they would not attempt to secede from the Russian Federation. The evidence suggests that historical mistrust and the present climate, to some degree, condition and reinforce hostility between the two groups. Russians, as an ethnic group, appear less impacted by the conflict, which might be an indication that ethnicity, though an important component of the conflict, is not as prevalent as in some of the other conflicts in the region . Thus, it might be argued that members of each group are seeking closer identification with their ascribed ethnic group, while demonstrating tolerance for members of ethnic groups who are not directly involved in the competition for property rights.

Chechnya

Chechnya, also situated on Russia's southern flank, shares a fifty-mile border with the Georgian Republic. Approximately two-thirds of the 1.1 million population is ethnic Chechen, and one-fourth ethnic Russian. Most of the population is Moslem. At one time Chechnya possessed tremendous oil reserves but, the war has damaged refineries and impacted income from the pipeline carrying Caspian reserves to the Black Sea. Russia fears the loss of the Chechen oil fields.

The Chechens, like the Ingushetians, were deported to Central Asia during the Stalinist era. However, in 1957 Nikita Khrushchev allowed the

Chechens to return and established the Chechen-Ingush ethnic republic. Things were relatively peaceful until Mikhail Gorbachev launched the ideas of Glasnost and Perestroika. In October of 1991, General Dzhokar Dudaev stirred up protests against Soviet backed rulers in Grozny, won 80 percent of the support in an election, and declared independence (*Russia Today*, September 11, 1997). Chechnya split from Ingushetia in June 1992.

President Boris Yeltsin ordered troops into Chechnya on December 11, 1994. A bloody and protracted war ensued. According to Specter (1996: A8), after twenty months of war, there were 40,000 casualties. Soviet soldiers were accused of killing innocent civilians, which exacerbated the disdain for Russians. The actual war between Moscow and Chechnya lasted almost two years, but tensions remain high. Moscow still considers Chechnya a part of the Russian Federation. The conflict is complicated by the kidnapping of locals, as well as foreigners, the imposition of Sharia Law, a range of reported criminal activities (Chechen Mafia), and other conflicts throughout the Russian Federation.

Russia is an old enemy of the Chechens, going back to czarist massacres of Chechen in the 1860s. In fact, the Chechens are attempting to bring to fruition a centuries-old vow to drive the occupiers from their land (Specter, 1996: A1, 12). Thus, historical animosities, the presence of political entrepreneurs (both Russian and Chechen), Moscow's military attacks, as well as religious and economic factors, combine to create an environment of mistrust and hatred, at least of Russians.

This conflict suggests that ethnicity is a primary factor that informs and drives Chechens' quest for independence from Moscow, while religion and economic factors have complicated the internal situation. It is likely that conflict between the Chechens and Russians will not disappear in the near future. Over 200 years of mutual disdain is at work.

South Ossetia

South Ossetia, an autonomous republic of Georgia, declared its autonomy in September 1990. Government troops were sent into the region to put down the independence drive. In June of 1992, the two sides agreed to a cease-fire; however, the Georgian government has effectively ceded control over South Ossetia.

The conflict in South Ossetia is impacted by other conflicts in Transcaucasia. Abkhazian separatists were also engaging the Georgian government in a secessionist war. Conflicts in North Ossetia and Chechnya, though a part of the Russian Federation, have caused concern for the government. Ostensibly, the South Ossetians identify with their brothers and sisters in the north, and their angst appears to be directed toward political independence. It does not seem that ethnicity per se is a primary factor in this conflict. The Georgian government is constrained in its ability to engage the Ossetians in military combat; thus, it can be argued that the environment moderately conditions and reinforces intolerance (Aves, 1993; Gachechiladze, 1996).

Nagorno-Karabakh

Nagorno-Karabakh is an enclave of Azerbaijan, which resulted from the

Soviet redrawing of territorial lines. The conflict between ethnic Armenians (Christians) and Azerbaijanis (Shi'ite Muslims) over the enclave produced thousands of causalities, over one million refugees and displaced persons, and considerable infrastructure damage. Moscow's refusal, in 1988, to allow Armenians in Nargono-Karabakh to enter into a political union with Armenia sparked protests and violence between the two groups.

The Armenians of Nargono-Karabakh declared their independence from Azerbaijan on September 2, 1991, and immediately created the State Committee of Defense, which possessed all executive and a part of the legislative power. This move facilitated secessionist efforts. The Armenians now occupy about 25 percent of Azerbaijan's territory (some owing to the seizure of areas during the conflict) and comprise about 75 percent of the population of Nargono-Karabakh (Seymore, 1994).

The Armenians' success is in large measure due to the assistance of soldiers from Armenia. It must also be noted that Azerbaijan, like Georgia, was and is experiencing internal political turmoil. For example, the government changed hands five times from 1991 to September 1993 (Seymore, 1994). Additionally, separatist movements were occurring in other parts of the country. It seems that the overall environment was conducive to the Armenian takeover of the reins of political power. Although ethnicity was a factor initially, it seems that other factors and events were more at work in this conflict. Religion is a tangential factor. Azerbaijan possesses valuable natural resources, vast off-shore oil reserves. It is reasonable to assume that economics is a primary factor in this conflict.

Hungary and Romania

Conflicts in the final two cases—Hungary and Romania—seem more akin to ethnic conflicts in the United States and Western Europe than to what is occurring in the cases discussed previously. In the United States, Germany, and France, for example, the spirit of exclusiveness and anti-foreign sentiments has increased with rapid increases of immigration in conjunction with major domestic or international crisis. During these times, society feels that national unity and the stability of societal institutions depend on cultural homogeneity (Citrin, Reingold, and Green, 1990: 1124).

Ethnic discrimination in Hungary is directed against the Roma (Gypsies) who are thought to have arrived there between 1416 and 1417. Immediately after World War II the government's policy toward the Roma was influenced by Stalin and involved persecution of the Roma. However, in the 1950s the government established an official policy to actively support the development of minority culture and education. By 1961 the government decreed that Roma did not constitute a national minority but retained the developmental and constitutional rights extended to other groups. Among the poorest people in the country, they were relegated to slums surrounding major cities and unwanted rural lands, and had a much lower life expectancy and literacy rates than the national average (Fox, 1995: 2). Local prejudices held that they were lazy, stupid, and prone to crime, much like stereotypes of African Americans.

These problems remain the same, if not worse. Much of the prejudice is supported by local governments and anti-discrimination laws are ineffective. Skinheads (Neo-Nazis) routinely launch vicious attacks on Roma and other non-Hungarian people. Prejudice, which is expressed openly, takes the form of graffiti on walls (especially in major cities, such as Budapest), racist literature, attacks by skinheads and other hate groups, and racist statements by both citizens and political figures. Government efforts to address the situation are resented by other Hungarians due to their cost at a time when unemployment is high and government social programs are being cut.

Similarly, ethnic Hungarians in Romania are targets of discrimination. Transylvania, which was formerly a part of Hungary, is comprised of a large Hungarian population. It is viewed by both Romanians and ethnic Hungarians as the cradle of their nation (*Central Europe Online*, September 19, 1997). One of the leading advocates of discrimination against ethnic Hungarians is Gheorghe Funar, mayor of Cluj. Funar's 1990 speech in Tirgu Mures, a major city in the heart of Transylvania, led to an altercation between Romanians and ethnic Hungarians in which four people died and dozens were injured (Tokes, 1993).

The primary antagonists are Romanian nationalists who are opposed to minority rights for ethnic Hungarians. There have been rallies and signs denouncing government concessions to official use of the Hungarian language. Romanian nationalists have argued that Hungarians have an undue influence in the country's affairs and that the president has lost touch with grassroots reality. Hungarians have accused the government of creating an anti-Hungarian atmosphere, and directly or indirectly aiding efforts aimed at national homogenization. Ironically, the government in Hungary has engaged the Romanian government in dialogues concerning the status of ethnic-Hungarian—ironic because the Hungarian government is accused of complicity in the situation of Roma. Thus, it can be argued that conflicts in both cases, revolve around fears that are more apparent than real.

Case Summary

Although it is quite difficult to place these conflicts definitively within the context of any one form of nationalism, taking into account ethnicity, religion, environmental stimuli and attending responses, and perceived benefits should enhance our ability to identify correlational patterns and to distinguish between conflicts. As indicated by Table 1, only one of the eight conflicts is thought to be a clearly simplistic form of classical nationalism. And, although religion and ethnicity are factors in the conflict, they appear to be secondary to the conflict.

Similarly, only one case—Bosnia—is placed in the ethnonationalism category. The Bosnian conflict, however, has an equally strong religious component. Moreover, the activism of political entrepreneurs (read nationalist presidents and party leaders) serves to exacerbate tensions along ethnic and religious lines. Thus, it might also be viewed as a religious nationalist conflict. The Chechen conflict also has a strong religious component. In fact, the present leadership has used religious laws to punish persons who have been convicted of crimes. Religion, however, appears to be less significant in the Nargono-Karabakh conflict.

Table I
Correlates Of Nationalism

	Sense of Ethnic Identity	Environmental Stimuli	Response	Perceived Benefit	Conflicts
Nationalism	Mild Flexible	Encourages identification state and support for elite agenda, and tolerance	Supports the established order	Total Control of state/region and resources	Tajikistan
Ethno-Nationalism	Strong Rigid	Strongly conditions and reinforces intolerance for outsiders	Total identification with ethnic group, overt hostility (armed violence, genocide)	Ethnically defined state total control over resources	Bosnia
Religious-Nationalism	Strong Rigid	Strongly conditions and reinforces intolerance for other ethno-religious groups	Total identification with religious group; overt hostility (armed violence)	Religiously defined state, total control over resources; stronger linkages between state and church	Bosnia *Tajikistan Chechnya *Nargono-Karabakh
Irredentist-Nationalism	Moderate Flexible	Moderately conditions and reinforces intolerance for outsiders	Challenge existing order, increased identification with subjective ethnic group but able to embrace others	Greater control over state and state and resources; increased societal homogeneity	Chechnya N. Ossetia S.Ossetia Nargono-Karabakh
Retrench.-Nationalism	Moderate Mildly Rigid	Weakly conditions and reinforces intolerance for outsiders	Identification primarily with own ethnic group; unequal hostility toward outsiders, isolated violence	Greater societal homogeneity, limits distribution of resources	
Xenophob-Nationalism	Moderate Mildly Rigid	Weakly conditions and reinforces intolerance for outsiders	Accepts existing order but identifies primarily with own ethnic group; unequal hostile reactions (limited or isolated violence)	Greater societal homogeneity; limits distribution of resources	Romania Hungary

*Indicates that the conflict is not primarily a religious conflict.

A number of the eight conflicts—North Ossetia, South Ossetia, and Nargono-Karabakh—are of the irredentist nationalist variety. In each case, the conflict revolves around secession from a Soviet successor state. However, it is noted that the Ingushetians might opt for greater autonomy within the Russian Federation, if their demands for a "homeland" are met. Clearly, the South Ossetians and the Armenians of Nagorno-Karabakh are in search of political independence, which is in part related to desires to control the economic resources within the contested areas. Ethnicity per se does not appear to be the predominate factor in either of these conflicts.

The final category, xenophobic nationalism, seems appropriate for the conflicts in Romania and Hungary. The two countries have not experienced the level of violence that permeates the other conflicts. Essentially, there have been attacks on Roma (Gypsies) in Hungary, and ethnic-Hungarians have been attacked in Romania. Essentially, these attacks stem from some citizens' fears that they will have to share the nation-states' ever shrinking resources and compete with "others" for jobs and services.

Conclusion and Implications for Future Research

Undoubtedly, ethnicity is related to the conflicts that mar the landscapes of Eastern Europe and Soviet successor states but it does not in and of itself cause those conflicts. It even appears not to be a primary factor in a number of the conflicts examined. The cases do, however, suggest that ethnic identification is dynamic. That is, the strength of one's ethnic identification is likely to be impacted by environmental stimuli, which can either move one closer to or further away from those who share ethnic, and/or religious identifications. To some extent the strength of ethnic identity will be impacted by one's perceptions about material and emotional benefits that might accrue from association with a particular ethnic group.

The cases confirm a link between nationalism and ethnicity but, they do not make clear which of the two will be the driving force in a given conflict. The patterns of ethnic conflict exhibited in the post-communist systems of Eastern Europe and Soviet successor states seem clearly to represent variants of nationalism, which also poses an analytical challenge. A simplistic conceptualization of nationalism views it as efforts directed at self-determination. Historical evidence and existing research, however, indicate that nationalism is a much more complex phenomenon (Seymore, 1994: 5). It takes on various forms, and homogenizes and differentiates, simultaneously. Nationalist discourse drives toward cultural standardization within the nation, which tends to mute genuine multiethnic and multinational expression. Nationalism advocates sovereignty over a sharply circumscribed community of inhabitants and a sharply circumscribed territory (Little, 1996). This view of nationalism is analogous to that which communist regimes throughout the Soviet bloc sought to repress. Generally, the approach utilized in this analysis provides evidence, albeit tentative, that these conflicts might be viewed within the context of nationalism and stages of ethnic identity, which moves us further in the direction of being able to identify the nature of and differentiate between post-communist conflicts.

Obviously, the correlational pattern presented in the analysis does not establish causation. Moreover, the underlying nature and reasons for the growth of ethnic conflict are not as apparent and easily definable as some of the extant research suggests. The problems associated with providing a definitive assessment of post-communist conflicts stems from the existence of multifaceted expressions of ethnicity, an inability to clearly and unequivocally identify the motives of key participants, and the overall multidimensionality of any given conflict. Additional research, which takes into account other variables, is necessary to accomplish that goal. For example, survey data designed to tap into how parties to the conflict view themselves, other ethnic groups, and their leaders would facilitate such an effort. Other variables that would allow for gauging the intensity of conflicts, mass consciousness, and level of perceived threats would facilitate efforts to establish causation, which, in turn, would move us toward the establishment of definitive categorization.

References

Aves, Jonathan. 1993. "Politics, Parties and Presidents in Transcaucasia." *Caucasian Regional Studies*, 1 (1996): 1–21.
Brown, M., ed. 1993. *Ethnic Conflict and International Security*, 21–41. Princeton, NJ: Princeton University Press.
Carment, D., and P. James. 1997. " International Constraints on Interstate Conflict: Toward a Crises Based Assessment of Irredentism." *Journal of Conflict Resolution*, 39 (1): 82–109.
Central Europe Online. 1997 (September 19). "Romanian Nationalists Call for Anti-Government Alliance." http://www.centraleurope.com/ceo/news/04.html.
Citrin, Jack, Beth Reingold, and Donald P. Green. 1990. "American Identity and the Politics of Ethnic Change." *Journal of Politics*, 52, 4: 1124–53.
Connor, W. 1994. *Ethnonationalism: The Quest for Understanding*. Princeton, NJ: Princeton University Press.
Diamond, Larry. 1994. "Introduction." In *Nationalism, Ethnic Conflict, and Democracy*, ed. L. Diamond and M. Platter. Baltimore: Johns Hopkins University Press.
Dreyer, June Teufel. 1993. "Tibetan Ethno-nationalism in International Politics." In *The Ethnic Dimension in International Relation*, ed. Bernard Schechterman and M. Slann, 43–56. Westport, CT: Greenwood.
Erlanger, Steven. 1993. "Troops in Ex-Soviet Lands: Occupiers or Needed Allies?" *New York Times* (November 30): A1, 12.
Esman, M. J. 1994. *Ethnic Politics*. Ithaca: Cornell University Press.
Fox, Jonathan. 1995. "Roma (Gypsies) in Hungary," unpublished manuscript.
Gachechiladze, Revaz. 1996. "Geographical and Historical Factors of State Building in Transcaucasia." *Caucasian Regional Studies* 1: 22–36.
Golden, Kathie Stromile. 1994. "Semantical Illusions or Disillusions?: U.S. Congressional Discourse on Bosnia-Herzegovina and Somalia." Paper presented at The National Conference of Black Political Scientists Twenty-Fifth Annual Meeting, Hampton, Virginia.
Gurr, Ted Robert. 1993. *Minorities at Risk*. Washington, DC: U.S. Institute of Peace.
Harff, Barbara. 1993. "Minorities, Rebellion, and Repression in North Africa and the Middle East." In *Minorities at Risk*, ed. Ted Gurr, 217–51. Washington, DC: U.S. Institute of Peace.
Horowitz, Donald. 1985. *Ethnic Groups in Conflict*. Berkeley: University of California Press.
———. 1994. "Democracy in Divided Societies." In *Nationalism, Ethnic Conflict, and*

Democracy, ed. Larry Diamond and Marc Platters, 35–55. Baltimore: Johns Hopkins University Press.

"Informe Sobre La Tragedia De La Poblacion Civil En Bosnia Y Hercegovina." 1993 (September). *Boletin del Central Informativo Croata de la Republica Argentina.*

Isaacs, Harold. 1975. *Idol of the Tribe: Group Identity and Political Change.* New York: Random House.

Jinadu, L. Adele. 1994. "The Dialectics of Theory and Research on Race and Ethnicity in Nigeria." In *"Race," Ethnicity, and Nation: International Perspectives on Social Conflict*, ed. Peter Radcliff, 163–78. London: UCL Press Limited.

Jentleson, Bruce. 1996. "Preventive Diplomacy and Ethnic Conflict: Possible, Difficult, Necessary." Policy Paper No. 27. Institute on Global Conflict and Cooperation.

Kasaev, Alan. 1996. "Ossetia-Ingushetia." Rand Organization Publication.

Lake, David, and Donald Rothchild. 1996. "Ethnic Fears and Global Engagement: The International Spread and Management of Ethnic Conflict." Policy Paper Number 20. Institute on Global Conflict and Cooperation.

Little, David. 1996. "Beliefs, Ethnicity, and Nationalism." Washington, DC: United States Institute of Peace.

Lipschutz, R., and B. Crawford. 1995. "Ethnic Conflict Isn't." Policy Brief. Institute on Global Conflict and Cooperation.

McGarry, John, and O'Leary, Brendan. 1993. *The Politics of Ethnic Conflict Regulation.* London: Routledge.

Nodia, Ghia. 1994. "Nationalism and Democracy." In *Nationalism, Ethnic Conflict, and Democracy*, ed. Diamond and Platter, 3–22. Baltimore: Johns Hopkins University Press.

Pajic, Zoran. 1995. "Bosnia-Herzegovina: From Multiethnic Coexistence to 'Apartheid'...and Back." In *Yugoslovia: The Former and Future*, ed. Payam Akhavan and Robert Howse, 152–63. Washington, DC: Brookings Institute.

Radcliff, Peter. 1994. *"Race," Ethnicity, and Nation: International Perspectives on Social Conflict.* London. UCL Press Limited.

Rapoport, D. C. 1996. "The Importance of Space in Violent Ethno-Religious Conflicts." Policy Paper Number 21. Institute of Global Conflict and Cooperation.

Reuters. 1996 (August 5). "Muslims, Croats Still Deadlock over Mostar."

Russia Today. 1997 (September 11). "Chechnya: Facts and Figures."

Saideman, Stephen. 1995. "Is Pandora's Box Half-Empty or Half-Full? The Limited Virulence of Secessionism and the Domestic Sources of Disintegration." Policy Paper Number 18. Institute on Global Conflict and Cooperation.

Schermerhorn, R. A. 1970. *Comparative Ethnic Relations: A Framework for Theory and Research.* New York: Random House.

Seymore, B, II. 1994. *The Access Guide to Ethnic Conflicts in Europe and the Former Soviet Union.* Washington, DC: ACESS.

Smith, Donald. 1993. "The Ethnic Sources of Nationalism." In *Ethnic Conflict and International Security*, ed. Michael Brown, 27–41. Princeton, NJ: Princeton University Press.

Specter, Michael. 1996. "How Chechens Surprised Foes to Retake Capital." *New York Times* (August 18): A1, 12.

———.1996. " The Chechen Buck Stops Where? Not in Kremlin." *New York Times* (August 29): A8.

Tashin, Hassan. 1997. "Israel Cashing in on the Kurdish Crisis." *Arab.net.* http://arab.net/arabview/articles/tahsin9.html.

Tokes, Laszlo. 1993. "What's Behind a Statement." Transylvania, Romania: Bishops' Office of Kiralyhagomellek Reformed Church District.

United States Institute of Peace. 1997. "The U.S. Contribution to Conflict Prevention, Management, and Resolution in Africa." A Report of a United States Institute of Peace Symposium. Washington, DC.

Walker, J. 1993. "International Mediation of Ethnic Conflicts." *Survival*, 35.
Weatherby, Joseph. 1994. "The Middle East and North Africa." In *The Other World: Politics of the Developing World*, ed. Joseph Weatherby, Randall L. Cruikshanks, Emmit B. Evans, Jr., Reginald Gooden, Earl D. Huff, Richard Kranzdorf, and Dianne Long, 192–233. New York: Longman.
Weber, Max. 1968. *Economy and Society: An Outline of Interpretive Sociology*, vol. 1, 385–98. New York: Bedminster Press.

African-American Politics in Constancy and Change

Thoreauvian Theater Impacting American Politics: Martin Luther King's Media and His Leadership

Glenda Suber

Benedict College

> *The political process has been much less thoroughly studied as a purveyor of symbols. [H]owever...there is a good deal of evidence...that symbols are a more central component of the process than is commonly recognized in political scientists' explicit or implicit models.*
> —Murray Edelman, "Symbols and Political Quiescence"

The Study of Politics as Theater: The Philosophical Context

The role of and presence of symbolic leadership in societies and in cultures throughout history is a phenomenon that has been studied and analyzed overtime by various scholars in many disciplines. From Plato's preferred philosopher-king to Orrin Klapp's treatise *Symbolic Leaders*, scholars have attempted to monitor the political aspects of dynamic leadership. As for political scientists, however, we still have not yet developed a generally accepted paradigm for analyzing, interpreting, or categorizing the theatrical aesthetics utilized by symbolic leaders in their positions of public responsibility.

A brief glance at the literature on "dramaturgism," suggests that since the 1960s there have been some limited cross-disciplinary efforts and discourse in the social sciences concerned with developing a paradigmatic framework to relate theatrical elements to dramatic politics. This rather young cross-disciplinary subfield came to be known as dramaturgy. No specific paradigms, however, have been firmly established within the political science discipline as a generally accepted barometer for making associative characterizations between politics and theater.

The origination of a seminal work on dramatic theory, *The Theater in Life*, by Nikolai Evreinov (1927), writing from the humanities' perspective, provides a basis for conducting further research in this area. In addition, Erving Goffman (1959), Orrin Klapp (1964), and Kenneth Burke (1968) have added more theoretical substance for pursuing generalizing concepts about politics and theater. However, since these classic works were produced, there has been little overlap in disciplinary specific studies on dramaturgy. Scholars in the fields of social psychology, anthropology, philosophy, political science, and sociology, as well as media theorists, have all posed independent, relevant questions about the presence of theatrical elements in dramatic politics.[1] Between 1960 and the mid-1980s, when the media's role in and effects on the political process grew at geometric proportions, political scientists did attempt to focus on symbolic leadership and mediated events. After Reagan's term in office, however, and after he successfully applied dramaturgical techniques, the scholarly research in this area began to wane even though the media continue to play a major role in political affairs.[2]

With pervasive media technology influencing the political environment, the dramatic context becomes even more important. The affinity for and linkage between political leadership and dramatic techniques represent a growing area and subfield within political science that needs further exploration. Mass media represents the "fourth estate" in American politics. Its influence and effects on cultural norms and trends are pervasive and growing. The dramatic qualities and theatrical aspects of politics, therefore, become important variables in conducting analysis of political leadership. Descriptive (if not prescriptive) concepts and a terminology that move scholars closer to paradigm consensus about the theatrical manifestations of politics are direly needed in political science .

Several key frameworks are outlined in this analysis. One is based on a Burkeanian interpretation that theatrical characteristics are inherent in the political domain (Burke, 1968; 1972). The other is based on postmodernist perspective (Wagner-Pacifici, 1986) that all political events are generated by and within a given nationalistic culture. She posits that any social or political drama is simply a dramatic reflection of the essential traits of the society in which it occurs. In the tradition of Orrin Klapp (1964), Wagner-Pacifici also argues on a macro-sociological level by recognizing the "phenomenological" place and moment in which dramatic events take place. Essentially, the political spectacle is constructed when socio-political reality confronts dynamic circumstance. It is at this point that the elements of theater necessarily become manifest as the emergent phenomenon interacts with the cultural reality and becomes reified political drama. Klapp argues that the "phenomenistic" circumstance becomes theatrical and symbolic at the point in the dialectic when dramatic confrontation occurs. As such, in the following dramaturgical analysis, this researcher assumes that politics generally and implicitly contain theatrical elements. Further in the view of post modernists, this researcher assumes more specifically that political theater is also consistently inherent in cultural dramatic confrontations. As a result, political drama necessarily produces emergent and phenomenistic theatrical elements that are significant to the eventual success of political leadership and to the definition of the type of theater taking place in the political culture.

While this paper does not attempt to specify a comprehensive paradigm for analyzing dramatic politics and symbolic leadership, it does seek to argue for the relevance in political science of utilizing "dramaturgical" characterizations in the study of political leadership. The paper also attempts to introduce briefly a tentative political concept, "media style," which could be used to define the way in which a political actor builds his image in the media for the purpose of projecting this image onto a mass audience. The "media style" concept could also be utilized to define any themes in the leader's message or actions that might be consistent with a particularly specific theory emanating from the classic literature of political science, which could be obvious in the leader's use of dramatic techniques. Further, the paper specifically attempts to illuminate and define, through a case study, the media strategies of one of television's first symbolic leaders and issue advocates, the Reverend Doctor Martin Luther King, Jr. As scholars broach the issues of significance about modern day symbolic leadership, I argue that it is the leader's media style—his interactions with the media to convey his message—that essentially shapes, molds, and casts the symbolic image of the individual leader onto the public mind.

Dramatic Politics on the Pluralistic American Political Stage

Increasingly, politicians attempt to create images of themselves to capture and hold public attention. These images are the more or less accurate reproduction of themselves. They are a collection of characteristics that each chooses to offer to public view.
—Roger-Gerard Schwartzenberg, *The Superstar Show of Government*

The years 1955 through 1968 in American political history represent a period of tumultuous unrest and dramatic confrontation in the public political domain. It was an era when various subcultures in America placed radical political ideas on the front of the political agenda, such as drugs, anti-war, free love morals, and civil rights. Particular to this analysis, it was an era when civil rights for blacks (as a priori unrecognized constitutional rights) were demanded. Essentially, it was an era when the nation's largest minority group erupted in a dramatic revolt against established institutions, laws, and practices in American political culture. It was a time when African Americans spoke out boldly for a change in the mores of the day. Slavery had placed them as subhuman in American sociological development and "Jim Crow," the western version of systematic apartheid, had placed them as inferior. A twelve-year drama resulted from the oppression inherent in these circumstances. The conflicts that resulted produced a political drama that clearly challenged the accepted framework of western liberal democratic pluralism.

In the pluralism polemic, Robert Dahl (1967) and Theodore Lowi (1969) disagree on the expediency to which interest groups can bring about changes in public policy. Essentially, they disagree on the effectiveness of the interaction and bargaining that goes on between established political groups and the policy-making process. So, the emergence and the effectiveness of protest groups in the 1960s (as a priori unestablished interest groups) indicated that there were certain dynamics of change that had been unaccounted for in the literature. Consequently, some social scientists began to focus on protest politics in an attempt to sort out the variables that played a vital role in social movements.[3] With a sensitizing impact, the civil rights movement made established political institutions become more responsive to those who were previously without a voice or without representation. As a result, several scholars, including Lipsky (1968), Gamson (1968), Lowi (1969), and Davidson (1972), challenged whether pluralism presents an accurate description of political interaction in America.[4]

These new issues about pluralism led these scholars to raise new questions about the role of race and protest in American politics. Then there were attempts to dissect the variables important to protest politics in a pluralistic culture and attempts to enumerate the factors that played a significant role. Michael Lipsky (1968), one of the scholars asking new questions, studied the issue and elaborated a model of protest politics that contained four key variables: the protestors, the opponents, the audience, and the media. Lipsky says, "Protest is correctly conceived as a strategy utilized by relatively powerless groups in order to increase their bargaining ability. As such, I have argued, it is successful to the extent that the reference publics of protest targets [the audience] can be activated to enter the conflict in ways favorable to protest goals" (1968: 1157).

It is this format, a "quadripartite model" of protest politics (the protestors, opponents, audience, and media) that provides a solid foundation for an examination of the theatrical techniques utilized by movement leaders and for analyzing the dramatic tactics used in the protest politics of the civil rights movement. Since it is up to the movement leaders or political leaders to shape and cast the drama, the images, the symbols, and the messages emanating from their cause onto the mass audience, an examination of their techniques as regarding any manipulation of images and techniques of impression management through the media becomes an important element in their ability to impact public opinion and becomes a crucial ingredient to understanding the factors behind their success or failure.

Even more important, Lipsky's model essentially places the notions of symbolic politics and leadership at the core of the interactions between the four parties involved in the conflict. Though these factors are implicit in the model, the importance of dramaturgical techniques as a function of the outcome of the conflict is evident. Lipsky's model does, however, clearly and explicitly establish the importance of both the audience as a factor in the outcome of the protest and the media as a mechanism for disseminating the message of the protest.

The importance of the audience in protest politics was noted as early as the 1920s. Not only did Walter Lippmann (1932), renowned for his writings on the significance of public opinion in public policy debates and decision making, comment on the role of the audience, but sociologist Clarence Case, in 1923, also noted the role of public opinion in the introduction to his work: "Disobedience without violence wins, if it wins, not so much by touching the conscience of the masters as by exciting the sympathy of disinterested onlookers. The spectacle of men suffering for a principle and not hitting back is a moving one. It obliges the power holders to condescend, to explain, to justify themselves. The weak get a change of venue from the will of the stronger to the court of public opinion, perhaps of world opinion."

Lipsky also discussed, in detail, the importance of the media to achieve the political objectives of protest groups. He said, "If protest tactics are not considered significant by the media, or if newspapers and television reporters or editors decide to overlook protest tactics, protest organizations will not succeed. Like the tree falling unheard in the forest, there is no protest unless protest is perceived and projected"(Lipsky, 1968: 1151). Likewise, Doris Graber says of the media, "The media often serve as attitude and behavior models. In the process of image creation, the media indicate which views and behaviors are acceptable and even praiseworthy in a given society and which are unacceptable or outside the mainstream"(1989: 3).

The discussion above establishes an important framework for the study of dramatic political conflict and the type of theatrical techniques that may be used by political leaders. Clearly, though theoretical, in addition to the combatants (the protagonist and the antagonist), the media and the audience are crucial factors in protest politics and political conflict. Therefore, the dramatic devices used by the political leader to influence the media and the observing public are also crucial elements in determining political outcome. Yet, with the exceptions of Murray Edelman and Richard Merelman, few political scientists have attempted to apply notions of the dramatic form to an understanding of politics. Merelman notes, "This fact does not mean that there are no analysts who implicitly and unconsciously recognize the relationship between politics and dramaturgy. On the contrary, the pervasiveness of unacknowledged dramatic interpretations of politics seems to demand the more systematic exploration"(Merelman, 1969: 219).

In order to conduct more systematic exploration into this case study, this researcher, therefore, explicitly acknowledges and attempts to justify the notion that in both theater and politics, all actors are concerned with "impression management." That is to say, "all drama [political, social, and theatrical] is concerned with the conveyance of impressions to a group of auditors" (Merelman, 1969: 217). Further, I argue that the notion of "impression management" is the fundamental objective of the "media style" of the political leader. Through his media style and strategy, the political actor attempts to influence media professionals and the observing public. Merelman, again, notes that "in addition to its other characteristics politics incorporates specific dramatic characteristics because politicians use dramatic devices"(216).

It is apparent that one of the reasons political actors may use dramaturgical techniques is because of the need, as Schnattschneider (1960) says, for "socialization of the conflict." In fact, this attempt to increase or socialize the audience's attention and intervention into the conflict is a key purpose for the leader's media style. Consequently, to achieve a mastery of impression management and socialization of the conflict, the leader seeks to interact with media professionals and to convey his message and the symbols of the drama in which he is involved.

Klapp (1964) discusses the roles of political actors as they assume a part on the stage of the pluralistic "dramatic domain." Klapp deals with issues related to the celebrity phenomenon of becoming a symbol. Of the possible roles that an actor can play, hero, villain, or fool, Klapp suggests ways to manage the image through the use of dramatic techniques. Among the issues he deals with are the dramatic encounter, image trouble, role reversals, and hero stuff. His work is aimed at providing a commentary on public dramas in a changing society and on the management of symbolically popular images. About the notion of the dramatic domain, Klapp says, "Certain persons have enormous effect, not because of achievement or vocation but because they stand for certain things; they play dramatic roles highly satisfying to their audiences; they are used psychologically and stir up followings." Perhaps most useful to this study is Klapp's explanation of the symbolic leader: "The symbolic leader is an emergent phenomenon, and that is why we so often do not know in advance—nor does he—what he will become. It is typical of a dialectic—an argument or other prolonged give-and-take in which interaction is creative—that neither party knows the outcome; it is a discovery for both" (1964: 32). Perhaps the most important point to be made in noting the applicability of these somewhat theoretical writings on drama and politics to political conflict is that few individuals, if any, have understood the dynamics and processes involved in dramatic politics better than Martin Luther King, Jr.

Thoreau Sets the Stage

Unbeknownst to him, in his unorthodox lifestyle, Henry David Thoreau provided the rational justification and method for twentieth-century protest politics. In his time, Thoreau displayed a willingness to step forward in opposition to the accepted modes of thought, policies, and actions of his contemporaries. He went into seclusion to ponder the great issues of the day and to rely on his own inner strength for his sustenance. His writings display an originality in radical thinking, wit, and power. His thought would be the basis for a generation of protest activity in America and in India as well: "Thoreau put into crisp and driving language what men of spirit instinctively feel wherever they confront a tyrannical State or social institutions that overpower the sense of personal independence.... He left in living language, so simple and so eloquent, the testament of a rebel against conventional restraints on personal freedom" (Baldwin, 1946: 34). In his essay "Civil Disobedience," Thoreau argued that man should not submit to an unjust government. He felt that every man had the individual responsibility to stand up for "right" but not necessarily the "law." He said,

> It is not desirable to cultivate a respect for the law, so much as for the right.... Unjust laws exist; shall we be content to obey them, or shall we endeavor to amend them, and obey them until we have succeeded or shall we transgress them at once?...if it [government] is of such a nature that it requires you to be the agent of injustice to another, then, I say, break the law...what I have to do is to see...that I do not lend myself to the wrong which I condemn. (Thoreau in Bode, 1947: 111, 119–20)

Saying that unjust laws exist in the civil society of American liberal democracy, Thoreau felt that civil disobedience offered a form of civil protest through nonviolent resistance. He advocated breaking the "law" to make a point for "right." Under a government that imprisons any unjustly, the true place for a just man is also a prison (Thoreau in Atkinson, 1937: 644).

Thoreau essentially elaborated the principles by which mass protest efforts could be mounted to affect public policy through civil disobedience. Having read *Bhagavad-Gita* and several of the sacred Hindu *Upanishads,* he was adamant about the moral force of noncooperation and resistance as a means to combat injustice. He was personally and particularly concerned about the issues of taxes, slavery, and war: "All men recognize the right of revolution; that is, the right to refuse allegiance to, and to resist, the government, when its tyranny or its inefficiency are great and unendurable"(Atkinson, 1937: 638).

Essentially it was Thoreau who laid the foundation for future protest activity both in India and the United States. Gandhi read Thoreau's "Civil Disobedience," was very impressed, and succeeded in changing British law in India. He converted Thoreau's theory into political reality and gave it practical application in the form of boycotts, strikes, and protest marches (Steger, 1993: 201). Martin Luther King was also impressed by Thoreau and embraced his theory of passive resistance to achieve legal rights and institutional respect for African Americans.

The Case of Martin Luther King, Jr.

Public relations is a very necessary part of any protest of civil disobedience. The main objective is to bring moral pressure to bear upon an unjust system or a particularly unjust law.

—Martin Luther King, Jr., October 31, 1961

Indeed, Martin Luther King, Jr., is one of the most dramatic political figures in modern American history. He seemed to innately understand the assumptions and principles of the "dramatic domain" and was able to successfully manipulate the media and his audience to reveal the horrors of the "Negro" experience in the modern south. King, unknowingly, employed many of the techniques recommended by Orrin Klapp (1964). King effectively engaged in impression management and was successful in socializing his conflict to the news media and to the American public. His symbolic leadership was indeed an emergent phenomenon.

Stephen Oates discusses King's introduction to Thoreau in 1944 as an undergraduate student at Morehouse College: "A class assignment in Thoreau's 'Civil Disobedience' offered a clue, introducing King to the idea of passive resistance.... He was infatuated with Thoreau's provocative argument that a creative minority—even a minority of 'one honest man'—could refuse to cooperate with an evil system and thereby set in motion a moral revolution" (Oates, 1989: 705–6).

King at that time was pondering how Negroes could combat discrimination in a country ruled by a white majority. He took away from Thoreau the lesson that by applying the idea of civil disobedience, a man is justified in rebellion without violence: "At this point for young King, the musing from Walden Pond could be only an academic stimulant. Later, combined with the teachings of other men, that stimulant would be a basis for social reform" (Smith, 1989: 829–30).

Indeed, many years later, on December 5, 1955, Martin Luther King, Jr., found himself standing in Montgomery, Alabama, as the new president of the newly organized Montgomery Improvement Association (MIA). The members of the group were angry about segregation on the city buses and about the arrest of Rosa Parks for refusing to give up her front seat in the bus and move to the back. They were about to figure out what to do. It was here, as historical retrospection can see, that King was alas in a position to apply the notions of civil disobedience. In a sense, he now had the challenge of giving form to Thoreau's content. He seemed to instinctively know that he should play to the press. But what he was to quickly learn was that his political positions would be readily captured by the news media and would be played often before a mass audience. A political drama protesting man's inhumanity to man and an argument for liberation were about to begin and to be cast on the stage of mid-twentieth-century American public policy debate. Having read Thoreau as one of his first intellectual challenges, Martin Luther King, Jr., had a solid philosophical foundation upon which to launch his efforts.

The key objective of this analysis is to present the "media style" (the dramatic rules and the roles) that King utilized to achieve effective political action. The idea of "rules" refers to the news manipulation techniques that King employed and the "roles" are the images King created for himself. The concepts of developing a "media style" involves employing the notion of "descriptive dramatics"—the presentation of the leader's arguments through verbal expressions—and the notion of "substantive symbolics"—the direct actions taken in the dramatic domain to promote the leader's agenda. In this case, the agenda was protesting and eradicating racial injustice in America.

The concepts of "descriptive dramatics" and "substantive symbolics" are important notions in an attempted dramaturgical characterization of the leader's efforts.[5] The methods of dissemination of information are also the primary tools of news manipulation. King's media style was forceful yet sensitive. His techniques were captured by the news writer's pen and portrayed in vivid pictures by television cameras. His primary channels for verbal expression were conduits that he could access fairly quickly as circumstances might dictate. These were the news conference and the formal speech.

King's Use of Descriptive Dramatics

The arguments of Martin Luther King, Jr., were disseminated to the public mind through an eclectic variety of channels utilizing both descriptive dramatics and substantive symbolics. Through these various methods, King spoke his mind about the issues of injustice, intolerance, and racism. Through these channels, he called on the larger society in vivid language and pictures to meet the challenges of the American democratic promise. His rhetorical messages, his sermonic style, and his peaceful protests appealed to the conscience of the nation and turned traditional policies into new, progressive laws. King was, indeed, conscious of the power of the media and of the time constraints of journalists. As such, he worked diligently to meet their needs as well as his own.[6]

The tactics and the strategies utilized by King and Southern Christian Leadership Conference (SCLC) were an attempt at "educational television," says King aide Andrew Young. He described King's awareness of the role of the media in the movement as "extremely conscious." According the Young, "He would always say we couldn't have a movement without television."[7]

My interviews with King's aides and colleagues reveal a consistent trend acknowledging King's ever-present awareness of his public image. While his strategy emerged over time, he had thoughtful, clear objectives in casting his argument before the public mind. He generally seemed to have a healthy relationship with the press and courted them even when he was criticized. King would regularly hold meetings with the editorial board of some of the major papers. He was aggressive internally at setting up public relations practices that served to disseminate the message of the movement. He attempted to appeal to the ideology of the journalists covering the story. His view was explained by Andrew Young. "Martin felt that you had to take the time to educate the press." The perspectives of King's colleagues indeed provide rich detail of movement activities. Young describes how King seemed to feel about all of the media attention he received:

> He was extremely sensitive to it. He used the analogy of a boil...that people are just not aware of injustice and it has to be brought to light. He said that one of the ways you heal injustice in society is by exposing it to the light of truth. So he saw the media as in many ways an ally.... He felt that he understood that his role as a black leader was helping to interpret the situation in America to the white majority. And he understood that the only way that he could do that was through the media.

Different from the strategies utilized by SNCC (the Student Nonviolent Coordinating Committee), King was pro-media, says Young: "One of the differences between SCLC and SNCC was that they were anti-press. They saw the press as somehow white and the enemies." King felt that educating the press was an important ingredient in his media efforts. Young elaborated,

> We were really trying to reach the American people. Martin used to say, for instance, that we had three minutes per night to say what we weregoing to say. That was roughly a minute on each network. So we even designed the demonstrations so that they would fit in the minute. For instance in those days in order to get on the six o'clock news the film had to be on the last plane out to New York which was usually around two o'clock. So demonstrations were always around 11 o'clock in the morning. And that was specifically designed and so were the press conferences and demonstrations. We were virtually through with everything we were going to do by noon because we wanted the reporters to have time to get the film on a plane and get it back to New York in time for the six o'clock news.

Essentially, Young says the point of the strategy was to expose the evils of racism: "Our strategy was to consistently demonstrate to the American public what segregation was all about. Our demonstrations were thought through with the idea of what is this going to say to the average American in Peoria."

By 1966, as he was nearing the end of his political career, King appeared to have dropped in popularity. He came out against the war on Vietnam and attempted more aggressive efforts toward conditions of poverty. Young says, "He agonized over that a long time. There were many of us who didn't think we were strong enough to fight three battles: simple racism in the south, poverty in the north, and he was taking on the war in Vietnam." Then after the 1964 Civil Rights Act and the 1965 Voting Rights Act, much of King's support from media editors and journalists and from northern liberals began to shift. His relationship with the press tended to turn adversarial.

> When that began to happen, the press began to not see the significance and the importance of continuation of the kind of coverage they had done previously, and as a result of that the relationship began to get more adversarial because Dr. King began to pick issues like the Vietnam war, which was unpopular and began to pick issues like poverty and raising the whole concern about the economic system, those issues put him in not the most favorable position and subsequently the relationship became more adversarial between he and the press.

King's successes by the time he reached Chicago (to protest against northern poverty and to speak out against the Vietnam War) had apparently satisfied the media that the initial mission had been fully accomplished. As such, he was not given the wide array of news coverage on these issues that he had received in the south in his battles against segregation. This result is very consistent with Lipsky's analysis, cited above, that, "If protest tactics are not considered significant by the media...protest organizations will not succeed. Like the tree falling unheard in the forest, there is no protest unless protest is perceived and projected" (Lipsky, 1968: 1151). By the time King entered Chicago and began to speak out against the Vietnam War, the news media essentially began to tune him out. His efforts to elaborate upon his message by adding an argument against economic injustice and arguing more forcefully for pacifism were at this point largely unsuccessful.

In addition to the news conference and the formal speech, King utilized several other channels of dissemination for conveying his descriptive dramatics to defend his cause. Included in these tactics are personal articles, news program appearances, news releases, news leaks, and books. These mechanisms not only represent the rules he used to cast his argument but also served to present the roles that he so adamantly defended.

Figure 1
King's Descriptive Dramatics

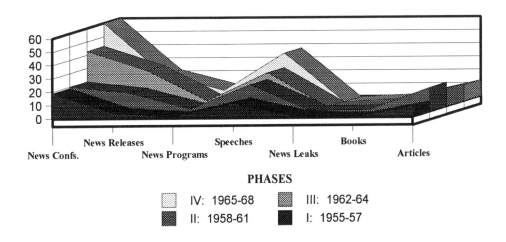

King's descriptive dramatics or the arguments of his thoughts were more skillfully presented as the movement progressed. Initially King relied more on the news conference (than he did on other methods) to expediently express his view and this trend largely continued throughout the entire spectrum of his leadership development. But the utilization of formal speeches also ran high in the emerging nature of King's leadership. In each phase of the eclectically divided four-phase era of his political leadership, there was also an increase in the number of news program appearances that King made.[8] In effect, King used the media successfully during most of his career as a political activist as a way of communicating the arguments of the movement. King's drama contained three key successful acts: Montgomery, Birmingham, and Selma. These stops by King created new legislation in American political development aimed at basic constitutional and civil rights for African American citizens.

King's Use of Substantive Symbolics

Essentially, the roles in which King presented himself comprised several main images of the developing political leader. The mass audience saw him as: the campaign leader, the political celebrity, the innocent protester, the political activist, or the diplomatic statesman. In each of these roles, King's image was one of either the "hero" or the "victim." During the third phase of his career, his image was bolstered by the national recognition he received as "Man of the Year" for 1963 by *Time* magazine and by being the recipient of the Nobel Peace Prize in 1964.[9] King was generally presented in the media as a credible, intelligent political activist who attempted to bring equity into the American democratic process through nonviolent means.

The civil rights movement, under King's leadership, used the premiering medium of television (and the national press) for the most dramatic appeal for social justice witnessed in American political culture. King had innate dramatic charisma. And he early on understood the notion that the management of impressions before an audience is a key component of political theater. He would also learn the importance of utilizing dramatic devices in capturing popular imagination. As the stirring voice and role of Martin Luther King, Jr., in American political culture increased, it was a voice and an image of the black male never before presented over the media. King was a minister, gifted with oratorical skills, eloquent in his argument, and committed to his cause. He spoke for the formerly voiceless. He successfully demonstrated that "people can effect change, especially when they have access to television" (Saldich, 1979: 57). He preached nonviolent resistance. He revealed the evils of racism. He unmasked the opponent. And he commanded a serious hearing of the issues. His evolving media style and eclectic use of dramaturgical techniques were successful in casting Negroes as the "victims" and their opponents in the role of the "villain." Roger-Gerard Schwartzenberg argues that for some leaders this trait is innate: "The real geniuses of practical politics, the charismatic leaders...seemed to know instinctively those principles of leadership which would capture popular imagination and enable an individual to rise from the most lowly estate to a position of world significance. This genius is clearly innate although not a few charismatic leaders have studied the techniques of their predecessors" (1980: foreword).

King and his colleagues did not of course always consciously script the details of their political conflicts. But in the efforts they did put forth, they created an image of a leader and an image of a democratic protest group being victimized by the injustices they abhorred. Their major successes in Montgomery in 1956, in Birmingham in 1963, and in Selma in 1965 contained appropriate levels of "impression management," and opinion change, and the efforts of King and his colleagues were rewarded.

King's public image or "substantive symbolics" developed through his media style of intermixed tactics. He utilized the direct action campaign as a means of visualizing and actualizing the issues of the struggle. He was portrayed as the "symbolic leader" of media events that he began to design to attract news coverage. He was portrayed as the nonviolent victim of racial intolerance through his arrests and convictions. He also presented symbolic images through experimental trial balloons. And he brought his celebrity image into direct interaction through personal patronage with renowned political leaders and the appropriate opinion makers.

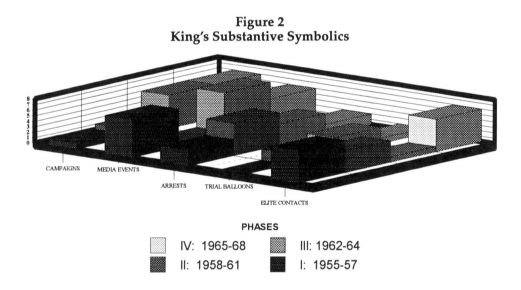

Figure 2
King's Substantive Symbolics

PHASES
IV: 1965-68   III: 1962-64
II: 1958-61   I: 1955-57

In the beginning phase of his activist career, King focused singularly on the problem of segregated buses in Montgomery. A bus boycott was organized and lasted for more than a year. Because of the intensity and success of his efforts, he began to receive national attention. In December 1956, the U.S. Supreme Court overturned Alabama state segregation laws and the movement had its first victory. The story made front page news in the *New York Times*. In the next phase of his career, King was busy building both his organization and his public image. His number of formal speaking engagements doubled, he was arrested a number of times, he issued more news releases, and he was readily available for impromptu news conferences. In this phase, he polished his media tactics and style.

In phase three of his career, however, King learned an important lesson about media attention. In Albany in 1962, despite the efforts of SCLC to protest segregation there, King and the movement received very little national media attention. Albany's chief of police, Laurie Pritchett, repeatedly made arrests of the protestors without incident. He then sought and won a federal court injunction barring local protest marches. King, initially uncertain about what to do, decided not to disobey the federal court order but complied instead. No news attention was garnered. SCLC leaders eventually left disappointed. And Albany remained segregated. Assessing this lesson, King moved on to Birmingham. King this time decided to rely on the notion of civil disobedience and decided to disobey a similar injunction prohibiting the protest marches and he went to jail. Pictures of the arrest were widely distributed in the news media. While there, the protesters were treated brutally as Chief of Police Bull Connor used water hoses and dogs attempting to deter the protestors. While incarcerated, as the protests continued, he penned his famous "Letter from a Birmingham Jail." Essentially, in Birmingham, King and the movement received a great deal of national attention and the pressure mounted on national officials. What King learned about civil disobedience was that it was effective for the purpose of impacting a larger political audience. The dramatic elements of the nonviolent resistors meeting violent opposition provided good substance for good political theater. Calling King "a Creative Extremist," Per Sveino writes, "Nonviolence as principle and method would have had small chances of success if it did not somehow or other appeal to the public, or perhaps better, sting their consciences. King not only counted on 'the conscience of the great decent majority,' but firmly believed that 'the oppressor, too, will be convinced and feel ashamed of his own barbarity'" (Sveino, 1989: 954). Motivated by the increasing interest in his efforts and refusing to give in and give up, King then organized the famous March on Washington. Shortly thereafter, the 1964 Civil Rights Act was passed. About the March on Washington, Miroff says, "It was the setting that initially supplied special drama to King's words: appearing before the Lincoln Memorial to an interracial throng of unprecedented size and to a national television audience, he found the kind of stage for his oratory ordinarily available only to presidents. It was also the passion of the occasion that led King to discard his planned peroration and to end his speech with extemporaneous fire" (Mitroff, 1989: 319).

In the final phase of his career, King again utilized the drama of protest to achieve what would become his last major impact on American public policy. In Selma, in 1965, protesters were again brutally treated, culminating in what came to be known as "Bloody Sunday." When protesters attempted to march across the Edmund Pettus Bridge, policemen on horses created vivid pictures of police violence as they attacked peaceful protesters. The violence again "stunned the nation and made federal voting rights legislation a political imperative.... President Johnson's superb speech introducing his voting-rights bill ensured the ultimate success of the drama" (Mitroff, 1989: 326). The 1965 Voting Rights Act was subsequently passed.

Thoreauvian Theater Impacting American Politics

"Theater," then, is an appropriate characterization for twentieth-century politics. Politics can often incorporate dramatic characteristics and principles of dramatic construction, which, in turn, play a significant role in public debate. Further, the increase in mass channels of communication expands the scope of possibilities for the "dramatic arrangement of political events."

Philosophically, King embraced Thoreau's position to respect the "right" over the "law" and projected the theory from an individual level into a mass protest movement and onto a mass audience of conscience. For Thoreau, it was the individual who must conform his ideology and act to protest social evils. Donald Smith said of Thoreau, "He was not especially interested in proselytizing but instead he sought to free himself from the guilt of acquiescence to evil" (1989: 829). King, on the other hand, through the principles of civil disobedience, transformed an individual application of nonviolent resistance into a broader national application. Through the use of this theory, King learned that it was a moral obligation to not cooperate with injustice, and to break manmade rules if need be. Said Thoreau: "Civil disobedience is not passive. Its immediate end is to clog the machinery of the State; it is counter-friction. Its ultimate end however, is to undermine expediency by introducing a standard higher than social right and authority—the moral law. Where the moral law becomes the fulcrum even the individual lever is an instrument of incalculable force" (Paul, 1960: 233).

Essentially, in phase one, King's image was automatically cast as a "symbolic leader" in the dramatic domain of twentieth-century American politics. In this phase, King focused singularly on the problem of segregated buses in Montgomery and he began to receive national attention. In December 1956, the U.S. Supreme Court overturned Alabama state segregation laws. After this victory, in phase two, King worked to build his organization while at the same time he worked to solidify his image in the national press and attempted to find new channels for his voice. In phase three, his message in Albany seemed to have lost its battle and its audience. After assessing the lesson, he went on to Birmingham to expose "the evil of racism," as pictures and stories of his arrest and of the racist actions of Bull Connor's water hoses and dogs were broadcast worldwide. In Washington, King conducted a national protest march against segregation and staged a scene of civil, nonviolent protesters gathering in large numbers. Here he rendered his infamous "I have a Dream" speech. This effort helped to push the lobby for civil rights legislation to victory. The 1964 Civil Rights Act was subsequently passed. As such, King was cited as both *Time* magazine's "Man of the Year" and a Nobel Peace Laureate. Essentially, in phase three, he took a geographical defeat in Albany and turned it into an American lesson on civil disobedience and civil rights. In phase four, in Selma, the "Bloody Sunday" March also rendered vivid pictures of police violence against peaceful protesters on the Edmund Pettus Bridge. In Selma, King essentially "unmasked the opponent" and cast him as the "villain" in the dramatic domain of American culture and cast the Negro race as the "victim" of Southern injustice. The 1965 Voting Rights Act was soon passed.

King struggled to expand the breadth of his movement into the urban North but was overshadowed in his efforts by the big city machine politics of Chicago and by lack of media coverage for the cause. Still determined, he returned to Memphis to expand upon the argument against economic injustice and unfair wages. While there, he was assassinated. It was perhaps his death that cast the most enduring image of all of the legacies he left behind. Upon his death he was cast as a martyr for the cause of political justice. He was further catapulted into the annals of American political development as a major player on the stage of political history. He was cast as a symbolic leader, a martyr, and as an "American hero."

Essentially then, Martin Luther King, Jr., led dramatic revolts of civilly disobedient political unrest. His voice burst onto the public scene, at the young age of 26, in December 1955. Through the use of his media style—dramaturgical techniques for impression management—he learned valuable lessons about the role of mass media in contemporary political culture. His image either as "hero" or "victim" was skillfully managed over the long run.

The outcome of political drama, then, is contingent on the successful interaction between the message and the audience and on highly controlled forms of media communication. Richard Merelman says about the dramaturgy of politics: "[T]he growth of mass communications expands the scope for dramatic techniques in politics...the mass media provide the politician with greatly expanded opportunities for the dramatic arrangement of political events. The desire of the mass media to hold their audiences also exaggerates the importance of dramaturgy in politics" (1969: 220–21).

Political conflict before large audiences requires impression management. Because this is so, an element of theater and drama is ever present for the political leader. Merelman says of King that he was but "twenty-six when he found his public voice, thirty-nine when he died, he was, in reality, very young to be so prominent" (1969: 317).

Fundamentally, King applied Thoreau's ideas and was able to cast a drama of civil protest into the mainstream political debate of the day. His message was strong and demanding. His cause was a fight for justice. He developed an image of civil disobedience that captured the public's attention and one that also held their interest. King's name essentially became a label and was synonymous with the civil rights movement. Though King had a great deal of help from his staff in planning his strategies, it was his name that became a trademark for the movement. King became, in Thoreau's words, the "one honest man" who stood for the "right" over the "law." And for American politics, his efforts made a difference. The drama of nonviolent resistance as advocated and implemented by King demonstrated significant consistency with the writings of the nineteenth-century American political thought of Walden's solitary Henry David Thoreau.

The protest activities of the civil rights movement presented, in theatrical and symbolic manifestations, the principles of Thoreau's ideas. The movement went as Thoreau did—deviating from the standards of American sociological norms and using, in principle, civil disobedience as a form of protest and nonviolent resistance. The civil rights era, utilizing Thoreauvian tactics, verified the dramaturgy of politics. The dramatic domain of this era therefore can be appropriately classified as "Thoreauvian Theater" on the stage of American political history. So for the annals of American political history, King's effort in the civil rights era 100 years after Thoreau's argument was an expression of Thoreau's ideas. After all, they were withdrawing their cooperation from an evil system. This is, in fact, what Thoreau had summoned moral men to do.

Conclusion

Essentially, King and the civil rights movement made a Thoreauvian argument about political injustice and about the effects of racial bigotry. King, the lead spokesman, in Thoreauvian terms, was the "one honest man" needed to stand up for right. Thus, the image was cast and the drama was performed. Martin Luther King, Jr., was able to display in pictures and images what Henry David Thoreau thought civil disobedience should be.

Summarily, then, it is a necessary condition in understanding the scope of the dramatic domain to acknowledge the role of media in determining the success or failure of a political cause. Image manipulation and impression management make political theater a significant variable for contemporary political leadership in a high tech media environment. These characteristics of political drama make dramaturgical analysis an important concern in the study of political leadership both for descriptive and prescriptive purposes and for both political scientists and other social scientists as well. Further study is needed. Dramatic metaphoric construction before the media increased King's level of success. Dramatic metaphoric construction in the media will continue to increase or destroy the image and cause of political leaders in the future for a long time to come.

Notes

1. Dramatist Art Borreca (1993: 57) presents a history of the development of the dramatist perspective and argues that scholars have often been confined to their own respective fields. Some of the leading works include Duncan (1968); Turner (1974); Geertz (1981); Klapp (1964); Edelman (1977); Boorstin (1987); McLuhan (1965); Postman (1986); Williams (1989); Chomsky (1988).
2. For some examples of the work done by political scientists, see Cohen (1963); Lipsky (1968); Merelman (1969); Schwartzenberg (1980); Edelman (1971, 1977, 1988); Kernell (1986); Iyengar and Kinder (1987); Graber (1989); Nimmo and Combs (1990); Greenstein (1992).
3. Several scholars have attempted to sort out the impact of protest politics. See in particular Huntington (1974); Parenti (1970); Easton (1969).
4. David Garrow (1978) elaborates on this notion of pluralism in American protest politics. This section will attempt to integrate his discussion on the development of the literature on the pluralism polemic into the relevance of the symbolic media style notion.
5. These are my terms for operationalizing the variables inherent in the media style concept.
6. In my interview with Andrew Young, Young talks about their efforts to accommodate the press to make sure journalists would be able to meet their technical deadlines on time. This effort was important to movement leaders so that they could facilitate the delivery of the news they wanted to have disseminated.
7. These comments and the other comments from Young in this section were extracted from my interview with Andrew Young, June 29, 1994.
8. Phases were divided into a random chronological sequence—phase one: 1955–57; phase two: 1958–61; phase three: 1962–64; phase four: 1965–68.

9. See *Time Magazine*, "Martin Luther King, Jr.: Man of the Year," January 3, 1964, cover story, pp. 14–27, and James Feron, "Dr. King Accepts Nobel Peace Prize as 'Trustee,'" *New York Times*, December 11, 1964, pp. 1, 9.

References

Atkinson, Brook, ed. 1937. *Walden and Other Writings of Henry David Thoreau*. New York: The Modern Library.
Baldwin, Roger N. 1946. "Thoreau the Libertarian." *Thoreau: The Cosmic Yankee*, ed. Frederick W. Roman. Los Angeles: The Roman Forum.
Bode, Carl, ed. 1947. *The Portable Thoreau*. New York: Viking Press.
Boorstin, Daniel. 1987. *The Image: A Guide to Pseudo-Events in America*. New York: Atheneum.
Borreca, Art. 1993. "Political Dramaturgy: A Dramaturg's (Re) View." *The Drama Review*, 37, 2 (Summer).
Branch, Taylor. 1988. *Parting the Waters: America in the King Years 1954–1963*. New York: Simon and Schuster.
Burke, Kenneth. 1968. "Dramatism." In *International Encyclopedia of Social Sciences*, vol. 7, ed. David Sills, 445–51. New York: Macmillan.
———. 1972. *Dramatism and Development*. Barre, MA: Clark University Press.
Carlyle, Thomas. 1840 (1907). *On Heroes, Hero-Worship, and the Heroic in History*. Boston: Houghton Mifflin.
Case, Clarence. 1923. *Nonviolent Coercion: A Study in Methods of Social Pressure*. New York: Century Co.
Chomsky, Noam. 1988. *Manufacturing Consent*. New York: Pantheon Books.
Cohen, Bernard. 1963. *The Press and Foreign Policy*. Princeton, NJ: Princeton University Press.
Dahl, Robert. 1967. *Pluralist Democracy in the United States: Conflict and Consent*. Chicago: Rand McNally.
Davidson, Chandler. 1972. *Biracial Politics*. Baton Rouge: Louisiana State University Press.
Duncan, Hug. 1968. *Symbols in Society*. New York: Oxford University Press.
Easton, David. 1969. "The New Revolution in Political Science." *American Political Science Review*, 63 (December): 1051–61.
Eckstein, Harry. 1975. "Case Study and Theory in Political Science." In *Handbook of Political Science*, vol. 7, ed. Fred Greenstein and Nelson Polsby. Reading, MA: Addison-Wesley.
Edelman, Murray. 1960. "Symbols and Political Quiescence." *The American Political Science Review*, 54: 695–704.
———. 1964. *The Symbolic Uses of Politics*. Chicago: University of Illinois Press.
———. 1971. *Politics as Symbolic Action*. New York: Academic Press.
———. 1977. *Political Language: Words That Succeed and Policies That Fail*. New York: Academic Press.
———. 1988. *Constructing the Political Spectacle*. Chicago: University of Chicago Press.
Evreinov, Nikolai. 1927. *The Theatre in Life*. New York: Benjamin Blom.
Gamson, William. 1968. "Stable Unrepresentation in America Society." *American Behavioral Scientist*, 12 (November-December): 15–21.
Garrow, David. 1978. *Protest at Selma: Martin Luther King, Jr. and the Voting Rights Act of 1965*. New Haven: Yale University Press.
———. 1986. *Bearing the Cross: Martin Luther King, Jr. and the Southern Christian Leadership Conference*. New York: Random House.
———. 1989. "The Intellectual Development of Martin Luther King, Jr.: Influences

and Commentaries." *Martin Luther King, Jr.: Civil Rights Leader, Theologian, Orator*, ed. David Garrow. Brooklyn, NY: Carlson Publishing, Inc.

Geertz, Clifford. 1981. *Negara: The Theater State in Nineteenth Century Bali.* Princeton, NJ: Princeton University Press.

Goffman, Erving. 1959. *The Presentation of Self in Everyday Life.* New York: Doubleday.

Graber, Doris. 1989. *Mass Media and American Politics*, 3d ed. Washington, DC: CQ Press.

Greenstein, Fred I. 1992. "Can Personality and Politics Be Studied Systematically?" *Political Psychology*, 13, 1: 105–28.

Huntington, Samuel. 1974. "Paradigms of American Politics: Beyond the One, the Two, and the Many." *Political Science Quarterly*, 89 (March): 1–26.

Shante Iyengar and Donald R. Kinder. 1987. *News That Matters: TV and American Opinion.* Chicago: University of Chicago Press.

Kernell, Samuel. 1986. *Going Public: New Strategies of Presidential Leadership.* Washington, DC: CQ Press.

Kielbowicz, Richard, and Scherer, Clifford. 1986. "The Role of the Press in the Dynamics of Social Movements." In *Research in Social Movements, Conflicts and Change*, vol. 9, ed. Louis Kriesberg, 71–96. Greenwich, CT: Jai Press.

King, Martin Luther, Jr. 1956. *Liberation Magazine*, April, King Papers, Martin Luther King, Jr., Center for Nonviolent Social Change, Archives, Atlanta, Georgia.

Klapp, Orrin. 1964. *Symbolic Leaders: Public Dramas and Public Men.* New York: Funk & Wagnalls.

Klapper, Joseph. 1984. "The Effectiveness of Mass Communication." *Media Power in Politics.* Washington, DC: CQ Press.

Lentz, Richard. 1990. *Symbols, The News Magazines, and Martin Luther King.* Baton Rouge: Louisiana State University.

Lippmann, Walter. 1932. *Public Opinion.* London: Allen & Unwin.

Lipsky, Michael. "Protest as a Political Resource." *American Political Science Review*, 62 (December 1968).

Lowi, Theodore. 1969. *The End of Liberalism.* New York: W.W. Norton.

McCombs, Maxwell, and Donald Shaw. 1972. "The Agenda-Setting Function of the Mass Media." *Public Opinion Quarterly*, 36: 176–87.

McLuhan, Marshall. 1965. *Understanding the Media: The Extensions of Man.* New York: McGraw Hill.

Merelman, Richard M. 1969. "The Dramaturgy of Politics." *Sociological Quarterly*, 10: 216–41.

Mickelson, Sig. 1989. *From Whistle Stop to Sound Bite: Four Decades of Politics and Television.* New York: Praeger.

Mitroff, Ian. 1989. *The Unreality Industry.* New York: Carol Publishing Group.

Nimmo, Dan, and Combs, James E. 1990. *Mediated Political Realities*, 2d ed. White Plains, NY: Longman Publishers.

Oates, Stephen. 1982. *Let the Trumpet Sound: The Life of Martin Luther King, Jr.* New York: Harper and Row.

———. 1989. "The Intellectual Odyssey of Martin Luther King." *Martin Luther King, Jr. and the Civil Rights Movement*, ed. David Garrow. Brooklyn, NY: Carlson Publishing, Inc.

Olien, Carice, Phillip Tichenor, and George Donohue. 1989. "Media Coverage and Social Movements." In *Information Campaigns: Balancing Social Values and Social Change*, ed. Charles Salmon, 139–63. Newbury Park: Sage Publications.

Parenti, Michael. 1970. "Power and Pluralism: A View from the Bottom." *Journal of Politics*, 32 (August): 501–30.

Paul, Sherman. 1960. *Walden and Civil Disobedience.* Boston: Houghton Mifflin Co.

Plato. 1955 (1986). *The Republic.* New York: Viking Penguin Inc.

Postman, Neil. 1986. *Amusing Ourselves to Death: Public Discourse in the Age of Show Business*. New York: Penguin Books.
Saldich, Anne Rawley. 1979. *Electronic Democracy: Television's Impact on the American Political Process*. New York: Praeger Publishers.
Schnattschneider, E. E. 1960. *The Semisovereign People*. New York: Holt, Rinehart & Winston.
Schwartzenberg, Roger-Gerard. 1980. *The Superstar Show of Government*, trans. Joseph A. Harriss. Woodbury, NY: Barron's Educational Series, Inc.
Smith, Donald. 1989. "An Exegesis of Martin Luther King, Jr.'s Social Philosophy." In *Martin Luther King, Jr., and the Civil Rights Movement*, ed. David Garrow. Brooklyn, NY: Carlson Publishing, Inc.
Steger, Manfred. 1993. "Mahatma Gandhi and the Anarchist Legacy of Henry David Thoreau." *Southern Humanities Review*, 27, 3: 201.
Sveino, Per. 1989. "Martin Luther King: A Creative Extremist." In *Martin Luther King, Jr. and the Civil Rights Movement*, ed. David Garrow. Brooklyn, NY: Carlson Publishing, Inc.
Turner, Victor. 1974. *Dramas Fields, and Metaphors: Symbolic Action in Human Society*. Ithaca, NY: Cornell University Press.
Wagner-Pacific, Robin E. 1986. *The Moro Morality Play: Terrorism as Social Drama*. Chicago: University of Chicago Press.
Williams, Raymond. 1989. "Drama in a Dramatised Society." In *Raymond Williams on Television*, ed. Alan O'Connor, 3–13. London and New York: Routledge.
Young, Andrew. 1971. "And Birmingham." *Drum Major*, 1 (Winter): 21–27.
———. 1994. Personal interview. June 29.

The Recruitment of Blacks to State Courts of Last Resort

Nicholas O. Alozie

Arizona State University

Because of the extensive litigation associated with the civil rights movement, along with other well-documented efforts to attain fully the promise of U.S. citizenship (National Research Council, 1989), American courts are more readily conceived of as institutions that blacks "employ" in a process, as opposed to being participating members. The practical reality, and the common perception, is that the relationship between blacks and the judicial system is changing, particularly at the policy-making levels. Since the beginning of the 1980s, the role of blacks in the judicial system has increased as more and more black jurists have become visible members of the judiciary at all levels. Presently, this changing role has become more salient than ever before (Graham, 1990a).

As part of their broader interest in the role of blacks in the country's highest policy-making institutions, analysts are beginning to show interest in the racial composition of the judiciary. The academic interest that ensued in the 1980s has spawned research exploring the factors associated with black access to the judiciary (Graham, 1990a, 1990b; Alozie, 1988, 1990; Fund for Modern Courts, 1985; DuBois, 1983; Goldman, 1979; Crockett, 1975). Not surprisingly, none of this research focuses on state courts of last resort. This is easily explained by the fact that the service of blacks in these institutions is a recent phenomenon. Emmert and Glick (1988: 464) found only two black jurists on state supreme courts during 1980–81. Graham (1990a) uncovered eleven in 1986. The 1993 survey upon which the present study is based revealed twenty. Thus, there are sufficient data points to begin exploring the factors that influence the racial composition of the highest courts in the states. While black service on state courts of last resort has symbolic appeal for black citizenship, the potential that the presence of black justices could sensitize these institutions to racial issues and inspire policies that are more responsive to the needs of the black community is particularly noteworthy.

The purpose of this study is twofold. First, the study explores the patterns of black representation on state courts of last resort (including region-by-region comparisons). Second, it probes the efficacy of several explanations for those patterns, including: judicial selection systems; eligible pool (Alozie, 1988, 1990; Cook, 1972); size of collegial body (Segal, 1983; Taebel, 1978); incumbency and the window of opportunity (Welch and Karnig, 1979); minority political power (Crockett, 1975); intergroup competition (Alozie, 1990; Welch and Karnig, 1979); and regionalism (Bullock and MacManus, 1991; Graham, 1990a, 1990b; Cook, 1972).

Black Service on State Judiciaries

The 1980s was a decade of profound debate and litigation over minority recruitment and participation on state judiciaries across the United States.[1] As Graham (1990a) predicted, that appraisal has persisted into the 1990s. At issue is how committed states are to a diverse judiciary where racial and ethnic minorities participate in molding judicial processes and outcomes. The data since the mid-1980s provide evidence that blacks continue to gain greater access to state judiciaries, although they are underrepresented with respect to their composition in the population and serve primarily on state courts of limited jurisdiction (Graham, 1990a: 30).[2] In short, the very institution which blacks relied upon in their crusade for civil rights have themselves come under public scrutiny.

At the center of the question of whether blacks and other minorities serve on the judiciary is the debate over the potential effects of judicial selection systems on court diversity. Broadly conceived, judicial selection systems employ two primary decision mechanisms—appointment or election. At its core, the debate over selection systems and minority (and indeed women's) service on the judiciary revolves around the relative efficacy of the appointive and elective mechanisms in recruiting members of these groups to the bench. Both the structural and interactive dynamics of the elements of appointment and election factor into the debate.

At present, there are five major formal judicial selection systems employed across the nation: (1) executive appointment; (2) commission or "merit" selection; (3) legislative election; (4) nonpartisan election; and (5) partisan election (Berkson et al., 1980). Regardless of their niceties, these selection systems are rooted in some form of appointment or election. While the recruitment of minorities and women has become a central issue, these selection systems actually evolved amid broader and long-standing concerns that the selection system may recruit judges of varying backgrounds and qualifications (Emmert and Glick, 1988; Glick and Emmert, 1986), as well as impact the balance between judicial independence and political accountability (DuBois, 1980). Despite the high anxiety (and popular sentiment) directed toward these selection systems, research findings on the relevance of formal selection system to black recruitment to the judiciary appear nebulous (Graham, 1990b; Alozie, 1988, 1990; Fund for Modern Courts, 1985).

Crockett (1975) asserted that black under-representation on the judiciary could only be remedied through partisan election of judges. Crockett's position is predicated upon the assumption that the increasing electoral strength of blacks would guarantee the election of more black judges in areas where blacks have a substantial voting bloc. To the contrary, Graham (1990b) established that "judicial elections have been a less successful way of increasing black representation on the state bench" (333), but cautioned that informal selection mechanisms in elective jurisdictions (e.g., interim appointment, often by the governor to fill vacancy between elections) may benefit blacks.

Given that judicial nominating commissions are dominated by white males (Dunn, 1981), not directly accountable to the electorate, some advocates suggest that these commissions may not be sensitive enough to the need for diversity. Accordingly, it has been suspected that minorities might not fare as well in merit selection courts, where commissions are an integral part of the selection process. For sure, diversity on judicial selection commissions itself is a worthy goal, although neither Graham (1990b) nor Alozie (1988, 1990) confirmed the suspicion that women and minorities will do less well with merit systems. Women and minorities appear to do equally poorly across selection systems.

Finally, some analysts suggest that executive appointment permits minorities greater access to the judiciary (Fund for Modern Courts, 1985). In part, it is reasoned that chief executives may be sensitive to the need for diversity and will more likely, as part of states' diversification efforts, appoint members of these groups to the judiciary. However, Alozie (1988, 1990) did not find significant selection-based differentials in the recruitment of black judges.

Thus, while the popular sentiment is to believe that formal selection systems are consequential to minority recruitment to the judiciary, research is yet to embrace that leaning. A significant dimension was added to this literature by Graham (1990b). In her survey, Graham discovered that informal recruitment mechanisms may well prove more consequential than formal mechanisms in recruiting minority judges. In particular, she discovered that interim appointment (often to fill vacancies pending election) is a common route through which minorities reach the bench initially in elective jurisdictions. Of course, once such an appointment is extended, the candidate attains incumbency status along with its attendant name recognition and other political resources (e.g., Fletcher, 1996). Indeed, a descriptive survey of the data gathered for the present study revealed that an overwhelming number of black justices in elective jurisdictions in the South reached states' courts of last resort initially through interim appointment.

Another dimension of the question of selection system and minority representation pertains to structural arrangements (at-large or district). This aspect of the selection debate has reached the courts. Minorities and their supporters (as plaintiffs) contend that, just as court rulings under section 2 of the Voting Rights Act of 1965 eliminated structural impediments to voting (particularly those imposed by at-large balloting) in legislative races, resulting in increased numbers of black elected legislators (Graham, 1990b: 333), so too should the removal of such structural impediments from judicial races enhance the success rate of minority candidates. In their rebuttal (as defendants), attorneys for the states maintain that judges cannot be seen as "representatives" as defined under the Voting Rights Act of 1965.

In 1991, the U.S. Supreme Court rejected the state argument, ruling instead that the provisions of section 2 of the Voting Rights Act of 1965 are applicable to judicial elections (U.S. Supreme Court, 1991). The Court's ruling aside, it is still premature to design a multivariate study that can assess the effects of structural arrangements in judicial elections. This is precisely because, although there are judicial districts at present, they are not drawn as vote-dilution-conscious remedies with respect to the justice department's *Totality of the Circumstances Test* (Bullock and MacManus, 1993). To the extent data allow, this study will shed some light on structural features and black representation on state courts of last resort. Beyond the debate over selection systems, analysts have been preoccupied with several other theoretical propositions.

Eligible Pool

Group under-representation in the eligible candidate pool for public office may influence the recruitment of minorities to office (Welch, 1978: 372; Cook, 1972). Age aside, almost anybody meeting the residency qualification can serve on a city council, state legislature, or Congress. Service on the judiciary is different insofar as it requires specialized training. Judges are usually chosen from the lawyer pool. MacManus (1992) illustrates the importance of the eligible pool when an office requires specialized training. Moreover, lawyers and their law firms constitute the first frontier of political resources for judicial candidates (Champagne, 1986). Where there are more black lawyers, one can anticipate both more effective networking and a viable black bar association (Segal, 1983). In judicial election states, lawyers and their law firms donate generously to judicial campaigns (DuBois, 1986; Nicholson and Weiss, 1986; Champagne, 1990). Minority lawyers also have been instrumental in initiating and litigating judicial vote dilution cases across the country. Minority lawyers may make an impression on commissions or any elected official making an appointment decision. Finally, lawyers also vote, and this is vital given the often abysmal voter response to judicial races (Champagne, 1986).

The relevance of black lawyers as a predictor of black service on the judiciary has been tested empirically (Alozie, 1988, 1990; Graham, 1990b; Cook, 1972; see also American Judicature Society, 1973; Shuman, 1971). The results affirm that the black lawyer pool is germane. However, the case of state courts of last resort presents a completely different set of considerations with respect to the eligible pool thesis. Justices typically come from the judge pool on the lower courts, not lawyers per se. Thus, black judges on lower courts constitute a more immediate eligible pool from which black justices are chosen. Accordingly, data have been gathered on black service on each state's judiciary.

Size of Collegial Body

The size of a collegial body might be relevant to minority service on that body (Taebel, 1978), particularly as it relates to whether or not minorities get an opportunity to serve at all, as opposed to their degree of representation (Alozie and Manganaro, 1993b). Welch and Karnig hypothesized that the greater the number of seats on a city council, the less prestigious and less attractive council membership. Assuming white males will show less desire for such offices, members of out-groups should acquire more seats. Service on a state court of last resort is a prestigious undertaking, court size notwithstanding. Indeed, except for the U.S. Supreme Court, membership on a state court of last resort is the pinnacle of the legal profession in each state. Thus, each seat is highly coveted and competition is stiff.

There are two interrelated reasons why one may expect blacks to fare better across larger courts. First, Taeble (1978) suggested that if there are more slices in the pie (court seats) the dominant majority may be more inclined to share. Second, competition is a relative phenomenon. All other things equal, the level of competition for seats on a court may well be a function of the number of positions to be competed for by qualified jurists. Either way, more seats may mean more opportunities for blacks to get to the court.

Incumbency and Window of Opportunity

Prior research assessing the potential impact of the length of term of a collegial body for women and minority service on that body has hypothesized that the longer the term, the more prestigious/desirable the office, the less likely women and minorities are to hold that office (Welch and Karnig, 1979; MacManus and Bullock, 1989). The peculiar case of state courts of last resort occasions a variant perspective on the potential negative effect of length of term. Relative to other offices, justices serve unusually long terms—indeed, life tenure is not unusual. The question is how previously excluded groups gain access if a window of opportunity is not created often enough. These groups may rely solely on vacancies generated by the infrequent cases of retirement, death, or impeachment and removal to enter the court. Of course, it is equally possible that shorter terms could escalate the vulnerability of current minority justices, precipitating service instability. Thus, the potential impact of term of office is not apparent.

Women and Minority Competition

Competition by women could impact black recruitment to public office. Sigelman (1976) suggested something of a zero-sum outcome between the employment prospects of women and minorities. Subsequent examinations of the hypothesis have been undertaken elsewhere also (see Welch and Karnig, 1979; Alozie, 1990; Alozie and Manganaro, 1993a, 1993b). At best, however, the hypothesis is very weakly supported by the extant literature.

Regionalism (Race Progressiveness Gap)

The idea that the South is more inhibitive of black political aspirations is a long-standing precept in black political studies. Although recent research indicates that the deleterious effect of southern location is dissipating (Welch, 1990), researchers still approach the perennial issue of the relevance of race in southern politics with considerable caution. For instance, a significant proportion of judicial vote dilution litigation is in the South.[3] This study explores the race progressiveness gap thesis, which hypothesizes that blacks will do less well in the South.

Data and Methodology

This study uses states as its units of analysis. Rather than 50 observations, however, there are 52. Oklahoma and Texas have both a Supreme Court and a Court of Criminal Appeals that are courts of last resort (Council of State Governments, 1992: 227). A decision was made not to combine both courts into one observation. The courts vary in their structure and functioning (e.g., size, presiding officer, finance) and should be treated as separate entities.

Data are drawn from several sources. The first are both written and telephone surveys of clerks of the court conducted in December 1993. Each clerk was asked to provide information on the number of justices, current racial, ethnic, and gender composition, and selection method(s) for the court. In elective jurisdictions, additional information on how each justice reached the court initially—for example, interim appointment—was solicited. Unlike judicial selection for lower courts, the selection of justices of courts of last resort is straightforward. Except in two states (Illinois and New Mexico) where two systems intersect at the retention level, selection systems are unidimensional.

In Illinois, justices acquire their seats initially on partisan ballot; retention is determined in uncontested elections. In New Mexico, justices begin with a merit selection plan; retention is determined in partisan, contested elections. Because of the significance of the incumbency effect in judicial elections (Champagne, 1986), justices in these two states are identified with the formal selection method that brought them to the bench initially. Information on length of term is reported in the 1992–1993 edition of the *Book of the States*. Data on black lower judgeships for each state were drawn from the *Equal Employment Opportunity Special File* of the 1990 Census.

The descriptive portion of the study examines two attributes of black representation on state courts of last resort. One is a measure of the percentage of court seats held by blacks. The other is a measure of whether blacks have court presence at all. It is scored 1 if a black justice serves on the court, and 0 otherwise. The merits of this dependent variable derive from both the realistic incidence of minority service on high level political office and the often limited results of affirmative action (Cook, 1978). Because of the current distributional patterns of black justices across state courts of last resort (largely one black justice per court where blacks served), the multivariate analysis examines only this binary measure as dependent variable. Thus, the multivariate analysis seeks to predict the presence or absence of a black justice on a court given the court's state characteristics as follows:

$$P(I = 1) = f(X) \quad (1)$$

where the dichotomous dummy dependent variable is the likelihood that a black justice serves on the court (I = 1 if a justice is present, 0 otherwise) and vector X defines court and state characteristics.

Each selection method is defined as a dummy variable, while black lower judgeships is measured as a percentage of the total in the state. Size of court is represented as the actual number of seats on the court. Length of term is coded 1 for courts providing terms in excess of six years, 0 if less. Women and black competition is measured by specifying the service levels of women on the court. If there is a zero-sum outcome, black court presence will covary negatively with the degree of women's representation. Region is measured by dummies for the Midwest, Northeast, South, and West. In the multivariate analysis, estimation is performed comparing the South (11 states of the Confederacy) to the non-South.

Findings

The Incidence of Black Service

There were 343 justiceship positions on state courts of last resort at the end of 1993. Blacks held 20 (6 percent). This frequency evidences growth when compared to the two blacks found on these courts in 1980–81 (Emmert and Glick, 1988), and to the 11 in 1990 (Graham, 1990a). Of the 52 courts, blacks had presence on 19 (37 percent). Except in Georgia where 2 black jurists served (1 male, 1 female), blacks held only 1 seat wherever they served. Overall, 2 black female justices were found (the other in Louisiana). Of the 52 Chief Justice/Presiding Officer positions on these courts, blacks (male) occupied one, in Pennsylvania.

The second part of Table 1 presents a region-by-region account of black service. The data reveal the highest degree (percentage) of black service in the South (mean = 9.6 percent). Moreover, black justices are also more likely to be found within southern courts. Because of the special interest the 11 states of the Confederacy retain in black politics, the courts in these states have been set aside for further exploration (final part of Table 1). The black service measures (percentage black on the court—12.0 percent—and courts with black presence—83.0 percent) indicate relatively more blacks on these courts than the norm nationally, or in any other region. Indeed, while a different kind of conclusion may be reached about representation once the distribution of the black population is accounted for, the numbers reported here

Table 1
Summary Statistics on Black Representation

		Census Regions				
Variable	All States (N = 52)	Midwest[a] (N = 12)	Northeast[b] (N = 11)	South[c] (N = 16)	West[d] (N = 13)	States of the Confederacy[e] (N = 12)
Total seats	343	80	69	115	79	89
Black justices	20(5.8)	3(3.8)	4(5.8)	11(9.6)	2(2.5)	11(12.0)
Black on court? (yes = 1)	19(37.0)	3(25.0)	4(36.4)	10(62.5)	2(15.4)	10(83.0)

Note: Numbers in parentheses are percentages.
[a]IL, IN, IA, KS, MI, MN, MO, NE, ND, OH, SD, and WI.
[b]CT, ED, ME, MD, MA, NH, NJ, NY, PA, RI, and VT.
[c]AL, AR, FL, GA, KY, LA, MS, NC, OK, SC, TN, TX, VA, and WV.
[d]AK, AZ, CA, CO, HI, ID, MT, NV, NM, OR, UT, WA, and WY.
[e]AL, AR, FL, GA, LA, MS, NC, SC, TN, TX, and VA.

Table 2
Selection Systems and Black Representation

Variable	At-Large (N = 43)	District (N = 9)	Partisan Election (N = 10)	Non-Partisan Election (N = 13)	Executive Appointment (N = 4)	Merit Selection (N = 22)	Legislative Election (N = 3)
Number of judges selected	279	64	74	90	26	136	17
Black justices	16(5.7)	4(6.3)	7(9.5)	6(6.7)	1(3.8)	4(2.9)	2(11.8)
Black on court? (yes = 1)	15(34.9)	4(44.4)	7(70.1)	5(38.5)	1(25.0)	4(18.2)	2(66.7)

Note: Numbers in parentheses are percentages.

do not support the contention that southern states will provide lesser opportunity for blacks to serve on their courts of last resort.

Selection Systems and Black Recruitment

The data in Table 2 compare the means for black representation across selection systems. The data suggest some advantage for district systems on both measures of black representation. The second part of Table 2 examines formal selection systems. The highest level of black service on the percentage measure occurred in legislative election courts (11.8 percent), with partisan election a close second (9.5 percent). As to whether a black is present on the court, partisan election (70.1 percent) slightly eclipses legislative election (66.7 percent). Two important outcomes for blacks in Table 2 are worthy of mention. First, blacks have the least representation under merit selection, and this is consistent across both measures of black service. Second, except for the comparison on partisan and legislative elections, all other systems show consistency with respect to the two measures of black representation.

Predicting Black Court Presence

As noted earlier, the current incidence of black justices across courts of last resort forced the multivariate analysis to be restricted to the 0 or 1 dependent variable. In this analysis, legislative election courts (Rhode Island, South Carolina, and Virginia) are omitted for too few cases. Thus, the final analysis is based on 49 observations. Cognizant of the binary (values of only 0 or 1) dependent variable, logit (a maximum likelihood estimator) regression was used to estimate the effects of the independent variables on black court presence. Maximum likelihood estimators are more efficient than ordinary least squares in instances where the dependent variable is discrete.

The results of the multivariate analysis are displayed in Table 3. These results probe directly whether individual selection systems grant blacks dif-

Table 3
Multivariate Analysis of Black Presence on State Courts of Last Resort

Variable	MLE	t-Ratio	Significance
Percent black judges on lower courts	0.34*	2.55	.05
Court size (total seats)	0.87+	1.79	.10
Percent women justices on the court	0.13*	2.08	.05
Term of office	1.22	1.00	ns
Region (South = 1)	1.11	0.72	ns
Merit selection	—a		
Partisan election	2.48	1.44	ns
Non-partisan election	0.32	0.25	ns
Executive appointment	−0.80	0.38	ns
Intercept	−12.317*		
Pseudo R-squared	.41		
χ^2 (df = 8)	34.51**		
Concordant pairs	93.8		
N	49		

aReference category for selection systems.
+p<.10. *p<.05. **p<.001.

ferential access to state courts of last resort. They also test directly the hypotheses related to the eligible black judge pool, women and minority competition, southern race progressiveness gap, size of collegial body, and incumbency and window of opportunity.

We turn first to the vital statistics reported in Table 3 (pseudo r-squared, .41, and chi-squared, 34.51, p<.001). These statistics suggest that the independent variables predict black court presence successfully. The coefficient for the effect of black representation among lower court judges in the state is positive and statistically significant (MLE = 0.34, p<.05). Thus, the greater blacks' share of a state's lower judgeships, the greater blacks' likelihood of securing a seat on that state's court of last resort. Clearly, the eligible pool hypothesis receives firm support.

The estimated effect of the degree of women's representation on the court (the competition hypothesis) also portrays a positive and significant effect (MLE = 0.13, p<.05). That is, the greater the degree of women's representation, the better blacks' chances of securing some presence on the court. This result is averse to the competition hypothesis, which expects that black and women's representation will co-vary negatively. Along with the results of an earlier study on women (Alozie, 1996), which revealed that women achieved greater representation on state courts of last resort where blacks also fared well, the findings on this competition hypothesis for courts of last resort appear to have come full circle. In the least, this dynamic obviates any reason to anticipate that policy undertaken by states to improve women's service on state courts of last resort will be detrimental to blacks' aspirations. Neither will those policy initiatives undertaken to strengthen the position of blacks undermine women's participation. If anything, these results underscore the fact that once the political system in any community is sensitized to the need for women and minority participation at a broader level, all groups stand to benefit.

The fact that increasing black representation on state courts of last resort may be largely an attribute of heightened selection politics and litigation could explain the relatively slow progress of black females in particular (as noted in the descriptive portion of the findings that showed only two black female jurists across the states). Prior research suggests that while the black community's resources are significant determinants of black political success, those resources are directed mostly toward the politics of black men, sometimes to the neglect of black females (Karnig, 1979).

The estimated effect of court size portrays a positive and significant coefficient (MLE = 0.87, p<10). Accordingly, there is some reason to infer that larger courts will provide greater opportunity for black recruitment. Conversely, the analysis indicates no significant effects for term of office, regional location, or judicial selection systems. In effect, the 11 states of the Confederacy do not differ significantly from the rest of the country with regard to the likelihood that black justices will be present on their courts of last resort. Similarly, selection systems do not diverge significantly in the degree of access they are likely to permit blacks to their courts. By implication, then, none of the hypotheses embodied in these latter variables is supported by the data. For selection systems, this means any disparities between elective and appointive systems are not a significant explanation for varying black access to state courts of last resort. In the case of the finding on regional location, increasing liberalization and the highly politicized judicial selection debate (and litigation) in the South since the 1980s may account for this outcome.

The last part of the puzzle pertains to the relevance of electoral structure: district and at-large arrangements. Several logit diagnostic regression models were estimated specifying a dummy independent variable that separated the district and at-large election systems. No significant differentials emerged between the two systems. The most basic of these runs was the one specifying a simple regression model with the district/at-large dummy as the independent variable. The result was as follows:

$$I = 0.731 + 0.508 \text{ (DISTRICT)} + e$$
$$(0.46)$$

(I is the probability that a black justice serves on the court; model chi-square = 0.46, n.s.; 0.731 is the intercept; 0.508 is the estimated [insignificant] MLE for the district system with t-ratio in parenthesis.)

The model chi-square did not attain significance. Overall, electoral arrangement does not predict the presence of a black justice. This outcome persisted even after entering and interacting the size of the black population. The conclusion that has been reached here on the effect of electoral structure is presented reechoing the caveat concerning both data limitation and the fact that judicial districts in existence at the time these data were collected were not designed as vote dilution conscious remedies per se.

Summary and Policy Implications

This is a baseline analysis that must not be considered the final word on the hypotheses examined here. More research is warranted as the number of blacks on state courts of last resort increases. There are clearly some data limitations with respect to the somewhat limited mean of the percent black representation measure (mean = 5.8), although sampling and generalization to some larger population is not at stake here. Moreover, the study analyzed cross-sectional data on a rapidly evolving phenomenon. Also, only formal judicial selection methods have been surveyed, and not informal mechanisms (Graham, 1990b). Nevertheless, the results provide a first insight into the factors associated with black recruitment on states' highest courts, and form a benchmark for comparison of future deviations.

The survey discovered more blacks serving on state courts of last resort than were recorded a decade or so ago, although the success rate of black females has clearly not kept pace with that of black males. Blacks show both their highest degree and incidence of service on southern courts. When other factors are taken into account, however, significant differentials do not emerge for the South and non-South. The multivariate analysis further revealed that blacks attained greater chances for representation in jurisdictions with larger black shares of lower judgeships and on those courts where women have achieved greater representation themselves.

Some important policy implications emerge from the study. These implications pertain both to the debate regarding judicial selection in particular and to regional politics and affirmative action in general. First, states are increasingly opting for some form of merit selection for recruiting judges (Emmert and Glick, 1988). If such a move is contemplated for courts of last resort, care must be taken to audit the potential for black under-recruitment (Table 2), especially if that action involves switching from partisan election. Moreover, there has been progress in black recruitment to state courts of last resort, particularly in the South. Indeed, if the trend of black progress observed in this study continues, there are good prospects for even greater success by blacks in the South in the foreseeable future.

Second, there is no reason to anticipate that policies undertaken to improve women's representation will hurt blacks. Neither will those implemented to assist blacks disadvantage women (Alozie, 1996). In short, the emerging general openness of the political culture to nontraditional officeholders such as women and blacks, rather than deleterious or zero-sum competition, appears to suggest that a rising tide will lift all boats.

Perhaps a particularly far-reaching policy implication of the study pertains to the effects of the black legal-profession-specific factor, namely, lower judgeships. While some political advocates are eager to confine the discourse on black under-recruitment on state courts to selection systems alone, the linkage with black lower judgeships must not be lost. This linkage highlights the importance of multifaceted remedies encompassing action throughout the structure of the legal profession—including law school attendance, admission to the bar and professional development, and attainment of lower judgeships (Segal, 1983). Only through such a comprehensive program may blacks become a permanent presence on state courts of last resort.

Yet, it is this last general observation that magnifies the importance of the result of the eligible-pool hypothesis. There is growing anxiety over the U.S. Supreme Court's increasing vacillation, even outright hostility (McClain, 1996: 872; Wasby: 1994), toward affirmative action programs that have been widely credited with much of the progress of women and minorities in the last three decades in all walks of life. Recently, the Supreme Court, as if in some haste to send a message before its recess, let stand an appeals court ruling that struck down a University of Texas law school affirmative action program that set apart a separate admissions procedure for blacks and Hispanics. Although that ruling was binding only in Texas, Louisiana, and Mississippi, it was the first federal court decision to mandate that race could not be used at all as a factor in public college admissions. As Wasby (1994: 58) aptly noted, "the Supreme Court seems to have returned to the late nineteenth century, even without a new Reconstruction." Only time will tell how this new posture will impact blacks in the legal profession.

Notes

The author wishes to thank Heather Campbell and Alvin Mushkatel for their comments. The anonymous reviewers for the *National Political Science Review* provided useful insights on the final draft of this manuscript.

1. Summaries of these cases appear in McDuff (1989) and Haydel (1989).
2. The present report is part of a larger survey of women and minority service on state courts of last resort, conducted by the author at the end of 1993. The survey also reported on Hispanics (4 Hispanic justices were reported in 4 separate courts).
3. There are relatively larger and more concentrated black populations in the South. Thus, it is easier to have the numbers needed to reach legal thresholds mandated by the justice department's battery of the Totality of the Circumstances Test, as well as meet important provisions of the Voting Rights Act for challenging at-large election systems.

Appendix
Distribution of Black Justices Across the States (1993)

State	All Justices	Black Justices
Alabama	9	1
Alaska	5	0
Arizona	5	0
Arkansas	7	0
California	7	0
Colorado	7	1
Connecticut	7	1
Delaware	5	0
Florida	7	1
Georgia	7	2
Hawaii	5	0
Idaho	5	0
Illinois	7	1
Indiana	5	0
Iowa	9	0
Kansas	7	0
Kentucky	7	0
Louisiana	8	1
Maine	7	0
Maryland	7	1
Massachusetts	7	0
Michigan	7	1
Minnesota	7	1
Mississippi	9	1
Missouri	7	0
Montana	7	0
Nebraska	7	0
Nevada	7	0
New Hampshire	5	0
New Jersey	7	0
New Mexico	5	0
New York	7	1
North Carolina	7	1
North Dakota	5	0
Ohio	7	0
Oklahoma (supreme)	9	0
Oklahoma (criminal)	5	0
Oregon	7	0
Pennsylvania	7	1*
Rhode Island	5	0
South Carolina	5	1
South Dakota	5	0
Tennessee	5	1
Texas (supreme)	9	0
Texas (criminal)	9	1
Utah	5	0
Vermont	5	0
Virginia	7	1
Washington	9	1
West Virginia	5	0
Wisconsin	7	0
Wyoming	5	0

*Chief Justice.

References

Alozie, N. O. 1988. "Black Representation on State Judiciaries." *Social Science Quarterly*, 69, 4: 979–86.
———. 1990. "Distribution of Women and Minority Judges." *Social Science Quarterly*, 71, 2: 315–25.
———. 1992. "Election of Asians to City Councils." *Social Science Quarterly*, 73, 1: 90–100.
———. 1996. "Selection Methods and the Recruitment of Women to State Courts of Last Resort." *Social Science Quarterly*, 77, 1: 110–26.
Alozie, N. O., and L. L. Manganaro. 1993a. Women's Council Representation. *Political Research Quarterly*, 46, 2: 383–98.
———. 1993b. "Black and Hispanic Council Representation." *Urban Affairs Quarterly*, 29, 2: 276–98.
American Judicature Society. 1973. "The Black Judge in America." *Judicature*, 57: 18–25.
Berkson, L., S. Beller, and M. Grimaldi. 1980. *Judicial Selection in the United States*. Chicago, IL: American Judicature Society.
Browning, R., D. Marshall, and D. Tabb. 1984. *Protest is Not Enough*. Berkeley: University of California Press.
Bullock, C., and S. MacManus. 1991. "Municipal Electoral Structure and the Election of Councilwomen." *Journal of Politics*, 53, 1: 75–89.
———. 1993. "Testing Assumptions of the Totality-of-the Circumstances Test." *American Politics Quarterly*, 21, 3: 290–306.
Champagne, A. 1986. "The Selection and Retention of Judges in Texas." *Southwestern Law Journal*, 40 (special issue): 53–117.
———. 1990. "Campaign Contributions in Texas Judicial Races." Paper read at the Annual Meetings of the Southwestern Political Science Association, Ft. Worth, Texas.
Cook, B. B. 1972. "Black Representation in the Third Branch." *Black Law Journal*, 1: 260–79.
———. 1978. "Women Judges: The End of Tokenism." In *Women in the Courts*, ed. W. L. Hepperle and L. Crites. Williamsburg, VA: National Center For Courts.
Council of State Governments. 1992. *Book of the States 1992–1993*. Lexington, KY: Council of State Governments.
Crockett, G. 1975. "Judicial Selection and the Black Experience." *Judicature*, 58: 438–42.
DuBois, P. 1980. *From Ballot to Bench: Judicial Elections and the Quest for Accountability*. Austin: University of Texas Press.
———. 1983. "The Influence of Selection System on the Characteristics of a Trial Court Bench." *Justice System Journal*, 8 (Spring): 59–87.
———. 1986. "Financing Trial Court Elections." *Judicature*, 70: 8–16.
Dunn, P. W. 1981. "Judicial Election and the Missouri Plan." In *Courts, Law, and Judicial Processes*, ed. S. Ulmer. New York: Free Press.
Elazar, D. 1973. *American Federalism: A View From the States*. New York: Crowell.
Emmert, C. F., and H. R. Glick. 1988. "The Selection of State Supreme Court Justices." *American Politics Quarterly*, 16, 4: 445–65.
Fletcher, M. A. 1996. "Is the South Becoming Colorblind? Five Incumbent Blacks Survive in Redrawn, Mostly White Districts." *Washington Post National Weekly Edition* (December 2–8): 13.
Fund for Modern Courts, Inc. 1985. *The Success of Women and Minorities in Achieving Judicial Office*. New York: Fund for Modern Courts, Inc.

Glick, H. R., and C. F. Emmert. 1986. "Stability and Change: Characteristics of State Supreme Court Judges." *Judicature*, 70, 2: 107–12.

Goldman, S. 1979. "Should There be Affirmative Action for the Judiciary?" *Judicature*, 62: 493.

Graham, B. L. 1990a. "Judicial Recruitment and Racial Diversity on State Courts." *Judicature*, 74: 28–34.

———. 1990b. "Do Judicial Selection Systems Matter?" *American Politics Quarterly*, 8, 3: 316–36.

———. 1991. "Federal Court Policy-Making and Political Equality." *Western Political Quarterly*, 44, 1: 101–19.

Haydel, J. 1989. "Section 2 of the Voting Rights Act of 1965: A Challenge to State Judicial Election Systems." *Judicature*, 73, 2: 68–73.

Karnig, A. K. 1979. "Black Resources and City Council Representation." *Journal of Politics*, 41: 134–49.

Karnig, A. K., and S. Welch. 1979. "Sex and Ethnic Differences in Municipal Representation." *Social Science Quarterly*, 60: 465–81.

MacManus, S. A. 1992. "How to Get More Women in Office." *Urban Affairs Quarterly*, 28, 1: 159–70.

MacManus, S. A., and C. Bullock III. 1989. "Women on Southern City Councils: A Decade of Change." *Journal of Politics*, 12: 32–49.

McClain, Paula D. 1996. "Black Politics at the Crossroads? Or in the Cross-Hairs?" *American Political Science Review*, 90: 867–73.

McDuff, R. 1989. "The Voting Rights Act and the Judicial Elections Litigant." *Judicature*, 73, 2: 82–85.

National Research Council. 1989. *A Common Destiny: Blacks and American Society*. Washington, DC: National Academy Press.

Nicholson, M. A., and B. S. Weiss. 1986. "Funding Judicial Campaigns in the Circuit Court of Cook County." *Judicature*, 70: 17–25.

Segal, G. R. 1983. *Blacks in the Law*. Philadelphia: University of Pennsylvania Press.

Shuman, J. 1971. "A Black Lawyer's Study." *Howard Law Journal*, 16: 225–62.

Sigelman, L. 1976. "The Curious Case of Women in State and Local Government." *Social Science Quarterly*, 56: 591–604.

Taebel, D. 1978. "Minority Representation on City Councils." *Social Science Quarterly*, 59: 142–52.

U.S. Supreme Court. 1991. *Slip Opinion*. Washington, DC: Government Printing Office.

Wasby, S. L. 1994. "Civil Rights and the Supreme Court: A Return of the Past." *National Political Science Review*, 4: 49–60.

Welch, S. 1978. "Recruitment of Women to Public Office." *Western Political Quarterly*, 31: 372–80.

———. 1990. "The Impact of At-Large Elections on the Representation of Blacks and Hispanics." *Journal of Politics*, 52, 4: 1050–76.

Welch, S., and A. Karnig. 1979. "Correlates of Female Office Holding in City Politics." *Journal of Politics*, 41: 478–91.

African-American Presidential Convention and Nomination Politics: Alan Keyes in the 1996 Republican Presidential Primaries and Convention

Hanes Walton, Jr.
Lester Spence

University of Michigan

Alan Keyes's historic and dramatic run for the Republican party's presidential nomination is, among other things, a clarion call to the students of African-American and national convention politics to reflect and reassess the state of affairs of this two-subfield area. For years after the behavioral movement in the discipline, key leaders of this movement have conceptualized and produced a systematic set of micro-level analyses of this political entity, national political conventions. In fact, even prior to the behavioral thrust, there were considerate institutional (macro-level) studies of national political conventions. And from these two types of studies have flowed testable propositions, hypothesis-generating ideas, and conformation theory.

In this literature, much in the way of uncovering significant variables and describing causal determinants of national convention behavior have evolved. Yet there is little in this rich and diverse literature on race. And that which exists is scattered and embedded in wide-ranging material. But beyond its scattered nature, it is piecemeal, unsystematic, and contains only tidbits of information. The Alan Keyes presidential campaign says that these initial tidbits of findings need to be pulled together, systematized, and structured so that initial theory building about African-American national convention political behavior can emerge in some comprehensive manner. It is the first intellectual step.

Data and Methodology

The purpose of this article is to use the Alan Keyes 1996 Republican presidential candidacy as a point of departure to develop in a comprehensive and systematic way: (1) an initial theory of African-American presidential convention behavior; and (2) posit this initial theory in such a manner that it can generate testable propositions that may be empirically tested in subsequent studies.

Keyes's candidacy is crucial to this theory-building foray because it offers for the first time a chance to bring the Republican party convention politics into the theory-building process. Prior to Keyes's pioneering campaign, African-American presidential candidates had only appeared in the political conventions of the Democratic and sundry third parties. Hence, if one wanted to initialize a theory of African-American convention behavior, it would have been incomplete because of the nonexistence of such candidates in Republican circles.

The data to be used in this initial theoretical effort will be drawn from the institutional, attitudinal, and/or individual and impact literature studies of Democratic, Republican, and third party conventions. It is from this literature that we shall draw the testable propositions about how African-American delegates and candidates behave politically. Our analysis will order, structure, and categorize this data in a tabular format. But this will provide only two-thirds of the bases for the initial theory.

Keyes's campaign will provide the final third. Here our data will consist of Keyes's electoral votes, his delegate support, his campaign and convention speeches, as well as coverage of his campaign. The focus of the analysis here is upon his performance in the primaries and at the convention for trends, patterns, and techniques. It is in these features that we hope to find the testable propositions.

The methodology for capturing the testable propositions from this data is a content analysis procedure. This technique uses a search of all of the pertinent literature on national political conventions to gather and evaluate all of the findings about African-American delegates and political candidates. From this evaluation, an assessment will be made to determine if any of the findings can be operationalized and empirically tested. The content analysis procedure will permit the identification, the collection, and finally the delineation of these scattered and diverse propositions into a holistic format, and if any testable propositions emerge, they will then be synthesized into an initial theory about African-American convention behavior.

The Historical Background

African-American delegates were present at the initial founding of the national political conventions as a device to nominate presidential candidates for major and minor political parties.[1] Before the emergence and use of national political conventions as a nominating device, these early political parties relied upon party caucuses. Born out of the meeting of factional blocs in Congress, these devices gradually evolved where they included congressional and sundry state party leaders in the decision-making process. Although broadened in scope in its formative years, the party caucus nominating device was an affair of the political elites.

Therefore, the further democratizing of the presidential nomination process came not from the major parties but from the rising third parties. Professor Fred Haynes, an authority on nineteenth-century third party movements, declares that third parties "were pioneers in the conversion of American politics from almost exclusive attention to constitutional and governmental matters to the vital needs of the people."[2] As Fred Haynes demonstrates, these parties socialized major parties on issues of social, economic, industrial justice, and, one can now add, racial equality.

There is a significant reason why these early third parties could transform the presidential game. Richard McCormick, the leading historian on this feature of the presidential process, reveals that in the beginning things had not yet congealed. McCormick notes,

> For roughly half a century, embracing fourteen presidential elections, the rules of the presidential game were quite unstable and even discontinuous. That is, the rules did not "evolve" in an orderly or sequential fashion.[3]
>
> The first four elections were conducted under extremely uncertain and even hazardous rules. The uncertainty derived chiefly from the variety and manipulability of the methods employed by the states for appointing electors.[4]

Therefore, when all of this settled down "between 1832 and 1844" and was transformed into the presidential party game, national political conventions became the central force in stabilizing the presidential selection process.[5] And this institution, the national political convention, would have a continuing and pioneering role and function in national politics. As this national institution began to evolve, African Americans evolved along with this national institution.

In the final analysis, two of the major innovations that third parties brought to American politics in this context are the National Political Convention and African-American delegates. They came together at a single moment in time.

The Origins of African-American Convention Politics

African-American delegates were present at the 1843 Liberty Party National Convention in Buffalo, New York. "Among these were the distinguished public figures of Henry Highland Garnet, Charles B. Ray, and Samuel R. Ward."[6]

> Garnet was appointed to the Committee on nominations of officers, the chairman of which was Solman P. Chase of Ohio. Charles B. Ray was appointed to the Committee to make a roll of the convention and was also elected one of the convention secretaries. Samuel R. Ward led the convention in prayer and delivered an address. This was the first time in American history that Negro citizens were actively in the leadership of a political convention.[7]

Besides the acceptance of African Americans at their national convention and giving them membership on convention committees, this became the first national political convention to give an African-American delegate a chance to present and have adopted a party resolution. And before it ended, this national convention adopted two resolutions in behalf of African Americans.[8]

The Liberty party action set into motion a pattern and trend that would continue. But this was just the first step. Another anti-slavery party, the Free Soiler Party of 1848 and 1852 followed the Liberty party's action. At this party's initial Convention of August 9, 1848, in Buffalo, New York, present were African-American leaders: "Samuel Ward, Henry Highland Garnet, Charles Remond, Henry Bibb and Frederick Douglass; and there were present...'other colored gentlemen.'"[9] With the arrival of this pattern and trend, and other parties following suit, African-American national convention delegates and participation had arrived. The only step left was to begin the process of attending and participating in the major party conventions. And that would come with the founding of the Republican party in 1854.

Thus, at the origin of the National Nominating Convention political device, African-American delegates could and did combine with their nomination politics, *a racial equality strategy*. The Liberty party was a party of principle; it had taken a forthright stand against slavery. But with the coming of the second anti-slavery party—the Free Soiler—the combining of a politics of nomination, that is, the selection of a candidate with a strategy of racial equality was now more difficult given the concern with compromise and expediency. The Free Soilers wanted to win, even if it meant the compromise of their anti-slavery principle. And they did compromise by allowing slavery in the old states but not in the new ones. African-American delegates were given half-a-loaf. Thus, African-American convention delegates went in search of a new reality. By 1856, they were in attendance at the initial Republican National Convention in Chicago. The hype here was the marriage of the racial equality concerns with a political candidate that had a principle position on anti-slavery. John C. Fremont the Republican nominee of that Convention, took such a position. A major party convention was now similar to the Liberty party Convention of 1843. The dilemma arose in 1860, and it has been present ever since.

The Republican party nominee, Abraham Lincoln, was unequivocal in his compromise position. He had established his compromise—nonprinciple—position in the well known Lincoln-Douglass Debates in the 1858 Illinois senatorial race In fact, in that race, Lincoln made his compromise position equal to that of a principle stand on anti-slavery. Here is the how he equated compromise with principles. He declared:

> I, as well as Judge Douglas, am in favor of the race to which I belong having the superior position. I have never said anything to the contrary, but I hold that notwithstanding all this, there is no reason in the world why the Negro is not entitled to all the natural rights enumerated in the Declaration of Independence—the right to life, liberty, and the pursuit of happiness. I hold that he is as much entitled to these as the white man. I agree with Judge Douglas, he is not my equal in many respects—certainly not in color, perhaps not in moral and intellectual endowment; but in the right to eat the bread without leave of anybody else which his own hands earns [sic], he is my equal and the equal of Judge Douglas, and the equal of every living man.[10]

Thus, Lincoln became not only a model, but a symbol for subsequent presidential nomination conventions. With Lincoln, the fledgling Republican party had now capitalized on the Liberty party's innovation, making compromise on the question of human equality a principled position. Needless to say, the Democratic party's national convention position was the reverse of the Liberty party's position. The Democrats upheld slavery.[11] Jean Baker, the eminent historian of this period, says:

> This explained why, no matter where they began, Democrats' set speeches invariably ended with blacks as the reason for higher taxes and tariffs, the impeachment of Andrew Johnson, inflationary greenbacks and Republican corruption. The Democrats looked at currency and saw the Negro, reviewed impeachment and ended with the Negro, debated the purchase of Alaska and concluded with the Negro.[12]

Therefore, "through the image of the politically impaired black man, Democrats saw themselves simultaneously as citizens of a unique nation and as members of a political party."[13] They used their national convention to carry the image forward.

Sadly, capitalizing on the third party invention resulted in the major parties: (1) taking a position supporting slavery; and/or (2) taking a compromise position on the institution. The third position was not seen as an alternative, that is, to take a stand completely opposing it. The major, parties had narrowed the alternatives. And this left African-American convention delegates, thereafter, in the very difficult dilemma of trying to wed a candidate strategy to a racial equality strategy. It is yet to happen.

The Literature on African-American National Nomination Politics and Convention Delegate Behavior

Long before African-American politics evolved into an academic subfield in the discipline, political scientists were developing institutional and individual analysis of national political conventions and their political participants. And inherent in *some* of these analyses are macro- (institutional) and micro- (delegates) level theories about these political entities of the American political process.

In the early and formative years of the discipline—1885 until 1960s—the studies of the national political conventions were essentially institutional analyses that focused upon: (1) the state delegations to these conventions; and/or (2) the balloting in these conventions as the central unit of analysis. Studies in this category poured forth and culminated in the five-volume, American Political Science Association-sponsored study of the 1952 national conventions.[14] Although a few institutional studies would emerge after this APSA effort, the high watermark was reached. Of this major effort, it has been said: "More than 100 political scientists, located at more than 70 cooperating colleges and universities, have contributed the field reports on which this five volume report...is primarily based."[15] However, before we make an exploration of the causal determinant of the decline of institutional studies of national political conventions, one caveat must be made. In addition to these studies' units of analysis being (1) convention ballots and (2) state delegations, they did provide some insights into delegate characteristics in a summary manner.[16] It was these data that helped to shift the focus from a macro- to a micro-level perspective.

Two things eventually transformed the institutional approach to national political conventions and led to their decline and displacement. First, there was a behavioral movement in the discipline, which shifted the focus and unit of analysis away from the institution and to the individual, which meant, in the case of national political conventions, an analysis of delegates to these national conventions.[17] Second, national political conventions lost their decision-making authority in the 1970s and 1980s."[18] Writing in 1957, one year after the 1956 national convention, "William Carlton argued that a major change in convention decision making had occurred and that the first ballot nominations of 1956 verified what he saw was a thirty-year trend to choose preconvention favorites."[19] Thus, as institutions, the national political conventions had no more real power, and therefore only the delegates became interesting and useful to analyze empirically and to focus upon. In the words of Professor Epstein, while the 1950s marked the beginning of a decline, "in retrospect, the conventions of the 1960s appear transitional...[hence]...the limited role of the national conventions of the 1970s and 1980s [were] the product of a long-term development began after 1952."[20] Therefore, "the post-1968 changes appear as culminating events in a fairly long historical process, rather than as an entirely novel departure from an established order, they were nevertheless rapid, broad, and durable enough to have remained in force for the two decades since their establishment."[21] Thus, in a word, national political conventions have no power and have not had much since the 1950s. Therefore, when one combines the shift of focus in the discipline with the convention's loss of decision-making power, the collapse of institutional studies is not surprising.

Jeane Kirkpatrick's study of the delegates to the 1972 national conventions firmly established the individual level approach with her quantitative analysis of delegate characteristics that went beyond the mere demographic features.[22] In addition to demographic factors, she provided a large array of other attitudinal characteristics. Needless to say, the Kirkpatrick work was built on the initial efforts of other pioneers:

> First among well known large scale studies concerned only with the characteristic of delegates is the work by McClosky, Hoffman, and O'Hara. It was conducted in 1957-58 through a mail questionnaire sent to delegates and alternates who had attended the Republican and Democratic conventions of 1956. Obtaining data from over three thousand participants, McClosky and his colleagues compared what they found with data from Gallup's sampling of Republican and Democratic voters.[23]

Following the path-breaking work of McClosky, Dwaine Marvick and Samuel Eldersveld obtained interviews with thirty-two Democratic and thirty-eight Republican delegation chairpersons at conventions in both 1952 and 1956. Their tabulated findings are "about the respondents' background, prior political experience, and actual convention procedure."[24]

Probing the delegates at the 1968 national convention, John Soule and James Clarke found differences between the convention delegates in the terms of their professional and amateur status.[25]

Thus, it was these works that the Kirkpatrick volume built upon. She significantly expanded the categories on which the delegates could be assessed.

But, the works on national conventions did not immediately follow in Kirkpatrick's tracks.

Denis Sullivan and his colleagues explained the 1972 and 1974 mini-conventions by analyzing interest group caucuses—such as the women's and black caucuses—and contrasted these with the power of the presidential candidate organizations. Caucuses, instead of delegates, became the units of analysis.[26] Some other works explored convention ballots and the number of roll calls needed to nominate.[27] But the Kirkpatrick volume had set the new groundwork. And to date, the pioneering work of M. Kent Jennings and Warren Miller have added a longitudinal dimension to the cross-sectional analysis began by Kirkpatrick.[28] Essentially, here is where the literature stands at the moment, having made the transition from institutional to individual analysis. Embedded in these institutional and individual analyses are some macro- and micro-level theories about African-American convention political behavior.

But these institutional and individual analyses do not exhaust the literature on African-American convention political behavior. William Nowlin's 1931 work *The Negro in National Politics* was an institutional look at political conventions up until this time.[29] Therefore, it focused essentially upon the Republican Convention, and African-American delegates, and their characteristics as well as the convention committees on which they served.

Following Nowlin's exploration of Republican convention politics until the 1930s, Edgar Lee Tatum, in his *The Changed Political Thought of the Negro*,[30] explored the Democratic national conventions, the African-American delegates and their characteristics, as well as the convention committees on which they served.

In V. O. Key's *Southern Politics*, the chapter "Negro Republicans" looks at the long history of African Americans' involvement with the party and the continual existence of Negro-state Republican delegations from the South to the national convention from 1888 until 1948. Key referred to these "Negro Republican delegates" as patronage farmers.[31]

Prior to Key's brief analysis of these convention delegates, Ralph Bunche in his memorandum "The Political Status of the Negro" for the Gunnar Myrdal study *An American Dilemma*, provided a more detailed assessment of these groups.[32] Finally, a comprehensive and systematic study of these southern black delegations to the Republican national conventions up to 1960 was made.[33] And a similar work on these delegations to the Democratic national convention was undertaken.[34] Again the focus was upon the contesting African-American delegations to both conventions.

The numbers of African-American delegates to both conventions from 1868 to 1972 were calculated to provide a longitudinal perspective of racial participation at these national political entities.[35] And a recent study updates this information through the 1984 national convention.[36]

In addition to these academic studies, the *Negro Yearbook and Handbook* as well as the Joint Center for Political Studies' monographs on each conventions since 1972 continued the emphasis and focus upon the African-American delegates and primarily upon their demographic characteristics.[37]

Professor Ronald Walters, with funds from the Ford Foundation, analyzed "black delegates to the 1976 and 1980 National Conventions" and one of their tentative conclusions is that there is "a systemic relationship between the delegate mix or composition, delegate perception on issues and candidates, and inferences concerning delegate behavior."[38] This study and subsequent efforts will move the focus upon demographic characteristics significantly further along and provide a basis for comparison with other attitudinal-based studies of African-American convention delegates.

But the upsurge in the number of African-American delegates to the national political conventions, particularly after the 1965 Voting Rights Act, did not exhaust African-American efforts to influence the outcome of candidate selection and platform stances at least in the Democratic party. While African Americans have used convention seating challenges to impact and influence national convention politics, these challenges gave way to a strategy of increasing the sheer number of delegates, which in turn increased their influence; eventually the increase in delegate strength evolved into a Black Caucus at the conventions of the 1970s.[39] But, like the seating challenges and greater delegate strength, the caucus technique gave way to the rise of an African-American presidential candidate in 1972 with Congressman Shirley Chisholm,[40] and in 1984 and 1988 with Reverend Jesse Jackson.[41] With the rise of an African-American candidate strategy to influence the political behavior and outcome of national political conventions came academic analyses that focused upon these candidate instead of the individual focus on delegate attributes.

With the focus upon these African-American political candidates that were seeking the Democratic and Republican party nominations arose a new type of study, the impact study. Initially, these impact studies arose in the area of judicial behavior. Scholars sought to find how Supreme Court decisions influenced the American populace. Following these initial impact studies in the area of judicial behavior came those that assessed how the American populace complied with federal bureaucratic enforcement of new civil rights policy and regulations.[42]

With the appearance of Congresswoman Shirley Chisolm and Reverend Jesse Jackson in presidential campaigns, impact studies took yet another focus. Numerous studies sought to determine what influence, if any, these candidates had upon the Democratic party's national conventions. Basically speaking, these new impact studies can be placed into two categories. First, what impact did the delegates of these candidates have? Second, what impact did the candidates themselves have upon the convention and the party's electoral fortunes in the fall campaign?

Political scientist Lucius Barker did the pioneering delegate study. He wrote of his own experiences as a Jesse Jackson delegate from Missouri to the 1984 Democratic national convention. In fact, his study is a diary of his entire experience and along the way reveals, through a participant observer's viewpoint, the strengths and weaknesses of Jackson's delegate strategies.[43]

Most notable among these studies is the one by Professor Ronald Walters.[44] Walters explored the Jackson candidacies of the 1980s and concluded that they were a form of dependent leverage and would have only limited impact and influence on the Democratic national convention. His implication is that since party candidates cannot have system-wide influence, the only way to achieve this was with an independent challenge not tied to either of the two parties.⁴⁵ Other studies of the Jackson effort concluded with an opposite point of view, that being that the Jackson candidacy hurt the liberal Democratic candidate and caused the loss of the White House for the party in both presidential elections.⁴⁶

Collectively these are institutional, individual, attitudinal, and impact studies. With the latter type of study being of recent vintage and the others being of a much older vintage. Moreover, the impact studies are a direct result of the political candidate strategy in African-American convention politics. In point of fact, as African Americans have developed and used different strategies to influence convention politics, so did the type of journalistic and academic studies on them. And it is from the data inherent in these different studies that we shall draw the testable propositions.

One further remark can be made about these studies. If we reorganize these studies into race relations and African-American political empowerment categories, additional insights are possible.

Overall, between the race-relation-oriented studies on national convention politics and the African-American-oriented studies there is this significant difference in interpretations: The former stresses what an African-American candidate strategy does to the Democratic candidates and the Democratic party, while the latter stresses the weaknesses and limitation of the strategy in improving and eliminating problems in the African American community. The differences are polar opposites of each other.⁴⁷

President Reagan and the Emergence of the Keyes Candidacy

In order to truly understand Keyes's presidential campaign, it is important to look at the role of President Ronald Reagan. His capture of the Republican party nomination had significant consequences for African-American Republicans already participating in the party. The majority of these African-American Republicans were like the African-American Senator Edward Brooke, economic conservatives and social liberals in terms of their beliefs about the government's role in protecting civil rights. They believed that when the party had power in the government, it should use those powers to eradicate the problems facing blacks and to enhance and protect the civil rights of African Americans. However, President Reagan's philosophy that government was the problem not only conflicted with the beliefs of this group, but was directly opposed to them. Hence, a month after his election, the president and his operatives began a search for a new group of African-American Republicans. The political recruitment of this new group began at the Fairmont Conference held in San Francisco in December 1980. The president's inner circle let it be known that those who agreed with and supported his philosophy of governmental nonintervention would receive significant political and economic patronage. Individuals came out of the political woodpile to take part. Hence, after the conference, the consensus was out and the new political recruitment scheme was in place. Of this new process, Smith and Walton have written: "The discrediting of the liberal black leadership was the official story. The hidden transcript was the displacement of the traditional black Republican leadership. This had to be done first because otherwise there would be no place to put the new 'leaders'."⁴⁸

Thus, President Reagan's strategy made Alan Keyes's candidacy possible. This strategy removed all of the African-American Republicans of Senator Brooke and Attorney J. Clay Smith, Jr.'s ideology. This permitted individuals like Keyes to rise and eventually launch a presidential candidacy.

There is more. President Reagan's dominance of the Republican Party (not only through his election, but through his re-election as well) permitted a change in the political context of the nation-state which carried a change in the political attitude of the white electorate. They not only became more conservative on racial issues but the majority accepted President Reagan's (and subsequently President Bush's) notion that the government should not play a role in the advancement of African-American civil rights. This was a reversal of the attitudes whites held on race in the 1960s. Hence, President Reagan and later President Bush not only modified the Republican party's recruitment strategy but brought in a new attitudinal change in the white electorate. In such a changed political context the rising Alan Keyes believed he could appeal to such a changed electorate and thus entered the Republican presidential primaries in 1996. His level of support strongly suggests the degree to which this changed attitudinal context was ready to support a messenger with a different skin color.

Alan Keyes and the 1996 Republican Presidential Primaries

Both perspectives were derived from analyzing the Democratic national conventions of 1984, 1988, and, to an extent, 1992. Yet in 1996, the Republican national convention saw its first candidate strategy effort by an African American. In the past, African-American Republicans had moved from a strategy of seating challenging essentially from the South in the form of "Black and Tan" delegates to political insurgents and mavericks that were civil rights stalwarts,[49] then to conservative clientage delegates (that is, as the Republican conservatives captured the nomination process, African-American delegates transformed themselves into supporters of the right-wing nominees beginning with the Nixon nomination),[50] and finally to an African-American candidate for president.

Keyes took advantage of the Fairmont Conference and was appointed by President Reagan as a delegate to the United Nations. After the end of the Reagan tenure, Keyes ran twice in the 1980s for a U.S. Senate seat from Maryland. In both election attempts Keyes lost to white Democrats. Following these electoral defeats, Keyes became a conservative media and talk show host and gave endless speeches to sundry conservative groups around the country.

Reagan, at the 1984 Republican national convention, and Bush, at the 1988 national convention, gave Keyes a chance to speak. It was a chance to show off the African-American conservatives and Keyes fit the bill. However, once in office, the Bush administration did not provide Keyes with a political appointment and Keyes went back to the chicken circuit. The Bush administration lost to Clinton in 1992 and Keyes decided to launch his own presidential campaign in those first years of the Clinton administrations. Here is how Keyes announced his campaign: "One side sees government action as the main solution; the other sees it mainly as part of the problem. Neither has rediscovered the concept that alone provides for the restoration of the community's moral power through an effective combination of private enterprise and community self-government at the grassroots level."[51] Modifying his position from one based on the economic conservatism of Jack Kemp to one based on the evangelical conservatism of Pat Robertson and Jerry Falwell, Keyes noted that America's moral foundation had to be rebuilt along conservative lines. This moral crusade would be his presidential agenda.[52]

Other analysts did not quite see Keyes's candidacy in this fashion. One group wrote: "Alan Keyes is not a presidential candidate. He's a radio talk show pro-life prophet haranguing the conscience of the nation from a bully electronic pulpit." They continue by noting that he "could be cast as 20th century John the Baptist, verbally flogging an inattentive and licentious populace to change their hedonist ways and restore moral and personal order to their lives, their community and the nation."[53] Thus, they see him as a "prophet in the political desert," with absolutely no chance to win the nomination. This is very similar to the way that many in the media approached Reverend Jesse Jackson's campaigns, though none noted that Keyes's campaign would in any way harm (or even benefit) the Republican presidential campaign as a whole.[54] In fact, an interesting comparison can be made between Keyes and Patrick Buchanan. Though undoubtedly there are some differences (most notable is Buchanan's status as a long-time party activist), the same argument made above—that Keyes was an unelectable rabble-rouser—could plausibly be made of Buchanan. But, not surprisingly, such an argument was never put forth of Buchanan in public circles.

Table 1
The Vote and Percentage for the 1996 Republican Presidential Primary Candidates in Savannah, Georgia: By Racial Districts*

Republican Candidates	Non-African American Election Districts		African American Election Districts	
Alan Keyes	421	(2.5%)	78	(5.4%)
Bob Dole	7,913	(46.3%)	636	(43.9%)
Pat Buchanan	3,745	(21.9%)	341	(23.5%)
Steve Forbes	2,608	(15.3%)	190	(13.1%)
Lamar Alexander	2,243	(13.1%)	190	(13.1%)
Others**	153	(0.9%)	13	(0.9%)
Total***	17,083	(100.0%)	1,448	(100.0%)

*The Non-African-American Election Districts are the five Chatham County Commissioner Districts, 1, 3, 4, 6, and 7, where whites constitute the majority of the registered electorate. The African-American Electorate Districts are the three Chatham County Commissioner Districts 2, 5, and 8, where African Americans constitute the majority of the registered districts. Moreover, each of these three districts have elected an African-American County Commissioner.
**The other category includes Republican candidates Robert K. Dornan, Phil Gramm, Charles Collins, Richard Lugar, and Maurice Taylor. They were still on the Chatham County ballot.
***The Chatham County returns included absentee ballots, but these totals were excluded from the final total because there was no way to put these votes into the two racial categories.
Source: Adapted from Chatham County Board of Elections, "Official Returns District Totals Presidential Primary and Special Election, Chatham County, Georgia," March 5, 1966, page 1. Calculations prepared by authors.

Table 2
The Percentage and Votes for Alan Keyes in
the 1996 Republican Presidential Primaries

State	Votes	%
Arizona	2,790	1
Colorado	9,049	4
Connecticut	2,209	2
Delaware	1,729	4
Florida	16,610	2
Georgia	17,538	3
Illinois	30,062	4
Louisiana		
Maine	1,229	2
Maryland	13,718	5
Michigan	15,995	3
Mississippi	2,907	2
Nevada	1,999	1
New Hampshire	5,572	3
North Dakota	2,030	3
Ohio	26,853	3
Oklahoma	6,306	2
Oregon	14,340	3
South Carolina	5,752	2
South Dakota	2,378	3
Tennessee	7,661	3
Washington	5,610	5
Wisconsin	18,028	3

Source: Adapted from the data supplied by the secretaries of state. Calculations prepared by authors.

Overall, Keyes entered some twenty-five primaries. But despite his right of center conservative stance, he encountered trouble in the South. First in South Carolina, Republican party leaders deliberately shut him out of the debate. Then in Georgia, at the WTBS television station he was arrested trying to get into the locally televised debate of Republican party candidates. After the debate was over, the charges against Keyes were dropped. Clearly, Southern Republicanism in these two states were not about to embrace this racial carrier of the message. The color of the messenger matters.[55]

There is more empirical evidence for the color of the messenger problem in the South. Taking voting data from Savannah, Georgia—of all of the southern primaries, Georgia gave Keyes the largest number of votes—and categorizing it into racial districts, African-American districts and non-African-American districts, it is possible to see not only how whites and African Americans voted for Keyes but how he performed in relationship to the white Republican candidates in the primaries.

Table 1 reveals that Keyes ran poorly in both of the racial districts. His vote totals gave him fifth place in a field of ten candidates. Moreover, Table

1 empirically suggests that he had little relevance in either racial district. And when compared to his white counterparts, it is highly probable that the color of the messenger mattered a lot.

Moving out of the South to the rest of the nation, Table 2 shows that Keyes's mean percentage stood at 3. Even in his own home state of Maryland, he was only able to secure 5 percent of the vote. Though support, in both the country overall and in the individual primaries, for social/religious conservatism ran particularly high, Keyes was unable to convince a significant number of voters to cast ballots for his presidential candidacy. Perhaps the tactics noted above may have diminished his chances somewhat, but even if such tactics were not employed it is doubtful that he would have been able to receive more than 4 or 5 percent of the vote from any one state.

Theory Building and African-American Presidential Convention Politics: A Concluding Note

In figure 1 one can see the percentage of African-American delegates to the Republican and Democratic national conventions. African Americans

Figure 1
The Percentage of African American Delegates at
the Republican National Conventions: 1868–1996

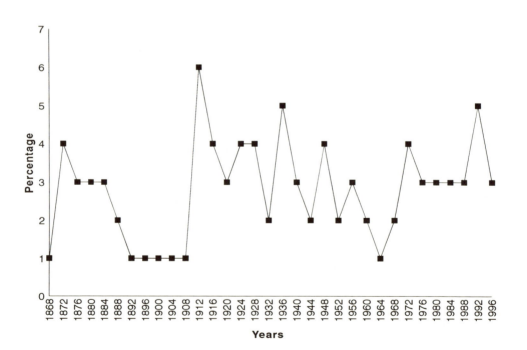

have had delegates at the Republican convention from 1868 to the present, while in 1924 an African-American alternate delegate attended the Democratic convention. "Beginning in 1932, the Democratic party allowed blacks in the Virgin Island two representatives at the Convention. But it was the 1936 Convention that the first black delegate (not alternates) had an opportunity to participate in the party's Convention politics"[56] This was the time of African-American party realignment.[57]

Thus, the institutional studies of national conventions basically commenced after the African Americans had realigned with the Democratic party and de-aligned from the Republican party. Hence, such studies pick up data on one party's convention. Moreover, when the discipline shifts its unit of analysis from state delegates and balloting to delegate attitudes, the number of African-American delegates to Republican conventions were significantly smaller than those to the Democratic conventions. And those smaller numbers provide even less and fewer insights into the psychological dimension of these delegates.

Finally these delegate studies make no adjustment for either Republican party shift to a conservative stance or (and more importantly) the party's choice to only promote African-American conservatives (rather than mod-

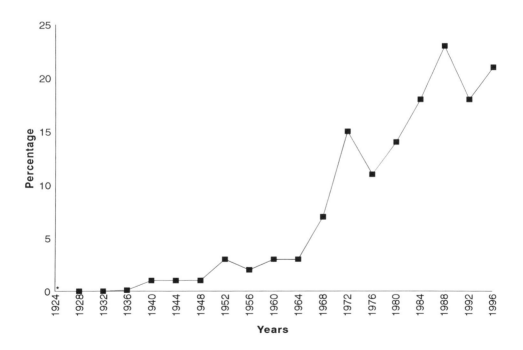

Figure 2
The Percentage of African American Delegates at
Democratic National Conventions: 1924–1996

erates or liberals) in their national political convention constituency. Also missing are studies of white delegates of Chisolm, Jackson, and Keyes.[58]

Besides these limitations and shortcomings of the institutional and individual literature there is at least one significant problem with the impact studies literature. This literature was built, like the others, by analyzing African-American Democrats at the Democratic national convention. Keyes's 1996 effort permits one to put the finding of a one-party focus into a two-party perspective. Or at least begin the process toward a two-party perspective. And to do that theory building, it is pertinent that we distill the literature into its embedded macro- and micro-level theories. The macro-level theories are taken from the institutional and impact literature while the micro-level theories are fashioned from the delegate characteristics—demographic and attitudinal—literature as well as the interest group/caucus data.

Table 3 lists the testable propositions that are embedded in this scattered and diverse literature. The differences in the three categories are due to the preoccupation of the discipline with specific areas. The larger number of findings about the institutional aspects of African-American convention behavior derives from the fact that this is the most studied aspect of African-American convention politics. Fewer findings about individual African-American delegates is due in part to the few studies on the subject and in part to the lack of interest in the subject. Finally, the testable propositions from the impact area reflect that one major study of the African-American presidential candidate strategy has been undertaken. Our analysis of the Keyes campaign adds additional insights in this area.

At the institutional level, Keyes's campaign reveals a strong ideological component that is synchronous with that of the Republican party, with that which prevailed at the level of his other Republican campaign, and with that which prevailed amongst the candidates in the presidential primary. Moreover, the candidates, the party, and the convention took a very strong conservative position and belief on the race issue.

At the individual level, the Republican primary votes are not only conservative but far to the right of the general populace voting for the party. Keyes, in the primary, went after the votes of the social, economic, and racial conservatives. Hence, his convention delegates, as well as his primary voters were essentially white. One can see his courting of these voters in his speeches, campaign appearances, and campaign strategy. Few African-American voters fall within these issue groups and networks.

Finally at the impact level, Keyes's strong denunciation of the government's affirmative action policies (which culminated in a demand for the end of all federal and state affirmative action) help to support the party and its electorate's public mood on this matter. Keyes also advocated nongovernmental intervention on other civil rights policy matters as well as no new governmental initiatives. This stance was a perfect fit with the party's general consensus. Impact wise, Keyes's candidacy was not designed to reshape the party, but to promote its positions.

Thus, from our analysis of Keyes's candidacy, we find potential testable propositions from all of the categories found in the literature review. And, as expected, with this data in hand, we can commence with our initial theory building. As noted in the beginning of the article, there is both macro- and

Table 3
The Testable Prepositions in the Institutional, Individual, and Impact Literature on African-American National Convention Delegates: 1868–1996

Institutional

1. The rhetoric and practice of the anti-slavery parties lead to the initial African-American (AA) convention delegates.
2. Republican party opposition to slavery lead to AA convention participation.
3. Republican party support of civil rights led to African-American convention delegates.
4. Resurgent racism in the South led to formation of a bifactional Republican party.
5. Competition between Republican presidential candidates sustained these dual southern convention delegations.
6. The patronage policies of the Republican nominees empowered the African American contesting delegations.
7. With its superior resources, the white Republican faction, eventually displaced the African-American faction.
8. As southern partisanship transformed itself, the lily-white factions built itself an electoral base and an office holding one.
9. Republican Convention rules are changed to favor delegates from areas of low African-American concentration.
10. Contextual charges like mass racial migration create majority population enclaves in the North.
11. Presence of Democratic machines transform these population enclaves into African-American Democratic elected officials.
12. African-American Democratic elected officials leads to alternate delegates and final delegates at Democratic national convention in 1936.
13. Increased number of African-American Democratic delegates lead to an African-American caucus at Democratic national convention in 1970s.
14. Increased number of African-American delegate at Democratic national conventions leads to increased number of convention appointive positions.
15. A state level caucus-convention system of selecting delegates will yield a higher percentage of blacks to national conventions.*

Individual

16. African-American convention delegates came from a higher socio-economic status. Corollary: African-American convention delegates come from a higher educational status.
17. African-American convention delegates are more liberal than the masses. Corollary: African-American *Republican* delegates are less liberal than the masses.
18. African-American convention delegates are overly concerned with civil rights laws. Corollary: African-American Republican delegates are overly concerned with the negation of civil rights laws.
19. African-American Convention delegates support social welfare policies. Corollary: African-American Republican delegates are overly concerned with the negation of social welfare policies.
20. Individual-level characteristics such as ideology and career ambition determine how black delegates represent the group at national conventions.*
21. The black percentage of Democratic party identifiers in the state favorably influences the percentage of blacks on state delegations to the party's national convention.*
22. Black socio-economic resources are a restricting condition for black representation at the national convention.*
23. The state's political culture provides an obstacle for blacks gaining delegate positions to the national convention.*

Table 3 (continued)

Impact

24. African-American convention delegates have engaged in several strategies to influence convention politics.
25. African-American presidential candidates strategy hurts Liberal democratic candidate and the party founders electorally.
26. African-American presidential candidates can be both liberal and conservative.
27. The one-party partisanship of the African-American electorate limits convention influence at both the Democratic and Republican conventions.
28. The race of the African-American presidential candidate impacts the support for the message.
29. There is very limited electoral support for African-American conservative candidates in both the Republican and Democratic parties even when both parties are conservative.
30. Black delegates have limited influence at national conventions in representing the black community.

*All of these testable propositions were taken from a pioneering dissertation on 1980 African-American convention delegates written by Professor Zelma A. Mosley.
Source: Adapted from a contextual analysis of the literature on African-American convention political behavior.

micro-level theory about national political conventions. Hence, we will start at the micro level. African-American convention behavior reflects both the contextual politics of the American political party system and the community politics as well.

African-American politics in general, and convention politics and behavior in particular, is *instrumentalist* in nature. Over the years, African-American delegates have generally developed and implemented political strategies to influence the outcome of the convention process. Thus, strategies have evolved from one of just sheer participation to the latest one of running presidential candidates. And most of these initial strategies have been played out in and around the Democratic national convention. Keyes's recent effort is a continuation of these strategies, but in a different party arena. And placed in context, Keyes's candidacy is an instrument.

More empirical evidence for this instrumentalist thesis can be seen in Table 4. Summarized in this table are the presidential candidates that African-American delegates helped to sponsor at the national conventions as well as the ones that the community supported in the presidential primaries. And whether these African-American presidential candidates were generated in the primaries or at the time of the national conventions, one can see the total delegate votes given to each candidate at both of the conventions. Thus, embedded in this table is the fact that long before African Americans started to run candidates in the presidential primaries to influence and impact conventions, these delegates employed a strategy of running candidates at both of the conventions to influence and impact the outcome. Therefore, when Keyes's candidacy is placed in context, it becomes clear that African Americans have had a dual instrumental strategy to shape convention behavior and outcomes at the institutional level.

At the micro level, African-American convention behavior is driven and

Table 4
The Vote Count for African-American Presidential Candidates at Major Party Conventions: 1880–1996

Year and Convention	African-American Convention Candidate	Office sought by African American	Votes received at Convention
Republican National Conventions			
1880	Blanche K. Bruce	Vice-President	8
1888	Blanche K. Bruce	Vice-President	11
	Frederick Douglas	President	1
1968	Edward W. Brooke	Vice-President	1
1992	Alan Keyes	President	1
1996	Alan Keyes*	President	1
Democratic National Conventions			
1968	Channing Phillips	President	68
	Julian Bond	Vice-President	49
1972	Shirley Chisolm*	President	152
	Shirley Chisolm	Vice-President	20
1976	Barbara Jordan	President	1
	Barbara Jordan	Vice-President	28
	Ronald V. Dellums	Vice-President	20
1980	Ronald V. Dellums	President	3
1984	Jesse Jackson*	President	466
	Shirley Chisolm	Vice-President	39
1988	Jesse Jackson*	President	1,219

*Each candidate ran in the primaries.
Source: Adapted from Michael Goldstein, *Guide to the 1996 Presidential Election* (Washington, DC: Congressional Quarterly, 1995), 43–44.

shaped by both personal ambition and party rules. After disenfranchisement, 1891–1901 Republican delegates from the South were patronage farmers, driven by a personal desire to achieve themselves via politics. In the Democratic party from 1924 to 1996, there was the personal desire to advance both as a group and as individuals as well. After 1960 the group concern re-asserted itself to a very significant degree and potentially subordinated the personal drive.

Rules, both party and convention rules, determine the number of delegates to each convention and to an extent the success and failure of convention strategies and politics of African Americans. And when these rules are coupled with party ideology and stance on race they significantly shape overall involvement and the degree of influence of that involvement.

Therefore, our initial theory at this stage reveals a broad instrumental strategy that includes a mix of personal and group-based motives played out essentially in Democratic national conventions. Thus, at this stage, African-American convention behavior is a one-party-at-a-time strategy. Hence, as these single party strategies have failed they have not only generated new ones—with the political candidate strategies being the most recent one—

but have set into motion similar strategies in the Republican party convention and in several third parties. African-American Democratic leaders and delegates have pioneered and set party convention behavioral parameters.

Notes

1. Hanes Walton, Jr., *The Negro in Third Party Politics* (Philadelphia: Dorrance & Company, 1969), 14.
2. Fred Haynes, *Third Party Movements Since the Civil War* (Iowa: State Historical Society of Iowa: 1916), 40.
3. Richard McCormick, *The Presidential Game: The Origins of American Presidential Politics* (New York: Oxford University Press, 1982), 4.
4. Ibid., 5.
5. Ibid., 207–38.
6. Charles Wesley, "The Participation of Negroes in Anti-Slavery Political Parties," *Journal of Negro History*, 29 (January 1944): 44.
7. Ibid., 44–45.
8. Ibid., 45.
9. Ibid., 53. At the August 11, 1852, Free Soil Convention, Douglass went with the New York delegation and was elected Secretary of the Convention, (ibid., 64).
10. Harold Holzer, ed., *The Lincoln-Douglass Debates: The First Complete Unexpurgated Text* (New York: Harper Perennial, 1993), 254.
11. Jean Baker, *Affairs of Party: The Political Culture of Northern Democrats in the Mid-Nineteenth Century* (Ithaca: Cornell University Press, 1983), chapter 6.
12. Ibid., 256.
13. Ibid., 257.
14. See Paul David, Malcolm Moos, and Ralph M. Goldman, eds., *Presidential Nomination Politics in 1952*, 5 volumes (Baltimore: Johns Hopkins University Press, 1960).
15. Ibid., vol. 1, xi.
16. Ibid.
17. Heinz Eulau, Samuel J. Eldersveld, and Morris Janovitz, eds., *Political Behavior* (New York: Free Press, 1956), 3–5.
18. Leon Epstein, "National Political Conventions: Changing Functions, New Research Strategies," in M. Kent Jennings and Thomas Mann, eds., *Election at Home and Abroad: Essays in Honor of Warren E. Miller* (Ann Arbor: University of Michigan Press, 1984), 267.
19. Ibid., 268. See also William G. Carleton, "The Revolution in the Presidential Nominating Conventions," *Political Science Quarterly*, 72 (June 1957): 224–40.
20. Ibid., 269–70.
21. Ibid.
22. Jeane Kirkpatrick, *The New Presidential Elite: Men and Women in National Political* (New York: Russell Sage, 1976).
23. Epstein, "National Political Conventions," p. 278. See Herbert McClosey, Paul Hoffman, and Rosemary O'Hara, "Issue Conflict and Consensus Among Party leaders and Followers," *American Political Science Review*, 54 (1910): 406–27.
24. Dwaine Marvick and Samuel Eldersveld, "National Convention Leadership: 1952 and 1956," *Western Political Quarterly*, 14 (March 1961): 176–94.
25. John Soule and John Clarke, "Amateurs and Professionals: A Study Delegates to the 1968 Democratic National Convention," *American Political Science Review*, 64 (September 1970): 888–98, and their "Issue Conflict and Consensus: A Comparative Study of Democratic and Republican Delegates to the 1968 National Conventions," *Journal of Politics*, 33 (February 1971): 72–91.

26. Denis Sullivan, Jeffrey Pressman, Benjamin Page, and John Lyons, *The Politics of Representatives: The Democratic Convention of 1972* (New York: St. Martin's, 1974), their *Explorations in Conventions Decision-Making: The Democratic Party in the 1970s* (San Francisco: W. H. Freeman, 1976), and Denis Sullivan, Robert Nakamura, Martha Weinberg, F. C. Arterton, and Jeffrey Pressman, "Exploring the 1976 Republican Convention," *Political Science Quarterly*, 92 (Winter 1977–78): 633–82.
27. Howard Reiter, "Party Factionalism: National Conventions in a New Era," *American Politics Quarterly*, 8 (July 1980): 303–18.
28. See Warren Miller and M. Kent Jennings, *Parties in Transition: A Longitudinal Study of Party Elites and Party Supporters* (New York: Russell Sage Foundation, 1986) and Miller's *Without Consent: Mass-Elite Linkages in Presidential Politics* (Lexington: University Press of Kentucky, 1988).
29. William Nowlin, *The Negro in American Politics* (Boston: Stanford, 1931).
30. Edgar Lee Tatum, *The Changed Political Thought of the Negro: 1915–1940* (New York: Exposition Press, 1941).
31. V. O. Key, *Southern Politics* (New York: Vintage Book, 1949), chapter 13.
32. Ralph Bunche, *The Political Status of the Negro in the Age of FDR*, ed. D. Grantham (Chicago: University of Chicago Press, 1973).
33. Hanes Walton, Jr., *Black Republicans: The Politics of the Black and Tans* (New York: Scarecrow Press, 1975).
34. Hanes Walton, Jr., *Black Political Parties* (New York: Free Press, 1972).
35. Hanes Walton, Jr., and C. Vernon Gray, "Black Politics at the National Republican and Democratic Conventions, 1868–1972," *Phylon*, 36 (Fall 1975): 269–78.
36. Hanes Walton, Jr., *Invisible Politics* (Albany: State University of New York Press, 1985), 161–65.
37. For the initial study, see Joint Center for Political Studies, *Guide to Black Political 1976: Part II—Republican National Convention* (Washington, DC: Joint Center for Political Studies, 1976). A monograph has appeared every four years.
38. Walton, *Invisible Politics*, 341. See also Ronald Walters and Diane Brown, *Black Presidential Politics in 1976: A Study of Black Delegates to the Democratic and Republican National Conventions in 1976* (Washington, DC: Institute for Urban Affairs & Research, n.d.).
39. Shirley Chisholm, *The Good Fight* (New York: Harper & Row, 1973).
40. Ibid.
41. Ronald Walters, *Black Presidential Politics* (Albany: State University of New York Press, 1988).
42. Hanes Walton, Jr., *When the Marching Stopped: The Politics of the Civil Rights Regulatory Agencies* (Albany: State University of New York Press, 1988), 20–27.
43. Lucius Barker, *Our Time has Come: A Delegate's Diary of Jesse Jackson's 1984 Presidential Campaign* (Urbana: University of Illinois Press, 1988).
44. Ronald Walters, *Black Presidential Politics*.
45. Ibid.
46. See Edward Carmines and James Stimson, *Issue Evolution: Race and the Transformation of American Politics* (Princeton, NJ: Princeton University Press, 1989), and Robert Huckfeldt and Carol Kohfeld, *Race and the Decline of Class in American Politics* (Urbana: University of Illinois Press, 1989).
47. Hanes Walton, Jr., Cheryl Miller, and Joseph McCormick, II, "Race and Political Science: The Dual Traditions of Race Relations Politics and African American Politics," in *Political Science in History*, ed. James Farr, John Dryzck, and Stephen Leonard (New York: Cambridge University Press, 1995), 145–74.
48. Robert C. Smith and Hanes Walton, Jr., "U-Turn: Martin Kilson and Black Conservatism," *Transition*, 62 (1993): 209–10.
49. For such a delegate, see David, Moos, Goldman, *The West*, pp. 172–173.

50. Paul Tillett, *Inside Politics: The National Conventions, 1960* (New York: Oceana Publications, 1962), 55–84. See chapter 6, Karl Lamb, "Civil Rights and the Republican Platform: Nixon Achieve Control."
51. Alan Keyes, *Master of the Dream: The Strength and Betrayal of Black America* (New York: Morrow, 1995), 167.
52. This moral agenda clearly provides the lynchpin for the three policy options Keyes addresses in his various campaign speeches: abortion, immigration, and foreign control of U.S. interests. On immigration, for example, he notes:

   > [Some]…have criticized the voters of California for demanding, through Proposition 187, that the integrity of residence and citizenship within our borders be supported with effective enforcement of the distinctions between legal and illegal immigration. They have implied that this demand is evidence of bigotry, intolerance, and racism. Since when is it racist to insist that laws, which no one denies our right to make, be enforced against foreign citizens who violate them? (Alan Keyes, Statement of Purpose)

   His ideas on abortion are even stronger. He argues, as have conservative theorists such as Robert Bork, that abortion is "the central issue of our time," and as such it is important to move towards legislation that would criminalize all abortions. And though the moral component is strong, it is also important to see how he ties the moral authority (invested by the Bible) into the political authority invested by the central documents of the United States. In his views on abortion, for example, Keyes argues that:

   > [W]hen…moral things violate the basic premises that establish our identity as a people, when those moral choices go against the immortal words of the Declaration of Independence that declare we are all created equal and endowed by our Creator with certain unalienable rights, then we not only have the right—we have the DUTY to stand up and say: NO! We will not sacrifice this nation's principles.

   It is perhaps important to note that when Keyes talks about "the Creator," he is not necessarily talking about the Christian God. Indeed he also argues that his moral agenda is religiously (as well as racially) inclusive—calling for a moral coalition of Jews, Muslims, Christians, and even Hindus. Keyes's ideas place him firmly within the realm of the cultural conservatives, and an interesting research project could trace his ideological movement from an economic conservative espousing Kempian economic policies, to a Falwellian cultural conservative.
53. Ralph Hallow and Bradley O'Leay, *Presidential Follies: Those Who Would be President and Those Who Should Think Again* (Texas: Brown Publishing, 1995), 103, 105.
54. Walton, *Invisible Politics*, 39–42.
55. Reading Keyes's speeches, it is not a stretch to argue that Keyes himself realized how his race affected his message. This can easily be detected by looking at the two speeches he made to explicitly black audiences (Black American Political Action Committee or BAMPAC, and Black Americans for Life), and comparing them to those made to predominantly white audiences. Though he often used the metaphors of racial harmony ("bringing whites and blacks together") and referred once in a New Hampshire speech to his ancestors (who have lived in Maryland "for the last 200 years, sometimes as free men and women and sometimes as slaves" [Alan Keyes, Speech to New Hampshire, 1/7/1996]) his tone in speeches given to predominantly white audiences was racially "neutered" so to speak. However in his speeches to black audiences he not only engaged in a subtle nationalist argument—positing how strong black families were even when

subjugated by oppressive forces—but also critiqued Colin Powell for attacking the cultural heritage of black Americans:

> [At] one point [Colin Powell] basically expresses the view, and apparently he's been known to say this before, that he didn't have a problem with a sense of self-worth because his parents were from Jamaica, and he therefore didn't look back to the heritage of slavery. As opposed, I guess, to folks like myself who *do* look back to the heritage of slavery and by implication therefore, have a problem with our sense of self worth. Now, I, would tell [Colin Powell] that, though he was a General and my father was only an NCO, I, grew up with a strong sense of self worth. It actually has something to do with a right understanding of that heritage of slavery. I also tell others that as long as he takes that view, I hope no one will insult me in the future with the suggestion that we are part of the same group, because we are NOT. If he has not learned how to look back at the Black American heritage and understand that in it is a cause for pride, then he had better step back, and learn again before he puts himself forward as anything which will symbolize that heritage. (Alan Keyes, Speech to BAMPAC, 9/22/95)

Interestingly enough, Keyes did not spend much time at all in addressing either affirmative action or welfare. In one speech he addressed what he felt was the central problem of welfare—that it mass produced illegitimate children (Alan Keyes, Statement of Purpose)—and he's touched briefly on this position elsewhere, but in NONE of his speeches did he address affirmative action.

56. Walton and Gray, "Black Politics," 274.
57. Hanes Walton, Jr., "Black Presidential Participation and the Critical Election Theory," in *The Social and Political Implications of the 1984 Jesse Jackson Presidential Campaign*, ed. Lorenz Morris (New York: Praeger, 1990), 49–64.
58. See James Bennett, "Clinton, Setting Out for Chicago, Denounces G.O.P. in Poll, Ardor for President, Faults and All." *New York Times* (August 26, 1996), A1, A1h; Bennett, "The Delegates: Where Image Meet Reality," *New York Times*, (August 12, 1996), A1, B8; and Janet Elder, "For Conventions Week Polls, Timing Can Be Everything," *New York Times* (August 20, 1996), A5. These newspapers articles were based on *The New York Times/CBS New Poll 1996 Democratic Delegate Survey—N-509* (with 377 follow-up interviews), August 8–August 22, 1996, and *The New York Times/CBS News Poll* (1996 Republican Delegate Survey, N=1,310), July 15–August 8, 1996. The Democratic delegate poll contained 17 percent (87) African Americans—while the Republican delegate poll contained 3 percent (39).

The Impact of Harold E. Ford, Sr.'s Endorsements on Memphis Mayoral Elections, 1975–1991

Sharon D. Wright

University of Missouri, Columbia

Introduction

Since 1974, the Ford organization has been the most powerful black political force in Memphis, Tennessee. Its members have included Memphis City Councilman Joe Ford, Shelby County Commissioner James Ford, Tennessee Senator John Ford, former Tennessee Representative Emmitt Ford, former U.S. Representative (for the ninth congressional district) Harold E. Ford, Sr., and current U.S. Representative Harold E. Ford, Jr. Because of their ability to win elections, popularity with black voters, and overall influence in Memphis politics, the Fords have been accused of running a political machine in the city.

In the first section of this research, I will provide an assessment of how the Fords gained their influence in Memphis politics. In the second section, I will examine former Congressman Harold Ford, Sr.'s endorsements in Memphis mayoral elections. Third, I will determine the impact of his endorsements by examining: whether they lead to an increase in black voter turnout; whether candidates who receive endorsements garner higher percentages of the black vote; and whether these candidates receive lower percentages of the white vote. In the final section, I will discuss the relationship that black citizens have traditionally had with political machines.

This research is significant because it analyzes the power that black political figures can establish in southern cities that have once been dominated by machines. Memphis is similar to many other southern cities that have made a transition from "machine politics" to "racial politics." In Atlanta, Baltimore, New Orleans, and other southern cities, black citizens have always voted, but white machines dominated the local political structure. Currently, predominantly black political structures govern these cities. An examination of the way in which the Fords gained their influence, the impact of Harold Ford, Sr.'s endorsements, the allegations of a Ford machine, and the transfer of power from Ford, Sr., to Ford, Jr., reveals a different relationship between machine politics and black politics. The ultimate question is whether a black political figure or organization can ever achieve the power to create a political machine.

Data and Methods

Precinct-level data provided the total number of votes received by each mayoral candidate, citywide turnout percentages, and the number of black and white registered voters. I then calculated regression estimates of their black and white vote percentages. According to newspaper reports, Harold Ford, Sr., endorsed Higgs in 1979, John Ford in 1983, and W. W. Herenton in 1991. Ford did not endorse J. O. Patterson, Jr., in the 1982 runoff or Otis Higgs in 1975.[1]

An analysis of variance (ANOVA) test is a statistical test of the difference of means for two or more groups. In order to test hypotheses in an ANOVA, one must identify the test criteria and calculate the test statistic, sum of squares (SS), degrees of freedom (df), mean square (MS), and the calculated value (F). If the calculated value falls in the critical region on the distribution curve, we can reject the null hypothesis. In an ANOVA, the critical region is always one-tailed to the right. I will determine whether we can reject the null hypothesis, which states that regardless of whether candidates received Ford endorsements, there is no significant difference in their mean black turnout or in black vote and white vote percentages.

The Ford Organization of Memphis

The Fords established an organization and maintained their positions mostly by relying upon their charisma and appeal. Although their father, the late N. J. Ford, ran unsuccessfully for the state senate in 1966, the Ford brothers lacked political connections during their first elective bids. Harold Ford was the first family member to win an elective office in 1970 after being elected to the Tennessee House of Representatives. After serving two terms in the House, Ford defeated Republican incumbent Dan Kuykendall by approximately 744 votes in 1974. He received almost 100 percent of the black vote and approximately 15 percent of the white vote. This victory made Harold Ford the first and only African American from the state of Tennessee to be elected to the U.S. House of Representatives. As shown in Table 1, he retired in 1996 after ten successful reelection bids and 22 years of service.

Initially, John, Emmitt, and James Ford benefited from Harold Ford's popularity and name recognition. In 1971, John Ford defeated Reverend James L. Netters for the district six seat on the Memphis City Council. In 1974, the Ford family established a political organization. Besides Harold Ford's congressional win, John Ford won election to the state senate and Emmitt Ford to the state house of representatives. The latter two garnered approximately 90 percent of the black vote. Their total vote percentages were double those of the second highest contenders. Since 1974, the Fords have usually received

Table 1
Regression Estimates of Harold E. Ford, Sr.'s Reelections, 1974–1994

Election Year	Democratic Primary	Black Vote	Primary Election	Black Vote
1974	63.3	92.5	49.9	94.6
1976	100.0	100.0	60.7	100.0
1978	80.6	93.6	69.7	94.2
1980	72.7	92.8	99.9	93.0
1982	84.4	96.2	72.4	96.4
1984	80.0	95.0	71.5	96.0
1986	80.0	95.0	83.0	97.0
1988	80.3	95.4	81.6	96.3
1990	69.2	96.2	58.1	97.0
1992	64.6	95.8	57.9	96.0
1994	55.5	96.0	57.8	96.0

Source: Shelby County Board of Election Commission

at least 80 percent of the black vote in their respective elections. In 1992, John Ford won reelection to the state senate and also became the first black contender to win a countywide race. Tennessee law did not prohibit him from serving both as a state senator and as the general sessions court clerk from 1992 to 1996. Ford continues to serve in the state senate, but was defeated in the court clerk reelection bid in 1996.

The majority of black politicians who were elected in the late 1960s and 1970s were veterans of the civil rights movement.[2] Unlike other black political families, such as the Mitchells of Baltimore and the Clays of St. Louis, the Fords were not civil rights activists.[3] They and others belonged to a new generation of young black politicians who had little involvement in the civil rights movement.

The Fords have not created a formal political organization with a leader and members who pursue the group's objectives.[4] During their careers, the Fords have held political offices and been replaced by family members when they either retired or sought other offices. For example, in 1979, voters chose Dr. James Ford to represent district six on the Memphis City Council, a position that was once held by Senator John Ford. Currently, Dr. Ford is a member of the Shelby County Commission and his brother Joe Ford is the district six representative. Finally, in 1996, Harold E. Ford, Jr., succeeded his father as U.S. Representative for the ninth congressional district of west Tennessee.

The first accusations that the Ford organization had developed a machine in the black community occurred during the 1970s. In 1979, groups consisting of black ministers and elected officials opposed the alleged practice of machine politics in a newspaper ad criticizing the organization's campaign tactics on behalf of James Ford's city council bid. After a last-minute announcement of entry in the race, James Ford relied primarily on the Ford name to get elected. Despite the fact that he had never held political office, James Ford defeated seven candidates.

More recently, Memphis Mayor W. W. Herenton and others have accused Congressman Harold Ford, Jr., of capitalizing on the Ford name, but lacking political experience. In his first political bid, the 26-year-old graduate of the University of Michigan law school defeated a number of candidates, including state legislators Steve Cohen and Rufus Jones for the Democratic nomination in August 1996. In November 1996, he defeated Republican Rod Deberry.

Over the years, the former congressman's opponents have described him as a "demagogue," a "political boss," a "god," and a "cancer in Memphis politics."[5] During the early 1990s, Harold Ford made two unsuccessful endorsements during the 1992 "Dream Team" campaign and the 1994 Shelby County mayoral race.[6] As a result of these defeats, particularly after W. W. Herenton's election as the first black mayor, many persons believed that Ford had lost some of his influence. Herenton and others have attempted to countervail Harold Ford, Sr.'s influence in the black community, but he continued to be the most powerful black political figure in Memphis before his retirement. In the next section, I examine the impact of Harold Ford, Sr.'s endorsements in mayoral elections.

Harold Ford's Endorsements in Memphis Mayoral Elections

When a well-known political figure endorses a candidate, the latter often benefits, especially if it is his first political race. As a result, contenders have sought backing from individuals, interest groups, labor unions, newspapers, and other sources for a number of years. Endorsements have been particularly important for candidates who lacked name recognition and who competed in at-large or citywide elections.[7]

Few studies have examined whether and to what extent these endorsements have affected voter preferences. The literature has found that they were more influential in local rather than state and national elections.[8] Others have discovered that voters relied to a larger degree on candidate endorsements, especially from newspapers, in nonpartisan elections.[9] However, an endorsement alone cannot guarantee a victory.

A number of Memphians have believed that candidates could not win without a substantial amount of support from Harold Ford, Sr. When Ford endorsed and actively campaigned for candidates, they allegedly benefited from a higher black turnout and black vote percentage, but Ford often alienated white voters. In many of the mayoral elections that occurred before 1991, black contenders blamed their losses on a lack of support from Harold Ford, Sr. Despite reports that he had wanted to become the city's first black mayor before the Herenton win, Ford has not run for the office. In this section, I will discuss his endorsements in Memphis mayoral elections from 1975 (when the first serious black contender ran for office) to 1991 (when the first black mayor was elected).

After the Ford brothers formed an organization in 1974, they began endorsing candidates for local and state offices. Harold Ford, Sr., created a separate ballot to endorse his preferred contenders. A larger number of candidates who were running for local and state offices sought endorsements from Ford as his popularity grew in Memphis. Some paid a small fee to have their names listed on the Harold Ford ballot.

According to James Q. Wilson, the leaders of organizations are primarily concerned with maintaining and enhancing their individual and organizational influence.[10] Mainly, Harold Ford, Sr., has endorsed candidates in order to strengthen his power base. When his preferred candidates won elections, Ford benefited from the perception that he delivered the black vote and a substantial black turnout at the polls. Many persons believed that black candidates could not win without a Ford endorsement.

In addition, Ford has supported candidates so that he could defeat his rivals. Former Memphis city council member and 1987 mayoral contender Minerva Johnican has had public battles with Harold Ford, Sr. In a 1980 congressional race, she became one of the few black candidates to make a credible run against him, but was defeated by a wide margin of approximately 40,700 to 11,300.[11] Two years later, Ford strongly endorsed and campaigned for newcomer Julian Bolton for the Shelby County Commission in an alleged retaliatory action. Bolton defeated Johnican, the incumbent, by 398 votes.

From 1975–1991, Harold Ford endorsed a number of mayoral candidates. In 1975, the first serious black contender, Otis Higgs, Jr., ran for mayor. The strength of Harold Ford's endorsements had not been determined because of his relatively brief political career. Although Higgs received approximately 96 percent of the black vote and 10 percent of the white vote in the runoff election, he was defeated primarily because of a higher white voter turnout of almost 20 percentage points.[12] During the 1979 mayoral election, Higgs received an endorsement from the now influential Harold Ford ballot, but lost the runoff primarily because of a low black voter turnout rate which trailed that of whites by approximately 15 percentage points.

In a 1982 special mayoral election, Harold Ford endorsed J. O. Patterson, Jr., in the primary, but not in the runoff race. Mostly as a result of a split white vote, Patterson emerged as the top contender in the primary election with 40.6 percent of the overall vote as compared to 30 percent for Richard C. Hackett. Harold Ford remained neutral during the runoff campaign. Final results showed that the 60 percent black voter turnout lagged 8 percent behind that of whites. Hackett defeated Patterson by receiving approximately 54.4 percent of the total vote to Patterson's 45.6 percent. On the day of Hackett's swearing-in ceremony, Patterson blamed his defeat on a lack of support from Ford. However, it resulted from a lack of white crossover support and low black voter turnout in a racially polarized election.[13]

In 1983, Senator John Ford competed against six other black contenders in the Memphis mayor's race. Despite Harold Ford's efforts to persuade voters to support the senator, he only received approximately 22 percent of the total vote (75 percent from black voters). Although this percentage was the highest received by a black candidate in 1983, it was not sufficient enough to prevent incumbent Richard Hackett's reelection with a 57 percent of the total vote.

Before the W. W. Herenton win, the 1987 mayoral race was the most promising for the election of a black mayor in Memphis. During the 1980s, the black population steadily increased by 7.2 percent while the white population decreased by 6.4 percent. According to the Shelby County Election Commission, the city gained a black majority in 1986.

Since Memphis had a predominantly black population, black candidates did not have to garner a substantial crossover vote from whites if they could encourage a large voter turnout among black voters. However, four black candidates competed in the election and the black turnout rate was disappointing. Minerva Johnican received the majority of the black vote (approximately 52 percent). Although Harold Ford did not endorse any of the candidates, John and James Ford supported white candidate Bill Gibbons. However, Mayor Richard Hackett won his second reelection bid.

In 1991, the Ford organization was preoccupied with Harold Ford's third mail and bank fraud trial, yet the congressman was strongly involved in the selection process for the one black consensus candidate to face Richard Hackett in the October primary election. During the last ten days of the Herenton campaign, the congressman endorsed Herenton, organized volunteers and gave speeches encouraging turnout during the get-out-the-vote campaign. Herenton won the election by approximately 172 votes. A final audit narrowed this margin to 142 votes.[14]

Findings and Data Analysis

The data in Table 2 seem to indicate weak correlations between the independent (Ford endorsements) and the dependent variables (black turnout rates, black vote percentages, and white vote percentages). Concerning turnout rates, Harold Ford did not endorse candidates Otis Higgs and J. O. Patterson, Jr., in the 1975 and 1982 runoff elections. However, approximately 56.5 and 60 percent of black citizens voted in these runoffs. Moreover, despite Harold Ford's support, black turnout decreased by 12 percent and lagged behind that of whites by almost 20 percent during John Ford's mayoral campaign in 1983. In 1991, the black turnout rate would probably have been substantial even if Ford had not gotten involved because black citizens wanted to elect the city's first black mayor. In addition, the candidates' black and white vote percentages may have resulted from the history of racially polarized voting in Memphis mayoral elections rather than from Ford endorsements.[15]

However, the analysis of variance shows that there is a significant difference in the candidates' mean black turnout, black vote percentage, and white

Table 2
Regression Estimates of Memphis Mayoral Election Results

Ford Endorsement	Mayoral Race	Mayoral Candidate	Black Vote	White Vote	Total Vote	Black Turnout	White Turnout
No	1975 Runoff	O. Higgs	96.8	10.1	42.0	56.5	59.1
Yes	1979 Runoff	O. Higgs	96.3	3.7	47.1	42.4	57.6
No	1982 Runoff	J.O. Patterson	96.5	9.0	45.6	60.0	68.0
Yes	1983 General	J. Ford	75.0	1.0	23.0	48.0	65.0
No	1987 General	M. Johnican	52.0	1.0	22.65	37.0	42.0
Yes	1991 General	W.W. Herenton	98.5	1.5	49.4	65.2	64.6

Source: Shelby County Board of Election Commission

Table 3
Calculation of the Test Statistic for the Data in Table 2

Black Turnout	x^2	Black Vote	x^2	White Vote	x^2
56.5	3192.25	96.8	9370.24	10.1	102.01
42.4	1797.76	96.3	9273.69	3.7	13.69
60.0	3600.00	96.5	9312.25	9.0	81.00
48.0	2304.00	75.0	5625.00	1.0	1.00
37.0	1369.00	52.0	2704.00	1.0	1.00
65.2	4251.04	98.5	9702.25	1.5	2.25
c^1= 309.1	16,514.05	c^2= 515.1	45987.43	c^3=26.3	200.95
n^1= 6		n^2= 6		n^3= 6	

$\Sigma x^2 = 62{,}702.43$
$\Sigma x = 850.0$
$N = 18$

Table 4
Summary of ANOVA for Ford Endorsements

Source of Variation	Sum of Squares	Degrees of Freedom	Mean Square	F
Between (factor)	20074.292	1	20074.292	41.10
Within (error)	2442.013	5	488.4026	
Total	22516.305	6		

vote percentage depending on whether they received Ford endorsements. In this research, the critical values are 16.258 at the .01 level and 6.61 at the .05 level. Tables 3 and 4 provide a calculation of the test statistic and a summary table of the ANOVA for Ford endorsements.[16] In this research, we can reject the null hypothesis because the calculated value (41.10) falls in the critical region at both the .01 and .05 levels.

The Possibility of a Black Political Machine

In *City Politics*, Edward Banfield and James Q. Wilson defined a political machine as:

> A business organization in a particular field [which is primarily concerned with] getting votes and winning elections.... It is interested only in making and distributing income—mainly money—to those who win and work for it.... The voter who is indifferent to issues, principles, and candidates puts little or no value on his vote and can be induced relatively easily (or cheaply) to put it at the machine's disposal.[17]

Primarily because of racial discrimination, black citizens have been among the most exploited groups by political machines, such as those in Baltimore,

Boston, Chicago, Cincinnati, Kansas City, Memphis, New York City, Philadelphia, and other cities. Robert K. Merton found that deprived classes and disadvantaged groups were more likely to accept machine rule.[18] Since black citizens usually comprised both a deprived class and a disadvantaged group, they relied on political machines to meet their needs.[19]

Hanes Walton pointed out that blacks usually were "of" not "in" political machines.[20] Machine bosses often allowed black community leaders to lead "submachines."[21] They persuaded black voters to support the machine's candidates, but were not appointed to high-level posts within the organizations nor provided with the authority to make crucial decisions.[22] In some cities, the existence of machine rule continues to be evident in cities with large black populations.[23]

Because a black political machine has never existed, one must question whether black politicians have ever possessed the power to create machines. Black family members have won offices and given influential endorsements in other cities that once had machine rule. In an article on St. Louis politics, Stein and Kohfeld stated, "[Congressman William Clay's] imprimatur means campaign support. Unless white opposition is very fragmented, this support is a necessary condition for success."[24] In Baltimore, members of the Mitchell family have been elected, given endorsements, and challenged both white and black machine politicians.[25] In New Orleans, Mayor Marc Morial was elected in a city that was once governed by his father Ernest "Dutch" Morial.[26] Thus, black family members have won offices in a number of cities.

Nevertheless, neither the Fords, Clays, Mitchells, nor Morials have established machines. According to its definition, a political machine provides incentives, influences vote choice, and wins elections.[27] Concerning incentives, the Fords have always been known for their high level of constituent service, but have not been able to provide the benefits such as patronage jobs, money, and others rewards to their supporters as did other machine leaders. Moreover because of the organization's size, the Fords cannot effectively mobilize all of the city's precincts as have other machine leaders and they have less support among white voters.

Conclusion

This research examined the dynamics of the Ford organization, the impact of Harold Ford, Sr.'s endorsements and the allegations of a Ford machine. The analysis of variance found a significant difference in the candidates' mean black turnout and in black vote and white vote percentages when they received endorsements. In essence, this analysis found that Harold Ford gave a number of influential endorsements during his political career, yet lacked the power and resources to control a political machine.

Notes

1. This article only examines the 1979 mayoral runoff election rather than the primary.
2. Steven F. Lawson, *Running for Freedom: Black Political and Civil Rights Since 1941* (Philadelphia: Temple University Press, 1991), 146–82.

3. Marion Orr, "The Struggle for Black Empowerment in Baltimore: Electoral Control and Governing Coalitions," in *Racial Politics in American Cities: Second Edition*, ed. Rufus Browning, Dale Rogers Marshall, and David Tabb (New York: Longman, 1997), 205; Lana Stein and Carol W. Kohfeld, "St. Louis's Black-White Elections: Products of Machine Factionalism and Polarization," *Urban Affairs Quarterly*, 27 (December 1991): 245.
4. James Q. Wilson, *Political Organizations* (New York: Basic Books Inc., 1973), 9.
5. Sharon D. Wright, *Hands Which Once Picked Cotton: Race, Power and Political Emergence in Memphis* (manuscript under review).
6. In August 1992, Harold Ford, John Ford, and Michael Hooks referred to themselves as the "dream team." Although the Fords won with massive percentages of the black vote (approximately 90 to 95 percent), Hooks lost his bid for Shelby County property assessor by approximately 1 percent. Ford's endorsement was said to have had a negative effect on the Hooks campaign during the final days before the election. As Ford made appearances on behalf of the "dream team," he was accused of heightening racial polarization and alienating white voters. Two years later in the 1994 Shelby County mayor's race, Harold Ford experienced a humiliating loss after he endorsed white independent candidate Jack Sammons despite the candidacy of Senator John Ford and three other black contenders. Republican Jim Rout later defeated Sammons by a large margin.
7. Susan Welch and Timothy Bledsoe, *Urban Reform and Its Consequences* (Chicago: University of Chicago Press, 1988), 60.
8. Dorothy Giobbe, "Endorsements: Influential or Irrelevant?," *Editor and Publisher*, 9 (April 6, 1974): 9.
9. Paul L. Hain, "How an Endorsement Affected a Non-Partisan Mayoral Vote," *Journalism Quarterly*, 52 (Summer 1977): 337; Lana Stein and Arnold Fleischmann, "Newspaper and Business Endorsements in Municipal Elections: A Test of the Conventional Wisdom," *Journal of Urban Affairs*, 9, 4 (1987): 328.
10. James Q. Wilson, *Political Organizations* (New York: Basic Books Inc., 1973), 9.
11. Shelby County Board of Election returns.
12. Before June 1991, a majority vote requirement stipulated that if none of the candidates in the primary election received a vote of at least 50 percent, a runoff election would be held approximately one month later. In June 1991, a federal judge ruled that this requirement as discriminatory because it diluted black voting strength.
13. Sharon D. Wright, *Hands Which Once Picked Cotton: Race, Power and Political Emergence in Memphis* (manuscript under review).
14. Harold Ford was not involved in the 1995 mayoral election in which W. W. Herenton received approximately 75 percent of the vote and defeated white candidate John Baker.
15. Sharon D. Wright, "The Failure of the Deracialization Strategy for Black Candidates in Memphis Mayoral Elections," in *Race, Politics and Governance in the U.S.*, ed. Huey L. Perry (Gainesville: University Press of Florida, 1997).
16. The calculated value (F) was determined by using the following equations:

Source of Variation	SS	df	MS	F
Between (factor)	$SS_b = å(\underline{c}^2) - (å\underline{x})_2 / (n)$	$k-1 / N$	$\frac{SS_b}{df_b}$	$\frac{MS_b}{MS_w}$
Within (error)	$SS_w = å x^2 - å(\underline{c}^2) / n$	$N-k / df_w$	$\underline{SS}_w$	
Total	$SS_t = å x^2 - (å\underline{x})^2 / N$	$N-1$		

See Victoria L. Mantzoupolos, *Statistics for the Social Sciences* (Englewood Cliffs, NJ: Prentice-Hall Inc., 1994), 332–44.
17. Edward C. Banfield and James Q. Wilson, *City Politics* (New York: Vintage Books, 1963), 115.
18. Robert K. Merton, *Social Structure and Social Theory* (New York: Free Press, 1968).
19. William J. Grimshaw, *Bitter Fruit: Black Politics and the Chicago Machine, 1931–1991* (Chicago: University of Chicago Press, 1992), 5; James Q. Wilson, *Negro Politics* (New York: Free Press, 1960), 54.
20. Hanes Walton, *Black Politics: A Theoretical and Structural Analysis* (Philadelphia: J.B. Lippincott, 1972).
21. Edward C. Banfield and James Q. Wilson, *City Politics* (New York: Vintage Books, 1963); William J. Grimshaw, *Bitter Fruit: Black Politics and the Chicago Machine, 1931–1991* (Chicago: University of Chicago Press, 1992), 72
22. Hanes Walton, *Black Politics: A Theoretical and Structural Analysis* (Philadelphia: J.B. Lippincott, 1972), 56–69.
23. John M. Allswang, *Bosses, Machines and Urban Voters* (Baltimore: Johns Hopkins University Press, 1986), 148–62; John J. Harrigan, *Political Change in the Metropolis: Fifth Edition* (New York: HarperCollins College Publishers, 1993), 94; John Mollenkopf, "New York: The Great Anomaly," in *Racial Politics in American Cities: Second Edition*, ed. Rufus Browning, Dale Rogers Marshall, and David Tabb (New York: Longman, 1997), 103–107.
24. Lana Stein and Carol W. Kohfeld, "St. Louis's Black-White Elections: Products of Machine Factionalism and Polarization," *Urban Affairs Quarterly*, 27 (December 1991): 245.
25. Marion Orr, "The Struggle for Black Empowerment in Baltimore: Electoral Control and Governing Coalitions," in *Racial Politics in American Cities: Second Edition*, ed. Rufus Browning, Dale Rogers Marshall, and David Tabb (New York: Longman, 1997), 205.
26. Richard L. Engstrom and Willie D. Kirkland, "The 1994 New Orleans Mayoral Election: Racial Divisions Continue," *Urban News*, 9 (Spring 1994): 6–9.
27. Harold E. Gosnell, *Machine Politics: Chicago Model* (Chicago: University of Chicago Press, 1937); William J. Grimshaw, *Bitter Fruit: Black Politics and the Chicago Machine, 1931–1991* (Chicago: University of Chicago Press, 1992), 5; James Q. Wilson, *Negro Politics* (New York: Free Press, 1960); Raymond Wolfinger, "Why Political Machines Have Not Withered Away and Other Revisionist Thoughts," *Journal of Politics* 34 (May 1982): 365–98.

References

Allswang, John M. 1986. *Bosses, Machines and Urban Voters*. Baltimore: Johns Hopkins University Press.

Banfield, Edward C., and James Q. Wilson. 1963. *City Politics*. New York: Vintage Books.

Engstrom, Richard L., and Willie D. Kirkland. 1995. "The 1994 New Orleans Mayoral Election: Racial Divisions Continue." *Urban News*, 9 (Spring): 6–9.

Giobbe, Dorothy. 1996. "Endorsements: Influential or Irrelevant?" *Editor and Publisher*, 129 (April 6): 9.

Gosnell, Harold Foote. 1937. *Machine Politics: Chicago Model*. Chicago: University of Chicago Press.

Gregg, James E. 1965. "Newspaper Editorial Endorsements and California Elections, 1948–1962." *Journalism Quarterly*, 42: 532–38.

Grimshaw, William, Jr. 1993. *Bitter Fruit: Black Politics and the Chicago Machine, 1931–1993*. Chicago: University of Chicago Press.

Hain, Paul L. 1977. "How an Endorsement Affected a Non-Partisan Mayoral Vote." *Journalism Quarterly*, 52 (Summer): 337–40.

Harrigan, John J. 1993. *Political Change in the Metropolis.: Fifth Edition*. New York: HarperCollins College Publishers.

Lawson, Steven F. 1991. *Running for Freedom: Black Politics and Civil Rights Since 1941*. Philadelphia: Temple University Press.

Mantzoupolos, Victoria L. 1994. *Statistics for the Social Sciences* Englewood Cliffs, NJ: Prentice-Hall Inc.

Merton, Robert K. 1968. *Social Structure and Social Theory*. New York: Free Press.

Mollenkopf, John. 1997. "New York: The Great Anomaly." In *Racial Politics in American Cities: Second Edition*, ed. Rufus Browning, Dale Rogers Marshall, and David Tabb. New York: Longman.

Orr, Marion. 1997. "The Struggle for Black Empowerment in Baltimore: Electoral Control and Governing Coalitions." In *Racial Politics in American Cities: Second Edition*, ed. Rufus Browning, Dale Rogers Marshall, and David Tabb. New York: Longman, 201–19.

Stein, Lana, and Arnold Fleischmann. "Newspaper and Business Endorsements in Municipal Elections: A Test of the Conventional Wisdom." *Journal of Urban Affairs*, 9, 4 (1987): 325–36.

Stein, Lana, and Carol W. Kohfeld. "St. Louis's Black-White Elections: Products of Machine Factionalism and Polarization." *Urban Affairs Quarterly*, 27 (December 1991): 227–48.

Walton, Hanes. 1972. *Black Politics: A Theoretical and Structural Analysis*. Philadelphia: J.B. Lippincott.

Welch, Susan, and Timothy Bledsoe. 1988. *Urban Reform and Its Consequences: A Study in Representation* Chicago: University of Chicago Press.

Wilson, James Q. 1960. *Negro Politics*. New York: Free Press.

———. 1973. *Political Organizations*. New York: Basic Books Inc.

Wolfinger, Raymond E. 1982. "Why Political Machines Have Not Withered Away and Other Revisionist Thoughts." *Journal of Politics*, 34 (May): 365–98.

Wright, Sharon D. 1997. "The Failure of the Deracialization Strategy for Black Candidates in Memphis Mayoral Elections." In *Race, Politics and Governance in the U.S.*, ed. Huey L. Perry. Gainesville: University Press of Florida.

———. *Hands Which Once Picked Cotton: Race, Power and Political Emergence in Memphis* (manuscript under review).

American Civilization, Name Change, and African-American Politics

S. N. Sangmpam

Syracuse University

In the winter of 1989, an old debate was rekindled among African Americans. It set those who prefer to be called "blacks" in opposition to those who prefer "African Americans." To advocates of the term "black," a change to "African American" is nothing more than a semantic exercise that would take the limelight away from the "real issues" of homelessness, drugs, and poverty in the ghettos. Those who push for the term "African American" favor it only halfheartedly over the term "black," which they do not categorically reject, and offer a predictable, if partially sound, reason to adopt it. For most, the term "African American" allows the cultural link with Africa. I argue that rather than take the limelight away from the "real issues" of poverty and homelessness, a name change helps solve them.

The Name Change Debate

Name changes for African Americans are not new. Simple name changes do not change people's lives. Why a name is changed and for what purpose has the potential to do so. Unfortunately, the gymnastics of name change has so far lacked this potential because it rests on the wrong reasons. The debate fails to identify its central issue, which trivializes it. In the 1989 debate, for instance, one of the debaters maintained that, "I'm willing to be called a Martian as long as I'm given economic equity and a real opportunity to expand." Apparently one can be called "nigger" or "brainless" and still be given economic equity—a contradiction in terms. Another debater likes the term "black" for its "poetry"—whatever that means—and is "not willing to give it up." The argument of still another advocate of the term "black" is apparently dictated by the sheer physical (mental?) exhaustion that results from the gymnastics of name change:

> I see no particular need to change. I am comfortable with the term "black." I've

gone through changes in the Deep South over the word "Negro." I fought with the press...to write the word "Negro" [with a] capital N. Then, we got them to go to Black. I don't see any need for me to make any changes at this time...I don't see any need to identify us as "African-Americans." (*Ebony*, July 1989: 80, 77, 80)

His exhaustion is understandable. The battles of name changes have been long and exhausting. Since the eighteenth century, the terms "black," "negro," "African," and "Afro-American" have been despised, adopted, dropped, and readopted. By the end of the nineteenth century, African Americans referred to themselves as "colored" or "negro." The battle of the 1930s consisted of changing the term "negro" with a small *n* to "Negro" with a capital *N*. In the post-1954 period, and especially in the 1960s, the term "black" replaced that of "Negro." The preeminence of the term "black" was justified by "black consciousness" that was associated with the "Black Power" movement.

Although used in different languages, the terms "negro" and "black" mean the same thing. "Negro" traces its origin to the Latin adjective "niger" (nigra, nigrum), from which is derived the Spanish and Portuguese term "negro" and the French adjectives "nègre" and "noir." The English translation is "black." It is plausible that the Romans and Greeks—when they did not use the term "Ethiopian"—referred to Africans with some descriptive term akin to "black." Indeed, the Germanic and English origins of the term "black" are traceable to Latin and Greek verbs that convey the idea of "to burn." The Greek and Roman reference to Africans was, then, descriptive/geographical in that it pointed to people "burnt by the sun." It is in this sense that ancient Egyptians, like people of the Axum (Ethiopia) and Kush (Nubia) kingdoms, were Kemites, that is, "people burnt by the sun." No ideological definition was involved. By the sixteenth century, the terms "black" and "negro" had acquired an ideological meaning in the face of "white." More importantly, before Europeans popularized the terms "negro" and "black," Africans did not refer to themselves as "black people." There is no shred of evidence for it, all the more so because Africans, like most cultures, have a negative perception of "black." By the same token, they did not refer to Europeans as "white" but by their geographical origins, functions, or social strata. Thus, *mbwel* and *bis a mpor* in Kibunda mean respectively "he who rules" (a reference to colonial occupation) and "those from Portugal" (a reference to the earlier arrival of and familiarity with the Portuguese; hence, today *Mpor* and *mpoto* in Zaire/Congo mean "Europe"); *mundele* in Kikongo and Lingala also means "he who rules," "he who possesses" (another reference to colonial stratification); and *muzungu* in Swahili means "European," as does *toubah* in the Senegambia region of West Africa.

In light of all this, the battle over "negro" and "black" by African Americans was off target. The battle was not about what Africans called themselves. Nor was it about recapturing the descriptive meaning of the identification term used by the Romans and Greeks because it had already been lost by the sixteenth century. Even if the Greek/Roman meaning had remained, there is no reason why their label should be preferred to that of the Africans themselves. One can only conclude that the battleground for name change was chosen and dictated to African Americans by the very racist ideology that they sought to combat. The fight over capitalizing "negro" or calling oneself "black" as opposed to "Negro" did not mean much as long as both terms said the same thing. Certainly one can sympathize with the attempt by those involved in the 1960s Black Power movement to preserve the "spirit of the struggle" by sticking to the term "black." But sympathy does not erase the fact that as a counter-ideology, the movement had reinforced what it attempted to avoid.

The recent argument in favor of substituting the term "African American" for "black" is generally based on what Jesse Jackson termed "cultural integrity," that is, as John Henrik Clarke put it, the need for African Americans "to find themselves on the map of human geography...and to know that they are an African people wherever [they] are on the face of the earth" (Clarke, 1989). This is only a small part of the reason. To be sure, given that the ritualized "white-black" dichotomy involves the fabrication of "black" as nothingness in history and civilization, it is understandable that African Americans call for "multiculturalism" and a connection with Africa to "deconstruct" this nothingness and to re-identify themselves with African civilization. In this sense, there is a link between the term "African American" and "cultural integrity/heritage."

Yet, dwelling on this cultural argument or on the term "African American" is to miss the point. The need felt today by African Americans to insert themselves into the Pan African world and to claim their African descent is less a "cultural" need than a political one. Indeed, multiculturalism implies that the "dominant culture" is claimed by European Americans as their sole property and that there is a need for other groups to fill the void by asserting their "own culture." But the "dominant culture" is no less nor more than American civilization. Claiming it to be "Western" (i.e., European) is the same as denying the contributions of other groups to it. This denial is only ideological, that is, illusionary, and does not square with the reality. The reality is that American civilization not only benefits from the African American contributions but *already contains* African culture/heritage in it. Melville Herskovitz and DuBois before him have, however imperfectly, proved this point (Herskovitz, 1990; DuBois, 1924). It is illusionary to think that slave labor, African-American technical inventions, their contribution to American democracy, religion, literature, music, and popular culture in general are not part of African heritage. Being misinformed and not being taught about it or about Africa is not the same as African culture/heritage not being part of American civilization. That all these contributions are part of the "unique experience" of African Americans, as some claim, does not negate this reality either. The "unique experience" of European Americans did not produce blues music that strikingly invokes the musical rhythms and melodies of the Congo Basin. (By the way, the origins of the blues are more fruitfully searched for in Central, not Western Africa). The point is that, culturally, African Americans are already, even when not acknowledged, linked to Africa, as European Americans are to Europe, through American culture. There would be no need for "multiculturalism" if every American were referred to as "American" and not as "white" and "black," that is, if no "out-of-place" feelings were imposed on some groups, which corresponds to their strikingly lower socio-economic status. Indeed, what is remarkably obvious as well as debilitating for the masses of African Americans is their low socio-economic status, not their "culture."

I argue that the lack of socio-economic and political equality for African Americans raises the issue of politics and socio-political rights. Socio-political rights, as opposed to natural rights, emanate from one's contribution to the social product (goods and services), the basis of any political competition. As an ideology, racism aims to deny the contributions of African Americans to American civilization (hence to the social product), which neutralizes them politically and reduces their share of the social product. The term "black" (and its predecessors "negro" or "nigger") and the black-white dichotomy are a major means of this ideological denial. Social and political struggles waged to correct the situation failed to identify this overriding goal of the ideology. By choosing to fight it with counter-ideologies (liberalism, civil rights, nationalism), the protagonists for change reinforced the ideological denial of the contributions of African Americans to the social product, hence their lower share of it. To be successful, a corrective struggle must rely, not on a counter-ideology, but on the political issue of the African-American contribution to the social product as the sine qua non for their claim to socio-political rights; as such, it involves inescapably a name change—a rejection of the terms "black" and "white"—to neutralize the white-black dichotomy and reassert the contributions of African Americans to the social product and their rights to an equal portion of it.

Posing the problem of name change today may seem a useless exercise given the increasingly wide acceptance of the term "African American" in lieu of "black." To avoid any misunderstanding, let me, at the outset, underscore the fact that the purpose here is not to advocate the use of the term "African American," to whose limitations I have just pointed. My intention is *not* to demonstrate that the term "African American" can help reaffirm the contributions of African Americans to the social product. The term "African American" does not display or contain in it the contributions of African Americans; it is not the issue. Although I use the term because of its increasing acceptance and more positive connotation, the essay's objective is different and broader. I argue that, if it can specify its main reasons, the name change itself (and not necessarily to "African American") *qua* a political struggle helps reassert the rights of African Americans to the social product. At the very least, I intend to show that the name change is a deeply political issue not only in the sense of competitive politics, but in the sense that it is an issue of interest for political theory.

Social Product, Politics, and Rights

Lack of social and political equality and rights for African Americans raises the issue of politics. Politics is a competition among social actors, groups, or classes over the distribution of the social product, that is, goods and services in a political community. Insofar as allocation of the social product is contingent upon the control of political power, politics is, at the same time, about the control and distribution of political power. The "common good" is a necessary effect and not the goal of politics, which is first about the competition over the social product. In Lasswell's suggestive phrase, politics is about "who gets what, when, and how" (Lasswell, 1936).

That politics is about the social product has been amply demonstrated in ancient and modern times. Aristotle subordinates politics (the ability to rule or not to rule) to property and distinguishes democracy from oligarchy on the basis of poverty and wealth (Aristotle, 1985: 4, 11, 1295; 3, 8, 1279b–39; 4, 3, 1290a30–b20). According to Hobbes, property caused war, hence politics (Hobbes, 1991: 118, 120, 124). Rousseau thinks of society as the cause of "obstacles" to the preservation of human beings. These "obstacles" result from the "generalized state of war" (politics) caused by the competition over social and natural resources. The competition over the social product and the "obstacles" that it generates require a "social contract," that is, the state to regulate them (Rousseau, 1950: Bk. 1, 13–14).

According to Adam Smith, political economy is a "science of a statesman or legislator" that aims to provide subsistence for the people" (Smith, 1937: 397, 670, 674). John Locke agrees when he maintains that government has no other end but the preservation of property (Locke, 1681). In American political thought, Alexander Hamilton, James Madison, Thomas Jefferson, and others hold opinions consonant with the subordination of politics to the social product. "The people who own the country ought to govern it," declared John Jay (Parenti, 1988: 5, 61). Marx, of course, does not differ from the above political theorists. He, too, defines politics in relation to the social product. In a class society, politics is a struggle pitting one class against another; one class exploits the other by virtue of its ownership and control over the means of production. The state and its implicit "contract" is structured and controlled by the exploiting class (Marx, 1954). In the African Kongo kingdom, government was not something established to govern a territory in the abstract but to represent the power of the senior lineage that controlled the land (Sangmpam, 1994: 45–103).

Thus, politics is the competition over property, goods and services—the "social product." The identification of politics with the social product has three important implications for discussions about African Americans. First, the notion of the "social product" implies that the claimable goods and services—the object of the competition—are a by-product of direct or indirect "social" involvement. That is, they have been contributed to by different social actors in different capacities, regardless of whether these goods are private or public property. This point is a logical derivative of the writings of some political theorists such as Montesquieu and Rousseau. Montesquieu's rejection of Hobbes's position on natural law was accompanied by his acceptance of the fact that society preceded the "generalized state of war." Rousseau did the same. In so doing, both Montesquieu and Rousseau accept that goods that are the object of the "state of war" (i.e., politics) are produced *ex ante* by the "forces" of the individuals who make up society (Althusser, 1977: 118–21). In other words, the objects of politics are collectively produced before they are placed at the center of the competition. This point is supported by Julius Nyerere, the former president of Tanzania, who rejects both Marxism and liberalism. "The wealth of the millionaire," he writes, "depends as little on the enterprise or abilities of the millionaire himself as the power of a feudal monarch depended on his own efforts, enterprise or brain. Both are users, exploiters of the abilities and enterprise of other people" (Nyerere, 1968: 2). Marx shares this view with respect to the capitalist society: "To be a capitalist is to have not only a purely personal, but a social status in production. Capital is a collective product, and only by the united action of many members, nay, in the last resort, only by the united action of all members of society, can it be set in motion. Capital is therefore not a personal, it is a social power" (Marx, 1954: 42). In short, the social product results from a whole civilization shaped, as it is, by the members of a given society in different capacities and roles. In American politics, the claimable goods and services constitute a "social" product for African Americans because of their contribution to it.

The *second* implication of the identification of politics with the social product is that the contribution to the social product involves *rights* for contributors. However strongly one may subscribe to a non-European communal mode of living or to the "natural instinct" of humans to live together in a community, this natural instinct does not provide an individual or a group or a class with equality or rights in the community. These are *earned* by contributing to what is distributable. Most of the political theorists discussed recognize not only the "social" nature of the goods and services at the center of politics but also the rights accrued to the contributors to the social product.

For Aristotle the contribution to the social product is to the citizens' rights what the amount of funds contributed to a commercial company's stock is to each shareholder's paid dividend (Newman, 1973: 250). According to Hobbes, the commodities of the Commonwealth are produced by the labor of its inhabitants, who have the right (presumably because of their labor) to expect that the sovereign distribute goods to them to avoid perpetual war (Hobbes, 1991: 170–76). The link is even more explicit according to Rousseau, "For the state, in relation to its members, is master of all their goods by the social contract, which, within the state, is the basis of all rights" (Rousseau, 1950: 19–20). He is echoed by Adam Smith who predicates the educational and defense policy of the state on the labor contributed by the citizens and subjects (Smith, 1937: 676, 734–35, 767, 773) and by James Mill who maintains that: "The greatest possible happiness of society is, therefore, attained by insuring to every man the greatest possible quantity of the produce of his labour" (Mill, 1978: 57). Marx, on the other hand, establishes a negative link between the contribution to the social product and rights. Because the proletariat feeds the bourgeoisie through its contribution to the social product/capital while it (the proletariat) sinks too low, it is the right of the proletariat to overthrow the bourgeoisie (Marx, 1954: 38). In Africa, despite the communal mode of living, rights were dictated by one's contribution to the social product. Julius Nyerere's attempt to establish African socialism (hence, equality and rights) in Tanzania in the late 1960s and the 1970s was predicated upon, among other things, the requirement in African pre-colonial societies that every able community member's claim to the social product depended on his or her share contributed to the social product:

> In traditional African society everybody was a worker. There was no other way of earning a living for the community.... The security that society gave to its members and the universal hospitality on which they could rely was the result of the fact that every member of society—barring only the children and the infirm—contributed his fair share of efforts towards the production of its wealth. (Nyerere, 1968: 3, 5)

Further evidence for the link between the contribution to the social product and rights is provided by immigration policies across the continents. Positively, they are based on the ability of the new immigrants to contribute to the national social product, and negatively, they prevent would-be immigrants from benefiting from the social product to which they did not contribute. The California-sparked debate about the allocation of social services to illegal and legal aliens is an example.

In light of the above, the *third* implication of the identification of politics with the social product is that the rights allocated to the contributors to the social product *are not abstract rights* or "natural rights." They, hence the civil rights involved, are *sociopolitical rights* emanating from their contribution to the social product.

> The main idea is that when a number of persons engage in a mutually advantageous cooperative venture according to rules, and thus restrict their liberty in ways necessary to yield advantages for all, those who have submitted to those restrictions have a *right to a similar acquiescence* on the part of those who have benefited from their submission. We are not to gain from the cooperative labors of others without doing our fair share. (Rawls, 1971: 112, emphasis added)

This discussion raises two types of questions: First, are these socio-political rights individual or group rights? Second, should they be proportionate to individual or group contributions to the social product? That I have referred to Western and non-Western political thought's three implications that derive from politics as competition over the social product does not mean that the two modes of thought share the same conception of right. Nor does it suggest that I subscribe to their respective notion of "right." Aristotle's concern, for instance, was not specifically "right" but "justice." According to him, the citizens' contribution to the social product allows them to have a share *proportionate* to their contribution. Differently put, Aristotle's view of justice implies unequal treatment based on one's contribution to the social product. It is no surprise, then, that he considers it "just" that those who are free citizens and equal (as opposed to those who are not) should have equality in other things and matters. This conception of "justice" is not necessarily synonymous with "right." The former implies "proportionate fairness," the latter entitlement. Proportionate fairness implies, among other things: (1) the assumption that some groups have contributed more than others to the social product, which is inconsistent with the very notion of the social product; and (2) the exclusion of some groups (e.g., slaves, ex-slaves, or possibly physically handicapped people) from the social product. To the extent that the notion of "fairness" must emanate, as I have argued, from one's contribution to the social product and not from "natural rights," it needs to be purged of this double Aristotelian import. Indeed, by rejecting the double import, fairness ceases to be proportionate to one's contribution and refers not to "justice" but to the "right" of individuals and *not* of a given group. It entitles (gives rights to) individual contributors to the social product *not* to a proportionate share of the social product but to the freedom from all types of political, economic, and social discriminations, marginalization, and oppression from other members of the political community. Because in all societies those who may not contribute to the social product (e.g., babies or mentally and physically handicapped people, etc.) are the progeny of some other members of the community who have contributed, they, too, are *entitled* to the same freedom (rights) by virtue of their relationship to their parents or relatives.

American Civilization and African Americans

Social product implies a whole civilization. Civilization, the accomplishments and ways of living of a people, involves: (1) the organization of material production and subsistence, which, in turn, relies on the development of technique and means of mastering nature; (2) social communication and interactions that include language, marriage, music, dance, literature, fine arts, sports, and so forth; (3) political organization, one aspect of which is military organization; and (4) ideological organization, of which religion is a major component. The contribution of African Americans to each of these components of American civilization is immense. For space reasons, I assume that these contributions by slaves and their descendants are well known today, and there is no need to rehearse them here.[1] DuBois sums them up: "The American Negro is and has been a distinct asset to this country and has brought a contribution without which America could not have been" (DuBois, 1924: 11). More recently, he was echoed by two sociologists who maintain that "not since ancient Rome conquered and then surrendered to the culture of its Greek slaves and freedmen has the culture of a dominant world civilization been so enormously influenced by so small a minority of people [African Americans]" (Patterson and Winship, 1992: 17).

Yet, at odds with the above prescriptions of the political theorists and philosophers, these contributions to the social product have not been translated into socio-political rights for African Americans, pointing to a relationship between their lower socio-economic status and race. Again, space precludes a repetition of these well-known facts. I will return to some of them as the argument proceeds. Suffice it to indicate that most striking is the growing number of what has been referred to as the "underclass." The median incomes for African-American families not only lag behind those of European Americans but have also dropped sharply since the 1980s. The number of homeless and penniless African Americans is disproportionately higher than that of European Americans. The educational infrastructure in African-American neighborhoods has deteriorated markedly; as a result, in contrast to the earlier rise, the number of African Americans enrolled in colleges and graduate schools has declined. The rate of joblessness for African Americans is disproportionately higher than that for the general population. Crime and violence, often drug related, disproportionately affect African-American neighborhoods. The result is the disproportionate number of incarcerated African Americans. African Americans have, on average, a shorter life expectancy than European Americans (Marable, 1983: 310–33).

Why, then, does a relationship exist between race and the lack of social and political equality and rights for African Americans despite the overwhelming evidence in favor of their contributions to American civilization, that is, to the social product?

Ideology of Denial and Neutralization

To answer this question, I return to the earlier proposition: As an ideological postulate, racism aims to deny the contributions of African Americans, which neutralizes them politically and reduces their share of the social product. The term "black" or its predecessors and the "black-white" dichotomy serve as a potent means of such denial. Political and ideological strategies of change reinforced this denial.

An ideology represents the imaginary relationship of individuals to their real conditions of existence. An imaginary relationship is not real; it is an illusion and an allusion to reality. The relationship is a two-tiered nexus. Ideology creates an imaginary relationship between individuals/groups (subjects, or s) and the bigger subject (S). The imaginary relationship, in turn, distorts the real conditions of existence of individuals/subjects; it conceals them by elevating itself through rituals, practices, and myths. Ideological practices and rituals so affect individuals and are taken so much for granted by them that these rituals become routine. Moreover, individuals are unaware of their involvement in the rituals that have become almost identical with real life. Individuals breathe ideology as they breathe air. In so doing, the imaginary relationship reproduces the conditions of existence of individuals/subjects in ways consistent with the prevailing interests and the goal of ideology. This property of ideology can be referred to as "ideological routinization or ritualization" (Sangmpam, 1994: 79–103).

With respect to the "black question" in the United States, this is accomplished by establishing an imaginary relationship between the "subjects/citizens" (s), of whom "blacks" are part, and the bigger subject (S), the "superior/white race." The imaginary relationship accomplishes two related objectives. It conceals and distorts the material interests involved and, more importantly, the contributions of African Americans to American civilization by elevating itself through the core dichotomous myth of "white-black races." This dichotomy involves a panoply of practices, myths, and rituals that evolves around the interchangeable terms "negro," "black," and "nigger." As terms of a relationship/comparison, "negro," "black," and "nigger" do not mean much by themselves; they acquire their meaning only through the other term of the relationship/comparison, that is, "white" and its accompanying myths (figure 1). "Negro/black" is antithetical to "white" the way, to use Sartre's phrase, that nothingness is antithetical to being. It is the very denial of what it represents. The "black-white" dichotomy is thus constructed

> in which the "white self" is created out of the violation of the black self, through its inclusion and degradation.... Thus the real being of the black person becomes insignificant in contrast to the intrinsically inconsequential color of his or her skin.... He or she becomes a thing, ultimately invisible. And this relation is mediated by the symbols of white and black. (Kovel, 1984: xliii, xliv)

To uncover the origins of the ideological role played by the dichotomy between "white and negro races," one has to go back to the pre-sixteenth-century period. It is fairly well established that during this period, anything black had a strangely negative connotation for Europeans (Kovel, 1984: 62–65)—not unlike Africans themselves. The earlier decline or stagnation of other

Figure 1
Black-White Dichotomy, Imaginary Relationships, and the Social Product

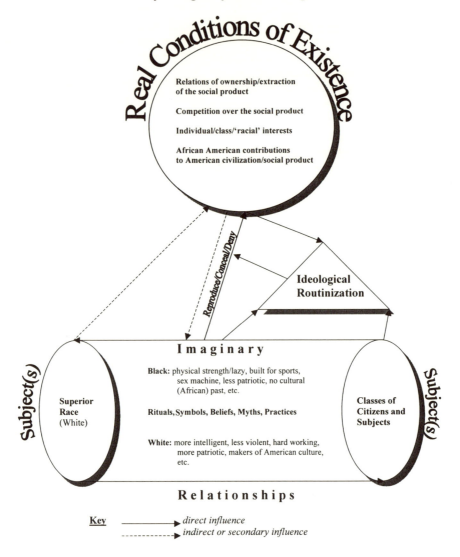

civilizations, including African ones, was followed by the rise of the European capitalist civilization by the sixteenth century. This period was accompanied by sustained contacts between Europeans and Africans whose dark complexion and different cultural patterns offered an easy target for European "fantasy of blackness," to use Joel Kovel's word. Attempts to justify and sustain the rise and dynamism of the new European civilization were accompanied by the need to deny/conceal those civilizations that preceded it, including the Axum-Nubian-Egyptian civilization. The need to deny gave rise to the fabrication of and dichotomy between "white and negro races." This process, which reached its highest point in the eighteenth century (see Diop, 1974; Bohannan, 1964; Bernal, 1987), resulted in the Atlantic slave trade, which, in a reciprocal manner, had allowed and strengthened the dichotomy. During slavery and in the post-slavery period, the ideological postulate served two interrelated purposes. The denial of African civilization became intertwined with the all- too-important goal of concealing African-American contributions to American civilization. The task was performed by the rituals associated with the terms "negro race" as opposed to "white race." This was, in turn, supported by "sociological" and pseudoscientific arguments that developed during the 1830–1860 period. Thus, for instance, combining biblical scriptures and pseudoscience, one apologist of slavery wrestled with ancient historians who asserted that Egypt "was originally inhabited by Negroes"; he proclaimed that "recent investigations have overthrown all previously received opinions on the subject, and that the Egyptians were a Caucasian race"; that "a marked moral and intellectual disparity [exists] between the races"; and that he had "proof of the moral and intellectual inferiority of the Negro and Indian when compared with the Caucasian" (Nott, 1981: 206–38). That the "negro" could not contribute to American civilization was consistent with this "racial inferiority." As another apologist put it, negro slaves provide vigor and docility whereas whites provide progress, civilization, and refinement (Hammond, 1981: 168–205).

This heritage has endured. The dependence of the real conditions of existence (racial and class interests) on ideological rituals ("white" vs. "black") make Americans breathe ideology the way they breathe air. Ideology is routinized through daily scenes and discourse in which "black" invokes automatic recognition and obviousness (that is nothingness), to use Louis Althusser's phrase. What is recognizable and obvious is that "blacks" are lazier, less intelligent, and more crime prone than "whites"; and that "blacks" did not, could not, and cannot contribute to American civilization.

Empirical and Historical Evidence

Longitudinal empirical evidence of this dichotomy is provided by studies done over the years. The situation under slavery has already been mentioned and needs not be repeated. Suffice it to say that the slavery period was so replete with dichotomic images and had so shaped the post-emancipation period that W. E. B. DuBois and Melville Herskovits were compelled, through their writings, to reconnect African Americans to their African past. In 1969, the dichotomy was confirmed in a study that recorded "whites'" opinions about "negroes." Values attributed to "negroes" were consistent with the ritualized images associated with "black/negro." For instance, concerning the predilection for pleasure seeking (lazy, happy-go-lucky, etc.) as opposed to responsibility, whites attributed this value to negroes with a frequency of 31 percent and only with a frequency of 9 percent to themselves. Concerning "high moral standards," they attributed them to negroes only with a frequency of 3 percent while reserving for themselves a frequency of 8 percent (Thune, 1969: 42). The situation was perhaps best summed up by two of the white interviewees: "You can't get a nigger to fool with a knitting machine. I don't think there's one in the United States," which is consistent with the fact that, "I guess I will always think of negroes as servants. I guess it's because the way I grew up" (Thune, 1969: 50, 103). A 1977 study, which correctly avoided survey questions and relied on in-depth interviews, echoed these sentiments. Among the dichotomic images associated with negroes or blacks were their instinctive violence, inferior intelligence, automatic inferior status, lack of ambition, happy-go-lucky (Wellman, 1977: 85, 86, 89, 117, 144, 153, 201). A January 9, 1991, *USA Today* survey of "whites" found that 62 percent think that "blacks" are lazier than "whites," 53 percent believe that "blacks" are less intelligent than "whites," 56 percent hold the view that "blacks" are more violent than "whites," and 54 percent believe that "blacks" are less patriotic than "whites." A 1996 survey of Syracuse, which was part of a class practicum for students in African-American politics, tends to support these views. The survey was not based on random sampling but on "geographical zone sampling." Both "whites" and "blacks" were surveyed and their opinions differed quite sharply. Three questions seeking to record the opinions of both groups on the white-black dichotomic naming yielded the following results: 84 percent (average) "blacks" think that the dichotomy creates ("always or often") the inferiority-superiority complex while 50 percent (average) "whites" think that this is "always or often" the case; whites do, however, supplement this with 50 percent agreeing that "white" implies "sometimes" more intelligent, less violent, and so forth.

The second aspect of the proposition I advanced above is that the white-black dichotomy leads to the denial of the contributions of African Americans, whether such a denial is accompanied by an explicitly contemptuous use of the term "black" ("negro/"nigger") or not. Here also evidence supports the claim. Under slavery, the ultimate consecration of the black-white dichotomy, the Confederate congress decreed in 1861 that if a slave invented a technical device, the pattern would be issued to the owner. The decree only codified a prevalent practice that had served to deny ownership of pattern to such slaves as Henry Blair, the inventor of the corn harvester. In 1857, in *Dred Scott v. Sandford*, Chief Justice of the Supreme Court Roger Taney, writing for the majority, declared that, "blacks had no rights which the white man was bound to respect." To be sure, there is no surprise here since the decision was consistent with slavery. But it does confirm my point. Because rights emanate from one's contribution to the social product, the dichotomic phrasing of the Supreme Court's decision clearly indicates that "blacks" were not granted rights because they represented nothingness to the "white man"; in other words, "black" implies lack of contribution to the social product generated by the "white man," who deserves all the rights. This point still stands even if one admits that Taney and other protagonists of slavery used from time to time "African race" to refer to "blacks" in Africa and the Americas. The term "African" was used not just marginally, but almost as a qualifier to "negro" or "black"; however, as indicated earlier, the purpose here is not to defend the term "African" or "African American."

One of the major contributions of African Americans to American civilization was the retention of aspects of African culture. Yet this contribution was denied (and is still denied by some) on the dichotomic grounds that enslaved negroes saw their own culture so inferior and that of their white masters so superior that they gave up their African aboriginal traditions to adopt those of their masters (Herskovits, 1990: 2). In other words, they did not contribute to American civilization. This view prevailed in both the pre-

and post-emancipation periods. Because it was reactionary, the overthrow of the Reconstruction strengthened this process of ideological denial and concealment. For instance, the movie *The Birth of a Nation* blunted the historically recognized accomplishments of African-American officials of the Reconstruction by equating "negro rule" with looting, lawlessness, ignorance, incompetence, and corruption (Franklin, 1989: 10–23). The demise of the Reconstruction led to the proliferation of negro-derived terms that sought to convey the idea of nothingness and of the noncontribution of African Americans to American civilization (see Logan, 1954). They ranged from "niggah" to "coon."

Because Elvis's debt to the African-American contribution to American musical heritage is well known, it is worth mentioning his oft-cited, albeit with no hard evidence, denial of this contribution. In his mind, indeed, "All black men were fit to do was shine my shoes and buy my records [and, presumably, not to be the source of his musical inspiration]." It is quite possible that Elvis never made the statement, but its persistence in the folklore only highlights the folk-like denial of African-American contributions. This folk-like denial is confirmed by some of the studies cited earlier. In the 1969 study, for instance, one interviewee maintained that, "Negroes have made progress.... This has been due to white people paying taxes and maintaining their schools and giving them privileges." For another, "these colored people that's not satisfied.... Load them on a ship and send them back. And say, 'Now here you are...we're going to run our country, you run yours'" (Thune, 1969: 50, 100). Those interviewed in the 1977 study frequently castigated "black impatience." In both studies, it is quite clear that "negroes" do not deserve material goods or to ask for them persistently because it is not their country and their contribution. This denial is perhaps best summed up by a 1990 anonymous flier addressed to "blacks":

> Basically, you have no black culture, only the white culture you've been taught. If a nigger desires to be successful in his career, he must act white.... What have niggers contributed to the world to be worthy of possessing a say in its affairs? Nothing! Everything has always been provided for you as if you were pets. Affirmative Action's...sole purpose was to try and get some of you off your lazy black asses and WORK.[2]

One understands then the invitation that is routinely extended to African Americans by racist groups (especially during racial confrontations) to "go back to Africa." In the 1996 Syracuse study both "blacks" and "whites" confirm this denial in different ways: 72 percent of blacks agree that the black-white dichotomy privileges ("always or often") white contributions at the expense of black contributions; 42.5 percent of whites say so. However, 48 percent of whites agree that this is "sometimes" the case.

Until recently and except in "black" studies, what strikes one most in the academia is the total absence of courses that make use of works by such African American thinkers as W. E. B. DuBois. The ongoing debate about "white canons," whatever its other objectives may be, has clearly highlighted this denial of African-American contributions. Henry Louis Gates, Jr., has argued for the need for an "alternative, minority canon of works" because, among other things, he does "not think white people are trained to see black intelligence" (D'Souza, 1991: 71). It is because "in classrooms across the nation...the contributions of black Americans to science and industry have been almost unknown" (Haber, 1970a: vii) that Louis Haber chronicles the lives of fourteen African-American inventors and scientists in *Black Pioneers of Science and Invention*. Ralph Ellison's *Invisible Man* and James Baldwin's *Nobody Knows My Name* are two of the best literary works that tell the story of nothingness imposed on African Americans by the denial of their contributions.

Any ideology has a programmatic aspect that sets priorities according to changing circumstances (see Rejai, 1984: 3–9). In this sense, despite its routinization, racist ideology changes programmatically to reflect new situations. One of these changes is in "whites' racial attitudes toward blacks" recorded in many survey studies (National Research Council, 1989; Tate et al., 1988). This change is accompanied by two concurrent events. First, the entrenched but openly offensive myths about "blacks" such as those discussed earlier are left dormant, although not profoundly as attested to by the *Bell Curve* debate; a new discourse based on "personal responsibility," "family values," and "morals" has been substituted for them. Yet "black" is still the target in the new discourse, since, as Walter Stafford points out, "both liberals and conservatives (believe) that many of the permissive trends in sex and drugs had originated in black lifestyles" (Pinkney, 1984: 31). The openly moralizing tone of the public debate in the 1980s and 1990s about "black responsibility" attests to it. Second, these changes of attitudes are accompanied by flagrant contradictions. Whites accept blacks now, but are unwilling to share residential neighborhoods with them, to integrate schools, to offer them jobs when they compete with white applicants, and so forth (Wellman, 1977: 131; Kovel, 1984: xxiii–xxiv; National Research Council, 1989).

Thus, because of social changes, to the earlier form of the denial of African-American contributions are added two new forms, wrapped up in a new ideological discourse: the moralizing discourse about "blacks" and the contradictory acceptance of "blacks" but refusal to share the social product with them. In all three forms, the white-black dichotomy sustains the ideological edifice, and the effect is the lowering of the African-American share of the social product.

From roughly 1877 to 1965, the denial translated into the denial of the rights to vote, of fair justice or economic opportunities under the Jim Crow laws. In all these instances, there was an excessively contemptuous use of the terms "nigger," "black," and "negro" that obviously supported this denial of African-American contributions to the social product. A 1930 study shows that among the reasons used to deny jobs to "negroes" were the beliefs about their mentality, limited intelligence, character, their general inability to perform the work required, and the claim that there were jobs exclusively reserved to the white race (Johnson, 1930: 73, 84). In the post-1965 period, despite obvious advances and the accurate assessment that "in the 1980s American society became more thoroughly integrated in terms of race relations than at any previous point in history" (Marable, 1991: 185–86), the effects of denial are more visible in the persistent and exacerbated social and political inequalities that affect African Americans. "Black lack of responsibility" means that African Americans are excluded from the social product because of their "own fault," and the contradictory refusal of whites to share with them means that they are kept out of the social product as well. The relationship between the white-black dichotomy and the denial of African-American contributions to American civilization is thus expressed in the form of joblessness, lack of education, lower income, homelessness or crime-infested neighborhoods, lack of political rights, and so forth. There is no need to rehearse here data about the lower socio-economic status of African Americans when compared to European Americans. Many studies have already done so (Farley and Allen, 1989; Pinkney, 1984; National Research Council, 1989; Barker and Jones, 1994). In almost all categories related to the social product, the white-black ratio disfavors blacks, which explains why 84.5 percent of African Americans feel that discrimination is a problem.

The proposition guiding this essay also suggests that, by denying African-American contributions and lowering their share of the social product, the ideological black-white construct conceals and enhances "whites'" racial interests. Empirical proof for this part of the proposition is not difficult to provide either. It is the other side of the same coin. Data provided by the studies just cited show in most categories how the share of whites is larger than that of blacks. From 1950 to 1980, the average black-white ratio in family income was 0.60 in favor of whites. In the 1996 Syracuse survey, 83 percent of blacks agreed that the characteristics associated with the term "white" (always or often) help whites advance their economic and political interests; 49 percent of whites think so, and 44 percent of them think that this is "sometimes" the case.

Americans' real conditions of existence are the economic, social, and political relations that govern their concrete existence in American civilization. They revolve around a set of individual, group, and class interests. In the racially conscious society these interests are "racial interests." They are consistent with allocating the bigger share of the social product to "whites." As James Baldwin so perceptively put it:

> Of course, it is true that many white people, including, certainly, the ancestors of many of our presidents, entered the country on similar terms—shipwrecks, criminals, and ladies fleeing to Salt Lake City to be married—but these all managed, and speedily enough, after all, to become White. They knew, at a glance, what would happen to them if they did *not* become White, and, by no means metaphorically, *on which side such bread as they might hope to find would be buttered.* I say, to "become" White, for they had not been White before their arrival, any more than I, in Africa, had been Black. In Africa, I had been part of a tribe and a language and a nation. (Baldwin, 1985: 29–30)

And as another observer put it, "to be 'white' essentially means that one's life chances improve dramatically over those of nonwhites, in terms of access to credit, capital, quality housing, health care, political influence, and equitable treatment in the criminal justice system" (Marable, 1991: 189). The 1977 study cited above found that the black-white dichotomy and its images "systematically provide economic, political, psychological, and social advantages for whites at the expense of blacks" (Wellman, 1977: 37). It did so by carefully relating the perceptions of its white interviewees to their political and material motivations and fears. In almost all cases, the negative connotations associated with "black" promote the interests of the "whites." As one of the interviewees put it, "somehow or other (whites) feel they are better than the colored fellow. They think they should have the choice of everything" (Wellman, 1977: 128–29).

Racial interests explain the contradictions and inconsistencies recorded in survey data dealing with "whites' attitude changes." Their unwillingness to share residential neighborhoods with blacks, to integrate schools, and to stop racial hirings despite the decline in prejudice and the moralizing ideological shift clearly reveal the point made earlier: despite its programmatic shift, ideological ritualization reproduces the prevailing racial interests. It is no surprise then that

> Young whites have learned to mimic African American music and singing styles, but they might vote against a black candidate for public office solely on racial grounds and oppose affirmative action program's adoption in their own businesses in order to avoid "reverse discrimination" against whites.... White students might purchase the latest taped recordings of black performing artists or cheer the exploits of black athletes at their university, but also bitterly oppose the adoption of academic requirements mandating courses in African-American or ethnic history, politics or literature. (Marable, 1991: 190)

The foregoing discussion helps understand what may be called the "invisible man syndrome." By reproducing racial interests, the racial imaginary relationship and its cohort of rituals strengthen themselves. Indeed, as racial segregation and discrimination become the policy reflection of the ideology, victimized African Americans cannot help but develop social behaviors that actualize the myths created by the ideology: "But to whom can I be responsible, and why should I be, when you refuse to see me," asks Ellison's *Invisible Man*. And this is true in real life of African Americans. The unbreakable link between job discrimination/unemployment and crime/welfare actualizes the myth that "blacks" are lazier, more welfare-dependent, and more violent than "whites"; the structural link between substandard education and high drop-out rate/crime/inability to excel in college or to be articulate reinforces the myth that "blacks" are less intelligent than "whites," and the link between the socio-economic status of African Americans and their grudge against the government reinforces the myth that "blacks" are less patriotic than "whites." This situation confirms Amiri Baraka's observation that "to name something [in this case, " black," "negro," or "nigger"] is to wait for it in the place you think it will pass" (Bell, 1986: 2).

The major effect of ideological routinization and denial is the political neutralization of African Americans. In the above quoted flier, this neutralization is well expressed by the claim that, because "niggers" did not contribute, they are not "worthy of possessing a say in (public) affairs." Although they may not succeed in sending them "back to Africa," the daily rituals and practices associated with the white-black dichotomy create an "out-of-place" feeling among African Americans. One senses this "out-of-place" feeling in their daily scenes, in their relationships with European Americans, and in their routine expressions, such as, "This is white America," "We came here by ship," "We are still slaves," "the man" (meaning "white man"), and "white supremacy" (a concept promoted unfortunately by African Americans to the delight of racist groups). In the 1977 study, a "negro" who received higher marks but was denied the chef job in favor of a white with lower marks thought that "that was life for a black man living in a white world" (Wellman, 1977: 109).

The consequences are immense. The ideological denial of African-American contributions, internalized by African Americans themselves, creates deep insecurities in them. In the 1969 study cited above, surveyed "negroes" attributed higher moral standards to "whites" and lower ones to themselves. The 1996 Syracuse survey shows that 54 percent of African Americans believe that "blacks" do (always or often) internalize and act according to what "whites" think of them; 43 percent think that they "sometimes" do so; 34.5 percent of "whites" think that this is always or often the case, and 55 percent think that it is "sometimes" the case. James Baldwin's father, we are told, "was defeated long before he died because, at the bottom of his heart, he really believed what white people said about him." By internalizing the denial of their contributions to American civilization, African Americans become politically neutralized. Political neutralization takes various forms, including "psychological" ones. Again, major African-American literary works best express this neutralization and its effects. One is reminded of the psychological beating suffered by Joe Youngblood despite his family's heroics in John O. Killens's *Youngblood* and Gus's sarcastic replies to Bigger who claims that he could fly a plane in Richard Wright's *Native Son*. James Baldwin captures the persistence of both the political and psychological neutralization when quipping about African-American apathy: "Yes, we've progressed. When I was a boy in Harlem, negroes got drunk and cursed each other out. Now they become junkies and don't say anything." "Don't say anything" means that politically African Americans, especially the masses, become resigned to their fate; the old blues song "Been down so long that down don't bother me" becomes their anthem.

Neutralization is inseparable from African-American alienation from American society, which is recorded by survey data. A 1974 study recorded its two highest scores in alienation index among African Americans on the issue of being "liked" by "whites" [19.0] and on their chances of getting ahead no matter how hard they work [10.9] (Schuman and Hatchet, 1974: 79). A comparison of "white" and "black" perception of twenty American institutions from the army to white churches confirms this alienation. The black support is, on the average, 30 percent and that of whites is 49 percent.[3] The earlier nationalist notion of a separate "black state" is additional clear evidence of alienation. Alienation leads to political neutralization, at odds with the picture of "active" participation painted by some studies.[4] Data show that, notwithstanding the civil rights activism and the apex of nationalism symbolized by the 1972 Gary Convention, participation for transformational politics is low among African Americans. Even at the apex of activism, the 1974 study reveals that 69 percent of African Americans did not think that it was worthwhile to organize into groups to protect against any violence by "whites" (Schuman and Hatchet, 1974: 83). Data on the 1984 elections confirm this fact: 60.1 percent, 78.2 percent, 81.4 percent, 80.4 percent, 82.4 percent, 70.5 percent, 84.8 percent, 91.3 percent, 72.5 percent, 66.2 percent, and 76.7 percent of African Americans answered "no" to questions dealing respectively with "showing people why they should vote," "attending meetings and rallies," "helping with a vote registration drive," "financial help for candidates," "campaigning for black candidates," "contacting public officials," "attending demonstrations," "sit-in/boycott," "working for party campaign," "calling public officials about a concern," and "membership in an organization."[5] The Syracuse study confirms these data, especially with regard to answers given by African Americans; 66 percent (an average for three questions asked) recognize the political neutralization that results from the denial of African-American contributions while 38 percent of European Americans think so. The latter do, however, agree that this is "sometimes" the case (an average of 55 percent). These data are quite consistent with other survey data on voting behavior, which have quite consistently shown that: (1) the lack of a "sense of belonging," hence of influencing the government; (2) the relative absence of African-American candidates; and (3) the socioeconomic status of African Americans are the leading reasons for their electoral apathy (Walton, 1985; Morris, 1975; Verba and Nye, 1972).

Neutralization is perhaps best revealed by the fate of the "underclass." Its members are for the most part the by-product of prior acts of denial of the contributions of their parents, who lived miserable lives that still haunt their offspring. The latter's lives are defined by "abject resignation to insufferable conditions [that] permeate lives compounded by a persistently nagging sense of despair, hopelessness, and frustration" (Blackwell, 1975: 89–91). Political participation under these conditions is impossible. At best, it is expressed in the form of escapism, and is misdirected toward easy targets, which explains "black on black" crime and the resentment against other "minorities." Their relationship with middle- and upper-class African Americans is filled with suspicion, the result of insecurities on both sides. This situation makes meaningful political alliances difficult, if not impossible. Political neutralization leads, in turn, to the denial of their contributions to the social product and to a lower share of it, a fact confirmed by 68 percent of African Americans in the Syracuse study.

Counter-ideologies of Denial and Neutralization

Neutralization is reinforced by the political solutions proposed to upgrade the socio-economic status of African Americans: liberalism, the Martin Luther King movement/civil rights, electoral politics, and the nationalist movement. Rather than solve the problem, they perpetuate it. Because they are counter-ideologies, these solutions/strategies fail to address the political issue of how to reaffirm the contributions of African Americans to the social product, the basis of any political competition.

To be sure, the King nonviolent movement and the post-civil rights electoral politics are not identical. The King movement relied on nonviolent protest to "get inside," whereas electoral politics "work from inside the system." Nevertheless, in addition to advocating the integration of all Americans, the two strategies share a common ideological root. They, like American independence, are derivatives of the built-in ideological contradictions of the liberal thought of the seventeenth and eighteenth centuries. Veering away from its own (European political thought) premise about the social nature of the goods of politics (the social product) and the subordination of rights to the social product, liberal thought focused on "natural rights." Despite the tremendous debate about how liberalism would influence the birth of the American Republic (see Hartz, 1970: 51–61), the Lockean brand of liberalism prevailed. "Natural rights" were at the very basis of the American Declaration of Independence: "We hold these truths to be self-evident that all men are created equal, that they are endowed by their Creator with certain unalienable Rights, that among these are Life, Liberty and the pursuit of Happiness." Insofar as the struggle for equality and rights for African Americans derives its inspiration from these liberal postulates of the Declaration of Independence, it is bound to be unsuccessful. As a counter-ideology, liberalism fails to specify the sine qua non criterion for one's claim to equality and rights. It is not self-evident that all men and women are born equal. The children of an aristocrat, a president, and a free person are not equal to the children of a peasant, a sharecropper, and a slave. Should the children of a peasant, a slave, and a sharecropper be equal to the children of an aristocrat, a free person, and a president in a political community? The answer is yes, but not because their claim to equality and rights is provided by nature or the Creator; rather, because, as I argued earlier, they *earn* it. They earn it because their parents—peasants, slaves, or sharecroppers—have *contributed*, if only through their exploitation, to the political community, hence to the social product.

Failure to come to grips with this specification and the focus on "natural rights" explain why the liberal thought was easily left open to attacks by pro-slavery and pro-segregation forces. Attempts by Christians to stop slavery, by arguing that slaves were "fellow creatures," were weak and useless because it could be easily argued that animals and trees are "fellow creatures" as well. Pro-slavery forces refuted the liberal thought by using its own premises. Having accepted the fact that slavery was God's creation, they argued that only God could end it (Hammond, 1981: 173). During the civil rights movement of the 1960s, the claim that all men are born equal was (logically) challenged by the segregationist J. B. Stoner. Accustomed since birth to "the inequality of races," it was logical for him that, "When the Constitution said all men are created equal, it wasn't talking about niggers" (Marable, 1991: 61). Thus, liberalism, a counter-ideology, fails to center the debate around the political issue of the contribution of African Americans to the social product. Its very vulnerability is symptomatic of its inability to upgrade their conditions.

As goes liberalism, so goes the civil rights movement, its derivative. Not only did it maintain all the premises of the liberal thought but it added a few of its own that further concealed the political issue. Consistent with his nonviolent philosophy, King said, "We will soon wear you down by our capacity to suffer, and in winning our freedom we will so appeal to your heart and conscience that we will win you in the process" (Oates, 1982: 236). Regardless of one's position about nonviolence—which is beside the point—the "capacity to suffer" and the "appeal to heart and conscience" clearly shift the debate from political terrain to the religious, emotional, and ideological field. Change had to come for African Americans not because they earned it but because their capacity to suffer incited sympathy. Like its liberal root, the King movement, unwittingly but effectively, neutralized African Americans politically in the long run by failing to posit their contribution to the social product as the reason for their claim to equality and rights. In this sense, the movement can be accurately referred to as "submissive integration." The disillusionment that characterized King and his followers after passage of the Civil Rights Act of 1964 and the Voting Act of 1965 amply testified to this.

Electoral politics, Bayard Rustin argued in 1965, had to replace protest politics (Rustin, 1966: 35–40). And so it did. In the post-1965 period African Americans have had recourse to institutional political participation. Because electoral politics is indissociable from liberalism, institutional participation rests on liberal premises. One of these is social liberty, or equal opportunity. According to the latter, any social actor, group, or social class can lay equal claims to the social product without knowing in advance the outcome of its demands. For this reason, the institutional setting of liberal democracy is tailored to resemble a lottery. Elections, the ballot, and the representation mechanism are aspects of such a system. Because it is ideological, equal opportunity is neither attainable nor unattainable for everyone in a liberal society. This is a puzzle that cannot be fully explored here (see Sangmpam, 1992). For African Americans, however, equal opportunity is not just a puzzle. Again, because it is the prolongation of "natural rights," the liberal notion of social equality/equal opportunity fails to address the political issue of African-American contribution to the social product. By definition, equal opportunity implies a recognition of the rights of the claimants to society's "now claimable" goods to which they had "previously" contributed in different capacities. In the case of African Americans for whom this recognition is ideologically denied, equal opportunity is highly vulnerable to routinized racist ideology. It is no surprise, then, that electoral politics has not altered the social status of most African Americans.

American electoral politics is based on a reality that further vitiates equal opportunity. What may be termed "pluralistic liberalism" rests on two principles: the "vector-sum" (balance-of-power) principle and the "referee" principle. According to the vector-sum principle, the major groups in society are the prime competitors in the electoral process. The referee principle supplements the vector-sum principle by assigning to the government the role of overseeing and regulating the competition among these recognized groups. It is debatable whether the "original" competing groups (ethnic, professional, religious, etc.) have remained the same. It can be said, however, that in general the same defined groups tend to be the major actors in the political competition. Social and demographic changes that occur have minimal impact on how these "original" groups are involved in politics because "once constructed, the picture becomes frozen, and when changes take place in the patterns of social or economic grouping, they tend not to be acknowledged because they deviate from that picture" (Wolff, 1965: 41). The picture is even more frozen for African Americans because their group is *ideologically* defined as "negro" or "black." Given that the vector-sum principle stipulates that political competition take place through groups, the ideological definition of "blacks" neutralizes them politically. As a "black" group opposed to the "white" group in the competition, "blacks" represent nothingness in the face of being. The result, to put it bluntly, is that they are always losers. Symptomatic of this situation is the fact that when forced to choose between "black" and "white" candidates with the same ideological orientations, educational background, and qualifications, most European Americans find it difficult to vote for the "black" candidate and choose the "white" candidate instead. Most do so even if the "black" candidate has better credentials than the "white" candidate. And because the government plays its role of referee by intervening between already pigeonholed groups, its role cannot alter the ideologically established imbalance in the competition.

Parallel to or in reaction to liberalism, submissive integration, and electoral politics, the nationalist movement has also sought to alter the socio-economic status of African Americans. The nationalist thought traces its origins back to slavery. As early as 1815 it was fused with the colonization movement that aimed to create overseas settlements for former slaves and quasi-free Africans. Openly or diffusely, most African American leaders of the nineteenth and early twentieth century, including W. E. B. DuBois, harbored nationalist sentiments. They did so often as a reaction to the deteriorating conditions of African Americans. When foreign settlements were not being proposed, nationalism advocated an inward-oriented, self-reliant, socio-economic development for African Americans as the solution. Booker T. Washington (to a certain extent), Marcus Garvey, Elijah Mohammad and the Nation of Islam, Malcolm X and the Black Power movement of the 1960s and 1970s are representative of the nationalist thought. Like their predecessors, most African Americans are diffusely nationalistic.

Try as it may, however, nationalism does not fare any better in its claim to salvage African Americans. Like the other counter-ideologies, it misses the political point of African-American contribution to the social product in three ways. First, in many cases nationalism is proclaimed by the African-American elite when submissive integration, of which they are the prime beneficiaries, fails them. As some doors are closed to them, the elite retreat to the masses of African Americans in "nationalistic and racial" solidarity. Needless to say, this opportunistic nationalism disappears as soon as new doors open to the elite, leaving unresolved the problems of the masses.

Second, the nationalist economic program, as articulated by the Black Power movement (see Carmichael and Hamilton, 1967), advocates economic self-sufficiency and self-reliance for African Americans. The realization of such a program is problematical because of the increasing monopoly exercised by gigantic corporations (e.g., monopoly over financial institutions and distribution channels) and the constraints imposed by the overall competing capitalist ventures (Allen, 1967: 45). These constraints and the unbreakable dependency of would-be "black businesses" on the overall national capitalist economy shed light on the weaknesses of economic nationalism. The latter constitutes a retreat from the means of production of the social product from which, to the extent allowed by capitalism, African Americans like all Americans must benefit. In other words, economic ventures by African Americans must be encouraged. But they need not be the result of an attempt to withdraw from the "white economy." Even if it were feasible, such an attempt contributes to the political neutralization of African Americans by reinforcing the idea that they did not contribute to American civilization. Malcolm X wrestled with this issue when by the end of his life he refrained from advocating a "black state" and "black nationalism" (Malcolm X, 1965: 197, 212).

Third, and more importantly, mass-based nationalism, which arises out of their sufferings, bears fundamental weaknesses. As their conditions deteriorate, the masses increase their resentment against "whites" and "white America." Because they want change that does not come, African-American masses internalize their revolt energies the way anti-colonial forces did in Africa, Asia, and South America. They retreat to themselves with a nationalistic fervor, liberating their revolt energies in escapism, religion, and "cultural"/artistic expression. Rap music and the movement around it are such an expression while addiction to drug, sex and "black on black" crime allow escapism. A "charismatic" nationalist leader can easily become successful by tapping into this raw energy. Marcus Garvey and the Nation of Islam owed their success to this situation. On the other hand, the absence of such leadership explains the incredible rebirth of Malcolm X among the frustrated African-American youth of the rap generation. Unfortunately, escapism or artistic expression associated with nationalism do not address the political issue. Rather than pose the problem in terms of how to reaffirm the claim to the social product, mass nationalism withdraws from the issue through an eminently counter-ideological discourse. Although Garvey's other ideas were highly liberating, his belief in "racial purity, racial integrity, and racial hegemony" (Garvey, 1987; Essien-Udom, 1962: 50) constitutes an example of this counter-ideology, as does the Nation of Islam's claim that the "white race" was created by Yakub, a "black scientist in rebellion against Allah" (Lincoln, 1961: 76–77). Although much of its scholarship that debunks racist fabrications about Egypt and Africa is solid (see Diop, 1991; Asante 1987, 1992), the now popular Afro-centric discourse also runs the risk of lending escapist ammunitions to the suffering African-American masses (and Africans for that matter). The point here is not to repeat the often misplaced critique leveled against Afro-centricity. There is nothing wrong with the Afro-centric position that Africans, when studied, should be subjects of historical experiences rather than objects on the fringes of Europe. Rather, I warn against creating, like in any movement, an army of ill-informed zealots whose views are not necessarily consistent with those of the founders of the movement. The escape and the danger lie in chasing a ghost (European racist ideology) with another ghost (African racist counter-ideology).

Thus, liberalism, the civil rights movement, and nationalism fail to place the political issue of the contributions of African Americans to the social product at the center of the debate. They reinforce the ideological denial of African-American contributions by the "black-white" dichotomy. Because they are ghosts chasing another ghost, they can never meet, and the chase cannot improve the socio-economic status of African Americans. And while they help the masses to avoid the political issue of how to reclaim what is owed them, the conditions of the masses worsen. The name change is part of the corrective solution.

Conclusion: Name Change and Integration from Strength

I have argued that as ideological rituals, the terms "negro" and "black" and the imaginary relationship built around the "white-black" dichotomy seek first to deny the contributions of African Americans to the social product. By neutralizing them politically, the denial perpetuates their socio-economic status. Various strategies proposed to solve the problem have failed because, as counter-ideologies, they fail to address the political issue of reaffirming African-American claim to the social product. Therefore, the challenge is to do maximum damage to the "white-black" dichotomy and to deprive the term "white" of its antithesis "black," and vice versa, through a name change. Because the term "black" is meaningless without its opposite "white," a repudiation of "black" requires a change from "white" to "European American," "American of European descent," or any combination that seeks to reject the term "white."

Whether the term chosen is "African American," "Americans of African descent," "Afro-Americans," or any other combination that seeks to reject the term "black" or "negro," the focus should be the name change itself as a political event and not the chosen name per se. As a political event, the name change strikes at the core issue of ideological denial of African-American contributions and political neutralization by striking the "white-black" dichotomy; it invalidates the term "white," the centerpiece of the ideological denial. In so doing, it brings to the forefront the political issue of African-American claim to the social product and helps reassert their socio-political rights. How so?

If in agreement with the political philosophers discussed earlier, we define politics as the competition over the social product and posit one's contribution to it as the sine qua non for socio-political rights, then it follows that these rights impose obligations on the members of the political community. And whenever the rights are denied to the contributors, the latter's obligations become "negative" ones. It is in asserting the importance of negative obligations that Rousseau maintained that those in the state who fail to accept the social contract may be "forced to be free," that is, to honor their part of the bargain; that Marx advocates the overthrow of the bourgeoisie; that in African societies the palaver broke the rule of secrecy of the power holders to expose their wrong deeds, and so forth. Because they miss the political point of the contribution of African Americans to the social product, liberalism/civil rights, electoral politics, and nationalism cannot fully draw these implications. Yet they remain (realistically) the only frameworks for African-American politics and discussions about changes because of the structural limits imposed by capitalism. Indeed capitalist democracy as exists in the United States can more easily accommodate these three types of politics/ideology, which are not a danger to its own survival, than it can a subversive ideology. The crucial question then becomes: How does one satisfy the requirements of "negative obligations" as advocated by political thinkers to re-assert the rights of African Americans within the limits of capitalist democracy? An answer to this question helps throw light on the issue of name change.

The answer lies in recovering the energy and commitment of the 1960s while avoiding the submissiveness of the civil rights movement and the insecurity-ridden exclusiveness of "Black Power"/nationalism. Because socio-political rights are earned, they require *self-confidence* in political struggles to reclaim one's share of the social product. A name change is consistent with this approach. Indeed, the rejection of the term "black" means ipso facto the rejection of ideology-based automatic recognition of the "white-black" dichotomy, in which "black" means nothingness and noncontribution. It reaffirms the hitherto ideologically concealed (by the dichotomy) African-American contributions to American civilization. In so doing, the name change gives lethargic masses of African Americans political self-confidence. The rejection of the terms "black" and "white" re-establishes the *philosophical and theoretical primacy* of the social product and African-American contribution to it as the basis of political competition.

Because the recognition of their contribution to the social product via the name change movement makes African Americans "sovereign" in the social contract, to use Rousseau's expression, it allows them to break James Baldwin's father syndrome by breaking their deep-seated insecurities about "white America." In other words, it allows African Americans to acquire political self-confidence, to reclaim, and not to beg for, what is owed them and to redirect the untapped energy that leads to escapism toward political organizing. Political self-confidence derived from the name change, hence from the recognition of African-American contributions, yields other beneficial effects; it helps African Americans to fight against degrading affirmative action and for *real* equal opportunities and to normalize their relationship with European Americans by breaking the superiority/inferiority complex in it.

To the extent that electoral politics is accepted as the means of political participation, the recognition of African-American contributions through the name change gives it a new impetus. By building the "sense of belonging," the name change movement helps solve the problem of electoral apathy among African-American masses by reasserting their self-confidence in influencing the government, which ceases to be viewed as a "white government" but rather as the contractual expression of all the contributors to the social product. This sense of belonging also means that African Americans will (or should) dare to become candidates in areas other than those traditionally "reserved" for them in "predominantly black cities and counties." They will (or should) compete for votes of European Americans in their neighborhoods the way the latter compete for votes in African-American neighborhoods. In this sense, despite the discouraging past record, candidacies for statewide and national offices, such as the Senate and the presidency, must be frequently targeted by African-American candidates. And because African-American voters tend to become more involved when an African-American candidate runs for office, the self-confidence of the African-American elite is likely to translate into higher participation of the African-American masses.

By invalidating "white" and by bringing to the forefront the issue of the claim to the social product, the name change prevents African Americans from sleeping on the comfortable bed of African history and civilization; it causes them to be confronted with today's harsh reality. The reality is that for the masses of African Americans, the reaffirmation of their contribution and claim to the social product is an arduous task. The history of social change in the United States shows that "such change occurs only when sufficient pressure is brought to bear on policymakers that they cannot continue business as usual" (Smith, 1991: 90–103). The name change implies a *social move-*

ment that re-arms African Americans with self-confidence to bring sufficient pressure on policymakers. In this sense, rather than divert the attention from the "real issues" of unemployment, crime, homelessness, and poverty, as the advocates of the term "black" claim, the shift to the term "African American" places these issues at the very center of the debate. It helps solve them.

Posing the central problem of African-American contributions sheds new light on "ethnic politics" in American pluralistic liberalism. The name change will not equalize opportunities between African Americans and other ethnic groups just because African Americans, like Italian Americans, Irish Americans, or Polish Americans, can claim their "ethnic heritage." Rather, it is because, by reaffirming their contribution to the social product, it allows them to claim their share on an equal basis. This point and the reference to "ethnic" grouping brings us back to the question raised earlier, namely, whether the claim to a share of the social product by African Americans translates into group-based proportionate rights. The answer, given earlier, is obviously negative. As an "ethnic" group, African American implies a sub-collectivity of individual actors. If, as argued, their contribution to the social product entitles individual African Americans, not to a proportionate share of the social product, but to freedom from political, social, and economic discrimination, marginalization, and oppression from other members or groups of American society, then the issue of discrimination against and rights for African Americans *qua* a group disappears. Rights become individualized. However, because African Americans will still be regarded as an "ethnic" group, this reaffirmation of individual rights should have implications for the group. It allows the group's integration from strength, and suggests new ways of looking at Pan Africanism, a point that cannot be pursued here.[6]

Notes

1. On African-American contributions, see Robert William Fogel and Stanley L. Engerman, *Time on the Cross* (Boston: Little Brown, 1974); Herbert G. Gutman, *Slavery and the Numbers Game: A Critique of Time on the Cross* (Urbana: The University of Illinois Press, 1975) and Paul David et al., *Reckoning with Slavery* (New York: Oxford University Press, 1976); Robert Starobin, *Industrial Slavery in the Old South* (London: Oxford University Press, 1970), 5; Franklin and Moss, *From Slavery to Freedom* (New York: Knopf, 1988), 122; Louis Haber, *Black Pioneers of Science* (New York: Harcourt, Brace & World, Inc., 1970); *Emerge* (October 1992): 26. Jack Fincher, "The Hard Fight Was Getting into the Fight at All," *Smithsonian*, 21, 7 (October 1990); LeRoi Jones, *Blues People* (New York: Morrow, 1963); Albert Murray, *Stomping the Blues* (New York: Da Capo Press, 1976); Derrick Stewart Baxter, *Ma Rainey and the Classic Blues Singers* (New York: Stein & Day, 1970); Giles Oakley, *The Devil's Music* (London: BBC, 1983); and *Ebony*, special issue, (August 1991); *U.S.A Today* (July 8, 1992): 2A; Milton G. Sernett, "Black Religion and the Question of Evangelical Identity," in *The Variety of American Evangelicalism*, ed. Ronald W. Dayton and Robert Johnston (Knoxville: The University of Tennessee Press, 1991), 135–47.
2. The flier was reprinted in "Fear Grips Students on College Campuses," *The Jewish Ledger* (November 1, 1990): 22.
3. Calculated from Alphonso Pinkney, *The Myth of Black Progress* (1984: 63, table 4.1).

4. See, for instance, Ronald Brown, "Political Action," in *Life in Black America*, ed. James S. Jackson (Sage, 1991), 254–63. His view of politically active African Americans, shaped by the activist civil rights politics, is not supported even by his own data.
5. Katherine Tate et al., *The 1984 National Black Election Study Sourcebook* (Institute for Social Research, The University of Michigan), tables 12.5, 12.6, 12.7, 12.8, 12.9, 12.10, 12.12, 12.13, 12.16, 12.17, and 12.18.
6. For a discussion in this direction, see Charles Hamilton, "Pan-Africanism and the Black Struggle in the US," in *Pan-Africanism*, ed. Robert Chrisman and Nathan Hare (Indianapolis: The Bobbs-Merill Co., 1974), 145–53.

References

Allen, Robert. 1969. *Black Awakening in Capitalist America*. Garden City, NY: Doubleday.
Althusser, Louis. 1977. *Politics and History*. London: NLB.
Aristotle. 1985. *The Politics*, ed. Carnes Lord. Chicago: University of Chicago Press.
Asante, Molefi K. 1987. *The Afrocentric Idea*. Philadelphia: Temple University Press.
———. 1990. *Kemet: Afrocentricity and Knowledge*. Trenton, NJ: Africa World Press.
Baldwin, James 1985. *The Evidence of Things Not Seen*. New York: Holt, Rinehart and Winston.
Barker, Lucius J, and Mack Jones. 1994. *African Americans and the American Political System*. Englewood Cliffs: Prentice Hall.
Bell, Janet C., ed. 1986. *Famous Black Quotations*. Chicago: Sabayt Publications.
Blackwell, James E. 1975. *The Black Community: Diversity and Unity*. New York: Dodd, Mead.
Bernal, Martin. 1987. *Black Athena*, vol. 1. New Brunswick, NJ: Rutgers University Press.
Bohannan, Paul. 1964. *Africa and Africans*. Garden City, NY: American Museum Science Books.
Carmichael, Stokely, and Charles Hamilton. 1967. *Black Power: The Politics of Liberation in America*. New York: Random House.
Clarke, John Henrik "We, the Named," *African Commentary* (November 1989).
Diop, Cheikh Anta. 1974. *The African Origin of Civilization: Myth or Reality*. Chicago: Lawrence Hills Books.
———. 1991. *Civilization or Barbarism*. New York: Laurence Hill Books.
D'Souza, Dinesh. "Illiberal Education," *The Atlantic Monthly* (March 1991).
DuBois, W. E. B. 1924. *The Gift of Black Folk*. Boston: The Stratford Co.
Ebony. "African-American or Black: What's in a Name?" (July 1989).
Essien-Udom, E. U. 1962. *Black Nationalism*. New York: Dell.
Farley, Reynolds, and Walter R. Allen. 1989. *The Color Line and the Quality of Life in America*. New York: Oxford University Press
Franklin, John H. 1988. *From Slavery to Freedom: A History of Negro Americans*. New York: Knopf.
———. 1989. *Race and History*. Baton Rouge: Louisiana State University Press.
Garvey, Marcus. 1987. *Life and Lessons*, ed. R. A. Hill. Berkeley: University of California Press.
Haber, Louis. 1970a. *Black Pioneers of Science and Invention*. New York: Harcourt, Brace & World.
———. 1970b. "John Locke and the Liberal Consensus." In *The Role of Ideology in the American Revolution*, ed. John R. Howe, Jr. New York: Holt, Rinehart and Winston.
Herskovitz, Melville. 1990. *The Myth of the Negro Past*. Boston: Beacon Press.

Hobbes, Thomas. 1991. *Leviathan*, ed. Richard Tuck. Cambridge: Cambridge University Press.
Johnson, Charles. 1930. *The Negro in American Civilization*. New York: Henry Holt and Company.
Kovel, Joel. 1984. *White Racism: A Psychohistory*. New York: Columbia University Press.
Lasswell, Harold D. 1936. *Politics: Who Gets What, When, How* New York: McGraw-Hill.
Lincoln, Eric C. 1961. *The Black Muslims in America*. Boston: Beacon Press.
Locke, John. 1689. *Two Treatises on Government*.
Logan, Rayford. 1954. *The Betrayal of the Negro*. New York: The MacMillan Co.
Malcolm X. 1965. *Malcolm X Speaks*, ed. George Breitman. New York: Grove Press.
Marable, Manning. 1983. *How Europe Underdeveloped Black America*. Boston: South End Press.
———. 1991. *Race, Reform, and Rebellion*. Jackson: University Press of Mississippi.
Marx, Karl. 1954. *The Communist Manifesto*. Chicago: Henry Regnery Company.
Mill, James. 1978. "Essay on Government." In *Utilitarian Logic and Politics*, ed. J. Lively and J. Rees. London: Oxford University Press.
Morris, Milton 1975. *The Politics of Black America*. New York: Harper and Row.
National Research Council. 1989. *A Common Destiny: Blacks and American Society*. Washington, DC: National Academy Press.
Newman, W. L. 1973. *The Politics of Aristotle*, vol. 1. New York: Arno Press.
Nott, Josiah C. 1981. "Two Lectures on the Natural History of the Caucasian and Negro Races." In *The Ideology of Slavery*, ed. Drew Gilpin Faust. Baton Rouge: Louisiana State University Press.
Nyerere, Julius. 1968. *Ujamaa: Essays on Socialism*. Dar es Salam: Oxford University Press.
Oates, Stephen B. 1982. *Let the Trumpet Sound: The Life of Martin Luther King, Jr.* New York: Harper & Row.
Parenti, Michael. 1988. *Democracy for the Few*. New York: St. Martin's Press.
Patterson, Orlando, and Chris Winship. "White Poor, Black Poor." *New York Times* (May 3, 1992).
Pinkney, Alphonso. 1984. *The Myth of Black Progress*. New York: Oxford University Press.
Rawls, John. 1971. *A Theory of Justice*. Cambridge: Harvard University Press.
Rejai, Mustafa. 1984. *Comparative Political Ideologies*. New York: St. Martin's Press.
Rousseau, Jean-Jacques. 1950. *Social Contract*. New York: E. P. Dutton.
Rustin, Bayard. "'Black Power' and Coalition Politics." *Commentary*, 42 (September 1966).
Sangmpam, S. N. 1992. "The Overpoliticized State and Democratization: A Theoretical Model." *Comparative Politics*, 24, 4 (July): 401–17.
———. 1994. *Pseudocapitalism and the Overpoliticized State: Reconciling Politics and Anthropology in Zaire*. Aldershot, England: Avebury.
Schuman, Howard, and Shirley Hatchet. 1974. *Black Racial Attitudes: Trends and Complexities*. Ann Arbor: Institute for Social Research, University of Michigan.
Smith, Adam. 1937. *The Wealth of Nations*. New York: The Modern Library.
Smith, Robert C. 1991. "Hammering at the Truth: The Civil Rights Era and After." *Transition*, 54: 90–103.
Tate, Katherine et al. 1988. *The 1984 National Black Election Study Sourcebook*. Ann Arbor: Institute for Social Research, The University of Michigan.
Thune, Jeanne M. 1969. *Group Portrait in Black and White*. Nashville: Senior Citizens.
Verba, Sidney, and Norman Nye. 1972. *Participation in America: Political Democracy and Social Equality*. New York: Harper and Row.

Walton, Hanes, Jr. 1985. *Invisible Politics: Black Political Behavior*. Albany: State University of New York Press.

Wellman, David T. 1977. *Portraits of White Racism*. Cambridge: Cambridge University Press.

Wolff, Robert P., Barrington Moore, and Herbert Marcuse. 1965. *A Critique of Pure Tolerance*. Boston: Beacon Press.

Reflections

Affirmative Action: What is the Question—Race or Oppression?

Mack H. Jones

Clark Atlanta University

At this point in American history, summer 1998, the most widely discussed question in the area of race and public policy is: Should individuals be given special consideration in seeking access to jobs, educational institutions, and other coveted societal positions because of their race? That was the question debated by the U.S. Supreme Court in the landmark affirmative action cases of *Richmond vs. Croson* (1989), *Miller vs. Johnson* (1995), and by the circuit court in *Hopwood vs. Texas* (1996) and that was how the issue was defined in the California referendum on Proposition 209. The issue was framed in a similar fashion in 1997 when the Michigan legislature called for an investigation of its flagship university for discriminating against "better qualified" whites while admitting "lesser qualified" black students. To ask whether one should be given special consideration merely because of race is to guarantee that the answer will be "no." No intelligent proponent of democracy would argue that special consideration should be given any individual or group merely because of their race. But in the context of the struggle for racial justice in America, that is not the appropriate question to raise now nor has it ever been the question. The pertinent question is: Should special consideration be given to individuals who belong to a group that was singled out for unequal treatment by the Constitution of the United States and by statutory law at all levels of American government, national, state, and local, whose unequal treatment was sanctioned by social custom and reinforced by the use of terror and economic intimidation, and who, as a result of that government-mandated and culturally sanctioned oppression, lag behind white Americans on practically every indicator of socio-economic well-being? The question is: Should members of that oppressed group receive special consideration until such time that the gap between them and the dominant group on these indicators of well-being is eliminated?

That is the question that history and ordinary logic would lead us to raise. And if that were the question that informed the public policy debate, the dialogue would certainly be different. But that is not how the question is phrased because the ordinary rules of logic are rarely if ever followed in the discussion or race and public policy in America. Questions about race are almost always raised in such a way as to deny the reality and severity of racial oppression as a fundamental force in American life and culture. To understand the contemporary debate about affirmative action and other so-called race-specific remedies, it is necessary to understand how this came to be. To do so we must go back to the very founding of the country.

On matters involving relations between European and other peoples of the world, the United States was founded on a fundamental contradiction. The Declaration of Independence and the Constitution adopted subsequently to bring about the new state envisaged in the Declaration spoke of the rights of man as the major pillar of human society. Yet the framers of these documents were slave holders in a slave-holding society that owed its very existence as an economically viable state to the then ongoing genocide of the native inhabitants and to the unrequited labor of millions of enslaved Africans. As a slave-holding, multiethnic, and multiracial society founded on the principle of white supremacy, America evolved a uniquely racist culture that made qualitative distinctions not only among the different socially constructed racial groups but between the various ethnic communities within the different racial groups as well. Europeans were placed at the apex of the racial hierarchy, followed by Asians, Native Americans, and Africans in that order. Within the European group, Aryan-featured Europeans received top billing with their more swarthy central and southern European compatriots occupying the lower rungs. The hierarchy among the ethnic groups in the Asian and African communities, such as Chinese vs. Koreans and West Indians vs. U.S.-born blacks, was more fluid depending upon white interests at any given historical moment.

The idea of white supremacy and its corollary, the notion of black inferiority, provided the ideological justification for this pernicious rank ordering of humanity and it created and sustained ideologies that justified the most inhumane treatment of people of color. At the same time, however, the basic documents of the country that proclaimed belief in the equality of all humanity were cleverly written to disguise the racist principles imbedded in them. For example, those who drafted Declaration of Independence managed to call for the creation of a new political system dedicated to the proposition that all men were created equal with the inalienable right to life, liberty, and property while at the same time enslaving millions of African people and holding countless thousands of their white compatriots as indentured servants.

Following their successful war of independence, these self-proclaimed democrats drafted a constitution that retained the legitimacy of slavery, forbade the new government from legislating on the matter for at least twenty years, and obligated the national government to use its powers to return those who managed to escape enslavement to their erstwhile slave masters. The framers put all of this in the Constitution without ever mentioning the words slavery, African people, or anything else that would indicate the real nature of the society they had built and were trying to maintain.

Since its inception, all of this shows, the United States has been a thoroughgoing racist society, but one in deep denial and one in which everything is done to maintain white supremacy and domination at home and abroad while denying that racism and racial oppression are major elements of American political culture and practice. Indeed the principle documents of American history raise self-deception to the level of art form. One of the results of this charade in self-deception has been the development of a culture in which the normal rules of logic are often suspended when the subject is race and racial oppression. Concepts and conceptual frameworks are developed to facilitate public policy discussions of the reality of racial oppression while at the same time denying that it exists. I have in mind concepts such as minorities, disadvantaged, inner cities, at risk, multiculturalism, and diversity, to name just a few.

The development of such concepts and their use in generating propositions about the nature of American life and the place of black folk in it defy the rules ordinarily used in developing empirically useful concepts and making logical inferences about experience. Instead we get discussions that are more illogical than logical. At the same time, however, those grounded in the American conceptualization of such matters are conditioned to accept this illogical discussion of race as if it makes sense. This spastic dance of self-deception is joined by practically every segment of American life, without regard to race, class, gender, creed, or color. Indeed an interplanetary visitor from Mars who observed America at work and play and saw the great racial divide manifested in these activities and then listened to the public discussion about it would certainly find it incredulous.

There is, however, a transcendental logic to this illogical dance. The transcendental logic is that it serves to maintain and reinforce the system of white supremacy and black subordination while, to borrow a term from a different but related area of inquiry, leaving space for plausible denial by those who have a need to do so.

Nowhere is this more apparent than in contemporary discussions of race and public policy, particularly discussions about affirmative action and other so-called race-specific remedies. When the question is stated as "should individuals be given special consideration because of race" it camouflages the historical reality and the systemic character of black oppression. And even more perniciously, by asserting that the pertinent category is race rather than oppression and that the question is should special consideration be given merely because of race, it equates the lived experiences of the various racial groups as theoretically and historically coordinate and prepares the public to accept the argument that what is done or not done for one should be done or not done for all others.

But the theoretical, historical, and empirically useful category that gives rise to affirmative action as an intervention strategy is oppression and not race nor minority status. Special consideration is being sought for members of a group that occupies a subordinate position in society not because of their race nor because of their minority status, but because of an empirically demonstrable specific pattern of historical and contemporary oppression. This concept of oppression, as inferred in the opening paragraph of this essay, can be easily and scientifically operationalized. No other group falls into that category. To be sure, other groups have suffered oppression in America, but none was the subject of slavery and constitutionally mandated oppression and none suffered through centuries of violence and terror. The matter of terror and violence is especially important, because, more than anything else, it prevented blacks from accumulating wealth during the early days of primitive accumulation in the Republic and as Oliver and Shapiro have demonstrated, the lack of wealth is perhaps the major factor that guarantees the continued subordination of black Americans.

To reinforce this point, many have forgotten and perhaps even more never knew that for almost a full century lynching was used as a primary tactic to maintain black subordination. The practice was so widespread that beginning in 1881, Tuskegee University began issuing annual reports on the lynching of black Americans. It was not until 1952, 71 years later, that Tuskegee reported that no lynchings had been brought to its attention (World Almanac, 1992: 88). It was through violence and terror that the southern planter class re-imposed its dominance on the emancipated black nation and sowed the seeds for the enduring "race problem." However, the ideology of white supremacy was so strong that Congress repeatedly refused to make lynching a federal crime.

Rather than acknowledge the reality of oppression and use it as the triggering mechanism for remedial legislation, policymakers prefer to use terms such as minority and diversity to justify affirmative action initiatives. Taken together, such terms paint a rather benign and self-serving portrait of the problem while reinforcing the image of the United States as a racially and ethnically diverse society in which some groups are overwhelmed because of their smaller numbers and as a result are underrepresented in various societal institutions. To compensate for this and because they believe that there is some special virtue in diversity, this portrait infers, dominant whites develop programs to increase the number of minorities in these institutions. Affirmative action becomes an act of majority benevolence rather than one of reparation to atone for past and continuing crimes against humanity.

But if we put the question of affirmative action and other so-called race-specific remedies in proper historical context, we begin with a quite different set of questions and a decidedly different and more useful discussion unfolds. We begin by asking how and why did blacks get so far behind white Americans on practically all indicators of socio-economic well-being. The answer, of course, is to be found in slavery and the century of state-mandated and culturally sanctioned oppression that followed emancipation. The angry white males and their sympathizers would prefer not to hear this. For them, slavery and its aftermath were merely accidents of history that have no connection to contemporary problems and should be forgotten. To insist on the salience of slavery as an important causal factor in the current unequal position of blacks is decried as whining victimization.

However, while we may will that slavery and its aftermath be forgotten, their social and systemic consequences have proven to be more stubborn. How else can we explain that none of the pressing societal problems of the current age, deteriorating inner cities, public welfare, the urban underclass, inadequate public schools, crime, poverty, structural unemployment, drugs, the militia movement, to name only a few, can be understood apart from the issue of race and racism in society?

At the time of emancipation, as even the most unenlightened cannot deny, blacks lagged behind whites on all measures of socio-economic well-being and after Sherman's aborted experiment in the sea islands, nothing was done to promote socio-economic equality. Instead states passed laws requiring segregation and discrimination and the national government through its own policies reinforced the discrimination and oppression mandated by the states. This was true in education, in government service, in corporations and labor unions, in sports, in the church, and in the military. These oppressive policies were culturally sanctioned and enforced by terror and violence. As a result, from the beginning of freedom blacks had higher unemployment rates, higher incidence of poverty, lower educational attainment, higher infant mortality rates, lower incomes, and lower life expectancy (U.S. Bureau of the Census, 1979). The gap between blacks and whites that existed following emancipation never went away. An elementary rule of causal analysis says that the cause must exist prior to the effect. Since the gap dates back to emancipation, more recent contemporary effects cannot be its cause.

When the civil rights movement erupted in the 1960s, these inequalities that initially developed during slavery and its aftermath still characterized black life. In spite of remedial laws and court decisions the gap between black and white well-being remained substantial. The realization that changing laws would not necessarily change the material conditions precipitated the push for what came to be known as affirmative action.

Affirmative action as an intervention strategy to reduce the gap between blacks and whites grew out of a particular understanding of the nature of the American political economy, which was viewed as analogous to a big gun that fires a shot and at the same time recoils. Out of one end it produces advantages, such as employment, good jobs, wealth, advanced education and training, comfortable housing, enviable health care, safe neighborhoods, and a host of other desirable outcomes. Simultaneously, out of the other end comes the debilities, unemployment, poverty level jobs, substandard education, poor and limited health care, and a litany of other undesirable outcomes. The important thing to understand here is that both the advantages and debilities, the good things and the bad, are all routine outcomes of the American political economy. Low-paying jobs are not created by the people who hold them. Both high- and low-paying jobs are systemic creations. The relative mix of high-paying and low-paying jobs at any given historical moment is a function of the dynamics of politico-economic processes. We see this in the current reduction of the number of high-paying industrial jobs and the concomitant rise in the volume of lesser-paying service sector positions. And we see it when increases in unemployment follow decisions of the federal reserve system to raise interest rates to temper inflation.

The compelling question in this regard is what forces determine who will get the advantages routinely produced by the system and who must settle for the debilities. American political thought says that individual initiative determines who gets ahead, but experiential reality is much more complex. As even the casual observer knows, individual initiative is exercised within a framework structured by major systemic forces. Thus, the critical question is: What forces structure the environment within which individuals strive and how does this structure impact the allocation of advantages and debilities?

The law is one major force. For a long time in America, the law guaranteed that whites would get more than their fair share of the advantages and correspondingly that blacks would get more than their fair share of the debilities. Laws limiting black access were put in place to regulate the lives of free blacks during the slave epoch and were carried over and elaborated upon following emancipation. For example, when the law denied blacks the right to enter the only state school that offered degrees in, say, engineering, medicine, or law, it insured that whites would get more than their fair share of the advantages and conversely that blacks would get more than their fair share of the debilities. Even when blacks managed to obtain such training in spite of the law, other social forces operated to insure their subordination The advantages for whites were cumulative and trans-generational. The sons and daughters of the graduates of such professional programs accumulated wealth that guaranteed that their children would start with even greater advantages over the sons and daughters of blacks whose opportunities had been constrained by the law. The systemic impact of such laws was recognized by the Supreme Court in *Sweat vs. Painter* (1950).

But it was not only the law that guaranteed racial inequality. The social, financial, cultural, educational, and economic systems functioned interdependently to insure that whites, particularly white men, got more of the advantages and less than their fair share of the debilities. We should keep in mind that in the decades immediately following emancipation, the preponderance of blacks lived in the southern states where they constituted substantial proportions of the population, in some areas approaching majority status. This meant that in the then existing racist, patriarchal, class-based society, white men of means had to compete only with themselves for the most coveted societal positions. Perhaps that should be designated as the first era of affirmative action. Under current conditions, the competition is much keener and perhaps hence their anger.

Oliver and Shapiro captured the systemic character of racial deprivation when they asserted that:

> Our examination...shows that unequal background and social conditions result in unequal resources. Whether it be a matter of education, occupation, family status, or other characteristics positively correlated with income and wealth, blacks are most likely to come out on the short end of the stick....We argue furthermore, that the racialization of the welfare state and institutional discrimination are fundamental reasons for the persistent wealth-disparities we observed. Government policies that have paved the way for whites to amass wealth have simultaneously discriminated against blacks in their quest for economic security. From the era of slavery on through the failure of the freedman to gain land and the Jim Crow laws that restricted black entrepreneurs, opportunity for asset accumulation rewarded whites and penalized blacks.(Oliver and Shapiro, 1997: 174)

To return to the argument of systemic deprivation and demonstrate how the various systems working interdependently reproduced and continue to produce racial inequalities, we might reflect on the plight of the child of a low-income black family living in inner-city America and compare it with that of a white child in suburbia. To make the comparison we might ask: How do the financial system and the labor market impact their respective chances for living in a safe and commodious neighborhood, how do the political and educational systems determine the quality of elementary and secondary schools each will attend, and how, in turn, do these systems influence their respective scores on college admission tests? We might ask also: How do they influence their respective performances on devices used for screening applicants for professional schools, such as law and medicine, and on their financial ability to matriculate at such institution? To raise these questions is to dramatize the extent to which individual initiative is constrained by systemic forces that predict group outcomes.

Here the phrase *group outcomes* is important because opponents of affirmative action are quick to point out that countless black individuals from such neighborhoods have succeeded and that their success is evidence that individual initiative rather than systemic conditions determines outcomes. However, the question or at least the one that interests me is not about individual success but about why there is such a wide gap in well-being between blacks and whites as groups and how can the gap be reduced. The argument being advanced here is that sustained intervention in the various systems reinforced by supportive changes in other societal institutions would change the systems themselves and eventually produce different group outcomes. Greater numbers of blacks would receive the advantages and fewer would get the debilities. Eventually more blacks would occupy pivotal positions in these systems and in turn, the systems would begin to produce different and more equitable outcomes.

Systems, of course, are resistant to change and can easily coopt limited and short-term interventions but systems can be transformed through concerted action. The hiring of a few black loan officers, for example, would not necessarily change lending policies, but the presence of significant numbers of black bank directors and bank officers committed to policy changes could over a long period of time change how the system works. Indeed the changing racial complexion of American institutions of higher education is evidence of the impact that sustained intervention may have. On the other hand, the deliberately deceptive debate over so-called political correctness and the present anti-affirmative action hysteria dramatize the resistance that systemic intervention generates.

Conclusion

Let me close this essay by commenting on the arguments of some of the critics of affirmative action and other so-called race-specific remedies. A popular argument among some whites is the lament that while affirmative action may have been necessary early on, that is no longer the case inasmuch as racial discrimination is a thing of the past (Cohen, 1996). Parenthetically, it is interesting to note that making this argument vehemently opposed efforts to end state-mandated segregation and discrimination in the 1950s. In response to the Supreme Court ruling in *Brown vs. Board* (1954), these opponents argued that segregation (and by inference, racism) was a valuable and enduring aspect of American culture and that cultures could not be transformed by legislative, judicial, or other political acts. Cultures, they argued further, could be transformed only through gradual, self-initiated change. Political actions, they continued, would only heighten tensions between the races and make things worse.

However, a few decades later, after fighting tooth and nail all efforts to overturn the racist order, these erstwhile proponents of state-mandated segregation declared that racism had indeed ended and that the question of race and oppression should no longer be a public concern. The inequities and inequalities that were carried over from the era of state-mandated discrimination are declared to be functions of individual and\or group failures. Indeed some go as far as to argue that affirmative action and other so-called race-specific remedies are the cause of current inequalities. As alluded to above such assertions contravene the elementary principles of causal inference.

There are other criticisms, particularly those coming from conservative black intellectuals, that merit consideration. Some argue that affirmative action only benefits the black middle class and as such its social divisiveness outweighs whatever benefits it may bring (Loury, 1984). Two responses to that criticism quickly come to mind. The first is that the validity of the claim has not been established. It is true that affirmative action and set-aside programs do not target low-income jobs, but no intervention strategy was necessary to give blacks access to low-paying, dead-end jobs. The important question is: Who are the people moving into the middle-income positions and university spaces made available through affirmative action? I am unaware of any systematic studies designed to answer such questions. I do know, however, scores of persons from poor families, myself included, who have achieved middle-class status with the assistance of such efforts.

The other response to the claim that affirmative action benefits the black middle class disproportionately is that the United States is a class-based society and that in such societies all public policies are biased in favor of the more well-to-do. All of the other government intervention programs favor those who are better off. This is true of the farm programs, the various housing/mortgage programs, programs offering assistance to businesses, and programs focusing on international trade, to name only a few. Even programs established expressly to assist poor individuals invariably do more for privileged classes than they do for the poor. So even if it is true that affirmative action has a class bias, that is no different from any other government-sponsored intervention program. Thus, the criticism is more of an indictment of America as a class-based society than an indictment of affirmative action as an intervention strategy.

The class issue, however, is central to any enlightened discussion of the controversy over affirmative action and other so-called race-specific remedies and it should be confronted head-on. To the extent that these programs benefit middle-income blacks, working-class whites with lesser incomes and material privileges may justifiably feel aggrieved. After all, they are being taxed in one way or another to assist those whose material conditions may already be greater than their own. But that is true for all of the government intervention programs mentioned above. The fact that the class bias of affirmative action and other race-specific remedies are recognized and opposed while the similar bias of other intervention programs are cheerfully indulged cries out for explanation. Those who oppose affirmative action because of its class bias, especially black intellectuals, could provide a useful public service by broadening their opposition to all class privileges. In doing so they would fulfill the role of enlightened dissenters called for by Martin Luther King, Jr.

On the other hand, underlying the argument for affirmative action and set-aside programs (though rarely clearly stated) was the commitment, however tepid, to create a class structure within the black community that mirrored that of the broader American society. That was the focus of the various government and privately sponsored black capitalism schemes including efforts to have franchises for capital intensive operations such as automobile dealerships and television stations awarded to prosperous blacks and to award multimillion dollar contracts to black construction firms. If properly structured, the debate over the class bias of affirmative action and set-asides could be used to educate all Americans about the systemic implications of the class character of American society and make white working-class people more conscious of their own self-interest.

Another anti-affirmative action argument advanced within the black community is the assertion that it is detrimental to black self-esteem because affirmative hires do not command the respect of their white colleagues (Carter, 1991). In response to this assertion, at the risk of sounding flippant, one could argue that the individual lack of white approbation may be a small price to pay for group advancement. I know of scores of black men and women who hold advanced degrees from prestigious universities, earn a comfortable living, and are in positions to advance the cause of racial justice as a result of the boost provided by affirmative action. Indeed some of the affirmative action critics would not have had access to the very forums from which they launch their criticisms were it not for affirmative action. This is especially true for the growing number of conservative black commentators in both the print and electronic media. They are hired and promoted because they are black (Jones, 1987). Yet their self-esteem seems intact.

On the matter of affirmative action and self-esteem, whites held negative stereotypical attitudes toward blacks long before affirmative action. Indeed it is instructive to remember that even an intellectual giant such as W. E. B. DuBois, who earned a Ph.D. from Harvard in the 1890s in the very shadow of slavery, never had the respect of his white peers. He was offered no positions commensurate with his training and talents.

To further clarify the issue of self-esteem and intercommunity approbation, it is worth noting that historically when whites achieved enviable status without having to compete with blacks, it did not cost them any self-esteem or loss of public approbation. Babe Ruth, the baseball hero, for example, was not ashamed of his home run record even though he did it without having to compete against Satchel Paige, the fabled black pitcher of his era. Nor has it tarnished his image among contemporary whites. Instead we know that Hank Aaron was censored by some for daring to challenge Ruth's record.

Finally there are those who argue that affirmative action is unnecessary because many blacks have excelled without it and their performance is sufficient evidence that any individual, no matter their color or previous condition of servitude, can do so if they put their mind to it. Suffice it to say that during slavery some enslaved Africans were so industrious that they were able not only to buy their freedom and that of other loved ones but also to become wealthy free persons whose material conditions outstripped that of many of their white neighbors (Berlin, 1974). However, individual successes, no matter how spectacular, do not change the reality of group oppression. Within every group the law of random distribution insures that there will be high and low achievers. The problem addressed by affirmative action is the negatively skewed distribution within the black community. Affirmative action and other so-called race-specific remedies are intervention strategies designed to correct that maldistribution.

Affirmative action, the critics should understand, is really a weak remedy designed to address an intractable problem that can be adequately resolved only through comprehensive reparations. However, as long as American culture remains in denial about the crimes for which reparations are due, affirmative action may be all that we can get. The struggle should be to expand rather than end it.

References

Berlin, Ira. 1974. *Slaves without Masters: The Free Negro in the Antebellum South.* New York: The New Press.

Carter, Stephen. 1991. *Reflections of an Affirmative Action Baby.* New York: Basic Books.

Cohen, Carl. 1996. *Naked Racial Preference: The Case Against Affirmative Action.* Madison: Madison Books.

Jones, Mack H. 1987. "The Political Thought of the New Black Conservatives: Analysis, Explanation and Interpretation." In *American Political Issues*, ed. Franklin Jones and Michael Adams. Dubuque: Kendall\Hunt.

Loury, Glen. 1984. "A New American Dilemma." *The New Republic*, 184 (December 31).

Oliver, Melvin, and Thomas Shapiro. 1997. *Black Wealth\White Wealth.* New York: Routledge.

U.S. Bureau of Census. 1979. *The Social and Economic Status of the Black Population in the United States: An Historical Overview, 1790–1979.* Washington, DC: Government Printing Office.

World Almanac. 1992. *Words That Set Us Free.* New York: Pharos Books.

Review Essays

Politicians, Political Scientists, and Congressional Reform

William F. Connelly, Jr.

Washington and Lee University

Fred R. Harris, *In Defense of Congress* (New York: St. Martin's Press, 1995), xiii + 177 pp.; ISBN 0-312-12304-3 (cloth)/0-312-09456-6 (paper).

Leroy N. Rieselbach, *Congressional Reform: The Changing Modern Congress* (Washington, DC: Congressional Quarterly Press, 1994), xi + 232 pp.; ISBN 0-87187-838-0 (paper).

Following the November 1994 electoral cataclysm in which House Republicans finally escaped from forty years of wandering in their "permanent minority" wilderness, most books on Congress are now dated. Former Senator Fred Harris's *In Defense of Congress* and political scientist Leroy Rieselbach's *Congressional Reform: The Changing Modern Congress* are not exceptions to this rule. The latter book, however, will prove more enduring than the former largely because it is based more on a principled political science than political partisanship. Rieselbach is widely and appropriately recognized as one of the leading authorities on congressional reform, thanks in part to an earlier "edition" of this book titled *Congressional Reform in the Seventies* (1977).

Both books are clearly written and highly readable. The Harris book may be more gripping because it is more topical, but the Rieselbach volume flows better. As a former member of Congress, Harris provides more of the flavor of Congress, while Rieselbach offers more insight into the character or nature of Congress. Harris targets the public, politicians, and pundits as his audience; Rieselbach targets his fellow political scientists and their students. Harris borrows heavily, albeit selectively, from the writings of political scientists, while Rieselbach clearly informs discussion about congressional reform among political scientists and serious reformers. Harris's purpose is political and partisan: he writes "in defense of Congress." Rieselbach first and foremost seeks to advance our understanding of Congress, only then does he recommend specific reforms of Congress.

The titles of the two books present underlying ironies. The title of Rieselbach's book unfortunately may suggest a narrow focus on reform, when in fact the book clearly serves the larger purpose of explicating the nature of Congress as an institution, including its evolution over the past five decades. Harris's "defense" of Congress incorporates many telling criticisms of the institution's limitations, along with his recommendations for needed reforms. Harris's political and partisan purpose might benefit greatly from Rieselbach's more principled political science.

The juxtaposition of the Harris and Rieselbach books is useful because it raises serious questions about politics and political science, including the tension between "politics" and "science," a tension inherent in the term "political science." This tension raises key questions that provide the framework for this review essay. First, what is the relationship between "politics" and "science"? Is political science inevitably political, or, for example, is a principled and nonpartisan discussion of political reform possible? Rieselbach's book is clearly less political and partisan than the Harris book, and yet Rieselbach suggests that all evaluations of reform are inevitably subjective (p. x).

Second, is "reform" all in the eye of the reformer, and does reform inevitably serve the interest of the reformer? Again, for example, is Harris's book a "defense" of Congress or a critique of Congress? He sharply criticizes "Congress-bashers" at the same time that he levels some rather pointed criticisms at Congress. Given GOP ascendancy in Congress, does Harris still favor making the legislative process more efficient? Does it all depend on where you stand, or perhaps on where you sit? Today Bill Clinton and congressional Democrats sound a lot like George Bush and congressional Republicans did when partisan control of the presidency and Congress differed (remember "PACs, perks, privileges, partisanship and paralysis"?). In 1995 eager conservative House Republican freshmen regularly lamented the ability of Senate Democrats to retard the Contract with America reforms by exercising the filibuster. Yet under unified Democratic control of the White House and Congress during the 103rd Congress (1993–94), Republicans were glad to have the filibuster. Similarly, President Clinton's criticism of Speaker Gingrich for failing to follow through quickly on the "New Hampshire handshake" over campaign finance reform rings hollow given the unwillingness of Democrats to seriously address campaign finance reform when they controlled both branches during the last Congress. Are all criticisms, analyses, and calls for reform merely relative to where one sits? Can commentators on Congress rise above partisanship and personal perspective?

The juxtaposition of the Harris and Rieselbach books helps us answer the above questions by raising a third question: What is the nature of Congress? Does Congress have an enduring and essential character or nature that we can understand? Both books talk about representation, deliberation, law making, and oversight as the essential functions of Congress. And both books speak of the importance of Congress being responsive, responsible, and accountable. Perhaps these functions and virtues of Congress constitute its essential nature, thus providing us with a means of discussing congressional reform in a principled, rather than merely partisan, manner. Finally, both authors clearly recognize that central to the functions and virtues of Congress is the constitutional separation of powers. Returning to the Founders' understanding of the separation of powers may provide us with a standard for gauging whether the analysis and advancement of congressional reform is merely partisan or political, or whether a principled understanding of congressional reform can provide a platform for promoting reform in the public interest. Must political science be indifferent to the welfare of a liberal regime, or can it contribute to promoting the common good?

Fred Harris's stated purpose in his book *In Defense of Congress* is to "stand up" for Congress and to suggest some improvements (p. 5). The author provides a somewhat journalistic account of recent scandals that have prompted calls for reform, to the point, for example, of almost wallowing in the John Tower and Clarence Thomas nomination episodes. At the same time, he is rather dismissive of the common contemporary criticisms of our national legislature. Consequently, his "defense" seems incomplete and not altogether convincing, although he does provide a more detailed discussion of the term limits movement than does Rieselbach. Harris's discussion of the term limits movement, perhaps the most prominent political reform movement today, makes for interesting reading. Still, if one wants a more complete picture of the term limits controversy, one should read *In Defense of Congress* in conjunction with commentator George Will's case for terms limits in his book *Restoration*.

Harris appropriately organizes his book into two parts, or two levels of analysis, individuals and institutions. Part one, a focus on members of Congress as individuals, discusses "price, pay, perks and personnel," along with member ethics, incumbency advantages, campaign finance, and term limits (p. 11). The key issue, Harris argues, is member accountability. Part two focuses on Congress as an institution, in particular, on the need to balance a more responsive Congress with a more responsible Congress. The book's prologue and epilogue provide useful summaries of what he is going to tell us and what he has just told us.

In part two Harris briefly touches on the "nature of Congress" as an institution (p. 82). He observes that Congress is slow, conflictual, partisan, and individualistic. Some of the institution's partisanship has rubbed off on former Senator Harris as evidenced by his list of "Congress-bashers" compared to his list of recommended reforms. The latter reflect his party and the former reflect the opposition party, thus leaving us again to wonder if "reform" is merely relative to the perspective of the reformer. Nevertheless, the book's discussion of the necessary trade-off between a responsive and responsible Congress, raises the possibility that reform can be founded on something less ephemeral than mere partisanship. Harris concludes: "Congress is still a responsive and representative institution, more so than at some times in the past, and its members could be made even more accountable. Congress is still the national lawmaking body, and its decision making could be facilitated and made more responsible and efficient" (p. 143). Perhaps the "responsive" and "responsible" virtues of Congress flow from the nature of its representative and law-making functions.

Harris concludes that Congress in the 1980s and early 1990s was more representative and responsive than the pre-reform Congress of the 1950s.

Yet he also notes that the heightened partisanship in Congress during the last decade ran contrary to the decrease in partisanship in the electorate. If Congress in the 1980s was more responsive, why did we have increased partisanship especially in the House in an era of weak parties-in-the-electorate and candidate-centered elections? Leading up to the 1994 election, term limits advocates frequently argued that Congress was out of touch *and* less responsive because elections were rigged in favor of incumbents. To his credit, Harris discusses such incumbency advantages at length, dwelling especially on how the existing campaign finance system favors incumbents over challengers. Yet given the book's heavy reliance on the political science literature, it is surprising that Harris fails to cite Morris Fiorina's considerable writings on this subject. This defect is all the more peculiar in light of how often Harris cites the "enormous growth in government" as an explanation for the changing nature of Congress (e.g., p. 136). Fiorina's *Congress: Keystone of the Washington Establishment* provides another fitting companion reading to *In Defense of Congress* precisely because Fiorina elaborates on how the growth of government has changed Congress.

Finally, Harris summarizes his proposed congressional reforms in the epilogue, including some substantial reforms in legislative rules and procedures, the committee system, and budget process, and an overhaul of the campaign finance system. A number of his ideas are particularly praiseworthy, including his call for eliminating one layer of the budget process and his suggestion that party leaders curb the inflation in committee memberships. Nevertheless, upon completing *In Defense of Congress*, one is left hungry for a more detailed discussion of potential reforms and a more careful development of their theoretical foundation. One place to look for both is in the two Norman Ornstein and Thomas Mann *Renewing Congress* project reports sponsored by the American Enterprise Institute and the Brookings Institution. Of course, another highly useful book on the theory and practice of congressional reform is Leroy Rieselbach's *Congressional Reform: The Changing Modern Congress*.

Rieselbach's book is a serious and careful examination of congressional reform over five decades. He begins appropriately by discussing Congress and the Constitution in order to offer a larger context for discussing reform. Rieselbach grounds his examination in a review of four theories or "broad visions" of our constitutional order: (1) the Executive Force theory; (2) the Responsible Parties theory; (3) the "Literary" theory; and (4) the Congressional Supremacy or "Whig" theory (pp. 14–16). To understand Congress one must understand the separation of powers.

Rieselbach next narrows his focus to more manageable standards for judging congressional reform. He proposes discussing congressional reform in terms of the trade-off between responsibility, responsiveness, and accountability. The author then uses this framework to examine the history of congressional reform from the pre-reform 1950s to the reform agenda in the 1990s. Finally, in his concluding chapter, Rieselbach offers a "middle ground" for reform that he calls "majoritarian democracy" (p. 199). The theoretical grounding provided by the majoritarian democracy ideal enables Rieselbach to plausibly set forth some specific reforms worthy of consideration. One cannot fairly or easily accept or reject the author's recommendations based merely on whether one is a Democrat or Republican, a member of the legislative minority or majority, or a denizen of the executive or legislative branch. Rather one must meet Rieselbach on his ground of grounds, namely, his discussion of the nature of Congress and the separation of powers.

To understand the nature of Congress, Rieselbach argues, one must begin by recognizing that congressional reform is only part of the change in Congress. Reform must be understood in terms of the mixture of individual reformers' motives ("electoral, policy and power motives" [p. 94]) and the larger institutional context for congressional change. "Reform is, after all, part and parcel of broader change. Crises outside Congress, new issues or the fundamental transformation of old ones, and new members of Congress may contribute as much as or more than specific reforms to the modification of legislative activity" (p. 94). Or, as he says elsewhere, "When the times, the membership, and the legislative agenda change, so do the ways Congress goes about its work" (p. 79). Congress and its context are enormously complex, thus one should not be surprised by the unintended consequences of reform. The daunting task of congressional reform presents a veritable Rubik's Cube of competing individuals, interests, ideas, and institutions. Understanding Congress and its environment, as a prelude to political reform, is no small challenge.

Rieselbach understands that the context for congressional reform is the established nature of Congress. He repeatedly articulates this insight:

> Lawmakers deal with reform as they do more "substantive" issues, incrementally. They are seldom if ever moved by broad visions or the ideal Congress; rather they respond, in the short run, to the circumstances of the moment. Reforms tend to be political, pragmatic, and more or less spontaneous reactions to seemingly irresistible forces. They have been piecemeal, not wholesale; individually modest, not radical; ad hoc, not the product of comprehensive planning. (pp. 46–7, see also pp. 172–3)

Rieselbach also recognizes that the roots of Congress's character can be found in the constitutional separation of powers and federalism: the president and Congress are independent and prone to competition, members of Congress are individualistic and parochial, and programmatic parties rarely prevail in the legislative process (p. 13). An understanding of the nature of Congress begins with the Constitution.

The constitutional order confronts reformers with a necessary trade-off between the competing trio of congressional values or virtues frequently mentioned by both Harris and Rieselbach, namely, responsibility, responsiveness, and accountability (p. 173). For example, in discussing accountability as an important aim of reform, Rieselbach concludes, "[m]ore accountability, however, is not without costs. Increased openness, or permeability, may inhibit both responsibility and responsiveness. The need to deliberate and decide in public, in the glare of the media spotlight may inhibit decisive decision making.... Here, too, efforts to maximize one value may interfere with the realization of the other two" (pp. 187–88). Rieselbach argues that in one sense these competing values are "complementary," though in another sense they are "incompatible" (p. 80). Ideally, reformers seek an "optimum blend" of the three (p. 168). Indeed, Rieselbach's own "majoritarian democracy" ideal seeks an "appropriate combination of congressional responsibility, responsiveness and accountability" (p. 173) or what he calls a "middle ground" (p. 199).

While Rieselbach is wise to narrow the focus of his discussion of congressional reform to the more narrow and manageable standards of responsibility, responsiveness, and accountability and away from the broad visions and grand theories of constitutional scholars, he cannot escape dependence on the latter. In fact, in his conclusion, Rieselbach reveals his own constitutional theory: "(m)ajoritarian democracy envisions an operative system of checks and balances—more precisely, a system of separate institutions, legislative and executive, with overlapping powers" (p. 196). Earlier the author makes even clearer his own acceptance of the common understanding of the constitutional separation of powers found in Richard Neustadt's formulation "separate institutions sharing power" (p. 10). Neustadt's understanding and formulation of the separation of powers is shared by both Leroy Rieselbach and Fred Harris (see, e.g., p. 94 of *In Defense of Congress*).

Both Rieselbach and Harris depend on a more or less implicit constitutional theory of the separation of powers as the necessary foundation for their discussions of congressional reform. But the "separate institutions sharing power" formulation as an interpretation of the Founders' constitutional intent is open to question. The separation of powers cannot be reduced to the checks and balances. As evidenced by Madison's Federalist # 10 and Hamilton's Federalist # 78, the Founding Fathers created the constitutional separation of powers to limit the abuse of power *and* to provide for the effective use of power. They wanted responsive, accountable *and* responsible, effective government. The means to these competing ends was the entire separation of powers or separation of functions system. The Founders' separation of powers system provides for a functional differentiation of three kinds of political power distinct in principle or by nature: executive, legislative, and judicial. They designed and organized each branch to best exercise the peculiar function given to it under the Constitution, based on the assumption that different institutions do different things. For example, they designed Congress to represent and deliberate effectively. Loosely speaking, they designed Congress to talk and the executive to act.

On the "maxim" or principle of the separation of powers, the Founders grounded their new "science of politics" (Federalist # 9, 31, 47, and 48). Their constitutional separation of powers was meant to endure and to serve the public interest, not just fleeting partisan interests. Principled congressional reform needs to be premised on an adequate and complete understanding of the constitutional separation of powers. Effective congressional reform depends on an understanding of the essential nature of Congress grounded on the Constitution.

The essential functions of Congress are representation, deliberation, law making, and oversight. These functions of Congress constitute its essential nature, thus providing us with a means of discussing congressional reform in a principled, rather than merely partisan, manner. A return to the Founders' understanding of the separation of powers can equip us with a standard for judging whether the analysis and advancement of congressional reform is merely partisan or political, or whether a principled understanding of congressional reform can provide a platform for promoting reform in the public interest. Leroy Rieselbach's *Congressional Reform: The Changing Modern Congress* offers a fine starting point for a serious examination of congressional reform; his book makes for an excellent classroom adoption. Joseph M. Bessette's new book *The Mild Voice of Reason* carries the argument about the constitutional nature of Congress even further.

The "Republican Revolution" of the 104th Congress may prompt many political scientists to rethink their understanding of Congress and congressional reform. Analysis, like reform, will endure only if grounded on the solid foundation of constitutional theory.

Conservatism, Extremism, and Ideology in a Post-Liberal Age

Euel Elliott

University of Texas, Dallas

Hans-George Betz, *Radical Right-Wing Populism in Western Europe* (New York: St. Martin's Press, 1994), x + 225 pp.; ISBN 0-312-08390-4 (cloth).

Paul Hockenos, *Free to Hate: The Rise of the Right in Post-Communist Eastern Europe* (New York and London: Routledge, 1993), x + 330 pp.; ISBN 0-415-91058-7 (paper).

Brian Girvin, *The Right in the Twentieth Century: Conservatism and Democracy* (London and New York: Pinter Publishers, 1994), xii + 230 pp.; ISBN 0-86187-981-3 (cloth).

Anthony Giddens, *Beyond Left and Right: The Future of Radical Politics* (Stanford, CA: Stanford University Press, 1994), vii + 276 pp.; ISBN 0-8047-2450-4 (cloth).

It has become a virtual truism to suggest that, as the century approaches its close, we are witnessing one of the most profound and sustained assaults on the established political order and its institutions in the past century. Events and processes as diverse as the collapse of the former Soviet Union and its client regimes in Eastern Europe, the seeming exhaustion, political and moral, of the welfare state, the rise of Margaret Thatcher and Ronald Reagan to power in the 1980s, together with the emergence of new conservative forces elsewhere—not to mention the more recent Republican victories in 1994—suggest a fundamental sea change in our political life. All of this has taken place in the midst of the ongoing integration of the world's economies with its attendant dislocations, which makes it an auspicious time to take stock of the political and ideological landscape.

While, in the view of this observer, much of what we consider "conservatism" contains important elements to be commended, such as the re-emergence of individual responsibility, a concern with moral values and efforts to seek nonstatist, nonbureaucratic solutions to our social ills, there are also more disturbing tendencies at work. These include the rise of authoritarian, nativist elements in Europe, and to a lesser extent the United States, as well as the social fragmentation that may be almost inherent in market-based, advanced industrial societies.

Four recent works go a long way toward helping us better understand and navigate the political contours of the post-liberal, post-Communist world. They explore an array of critical issues from the rise of right-wing nationalism in Eastern Europe and the emergence of populist conservative forces in Western Europe to a broad elucidation of more mainstream, broad-based conservatism and its relationship to democracy and speculations on the future of radical politics.

Two authors, Hockenos and Betz, concern themselves, respectively, with the rise of the right in Eastern and Western Europe. Paul Hockenos's study, *Free to Hate*, is concerned with the emergence of the right in Eastern Europe following the collapse of the Soviet Union and the dissolution of Communist governments in those countries. Hockenos systematically evaluates political dynamics in Germany, Hungary, Romania, Czechoslovakia, and Poland. Drawing heavily upon interviews with a wide range of individuals, Hockenos's work is perhaps somewhat more polemical in style than some might prefer. As the author notes in his introduction, "Across the region, deeply conservative, radical nationalist, and even neo-fascist movements arose from Communism's ruins. A diverse spectrum of right-wing forces surfaced in every country, each brandishing nationalist ideologies with authoritarian and social underpinnings" (p. 5). Still, Hockenos does a thorough job in documenting the historical antecedents of the rise of ultra-nationalist political movements across Eastern Europe that reflect deep-seated anti-Semitic and racist elements.

The author is careful to point out significant historical differences often grounded in the unique cultures of the countries examined. Nonetheless, in each country, including the former East Germany, the extremist political milieu had its roots in unique historical and cultural circumstances. Indeed, the author rejects (p. 102) the modernization theories of extremism that Betz and Giddens adopt. The nationalist movements that thrive in the wake of the Soviet empire's collapse in some respects find their ideology in the subordination of the individual to the collective with a stress on family, tradition, and religion. Perhaps not surprisingly, anti-modernist and anti-market forces flourish in this social milieu. The critical role of the Catholic church in Poland, for example—a nation unique in the role played by religion—has been profoundly opposed to the modernity of late twentieth-century liberalism and capitalism. Hockenos aptly describes the nationalist right in Hungary as "seek[ing] to revive the values and traditions that had flourished in Hungary before the rude interruption of Communism and other 'foreign' ideologies, such as liberalism" (p. 112), or the ultra-nationalist forces in Rumania that were loyal to the Ceaucescu regime prior to his downfall in 1989. Illustrative of the new political dynamic in Rumania is the rehabilitation of Marshal Ion Antonescu, executed in 1946 following the seizure of control by the Communists and their allies. Antonescu, who had fought the Soviets on the Eastern Front, was responsible for sending more than 300,000 Jews to their death in labor camps.

Hockenos is not totally pessimistic about the future, although the author of this essay questions the prescriptions put forth to rein in the nonviolent elements of extremism. Legal crackdowns, which he acknowledges as posing a risk, would violate the very constitutional ideals that are in danger. A rejuvenated "democratic left," with the implied rejection or drastic paring back of market reforms, could be an even greater threat, especially given that much of the "democratic left" consists of supposedly reformed members of the old Communist apparatus. It seems unlikely there can be a turning back from the capitalist road. Autarky is no longer an option. While his recommendations are to be occasionally questioned, Hockenos has done a workman-like job in documenting the threat to the constitutional order from the right. A greater recognition of the role the previous Communist regimes played in destroying any semblance of civil society, and the continued threat of the remnants of the totalitarian left, could have added to this effort.

Hans-George Betz's *Radical Right-Wing Populism in Western Europe* focuses on the increased social fragmentation and alienation from the established political order. Bringing somewhat more of a traditional social science approach to his discussion than is seen with Hockenos's work, Betz's fundamental argument can be found in chapter 1. He contends that the final victory of capitalism reflected in the collapse of the Soviet Union, in its East European states, and in the parallel developments of market institutions in China, together with the globalization of the world economy and the rapid innovations in information technologies have created a fundamentally a new post-industrial order. Importantly, it is an order in which "established subcultures, milieus and institutions...are getting eroded and/or being destroyed...by hyping up the new, fleeting and contingent in modern-day life, rather than the more solid values of the past, and by promising individuality in choice and life-style" (p. 29).

Together with the increased vulnerability experienced especially by those with modest education and job skills, the political environment has become ripe for a new politics of protest. Politics, Betz notes, has become dominated by resentment and alienation, a theme that is all too familiar to students of American politics.

Betz documents the decline of traditional party system alignments in Western Europe and the emergence of immigration and law and order as defining issues for the parties of the far right, from the national Front in France to the Republican party of Germany, the Vlaams Blok of Belgium, or the Automobile party of Switzerland. It is immigration, however, that appears to have been most successful in mobilizing support for these new political entities, another theme that hits close to home for Americans. Betz is sensitive to the nuances that differentiate the parties as well as the broad similarities, particularly in his analyses of the class basis of right-wing support, which tends to be concentrated among low-skilled, low-educated, working-class voters.

What is striking about the "new right" in Western Europe are the parallels with recent development in the United States, particularly the backlash against liberal immigration and social preference policies. Moreover, Betz's view suggests obvious, strong parallels with the nativist political forces at work in Eastern Europe, although a difference can be found in the presence—to a greater or lesser degree—of neo-liberal (pro-market) orientations among these parties. Still, Betz seems on safe ground in arguing that such "libertarian" elements of the radical right platform are overshadowed by more populist, and authoritarian, elements. Like Hockenos, the author of *radical* right-wing populism sees no easy solutions to what will almost certainly be a continuing phenomena.

Brian Girvin's *The Right in the Twentieth Century* is a sweeping analysis of the evolution of conservative ideology. Though primarily concerned with the contemporary era, Girvin begins with a discussion relevant especially to Betz and Giddens, that being the relationship between conservatism and modernity. He points out that conservatism was, "born at the moment of modernity and has maintained an ambiguous relationship to that process ever since" (p. 3) and proceeds to an illuminating discussion of the relationship between absolutism and conservatism under the English monarchy, then moving to an analysis of conservatism during the American Revolution and the restoration of monarchy in Europe in the early decades of the nineteenth century.

Girvin makes an important point in stressing current differences between conservative elites in Europe and the United States in the first half of the twentieth century and the unwillingness in the former to make concessions to "democracy, republicanism or nationalism" (p. 31). Of course, it is nationalism that would ultimately come to symbolize much of the conservative creed by the late nineteenth and early twentieth century, and it is a theme that plays a key role in both Hockenos's and Betz's earlier analyses of the new political reality in both Eastern and Western Europe.

Girvin's discussion of the post World War II period, unlike much of his earlier account, concentrates heavily on political developments in Britain and the United States. He argues essentially that British politics during the 1950s and 1960s reflected a political consensus between the Conservative party and Labor—the policy of "Buttskellism," named for the labor leader of the 1950s Hugh Gaitskell and the prominent Tory "Rab" Butler. He also views American politics as veering right during the Eisenhower years. Yet, there was virtually no enthusiasm for an actual rollback of the welfare state in the United States during the 1950s, nor did Eisenhower and most "moderate" Republicans advocate such a course. Indeed, one could argue the Republican argument for being kept in power was that they were more efficient and frugal managers of the welfare state. Germany, France, and virtually every other Western nation witnessed the new "politics of accommodation." While the political achievements of the 1950s should not be dismissed, economic and social politics almost certainly played a role in the establishment of politically stable political regimes throughout Europe in the years immediately following World War II. Still, there were real long-term consequences.

The policy consensus of the 1950s and 1960s, in Europe as well as the United States, helped produce a dramatic expansion of the welfare state and contributed to a greater or lesser extent to the structural deficits and its attendant problems—sluggish growth, high inflation—of the late 1970s that helped bring about a conservative revival.

Girvin does a commendable job in clarifying the reasons for conservative triumphs in the 1980s, showing, correctly in the view of this observer, that the economic crises of the late 1970s called into question the crucial tenets of the welfare state, in particular the belief in full employment. In conjunction with the rapid social changes of the prior two decades that upset the traditional order, the time was ripe for conservative parties such as Margaret Thatcher's Tories to assert traditional values and economic beliefs. However, the kind of aggressive free-market conservatism seen in England after 1979 was not repeated everywhere. Clearly, for example, Germany, governed by a center—right coalition—maintained many of the economic and social policies that had flowered under previous social Democratic governments. Many would also question Girvin's assessment of the ill-fated Bush presidency as being "conservative" in the same vein as his predecessor's.

Girvin could also have paid a little more attention to the kind of nationalist forces that Betz discussed so ably. Moreover, the author, while noting the role that conservative mainstream parties have played in reasserting traditional economic and social roles ignores the tendency—employed by Betz and Giddens—for market forces to contribute mightily to the very breakdown of traditional social structures that conservatives want to repair.

The prominence of the "New Right" movements in Western Europe, as well as in the United States, reflects, as Betz emphasizes (ch. 2, esp. p. 39), the decline of traditional electoral alignments. Along with this decline has come a fundamental challenge to the traditional ideological cleavages that allowed citizens to make some sense of the political landscape. It is, in the view of Anthony Giddens, essential that we move beyond the stifling strictures of traditional ideological thinking if we are to successfully face the political challenges of the future. Giddens begins with the not unreasonable contention that "conservatism" really exists in two forms: the "New Right" or neo-liberals with their emphasis on the expansion of market forces; the neo-conservatives with their acceptance of capitalism and liberal democracy but who "see the bourgeois order as destroying the traditional symbols and practices in which a meaningful social existence depends" (p. 30). It is Giddens's notion of "philosophic conservatism," found in the writings of Michael Oakeshott and with its emphasis on authority, in this sense the transcendent qualities of established institutions—allegiance and tradition—that he uses in the sense of formulating a new radical politics.

Rejecting what he views as the political and moral exhaustion of those on the right who proclaim the triumph of markets and the failed utopia of socialism, Giddens offers a version of a post-scarcity world based on a conception of generative and life politics. The former, while defending the notion of a public domain that is rejected by market forces, allows individuals and groups to "have things done for them" (p. 15), and the latter recognizes that technology and globalization have produced a world in which tradition and nature, as a force that exists independently of human action, have vanished.

Using this radical framework, Giddens proceeds to develop what he views as the core of a post-scarcity order. The application of generative politics to welfare and welfare policy, issues of poverty and violence (especially toward women) are explored, though the linchpin of a post-scarcity society lies in the formulation of a new ecological politics. While often thought provoking, he arrives at some conclusions relating to concepts of welfare that challenge left-wing orthodoxy, particularly in a redefining of equality, and of poverty and its relationship to human happiness and satisfaction. Further, elements of his discussion on the breakdown of families and the relationship to violence against women are sophisticated and not unsympathetic to traditionalist views of gender roles.

As noted already, the linchpin of the post-scarcity society is a new ecological politics, and it is here that Giddens veers off into the swamp of postmodernist orthodoxy. Here, also, we have disinterred the old "small is beautiful" mantra of the 1960s together with discredited notions of "limits to growth" that have been making the rounds for the last several years.

The "deep ecology" proposed by Giddens "proposes that a new political and moral philosophy is needed which sees beings as in, and of, nature, rather than superior to it; 'biospheric equality' places humans on an equal level with all other living things" (p. 199). A society based upon such principles would promote local, self-governing communities and "small" technologies.

Besides presenting no clear mechanism by which any of the proposed transformations of society could occur, the focus on a "post-scarcity society" even as a realistic goal in the advanced capitalist democracies seems hopelessly naive, given the kinds of economic pressures we are experiencing and will continue to experience. To simply say we are going to change the rules of the game is not enough. In short, Giddens's efforts to link his definition of philosophic conservatism to some of his suggested deep reforms are simply not convincing.

The ongoing massive and simultaneous political, economic, cultural, and technological changes in society are breaking down old partisan and ideological alignments. Social scientists over the next few decades will have an abundance of topics to dissect. The works discussed, in spite of occasional limitations, offer both tantalizing perspectives on the recent past as well as glimpses into the near future of politics and their possibly profound consequences.

U.S. Foreign Policy in a Changing World: Domestic Salience—Emerging Agenda

Karin Stanford

University of Georgia

David A. Deese, ed., *The New Politics of American Foreign Policy* (New York: St. Martin's Press, Inc., 1994), 284 pp.; ISBN 0-312-09133-8 (cloth).

Charles W. Kegley, Jr., and Eugene R. Wittkopf, eds., *The Future of American Foreign Policy* (New York: St. Martin's Press, Inc., 1995), 350 pp.; ISBN 0-312-03574-8 (paper).

James E. Winkates, J. Richard Walsh, and Joseph M. Scolnick, Jr., eds., *U.S. Foreign Policy in Transition* (Chicago: Nelson-Hall Publishers, 1994), 284 pp.; ISBN 0-8304-1343 (paper).

The fall of 1989 marked the beginning of numerous significant changes in the world that prompted a thorough analysis of the American role in international politics. Communism in the Soviet Union and Eastern Europe collapsed, the Soviet Union lost its direct control over other nations in its hemisphere, the Warsaw Pact perished, and the previously divided Germany merged. By the signing of various weapons and trade agreements at a summit in June 1990, Presidents George Bush and Mikhail Gorbachev essentially pronounced the end of the cold war between the Soviet Union and the United States.[1]

A defining event for the new post-cold war world was Soviet support of the United States during the 1991 Persian Gulf War. Also telling was U.S. determination to gain approval to use force against Iraq as part of a United Nations action. These acts signify that international politics is no longer restrained by a bipolar competition between two superpowers. Bipolarism has been replaced with multilateralism, in which the decision making for the world is shared by a multitude of nations with interests and resources great enough to influence a particular international issue. Without a looming and menacing security threat, nations who are financially secure and economically productive, such as Germany and Japan, have the opportunity for greater political impact in world politics.

In addition to the changes in the international system, the United States has also had to confront its own devastating domestic problems. Among the most prominent are fiscal problems, which include serious governmental budget and trade deficits as well as chronic poverty, a deteriorating physical infrastructure, a degenerating educational system, and an increase in violent crime. These domestic issues constrain the ability for U.S. leaders to act effectively abroad and therefore affect U.S. standing in global politics. Moreover, the American public is demanding that the nation's scarce resources be used to combat these overwhelming social problems rather than intervene in the affairs of other nation-states. U.S. policymakers, therefore, must confront the new challenges in the international system in an era of declining political and economic clout, and with the knowledge of waning public support for international action.[2]

The elimination of anti-communism and containment as the premier goals of U.S. foreign policy and the erosion of domestic power has lead to a passionate debate among scholars and practitioners about the nature and course of U.S. foreign policy. The fundamental debate revolves around the goals and objectives of U.S. foreign policy in a post-cold war world. Core questions underscore America's international interests or foreign policy priorities. For instance, should the United States continue its global activism, revert to isolationism, or reorient its role in the world in other ways? Closely related questions include whether or not the foreign policy-making process has changed? How will the changes impact relationships with former allies and adversaries? Does the United States have the ability to match capabilities with international commitments? Are there new issues impacting U.S. foreign policy?

Although the debate on American foreign policy in the post-cold war era is varied, most of the discussion remains state-centered and continues along traditional arguments between global activism versus isolationism and realism versus idealism. The most striking aspect of the contemporary discussion is the salience of domestic issues and concerns on the goals and objectives of U.S. policy. The premier question is whether or not the United States can remain a superpower given the constraints of domestic issues and the growing distaste of Americans for international intervention.

Using analysis, critique, and historical description, the edited volumes by James E. Winkates, J. Richard Walsh, and Joseph M. Scolnick, Jr.; Charles W. Kegley and Eugene R. Wittkopt; and David A. Deese address the transformation in U.S. foreign policy since the end of the cold war. These volumes raise important questions and offer bold proscriptions on how U.S. policymakers might formulate and implement policy and strategies for the changing world. Most authors agree that the United States has emerged as the only dominant world power, in view of its political stability, military power, and economic strength, and ideological and cultural attractions. However, they argue that the U.S. position in the world has declined in many ways—which has increased U.S. reliance on other nations to hold key roles in solving the world's problems.

U.S. Foreign Policy in Transition, edited by Joseph M. Scolnick, Jr., James E.

Winkates, and J. Richard Walsh, utilizes the concept of "transition" as one way of explaining contemporary U.S. foreign policy. Transition connotes the uncertainty and changes that U.S. policy has and will continue to undergo as a result of changes in the international system and U.S. domestic and international power. The primary contention is that U.S. foreign policy is in transition toward a new orientation to international politics. Essentially, U.S. foreign policy is transcending its narrow globalism to emphasize "inter-mestic" issues. "Inter-mestic" policies refer to those matters of international relations which by their nature closely involve the domestic economy of the nation, such as international trade, immigration, or oil imports (Winkates et al.: 4). "Inter-mestic" issues mobilize the same actors as domestic policies—executive agencies, Congress, interest groups, and public opinion.[3]

A second assertion made by these authors is that the domestic emphasis on U.S. foreign policy and the changes in the international system have forced the United States to change its style. Its role is shifting from directing leadership to one of advising, encouraging, and sanctioning the behavior of others. In the post-cold war world, the United States will attempt to become an honest broker more often and will deal with issues in broader contexts and in multilateral rather than bilateral settings.

The collection of essays in *The Future of American Foreign Policy*, edited by Charles W. Kegley, Jr., and Eugene R. Wittkopf, promotes issues and arguments that are very similar to those in the Winkates, Walsh, and Scolnick volume. The emphasis, however, is not on explaining the shift in foreign policy orientation but on predicting what a future U.S. foreign policy might look like and what forces will shape it. The primary question is whether the grand strategy designed to promote U.S. interests and protect its security after World War II will continue to serve in the post-cold war era. The contention is that the United States must confront the changes in the international system without the domestic and international power it once possessed. Therefore, the United States must begin to reassess its strengths and weaknesses to determine whether it has the will and capabilities to accomplish its objectives in a changing global environment and to deal with the new issues that challenge its leadership (Kegley and Wittkopt: 2).

The objective of *The New Politics of American Foreign Policy*, edited by David Deese, is to analyze the specific ways in which domestic politics and global politics shape U.S. foreign policy processes. The book highlights the newer and fundamental roles of voters, interest groups, social and political movements, the media, and Congress in foreign affairs. Unlike the two aforementioned books, which focus specifically on post-cold war foreign policy, the Deese book delineates political transformations in the foreign policy process since the 1960s.

Its main argument is that new issues, more actors, and a wider range of interests do not necessarily create a less effective foreign policy process. Indeed, U.S. foreign policy could be strengthened by a more consensus-oriented process that is driven by deliberative politics in which a greater degree of debate, involving a greater number of participants in the process, takes hold. The authors essentially declare that a longer, more deliberative discussion and debating process does not necessarily indicate weakness.

Most authors criticize the conventional, "top-down" view, which focuses heavily on the president as the dominant player in U.S. foreign policy. Public opinion in this view is volatile, unpredictable, inconsistent, and generally not very important to U.S. foreign policy processes. The media and Congress are viewed as hindrances that must be controlled in order to pursue an effective foreign policy. This view also tends to emphasize the "high-politics" nature of foreign policy as opposed to the domestic sphere, and the need to re-establish "bipartisanship" in foreign affairs. Those who adhere to this approach are likely to be particularly concerned about any erosion of presidential or American power that may be brought about by the new global environment of the 1990s (Deese: 262).

These authors, however, argue that since the 1960s foreign policy has been politicized, which makes it subject to many of the same populist pressures as domestic policy. And populist pressure in foreign policy is usually isolationist (Deese: xiv, xvi; Rockman in Deese: 70). The effectiveness of U.S. leadership in world affairs under the new conditions will depend upon America's ability to understand the concerns of the American public and view their participation as leading to the possibility of a stronger, more effective, and more democratic policy process.

Considered together, all three volumes attempt to discover the challenges of U.S. foreign policy in the post-cold war era. Four areas of concern become salient: goals, relationships, capabilities, and new agenda items. With a unique focus each volume addresses each issue area. The Winkates, Walsh, and Scolnick book concentrates on five functional issue-areas: defense, arms control, intelligence, international economic policy, and "new agenda" issues. They attempt to discern how the United States will reorient its policy in each area. Kegley and Wittkopt grapple with the dilemmas of the objectives, relationships, and capabilities of U.S. foreign policy in the 1990s and beyond. The Deese volume concentrates on the fundamental roles of institutions, social groups, and individuals in U.S. foreign policy processes. Most authors distinctively emphasize how domestic concerns will impact each issue area and the policy process. In addition, each author offers a perspective of the needs of the United States in the changing global arena and then addresses the concerns and the constraints offered by the domestic environment.

The first area is the objectives of U.S. foreign policy in the post-cold war era. The nature of the post-cold war environment, however, is complex and has not been clearly defined, which is why the debate over the future of American foreign policy often leads to divergent prescriptions. Those who adhere to a realist conception of U.S. interests assert that the end of the cold war requires no fundamental redefinition of American interests and politics. The search for power, prestige, and position should continue in much the same way it has been. They assert that, as before the collapse of the Soviet Union, there continues to be a threat of global instability and competition in arms that can only be controlled by maintaining a U.S. presence. In "Entangled Forever," Josef Joffe argues that communism may be dead, but realpolitik continues: "The death of communism spells neither the birth of a new world order nor the end of conflict" (Joffe in Kegley and Wittkopf: 39). The Soviet Union remains formidable; new centers of power are emerging;

and new conflicts are coming to the fore. In addition, because of internal problems and lack of military might, the new centers of power—Germany, Japan, and China are not ready to assume the burden of global management. Therefore, the United States must maintain a presence. Other authors, such as John J. Mearsheimer, take this argument one step further by asserting that global stability requires that we prolong the cold war. In "Why We Will Soon Miss The Cold War," he asserts that the bipolar systems tend to be stable and the nuclear weapons breed caution. If these restraints are lifted and Europe reverts to multipolarity, he warns, a new era of major crises and wars could result. Mearsheimer's proscription is that the cold war should be maintained at lower levels of East-West tensions by U.S. encouragement of limited, managed nuclear weapons in Europe for nuclear deterrence (Mearsheimer, in Kegley and Wittkopf: 48). John Gaddis considers the competing processes of integration versus fragmentation as the issues that will retain a U.S. presence in the world. Ethnic conflict as a result of nationalism, aggressive fundamentalist religious movements, and other violent secessionist activity will have to be contained in order to ensure global peace. (Gaddis in Kegley and Wittkopf: 16). Ultimately, the realists argue that the United States cannot return to isolationism; it must counter aggression.

In contrast, idealists argue that the end of the cold war provides the United States with the opportunity to play a more modest role in the world. Without containment as a guiding philosophy other problems can now receive attention. For instance, economic security issues can now receive the attention they have warranted for decades. Theodore C. Sorensen proposes a thorough re-evaluation of national security to include "the preservation of this nation's economic effectiveness and independence in the global marketplace" (Theodore Sorensen in Kegley and Wittkopt: 74). In addition, a focus on more altruistic issues, such as the peaceful enhancement of democracy to make the world a safer and congenial place, can now take place. Hence, U.S. financial and military support to corrupt regimes in Africa, Asia, the Middle East, and Latin America can now cease.

A second set of issues pertains to how foreign policy processes will adapt to fundamental changes in American society and political institutions. At issue is the politicization of U.S. foreign policy processes which many scholars agree began in the 1960s when the Vietnam War broke the pattern of consensus and congressional deference in foreign policy.[4] John T. Tierney describes how the politics of American foreign policy has become more like U.S. domestic policy—fractious and ideologically driven (Tierney in Deese). With a more diverse and active population in foreign affairs, congressional and executive action are more heavily influenced by public demands. Bert A. Rockman also elucidates how the environment of foreign policy-making today has become more politicized. One result, Rockman argues, is that the role of the president as exclusive shaper of foreign policy has been reduced (Rockman in Deese).

Several authors in the Deese volume view the media as a key player in the politicization process and a shaper of American public opinion, (Bennett, Graham, Shapiro, and Page, and Thomas Risse-Kappan in Deese). Lance Bennett, in particular, points to the extent of executive branch and executive congressional disagreement as critical in determining the extent of media coverage, public debate and participation, and overall openness of the foreign policy-making process. In the past, a handful of foreign policy elites controlled consensus on policy goals and provided information to the media. Images that the public received were designed to create public support for policies, not bring the public into the decision-making process. The crumbling of elite consensus contributed to the changes in news coverage patterns (Bennett in Deese: 170). The ensuing controversies over issues engage congressional attention and opposition, which in turn almost guarantees significant media coverage and the availability of much more information to the public and interest groups.

An essential question is: How critical a role will public opinion play in the policy process? John Reilly discusses recent trends in the foreign policy attitudes of Americans that discredited the elitist paradigm that public opinion is volatile or moody, unstructured and poorly informed, and not particularly significant to decision making (Reilly in Kegley and Wittkopt). The emerging new paradigm holds that public opinion is now a stable and independent actor in the process. Basing his discussion on late 1990 surveys of leaders and the public, he documents important shifts in attitudes since the collapse of communism. The results reinforce earlier findings that demonstrate Americans no longer view the Soviet Union as the principle threat but believe the former adversary is one of the three leading countries in which the United States has a vital interest. In addition, Reilly's findings suggest that the American public saw domestic issues as one of the greatest threat to U.S. stability. These opinions do shape policymakers' responses to issues. International crises of the 1990s in Haiti, Bosnia, and Rwanda indicate the reluctance of American voters to support intervention and therefore the reluctance of politicians to intervene. U.S. activity related to these crises has been restrained and lacked the resource commitment, militarily and financially, to eliminate aggression and rebuild democracy.

A key part of the debate on the transformation of U.S. foreign policy centers on the impact of changes on U.S. relationships with former allies and enemies, as well as regional international organizations. The question of the relationship between the U.S. and the former Soviet Union and Europe are paramount. Realist authors offer several reasons why the United States should remain involved with the former Soviet Union and Europe. First, they argue that it is in the interest of the United States to seek the survival of the former Soviet Union as a great power in order to maintain a stable bipolarity. In addition, the United States cannot assume that Russia will remain a friend forever. Moreover, it is possible to construct scenarios in which geo-strategic threats to the United States, with or without the former Soviet Union, could become pronounced (Goldberg and Gaddis in Kegley and Wittkopt). For instance, it is possible for an aggressive Germany to return to power. With regard to economics, these same authors view the European Economic Community (EEC) as a serious economic competitor, and therefore the United States must remain active in its attempts to reduce trade barriers and enhance its standing in the world's economic wars.

Irrespective of the fact that there has been no shifting of alliances, the American public would advocate a withdrawal from entrenched relationships that require an abundance of its resources and would like to focus on issues that provide direct benefits to America, such as free trade. Ronald Steel asserts in "Europe After the Superpowers" that, "Americans want to disregard Atlanticism—the organizing principle of U.S. postwar policy toward Europe which encouraged European dependence on the U.S." (Steel in Kegley and Wittkopt: 164). This view advocates that the United States should devolve greater responsibility for European security on the Europeans themselves and encourages more cuts in U.S. forces in Europe. On trade issues, this approach suggests that the American public would like to keep the ECC open to U.S. trade and investment, but U.S. financial well-being must always be considered primary (Shapiro and Page in Deese: 233).

The issue of trade is perhaps the most pressing issue affecting U.S. relationships with Japan and other parts of Asia. Selig S. Harrison and Clyde V. Prestowitz, Jr., point out, however, that U.S. economic difficulties with Asia stem from its emphasis on military rather than economic security, which gave Japan the resources to develop economically and to gain great trade surpluses with the United States (Harrison and Prestowitz, Jr., in Kegley and Wittkopt). The isolationist and idealist authors consider the military emphasis anachronistic since the fall of Soviet Union and assert that the United States must disentangle economic and security issues and put economic priorities first. On conflict resolution in the East, the argument is that the United States should develop multilateral approaches and engage in burden-sharing with these countries instead of pursuing a dominate role.

U.S. goals in the Middle East, Latin America, Africa and other parts of the third world are also changing. Because the goal of containing the Soviet Union no longer exists, the United States has begun to focus on other issues, such as democratization. In addition, a political repositioning has taken place among many Middle East states as a result of shifting alliances caused by the Iraqi invasion of Kuwait and the subsequent Persian Gulf War (Dowdy in Winkates et al.: 187). This has caused a slight change in the U.S./Israel relationship. For example, for the first time President George Bush asked the Israeli government to delay its request for loan guarantees for 120 days in order to avoid jeopardizing a Middle East Peace Conference. The Bush administration also demonstrated a change in its relationship with many Latin American nations. The preoccupation with the prevention of revolutionary activity dissipated and attention is now being spread to problems that affect U.S. domestic interest, including debt, free trade, terrorism, and drug production and prevention. Although there are some interest groups who take issue with the U.S. shift in policy orientation, there appears to be no serious opposition from realists or idealists. (Farnsworth in Winkates). There is, however, a raging debate about U.S. involvement in Africa and other parts of the third world. Some see the end of the cold war as an opportunity to disengage from the third world, much as they urge disengagement from Europe. Geoffrey Kemp believes that the answer to these issues rest in geopolitics and therefore neither Russia nor the United States will consider their vital interests at stake in most regions outside of their hemisphere or where there is not an acute global security question or financial interest, such as Africa (Kemp in Kegley and Wittkopt).

Other authors see U.S. national interests in the third world as continuing but less varied. Advocates of this school of thought concede that promotion of democratic government, economic development, and issues of peace and stability remain important. Without peace, neither democracy nor growth nor other values are likely to take root and develop. The issue of stability is so paramount that Pentagon military planners have also begun to redesign U.S. conventional military forces to deal with third world contingencies (Ikle in Kegley and Wittkopt). Emphasizing the domestic constraints to U.S. involvement in Africa and other parts of the Third World, John W. Sewell argues that U.S. leadership will be required to meet the challenge of these emergent issues, but he recognizes that the changed international economic position of the United States will impose constraints on what can be accomplished (Sewell in Kegley and Wittkopt).

The discourse on the instruments and capabilities of U.S. policy in the post-cold war era centers on defense and intelligence issues. Most authors agree that decisions about the future of U.S. military will be based on domestic values, politics, and economic conditions as well as perceptions of foreign threats. There is also an agreement that the new approach to defense policy will be based on a variant of what James E. Winkates calls "peacetime engagement" (Winkates and Hoover in Winkates et al). It posits a new form of broad-based deterrence which will encompass small and largely symbolic military forces to maintain a U.S. presence, rapid reaction capability, and the ability to reconstitute a larger force structure if massive overt threats reemerge. The difference is that previously the emphasis was on large military units to support major alliance commitments or to sustain U.S. security arrangements in multiple places. Because the American public will rarely support military efforts where its vital interests are only marginally at stake, the new era will consist of selective engagements that will consist of ad hoc coalitions based on shared goals. On intelligence issues, Loch Johnson maintains that although the cold war has ended, the need for accurate information about the world remains. In two articles on U.S. intelligence in the post-cold war era, Johnson argues that the U.S. intelligence needs will continue in the former Soviet Union and in other regions. In addition, new issues, such as terrorism, narcotics, and counterintelligence will require adequate U.S. intelligence. Therefore, the intelligence community must continue in its efforts to identify foreign threats, while expanding its responsibilities (Johnson in Kegley and Wittkopt and in Winkates).

The premier new agenda item reflected in these books is international economic policy. Although issues of international economic stability have always existed, they had not received extensive attention because of U.S. preoccupation with the cold war. Primarily because the future of U.S. prosperity and global influence will depend on steps to strengthen domestic economic performance, international economic issues are the premier new agenda item (Hammond in Winkates).

Issues of process are very important to this discussion. Hammond and Destler argue that the once separate security and economic issue areas are merging as one positive result of the end of the cold war. Although George Bush's administration provided some attention to these issues by focusing on increased free-trade zones, interest rates, trade sanctions, and increased opportunities for American business in the Soviet Union and the Middle East, it did not deal adequately with funding for education, job training, infrastructure, health care, an overcrowded criminal justice system, and constructive tax reform to increase savings and investment. The security/economic merger should soften or reverse the security over economic hierarchy. One example of how this shift has occurred is the implementation of the Clinton administration's new National Economic Council, which has joint responsibility for domestic and international economic policy. The Council's approach begins with the premise that the most serious flaw in U.S. economic policy is disinvestment in its people. The contemporary discussion of U.S. foreign policy begins with that premise (Hammond in Winkates, Destler in Deese).

In summary, the three volumes affirm that an interdependent world requires the interconnection of foreign and domestic policy. Therefore, part of the answer to how the United States will readjust its policies in the post-cold war period lies in how it organizes itself internally for making choices. Domestic interests, which will constitute the bases for political and institutional pressures on the foreign policy decision-making process, will provide the impetus for international policies. The challenge for scholars and practitioners is to deconstruct domestic interests along lines that take into account not only the concerns of economic and security interests, but also explore the ramification of gender, ethnicity, and class on U.S. foreign policy processes in order to determine which segments of society engender the most impact on policy goals, capabilities, and relationships in the post-cold war era.

Notes

1. Don Oberdorf and David Hoffman. 1990. "Superpowers Agree on Nuclear Arms Cuts, Sign Chemical Weapons, Grain, Trade Pacts." *The Washington Post* (June 2): sec. 1, A1.
2. For instance, Robert Shapiro and Benjamin Page cite several public polls taken by Roper and The National Public Opinion Research Center. They conclude that the American public is willing to intervene when it perceives that there is a clear threat to U.S. interests, but is very reluctant to do so when there is no alternative. See pages 219–25 specifically in the Deese book.
3. See John Spanier and Eric Uslaner. 1985. *American Foreign Policy Making and the Democratic Dilemmas*, 17–22. New York: Holt, Rinehart and Winston, 1985.
4. Ralph B. Levering. 1978. *The Public and American Foreign Policy, 1918–1978*. New York: William Morrow. Ole R. Holsti and James N. Rosenau. 1984. *American Leadership in World Affairs: Vietnam and the Breakdown of Consensus*. Boston: Allen and Unwin.

Book Reviews

Raphael J. Sonenshein. *Politics in Black and White: Race and Power in Los Angeles* (Princeton: Princeton University Press, 1993), xxii + 301 pp.; ISBN 0-691-08634-6 (cloth).

With the publication of this book on the regime of former Los Angeles Mayor Tom Bradley, Raphael Sonenshein has made an outstanding contribution to the study of both urban and racial politics in the United States (as the American Political Science Association recognized by awarding his book the 1994 Ralph Bunche Cultural Pluralism Award). A significant book that should be read widely, it has important strengths and weaknesses that deserve to be aired and discussed widely as well.

Taking the claims of its titles seriously reveals the major contributions and limitations of Sonenshein's book. Focusing on the main title of the book—*Politics in Black and White*—best brings into view its strengths and important contributions. Taking its subtitle—*Race and Power in Los Angeles*—seriously, however, discloses important weaknesses that will be addressed below.

As a study of "politics in black and white" in Los Angeles during the Bradley era, Sonenshein's book is excellent. The author has two primary aims, one social scientific and the other political, both of which may be seen as powerfully advanced when viewed through the prism of the book's main title. The central *social scientific aim* is to contribute to the literature on the political incorporation of peoples of color in U.S. urban governments. The book does this through a detailed description and analysis of the successful "biracial coalition" that governed the nation's second largest city for twenty years. Sonenshein sets the stage with a brief history of racial politics in Los Angeles, and then traces the origins, foundations, growth, and ultimate electoral success of Bradley's coalition. In a masterful historical narrative, he continues by tracing and analyzing Tom Bradley's twenty years in the mayor's office in some detail, including the electoral contests that affected the regime's power and the ups and downs of the policy aims that Bradley pursued while in power. Sonenshein shows Bradley to be a sophisticated and progressive political leader of one of the most difficult-to-govern cities in the world.

Interspersed with this narrative, Sonenshein moves beyond Browning, Marshall and Tabb's seminal work (1984) to articulate and flesh out a "Western model" of biracial political incorporation that challenges the conventional wisdom of Eastern and Midwestern urban racial politics. In Sonenshein's view, that conventional wisdom takes its bearings from the decades-old "black power" analysis of Stokely Carmichael (now Kwame Turè) and Charles V. Hamilton (1967). Contrary to the Carmichael/Turè and Hamilton argument, Sonenshein's principal theoretical claim (and this reveals the book's *political aim* as well) is that the Bradley regime—the "Western model"—demonstrates that successful and progressive political coalition between African Americans and white liberals *is* possible and mutually advantageous in large cities where the right conditions exist and are recognized and fostered. The key to this model's success, Sonenshein argues throughout, is the interweaving of three crucial factors: a shared *ideology* of liberalism, shared *interests*, and effective biracial *leadership*. Introduced at the outset, these three ingredients of successful biracial coalition politics are used very effectively by Sonenshein to organize and assess the materials of his historical narrative. Thus, Sonenshein goes beyond historical narrative and builds upon the analyses of predecessors to add sensible and insightful reflections on the nature of contemporary electoral politics and their connections to both the maintenance of political power in urban settings and to the conditions under which biracial coalition can flourish.

In all of these ways, the book is highly successful. As noted above, however, viewing Sonenshein's book through the lens of its subtitle, "Race and Power in Los Angeles," reveals serious weaknesses that deserve attention as well. First, while Sonenshein's emphasis on biracial coalition politics makes perfect sense in a study of the Bradley regime (African Americans and Westside white liberals were, after all, the core of the Bradley coalition), there is something fundamentally distorting about such a focus in a study of *race and power* in Los Angeles. The issue of *race* in southern California has never been understood in terms of "black and white" only, and the classic patterns of racial domination—for example, official and "private" violence, racially segmented labor markets, exclusion and segregation in multiple arenas of civil society—have been applied variously to all peoples of color in southern California and not just to African Americans. Mexicans and Mexican Americans, Asian Americans, and American Indians have been a part of the political landscape in Los Angeles from the beginning of the city's incorporation into the United States in 1848 to the present.

If the book's real focus was "race and power in Los Angeles," then one would want to know more about why these "other" racialized ethnic groups were not a part of the Bradley regime's governing coalition, and what their real status has been in the public world and civil society of Los Angeles. While Sonenshein does address these questions briefly (in the book's early pages and especially in a late chapter on the potential for multiracial coalition politics in Los Angeles's future), they are simply not a major focus for him. And this is because his book is really a study of the Bradley regime and not of "race and power in Los Angeles."

Sonenshein's unabashed liberalism has telling consequences for his analysis. The simplest way to make my point here is to suggest a comparison of Sonenshein's book with that of Mike Davis (1990). For Sonenshein, gaining *power* has to do with forming an *electoral* coalition that can garner enough votes to gain control of a city's *electoral* governing institutions. Since Latinos and Asian Americans played such a small role in Bradley's electoral coalition, from this liberal perspective it makes sense that a study of "power" in Los Angeles does not focus on these populations. For an analyst with Davis's more structural view, however, electoral institutions play a relatively minor (though not insignificant) role among a city's institutions exercising "power."

Sonenshein's assessment of the historic political strength of Los Angeles police chiefs indicates some awareness of the reality of the nonelectoral exercise of power. But once again, his liberal focus on electoral politics distorts his analysis of the nature of power in Los Angeles. A more structural theoretical foundation could have helped the book address with greater success not only the nature of racial politics in Los Angeles but also such public policy issues as Bradley's economic development agenda. This last is assessed with little attention to the structure of *economic* power in the Los Angeles region or to the global politico-economic changes that were impacting Los Angeles during Bradley's regime. As a consequence, he does not probe deeply for linkages between the limitations of Bradley's liberal program and the multiracial lower class anger that erupted in the Los Angeles uprising of 1992. (It is noteworthy that this *class* dimension of U.S. racial politics was a point of emphasis for Carmichael/Turè and Hamilton, an angle missing from Sonenshein's discussion of their book.)

In sum, Sonenshein's book succeeds very well as a narrative analysis of Tom Bradley's electoral coalition. As a study of "race and power in Los Angeles," however, the book has real limitations. And surely the multiracial demography of urban politics *and* the structural nature of power need to be addressed more directly by those of us elaborating the political incorporation paradigm in the study of urban political life.

References

Browning, Rufus P., Dale Rogers Marshall, and David Tabb. 1984. *Protest is Not Enough: The Struggle of Blacks and Hispanics for Equality in City Politics.* Berkeley: University of California Press.

Carmichael, Stokely, and Charles V. Hamilton. 1967. *Black Power: The Politics of Liberation in America.* New York: Random House.

Davis, Mike. 1990. *City of Quartz: Excavating the Future of Los Angeles.* London: Verso.

Ron Schmidt, Jr.
California State University,
Long Beach

Douglas J. Amy. *Real Choices/New Voices: The Case for Proportional Representation Elections in the United States* (New York: Columbia University Press, 1993), xi + 278 pp.; ISBN 0-231-08154-5 (cloth)/0-231-08155-3 (paper).

Recent U.S. Supreme Court decisions limiting the use of affirmative districting to increase minority representation in legislative bodies has stimulated interest in alternatives to the use of winner-take-all elections in the United States. Douglas Amy's book, *Real Choices/New Voices*, makes a powerful case for adoption of proportional representation (PR) elections for local councils, state legislatures, and Congress.

While frankly a work of advocacy, this book includes an incisive analysis of the arguments made against PR elections, taking each objection in turn and subjecting it to careful dissection. The conclusion, that PR systems best provide the opportunity for racial and ethnic minorities, women, and self-defined political groups, to gain fair representation, remains unshaken. Currently, while African Americans strive to maintain recent gains in representation and build on their electoral successes, many other American voters exhibit a growing interest in a viable third party. These diverse political aspirations toward a more open democratic system converge to make this work particularly timely.

At the outset, Amy lucidly exposes the flaws of single-member plurality (SMP) elections, a system that most American voters consider so natural that they do not think of it as a choice. Yet the United States, Canada, and Great Britain are among the very few countries in the democratic world to use these winner-take-all elections that produce such unrepresentative results. As Amy shows, the lead vote-getter in a single-member district wins all of the representation, whether by plurality or majority, while all other votes are wasted. Summing a large number of single-member districts adds to the distortion, and a council or legislative body becomes a "fun-house mirror, enlarging some features of our body politic and shrinking others" (p. 27), to the detriment of representative policy-making.

While these unfair outcomes are built into a plurality voting system, they also can be deliberately created by the way district lines are drawn. Amy shows how the gerrymander has been used historically to advantage or disadvantage a party, to protect an incumbent, or to exclude groups such as African Americans from representation by "packing" or "cracking" minority populations. The more recent use of the affirmative gerrymander has increased black representation in some areas, but depends for its success on residential segregation, cooperative districting authorities, and decisions in the judicial arena where support is rapidly eroding. Moreover, in diverse areas, one minority's gain from creative districting may mean another minority's loss, an outcome shaped by line-drawers, not by voters.

The alternative, which Amy calls "the simple solution" (p. 128), is to recognize that there are other options, specifically a number of PR systems that could be used in American elections to ensure fair minority representation, encourage women's candidacies, open up the party system to more choices, and facilitate issue-oriented elections that would give voters more input into policy-making.

The impact of electoral systems on voter turnout is difficult to establish, owing to the complexity of factors shaping the voter's decision to go to the polls. However, Amy presents compelling statistics showing that among industrialized democracies, those using PR elections turn out significantly higher percentages of voters than the United States does with its plurality elections (p. 141). While presidential elections bring out the American peak turnout of about half the eligible adults, turnout in PR elections in European countries ranges from a low of about 70 percent in Spain to over 90 percent in Austria and Belgium.

Assembling the pieces of the turnout puzzle, Amy identifies distrust of government and political alienation as factors depressing American turnout, and finds linkages between these characteristics and the single-member plurality voting system. The wasted votes of winner-take-all elections most obviously discourage voters from participating. In a two-person encounter, up to half of the voters may win no representation; in a three-way contest, close to two-thirds may be shut out. While this seems normal to most American voters, who are accustomed to winning or losing, it is not a necessary feature of elections. In the multi-seat contests of PR systems, up to 90 percent of voters typically win some representation, with seats allocated in proportion to votes.

The growing American phenomenon of safe legislative seats, strengthened by incumbent influence on redistricting, increases the numbers of wasted votes and further discourages minorities in a district, whether racial, ethnic, or partisan, from bothering to vote. Not only should the competitive elections of a PR system increase individual turnout, but party mobilization of voters should thrive in the climate of competition.

The party system is itself shaped by the electoral rules of the game. Many defenders of single-member plurality elections concede their flaws, but insist on their critical importance to the maintenance of a two-party system. On that point, Amy would agree. But he, like growing numbers of Americans, believes that new parties are needed to revitalize our political system, to expand options on the ballot for voters who feel unrepresented by the political duopoly which the ossified major parties have established in this country. PR elections would clearly encourage this development.

Amy analyzes at some length the fear of instability which many Americans feel would occur were multiparty elections to develop. He calls instability "one of the great myths surrounding PR" (p. 159). Evidence is cited of both single-party and coalition governments chosen in PR elections. While coalition governments are more frequently found in PR systems, they are not necessarily unstable. Indeed, in the plurality-elected U.S. Congress, coalition-building within the major parties and across parties is an essential component of the policy-making process.

The fear of instability is related to concern that fragmentation of society into groups would be further stimulated by small political parties representing diverse interests. Amy argues to the contrary that "the best way to attempt to ease racial and ethnic tensions in the United States is not by denying these groups their fair share of representation but by including them in the policy-making process" (p. 166).

For those oriented to the technical aspects of electoral systems, chapter 9 will be compelling. Here Amy compares the benefits of various PR systems for American adoption, and finds two that fit especially well. His recommendation for local nonpartisan elections is the single transferable vote (STV), sometimes called "preference voting," which was used by a number of cities in the United States between 1915 and 1960, and is still used in Cambridge, Massachusetts. For the U.S. House of Representatives and state legislatures, either STV in five- to nine-member districts or the additional-member system, a hybrid that combines geographical representation with a party list, would fill the bill.

Amy concludes his cogent treatment of electoral systems with a realistic assessment of the political prospects for PR in the United States. Procedural barriers that would have to be overcome are clearly identified, but the author correctly recognizes that the greatest barrier is the lack of public awareness of alternative electoral systems and the opportunities they could offer for opening up the political system. This book is a major contribution to building that awareness.

Kathleen Barber
Case Western Reserve University

George Kennan. *Around the Cragged Hill: A Personal and Political Philosophy* (New York: W. W. Norton & Company, 1993), 259 pp.; ISBN 0-393-31145-7 (paper).

The title of this book is taken from a poem by John Donne in which one must strive to reach "truth," which sits atop a huge, steep, and cragged hill. Others might apply this metaphor to their efforts to traverse the cragged hill of George Kennan's writings and speeches in order to identify a personal and political philosophy. It is the frustration and confusion of the latter that motivated Kennan to write this book. However, he readily admits that he has not succeeded where others failed and the book is less a struggle for truth than, in Kennan's words, "a collection of critical observations" and basic preferences that do not provide a consistent or coherent philosophy. Nevertheless, in addressing issues such as humankind's selfish nature, religion, governments, nationalism, foreign policy, and the problems facing the United States, Kennan does reveal an underlying set of values that are realist, conservative, and unabashedly elitist.

Kennan takes a dualist view of human beings as cracked vessels struggling between our more animalistic and civilizing tendencies. We are not perfectible but should do our best to address the problems and challenges we face. He identifies what he perceives to be the disturbing and crucial issues of our times and offers his view of how they should be approached. There is much here that is interesting, thoughtful, perceptive and provocative. Many will disagree with, if not be offended by, some of the opinions he offers. However, it is the degree to which Kennan seems divorced from, if not disparaging of, the social, economic, and political forces operating in the world today that make much of his analysis and many of his prescriptions seem naive and irrelevant.

He complains that America is too big, decries the emphasis on growth for growth's sake in economic policy, and fears the effects of immigration on our culture. He views the automobile, television, and advertising as evil "addictions" that are destructive to our social system. Egalitarianism breeds sameness and in appealing to the masses the leadership frequently plays to the lowest common denominator. He is concerned that automation and technological development have become separated from the qualitative improvement of life and bemoans the "monstrous expansion of cities and urban regions." He advocates free enterprise, but recognizes the need for the establishment of governmental regulation that corresponds to the size and importance of the enterprise. While we may share some of his concerns, at times he simply sounds like an old man longing for a past era (or at least his idealized vision of a past era), when America was smaller, less bureaucratized, and more homogeneous, when mass culture and influence was less pervasive, and when the elite were more respected and influential. Thus, he calls for breaking the federal structure into regional parts, limits on immigration, and the creation of a nine-person Council of State to study long-range problems and offer policy prescriptions.

The most recent election indicates that many share his sentiments about immigration and the federal government. Nevertheless, the implicit racism of his views on immigration is offensive. It is one thing to argue that there are limits to the population that America can absorb, it is quite another to compare our acceptance of immigrants who do low-skill menial labor to the dependency of Romans on barbarians to fill their military ranks. While he advocates the creation of regional structures, he does not believe this will occur and offers no real evidence that this structural change would be any better able to solve the complex problems facing the nation. Indeed, he contradicts his view that the grave problems facing America cannot be anticipated or confronted at the national political level when he advocates the creation of a Council of State to do just that. Kennan views government and politics as an unpleasant but necessary business and many would agree with this. However, he seeks solutions that assume we can avoid politics. The idea that we could avoid politics in the creation of such a nine-person advisory committee and that it really would be able to take a long-term, objective, nonpolitical (whatever that means when talking about political policies) view and recommend policies is dubious. Even if such a rarefied elite of people, who probably, like Kennan, would be out of touch with (and perhaps disdainful of) everyday life and people, could be selected, it is naive to assume that their pronouncements from on high could escape the political bargaining and conflict of other policy recommendations. Likewise, Kennan seems never to have considered that many of the problems we face, and poor policy choices we may have made that brought us to the situation we are in, are not simply the result of increased growth, population, and mass participation in politics but decisions developed and advocated by the very elite who now are assumed to be able to guide us into a better future.

Such views are not surprising when we consider that Kennan served this country so impressively in the field of foreign relations, which traditionally has been more of an elite decision-making enterprise. Indeed, the Council of State is comparable to the Policy Planning Staff headed by Kennan at the State Department. And it is in the sphere of America's relation to the world that Kennan is on sounder footing. He does disparage the struggle between domestic factions and the broader national interest that has caused too much attention to be given to what he describes as the sometimes sanctimonious advocacy of human rights. Arguing that just as people cannot be perfected, neither can governments and that over the long run people tend to get the form of government they deserve. While many will not share Kennan's views, the logic of his argument is more impressive than in his discussion of domestic politics. His concern with solving America's problems leads him to suggest greater focus on internal affairs and "very modest and restrained foreign policy." Arguing that America cannot solve the world's problems, he favors letting various regions accept more responsibility for their problems and favors multilateral institutions and actions over U.S. unilateralism. While recognizing the need for some changes, he nevertheless stresses our relations and alliances with Japan and Europe. He calls for an end to our fixation on nuclear weapons and downsizing of the defense establishment. He also wishes to streamline the bureaucracy and decision-making processes in the foreign policy field. He sees an improved and expanding role for the United Nations and one wonders whether recent events in the former Yugoslavia would cause him to reconsider whether multilateral institutions are capable of managing conflicts. Although one suspects that he might see such problems as unresolvable and not significant to the national interests of the United States.

As concerned, disappointed, and pessimistic as Kennan is in his analysis of America's ills, he continues to believe in this country and reflects a certain optimism about our ability to find answers to our problems. As George Kennan has traversed the cragged hill he finds the answer dependent on our civilizing tendencies being stronger than our animalistic ones and sees the elite as showing us the path to this.

Sandra Gubin
University of Virginia

Charles O. Jones. *The Presidency in a Separated System* (Washington: DC: Brookings Institution, 1994), xviii + 338 pp.; ISBN 0-8157-4710-1 (cloth); 0-8157-4709-8 (paper).

Quantification and specialization, two of the most pronounced tendencies in contemporary American political science, create particular problems for the study of the presidency. An institution centered around a small number of individuals supplies relatively few of the recurring patterns that practitioners of quantitative methods require. Political scientists of a strongly empirical bent tend to look elsewhere rather than wrestle with the complex interplay of individual, institutional, and political factors involved. Specialization, arising both from professional incentives and the organization of American politics courses, often results in disembodied treatments of the presidency, rather than works that place the institution within the constitutional system of which it is only one part. In this extraordinary study, Charles O. Jones provides an analysis of the modern presidency that is both resolutely empirical and systemic in scope. The result is a book that makes a compelling case for the view that the modern presidency—as it operates in the realm of domestic policy—must be understood in relation to the lawmaking capacities of Congress under the constitutional separation of powers, the complex representational activity that occurs through a system of separate presidential and congressional elections, and the constraints defined by the post-New Deal domestic agenda.

Jones begins by contrasting his "separationist, diffused responsibility" perspective with the dominant responsible party view that has been advanced by scholars such as James MacGregor Burns and James Sundquist, and adopted either explicitly or implicitly by many who interpret American politics in the news media. A perspective in which presidents set the national agenda through issue-oriented elections, win popular mandates, and govern with the support of party majorities in Congress, according to Jones, falls short both as a descriptive and as a normative model of the operation of the American constitutional system. Instead, he argues, analysts of the presidency need to be attentive to the diffused representation that occurs throughout the system, the constraints on presidential agenda-setting created by existing programs and commitments, and the variation in appropriate presidential roles and strategies associated with different political situations that occur across and *within* different administrations. Of particular importance are the variations in partisan politics that can and do occur within our constitutional forms.

In one of the most important conceptual contributions of the book, Jones defines four types of partisan interactions (partisanship, co-partisanship, bipartisanship, and cross-partisanship) and uses these categories to bring greater precision to our understanding of the range of patterns that have been present in interactions between the president and Congress and within Congress during the postwar years. The book then applies the separationist perspective to the presidents and presidencies from Truman to Bush. First, Jones looks at the interplay of personal, political, and policy factors associated with the beginning of each presidency. Different modes of assuming office, different personal qualities and political backgrounds, and different electoral and policy conditions, according to Jones, suggest a variety of governing strategies: assertive, compensatory, custodial, guardian, and restorative. What is striking is how rare conditions for assertive, partisan-based presidential leadership have been in the postwar era. Linking the empirical with the normative, Jones argues that our standards for evaluating presidents need to take these variable conditions into account. Next the analysis turns to the organizational side of the presidency, noting the inadequacy of conventional models (pyramid, spokes of a wheel) for describing the variation across presidencies. Here again Jones blends careful empirical analysis (and some ingenious figures documenting personnel changes) with normative argument, offering realistic assessments of problems all presidents encounter in managing the presidency and cabinet relations.

Before turning to the central matter of presidential-congressional interaction in lawmaking, Jones also addresses the influence of public approval on the presidency. Patterns in both long-term and short-term public approval of each of the presidents from Truman to Bush are analyzed. While acknowledging that the perception of strong popular support may enhance the president's bargaining position with Congress under certain conditions, Jones makes a persuasive case for his conclusions that the growing emphasis on short-term approval as a condition for presidential leadership is primarily a media-driven phenomenon, and that presidents are advised to pay greater attention to underlying political conditions and longer-term policy outcomes in developing governing strategies.

The real heart of the book is the analysis of presidential-congressional relations in chapters 5–7. Here, Jones begins with a critical discussion of the concept of a mandate, demonstrating that elections providing the conditions for conferring a mandate for presidential policy leadership have been the exception in postwar American politics. Jones argues that some presidents have had greater leeway in agenda-setting than others, but demonstrates clearly how each has had to work with Congress on a continuing agenda that evolves mostly independently of electoral cycles. In chapter 6, a theoretical framework for analyzing lawmaking in a separated system is developed, and previous empirical work on presidential-congressional interaction in lawmaking is surveyed. In a system in which the executive and two legislative bodies have different electoral/representational bases, work on a continuing agenda, may have different partisan configurations, and legitimately compete for influence, Jones argues that we should expect variable presidential participation in a lawmaking process that is continuous, iterative, representative, sequential, orderly, and declarative. Jones finds support for this framework in earlier studies of lawmaking activity (by Chamberlain, Moe, and Teel, and Mayhew), and offers a critical analysis of studies focusing on presidential support as measured in congressional roll calls. The latter, he contends, may be unreliable and focus too narrowly on presidential success rather than the more important question of systemic outcomes.

Chapter 7, entitled "Making Laws," is a masterful work of empirical political analysis. Twenty-eight major laws enacted during the nine presidencies are examined and categorized in terms of institutional participation (presidential preponderance, congressional preponderance, joint participation), degree of iteration, and patterns of partisan interaction. Consistent with the expectations of the separationist framework, major legislation was enacted under both unified and divided party control, and the majority (15) of the 28 laws involved significant joint participation by the president and Congress. Other significant findings are that a surprising degree of iteration or revision occurred at the floor stage in these cases, that patterns of party interaction varied widely, and that presidential support scores reported on these bills proved highly unreliable as indicators of presidential participation. Jones readily concedes that he has not necessarily chosen a representative sample of laws, and that his analysis involves numerous judgment calls on his part. These features of the study will undoubtedly be singled out for criticism by textbook empiricists and first-year graduate students, but these types of criticisms will miss the point that the force of the analysis lies in the substantive importance of the laws chosen and the unmistakable variation in presidential influence and partisan interaction that is documented. Suffice it to say that this part of the book will stand for a long time as the starting point for all future serious discussions of modern presidential-congressional relations.

In the concluding chapter Jones turns to the issue of constitutional reform, which has been a continuing theme in the works of presidentialist/responsible party advocates. Jones makes an original contribution to this debate by noting that evaluations of systemic performance need to take into account the problem of "policy escalation" as well as the more often discussed problem of policy stalemate. Jones suggests that reforms of the type favored by responsible party advocates are more likely to exacerbate the problem of ill-considered lawmaking driven by presidents seeking to reorder the national agenda in a very short period of time. The book concludes with a number of recommendations for presidents and reformers, the most important of which counsel respect for the true complexity of the constitutional system and the limits of presidential influence within it.

The careful empiricism and systemic scope of *The Presidency in a Separated System* make it an important and distinctive contribution to the literature on the American presidency. This book should be read carefully by all students of American politics and political institutions, and especially by those who seek to reform those institutions or explain them to others.

Randall Strahan
Emory University

Barbara Hinkson Craig and David M. O'Brien. *Abortion and American Politics* (Chatham, NJ: Chatham House Publishers, Inc., 1993), xi + 382 pp.; ISBN 0-934540-88-8 (cloth).

Abortion and American Politics is an informative and comprehensive analysis of both the moral and political dimensions of the abortion issue. The text focuses on the activities of major actors, including interest groups, state legislatures and Congress, the executive branch, the Supreme Court, and the public. Those who seek an answer to the compelling questions of how and why did abortion become such a divisive issue in American life will find it in *Abortion and American Politics*.

The first chapter discusses the landmark 1973 *Roe vs. Wade* decision. The authors also analyze earlier abortion cases that arose between 1943 and 1965. Usually these were dismissed because the plaintiffs lacked the standing to challenge state reproductive laws. Craig and O'Brien then examine the issues of standing, privacy, and reproductive freedom in *Roe*. Since the Burger court announced its majority opinion on the day of President Lyndon B. Johnson's death, the case received little attention initially. However, since 1973, the subject of abortion has escalated into a passionate one for those with both the pro-life and pro-choice stance. As stated in the text, interest groups that addressed abortion were virtually nonexistent before the late 1950s. Currently, numerous organizations file *amicus curiae* briefs in attempts to sway federal courts both in favor of and in opposition to restrictive laws. Also, tables in the text reveal massive increases in turnout for abortion marches from 1974 to 1989.

Abortion and American Politics is factual yet not too descriptive. Although many of the chapters have a heavy reliance on newspapers as a data source, the text is not lacking in analysis. The authors examine the often "surprising and ironic" decisions of the Burger and Rehnquist courts with emphasis on *Roe* and *Webster*. Just as scholars were surprised by the majority opinion in *Roe* due to Richard Nixon's four conservative appointments, others have described the conservative justices in the Rehnquist court as the "wimp block" out of disappointment that they have not more strongly upheld state laws placing harsher restrictions on abortion. Yet, many fail to realize that since the Burger court did not rule as expected in *Roe* and thereafter, there is no guarantee that the conservative majority on the Rehnquist court will overturn or narrow the scope of an established precedent. In the future, it will also be interesting to view the effect of President Clinton's two appointments and their position on the subject.

In their analysis of abortion as a political issue, the authors focus on activity in state legislatures and Congress as well as that of the president. Since Republicans now constitute the majority in Congress and in an increased number of state legislative bodies, it cannot necessarily be assumed that more restrictive federal and state laws will be passed. Yet it may be inferred that a higher probability exists of both their introduction and passage. Craig and O'Brien provide evidence that the Democrats appear as being more liberal on the subject of abortion. Democratic platforms usually take a pro-choice position while Republicans emphasize the right to life. For example, in 1984, the Republican party overwhelmingly supported President Reagan's anti-abortion views, his suggestion of a constitutional amendment, and his conservative Supreme Court appointments.

Since the 1970s, states have used a variety of tactics in their attempts to restrict a woman's right to choose. According to the authors, these include regulations on advertising and promotion; laws and policies to save the life of an aborted fetus (fetal-protection statutes); consent and notification laws (parental, spousal consent or notification); restricting public funding and use of public facilities. Many pro-life advocates have also lobbied before Congress for a constitutional amendment prohibiting abortions. Future research can build upon the *Abortion and American Politics* study and analyze the positions of female legislators, Republican and Democratic legislators (influence of partisan affiliation), and African-American and minority legislators, especially those who serve in the congressional Black and Hispanic Caucuses.

Abortion and American Politics leaves many other avenues for future research such as the willingness of many pro-life supporters to commit violent acts at abortion clinics. Recently, such has resulted in armed gunfire and murder at Florida and Massachusetts clinics. A crucial question for further examination concerns whether pro-life advocates are more likely to commit violence or does the media place more of a focus on their actions while neglecting those of pro-choice supporters.

Another subject for additional inquiry concerns the future relationship among abortion and presidential politics. In chapter 5, the authors discussed the actions of the Nixon, Ford, Carter, Reagan, and Bush administrations including the use of abortion in Republican and Democratic platforms during the 1980, 1984, 1988, and 1992 presidential campaigns. Ronald Reagan was the only president during this time to publicly oppose *Roe vs. Wade*. George Bush pursued the same strategies and tactics as the Reagan administration. It is difficult to ascertain Bill Clinton's stance on the abortion. Although he claims to be pro-choice, he is now taking a more moderate position on a number of views. If Clinton is defeated during his reelection bid by a conservative, a strong probability exists of a federal law or constitutional amendment making abortions illegal. An explosive situation would surely result as members of the public and pro-choice groups react to the constitutionality of abortions.

Concerning public opinion, Craig and O'Brien point out the problems with the numerous polls that seek to predict American views on abortion. Despite the many problems with public opinion polls, a heavy reliance is placed on their results. The authors state it thusly, "Ironically, the public opinion survey has become so commonplace in our society that questions about its utility and validity in the democratic process are all but ignored.... Polling is at best inexact because error can creep in at many points." Since the various polls often have differing results, Americans are even further confused and divided on the abortion issue. The probability may also exist of polls being manipulated to support the author's biases. In addition, the question arises as to ways to analyze views on abortion other than polls and whether these problems can be avoided.

In *Abortion and American Politics*, Barbara H. Craig and David M. O'Brien provide a thorough analysis of the relationship between abortion and American politics. The inclusion of clear and accurate tables and other useful information aids in making their text one of the most comprehensive ones written to date on the subject of abortion. It also leaves many research questions open for further discussion of one of the most divisive issues in American life.

Sharon D. Wright
University of Missouri

Gary Gereffi and Miguel Korzeniewicz, eds. *Commodity Chains and Global Capitalism* (Westport, CT: Praeger Press, 1994), xi + 334 pp.; ISBN 0-275-94573-1 (paper); 0-313-28914-X (cloth).

Sweet Honey in the Rock have an interesting song, "Are My Hands Clean," in which they trace the production path of a typical shirt from a Venezuelan oil field to Sears sales counter. This book is an extremely uneven effort to do the same from an academic perspective. The book is organized around three concepts appropriated by Wallersteinian world systems analysis from other disciplines: commodity chains, the constancy of change, and the importance of a systemic (i.e., international) perspective.

Commodity chains (CCs) are the interorganizational networks structuring the production of discrete final commodities. The textiles chain, for example, connects agriculture (fiber production) with a variety of chemical and mechanical industries (dying, spinning, weaving, garment assembly), with designers, advertisers, and wholesalers and retailers. The great strength of the CC approach is that it permits the analyst to evaluate precisely who has the economic upper hand in a given production process, and which organizations, to steal a phrase, control the commanding heights and by doing so the distribution of profits in a given chain. This focus on power and unequal distribution of profit distinguishes CC analysis on the one hand from typical business school analysis of the "value chain," like that of Michael Porter, and on the other hand from typical industrial policy research centered on manufacturing per se, like that of Laura

Tyson. These days, in the textiles chain, for example, manufacturing turns out not to be the dominant step in the chain. Current consumers are buying ephemeral image as much as concrete fabric. So control over information about the semiotic values consumers wish to consume, accumulated via proprietary retail outlets and realized via in house design, conveys control over the entire chain. In contrast a Porteresque analysis would only provide a listing of those factors contributing to competitiveness, and a Tysonian analysis would focus too closely on manufacturing itself.

The various articles in the book also stress the constancy of change and the need for historical perspective. In any given chain the production processes, technology, or organizational form that convey control change in response to changing technologies, labor movements, political intervention, and so forth. After all, through the nineteenth century manufacturing, not distribution, dominated the textiles chain.

Finally, the articles all stress the degree to which production is a global phenomenon, with production and distribution steps dispersed globally even if they are often concentrated in specific industrial districts. The book's strengths are geography, history, and the CC approach itself, which shows that "competitiveness," already recognized as something that cannot be accurately attributed to nations, hardly applies to sectors either. Instead, a great variety of regions, using a great variety of organizational approaches, have created competitive advantages in specific parts of the production process, sometimes with outside help or pressure, and sometimes endogenously. Looking at CCs thus allows for a more finely tuned appreciation of who stands to win and lose from trade and trade policy.

The articles themselves lay out the CC approach, then turn to a set of explorations focused on the organization of CCs, their geographical span, and the relationship between consumption and especially the deliberate organization of consumption and CCs. The strongest articles are by Gereffi, reiterating his work elsewhere on buyer-driven CCs; Erica Schoenberger, condensing—too much so—her fine work on how space and time increasingly affect competition; Hyung Kook Kim and Su-Hoon Lee on the South Korean automobile industry's place in the global auto industry; and Korzeniewicz on the Nike shoe company's metastasis inside the shoe chain. All of these demonstrate how control over design, distribution, and desire—the *shaping* of consumer preferences—mesh in ways that allow firms with no manufacturing capacity per se to extract the lion's share of profits from sales of a given commodity.

The book's major weaknesses emerge from the mechanical application of the world systems and commodity chain models. World systems writing has a tendency to substitute often ill-defined labels for analysis. And CC analysis sometimes falls into a narrow analysis of the value chain even though the whole purpose is to highlight the importance of politically constructed economic power. All these flaws characterize the weakest articles: a pair of extremely mechanical applications of world systems logic to the grain trade and ship building in the period before 1800; analyses of the service sector's role and the applicability of "fordist" and "post-fordist" production methods in agriculture which analysis got lost in jargon; and a statistical effort to assess the global distribution of six different commodities that seems to miss the whole point of the CC approach, namely, that the relationships among different organizations in the chain are what matter. These papers also display a very uneven level of research and writing, with some reading like little more than graduate student exercises. The grain and shipping chapters, which build off a research effort launched in 1986 by Immanuel Wallerstein and Terence Hopkins, are particularly disappointing.

The book has a failing generic to edited volumes, lacking cross-connections among chapters. It takes too much of a middle-of-the-road approach in its choice of cases. Rather than trying to pick one or at most two sectors and analyze all sides in order to show the connections between organizational formats, political structures, and international trade in-depth, or to analyze a wide variety of commodities to show the utility of CC analysis, the book does a bit of both. It concentrates on garments and autos, respectively buyer- and producer-driven chains, but also throws in services, shoes, drugs, and fresh fruit. The book also contains a number of grammatical and factual inaccuracies. For example, GM's Saturn factory in Tennessee is described as a Japanese transplant factory.

Overall the book seems like an effort to apply and confirm mechanically assertions made by Wallerstein, Hopkins, and Gereffi in previous (and better) work. At best it is suited for classroom use, as there is neither much original research here, nor enough elaboration of the conceptual apparatus involved in CC analysis to allow an uninitiated scholar to incorporate these techniques in his/her own work. In many ways it might be better to go back not only to the original articles on CC analysis but also to the original insights of Christian Palloix on the internationalization of capital and to Nicos Poulantzas's insightful, if turgidly formulated, analysis of how internationalization generated different types of bourgeoisie with very different politics and policy preferences.

Herman Schwartz
University of Virginia

Thomas M. Callaghy and John Ravenhill, eds. *Hemmed In: Responses to Africa's Economic Decline* (New York: Columbia University Press, 1993), xviii + 573 pp.; ISBN 0-231-08229-0 (paper).

When the subject of sub-Sahara Africa's (SSA) economic decline is broached, inevitably the question is asked: Who is responsible for such decline? Critics of the International Financial Institutions (IFIs), such as the World Bank and the International Monetary Fund (IMF), often put the blame on these institutions as well as the economically powerful Western industrialized nations. On the other hand, IMF and World Bank supporters and Western governments tend to put the onus on inefficient and corrupt political and economic structures in Africa. In *Hemmed In: Responses to Africa's Economic Decline*, the IFIs, the Western nations, and the African governments all share partial responsibility for the predicament in which Africa finds itself. Similarly, if the decline is to be reversed, all must be involved in helping Africa to become less "hemmed in."

In the Introduction, Thomas M. Callaghy and John Ravenhill note that the volume surveys the major economic, political, and social aspects of Africa's first decade plus of adjustment to derive lessons from African governments, the international financial institutions, bilateral donors, and all those who have an interest in the welfare of Africa's rapidly growing population, in short, those concerned with Africa becoming less "hemmed in" (p. 2). The volume is divided into thirteen chapters that include overall analyses of the continent, as well as country and sectoral studies.

In his chapter, "A Second Decade of Adjustment: Greater Complexity, Greater Uncertainty," Ravenhill posits that during Africa's first decade of structural adjustment, the World Bank and the IMF were experimenting with Africa, and therefore "learning by doing." The failure of structural adjustment in Africa caused these institutions to begin to reassess their assumptions, including the idea that the "initial prescriptions of short-term stabilization and getting the prices right" was the appropriate strategy to pursue to reconstruct African economies (p. 48).

Although acknowledging that structural adjustment has not worked to date in Africa, and that the context for economic growth has been weakened by structural adjustment, Ravenhill nonetheless feels that African governments have no alternative but to adjust because nonadjustment would result in even greater economic decline. For Ravenhill, the solution to this obvious conflict is that for the second decade of adjustment, the priority must "be to identify those elements that can be improved in the immediate future, and to provide the necessary finance to enable such improvements to be engineered" (p. 49).

Although Ravenhill provides a good summary of the first decade of adjustment in Africa, we learn very little about what can be done to alter Africa's economic decline. Will a modified IMF/World Bank structural adjustment model leave African countries in a more advantageous economic position during the second decade?

In his chapter "The IMF and the World Bank in Africa: How Much Learning?" Reginald Herbold Green feels that the IFIs can enhance structural adjustment in Africa if they transform themselves from being "Platonic Guardians" to "Pragmatic Partners." As the former, the IFIs see SSA "governments, other institutions, businessmen and select academics as, at most, junior warriors (to advise marginally and implement unqualifiedly) and the rest of the Africans (and academics) as workers who are to do as told for their own good" (p. 78). As part of this mentality, the Bank, for example, will not assume responsibility for bad advice it gives to member states, projects that are botched, or its failure to mobilize funding that it has agreed upon.

Green argues that the Bank must recognize not only the expertise that Africans have about their own countries, but also that often such expertise is superior to the Bank. Given the Bank's attitude toward African officials, perhaps we shouldn't be surprised at major problems with the implementation of structural adjustment programs.

Although Green, like Ravenhill, acknowledges that there is no alternative to adjustment, Green gives us more to ponder. For example, future strategies include examining "possible alternative paces, instruments, sectoral emphases, and social priorities within structural adjustment" (p. 82). Since in many African countries economic policy failure is a reflection of social and political pathologies, Green suggests that perhaps in some countries structural adjustment programs should be halted. The available resources for heretofore adjustment should then be given as humanitarian and survival assistance to the masses until political change occurs.

While the above is seemingly the logical thing to do, unfortunately it is not very realistic. In the first place, the IFIs and bilateral donors have not been successful to date in using the economic stick against African dictators. Such individuals have never exhibited concern about the suffering of the masses, and they tend to be able to continue to live lavishly as a result of the wealth they have accumulated, much of it taken from international financial flows slated for the masses. In the second place, delaying structural adjustment will leave these countries further marginalized economically.

In his chapter "Debt, Conditionality, and Reform: The Economic Relations of Economic Restructuring in Sub-Saharan Africa," David F. Gordon discusses how noncompliance with conditionality has contributed to the lack of economic reform in Africa. While the IFIs impose conditions on countries who agree to structurally adjust their economies, the reality is that the IMF and the World Bank have a limited ability to enforce conditionality. African governments therefore agree to structural adjustment knowing that they have no intentions of complying with the conditions. In the end, Gordon notes that, "what has transpired under conditionality-driven structural adjustment programs in Africa is thus not fundamental economic restructuring but 'partial reform.'" Using Asian and Latin American countries as models, Gordon suggests that fundamental reform will only take place in Africa when African leaders implement policy that goes far beyond what the IMF and World Bank suggest. Unfortunately, he may be correct in his assessment.

In the final analysis, Gordon feels that Africa has been "hemmed in" in a very peculiar way by donors and donor conditionality. They have done so "not by imposing inappropriate strategies or policies, but by substituting external pressure and financial resources for domestic leadership and an indigenous process" (p. 126).

The proverbial question of whether political liberalization is required in order to have economic reform, or whether economic reform is more likely under conditions that are less democratic, is discussed in the chapters by Naomi Chazan and Donald Rothchild ("The Political Repercussion of Economic Malaise") and Thomas M. Callaghy ("Political Passions and Economic Interests: Economic Reform and Political Structure in Africa."). In the former, the authors argue that political liberalization will greatly enhance the prospects for sustained economic reform.

Callaghy, on the other hand, argues that while the IFIs and Western governments tend to assume that political liberalization and economic structural adjustment are mutually reinforcing processes, that these assumptions may be incorrect. For example, Callaghy notes that "evidence from the Third World over the past decades, and now from the former Second World, does not support widespread optimism about the mutually reinforcing character of economic reform and political liberalization in a large number of cases" (p. 482). Political liberalization, if not handled properly, Gordon argues, could actually impede, rather than facilitate, Africa's chance of being relinked productively to the world economy. In a final note of caution, he refers to democracy as being risky, and often lacks brilliance and grandeur. African leaders interested in the maintenance of one-party political structures would certainly be pleased to read Gordon's analysis.

No doubt there is a significant difference between being on the outside promoting democracy and being on the inside attempting to implement it. Frederick Chiluba, who became President of Zambia in 1991, certainly knows this dilemma well. For example, in his 1991 inauguration speech, Chiliba stated, "The stream of democracy...is finally free to run its course as a mighty African river" (p. 520). Three years later, however, Chiluba was quoted as saying, "Maybe Africa was not really cut out for Western-style democracy.... How could a president get anything done with opponents constantly carping at him? Maybe the one-party state was the way to go, after all." Perhaps for the second decade of adjustment, attempts at economic reform under authoritarian one-party structures will be revitalized.

In the final chapter of the book, "How Hemmed In? Lessons and Prospects of Africa's Responses to Decline," Callaghy and Ravenhill discuss the "Back to the Future" vision that Western actors have for Africa, which "is an attempt to take African countries back to the 1960s, both economically and now politically, in order to start the development process over and do it right this time" (pp. 524-25). The vision that the industrialized democracies have for the world as a whole is of global transformation through the ballot box and the magic of the market. This vision, the authors contend, is flawed and will not be realized in many places in the Third World or the former Second World. Instead, "differentiation rather than convergence between regions and countries will mark the coming decade with confrontational rather than harmonious consequences" (p. 556).

In assessing how "hemmed in" Africa is, this volume does not give a promising future for Africa's second decade of adjustment. In the final analysis, as several authors note, it is ultimately up to African governments to reverse the economic and political decline of the continent.

Overall this volume captures the complexity of the social, political, and economic problems with which African governments are confronted. I therefore highly recommend that it be read by those seeking a greater understanding of the continent.

Margaret C. Lee
Spelman College

Steven R. Reed. *Making Common Sense of Japan* (Pittsburgh, PA: University of Pittsburgh Press, 1993), 188 pp.; ISBN 0-8229-5510-5 (paper).

This book begins with a commonly shared assumption that the Japanese are different from the Americans and the Japanese do many things that go counter to American common sense. Based on this premise, the author explores answers to two fundamental questions: How and why are the Japanese different? The two prime examples Reed cites are Japanese permanent employment, which makes no sense to American management or to American labor, and the cooperation between the Japanese government and business, which contradicts the basic American assumption that business and government are natural enemies.

In searching for answers to the key questions, the author rejects the cultural approach that attributes the Japanese "noncommon sense" behavior to different ways of thinking and different values of the Japanese. Reed argues that such a cultural explanation is not a real explanation but an admission of ignorance; it amounts to no more than saying that the Japanese do things differently from us because "that is the way they are." He dismisses the "mystical cultural explanation" as committing the "fundamental attribution error" and oversimplified stereotyping. He also maintains that the "Japan being culturally unique" explanation does not contribute to comparative analysis in political science. As a comparativist, the author is not in search of uniqueness but is interested in demonstrating that Japan can be understood by employing the same theories that explain other industrial democracies.

Reed, in fact, demystifies Japan by identifying common denominators that are applicable to Western industrial democracies. The simplest common denominator, the physical size of a country, reveals that Japan is not a small country but one significantly larger than the reunified Germany, Italy, and the United Kingdom. The author considers that Japan is situated "a bit north of France and just south of Germany" in terms of its levels of development and modernization. By showing that Japan is a "normal" country according to European common sense, he argues that America is a unique country.

Reed offers a "structural learning" approach as an alternative to the "culture as common sense" approach. He argues that behavior is determined by the structure, defined as "stable and repetitive characteristics of the actor's environment or situations." Behavioral patterns, in turn, are formed through the feedback between structure (independent variable) and behavior (dependent variable). As to the intervening variable between structure and behavior, Reed thinks that it is not rationality, as rational choice theorists would argue, but learning. According to the "structural learning approach," the actor adapts his behavior to specific situations and conditions through learning and, in this process, a stable set of rules is established. Reed applies this theory to two cases. First, he demystifies Japanese permanent employment by noting that the system is not a uniquely Japanese phenomenon, that employment is not really permanent in Japan, and that there is a continuum among industrial democracies from high job security to high-turnover systems. He demonstrates that the permanent employment system has evolved in Japan through a bargaining and learning process between management and labor. The structuralist generalizes that workers do not quit because there are concrete costs to quitting, while managers do not fire people because there are concrete costs to firing people. Once the system becomes institutionalized, it is hard to change, even if no one values the system as its stands.

Next, the author embarks on a structural explanation of Japanese government-business cooperation. Reed argues that the level of cooperation between government and business in Japan is much higher than in the United States, but not that much higher than in most other industrial democracies. He illustrates this cooperative relationship by introducing game theories: Japanese bureaucrats and business people have learned to deal with each other in an effective manner over a long period of time, through which a formula evolved that combines the best of self-control by business with the best of state control. It should be noted here that the author recognizes that nemawashi, or a consensus-building decision-making style rooted in Japanese culture, also explains cooperation between the two sectors.

The significance of this study lies in its endeavor to identify "common sense" factors that enable us to conduct comparative analysis of the "uncommon sense," Japanese way of doing things. By applying these common denominators to two cases, the author tries to demonstrate that Japan is not a mystical country but a normal nation, with a normal people living in it.

The problem of the book lies in the fact that the determinant of Japanese behavioral patterns is not as clear-cut as the author's structural generalization approach suggests. The fundamental problem is that overemphasizing structure as a determinant of behavior overlooks the role of culture as another determinant. The author defines culture as "the system of empirical beliefs, expressive symbols, and values that defines the situation in which political action takes place." He also views history as changing situations and argues that cultural repertoires that define conditions and situations change as well. His understanding of culture indicates that culture is a filter through which the actor sees situations and that culture is a determinant of structure. However, his structural approach does not clearly account for the linkage between culture and structure, or the distinction between the two. The reality is that culture is an integral part of the structural learning process and that both culture and structure closely interact with each other in the learning process. The author admits as much when he says that culture helps explain government-business cooperation. The point is that no single theory can fully explain behavior. In order to downplay culture, the author seems to have gone too far in the direction of structure.

The structural approach would have been more convincing had the author provided more cases, in which Japanese behavioral patterns are definitely shaped by structure rather than culture. Also, it would have strengthened the structural approach had he illustrated the cases in which two countries with different cultural constructs exhibited the same behavioral patterns in the same situations. Politically, Reed rejects being labeled either as a Japan basher or a Japan apologist. Instead, he argues that the goal of a political scientist should be to increase American understanding of Japan, although he quickly adds that understanding should not be equated with acceptance (as the Japanese would do).

In summary, the book offers an interesting alternative explanation to the cultural approach of Japanese behavior. This study accounts for Japanese "uncommon sense" behavior in ways that American common sense can comprehend. The author also provides an unbiased analysis of Japan by applying an objective analytical framework with a comparative perspective. His common sense approach, viewing Japan as a normal country, is a welcome addition to Japanese studies and to comparative politics.

Mayumi Itah
University of Nevada, Las Vegas

Dennis Dalton. *Mahatma Gandhi: Nonviolent Power in Action* (New York: Columbia University Press, 1993), xii + 279 pp.; ISBN 0-231-08118-9 (cloth).

James MacGregor Burns describes Mahatma Gandhi as the best modern example of a transforming leader. Unlike transactional leaders, such leaders transform the political imagination and the ethical and moral compass of those around them. Dennis Dalton's sensitive, sympathetic, and lucid book enriches our understanding of Gandhi as a transforming leader. A comparison of Gandhi with Martin Luther King and Malcolm X adds to the value of the book.

Swaraj and satyagraha are central concepts that guided Gandhi's political life. Dalton's elaboration of these two concepts is a valuable contribution to our understanding of Gandhi's view of freedom and power. Swaraj or freedom, for Gandhi, was not only about India's independence from British colonial rule. In Gandhi's words, swaraj means "self-rule or self-control." Satyagraha—Gandhi's term for civil disobedience—literally means truth force; Gandhi said that the way to swaraj is satyagraha: the power of truth and love." Satyagraha encourages reflection on one's actions and values not only on the part of those who engage in civil disobedience, but also on the part of those in authority. Thus, when Gandhi launched his programs of civil disobedience, he wrote to colonial officials, typically addressing them as "Dear Friend," informing them of his plans. A "please help, we both need it," quality to such pleas, as Dalton nicely describes them, are examples of how Gandhi sought to appeal to the shared humanity and morality of his adversaries.

In one of the blurbs on the book's jacket, Ainslie T. Embree calls Dalton's book "extraordinarily timely for an understanding of the redefinition of Indian nationalism that is taking place at the end of the twentieth century." In my view this otherwise valuable book does not quite keep up with that promise. It fails to do so because Dalton does not seriously engage the tensions between Gandhi's ideas and values and those currents that came to define India's nationalist movement. Dalton describes the tension quite well: "One might worship Gandhi from afar as a Mahatma or—as the alternative most Congressmen took—accept his judgements as 'policy' but not as a 'creed'.... (Each undermined Gandhi's thought and message for neither could give him support when the going became rough. At the very end, when it was indeed the roughest, Gandhi stood, tragically alone). My quarrel with Dalton is that he does not tell us in what sense and why Gandhi—whom official India regards as the "father of the nation"—stood "tragically alone" at the end.

Historians of modern India associated with the subaltern studies tradition have given serious attention to the tensions among competing themes within India's anti-colonial nationalist movement. Partha Chatteriee, for instance, in *Nationalist Thought and the Colonial World: A Derivative Discourse* (Zed Books, 1986), argues that the critique of modernity—that Gandhi articulated most effectively—was in conflict with the more limited goals of national independence and the quest for modernization and progress that came to define the nationalist movement.

The locus classicus of Gandhi's critique of modern civilization is *Hind Swarai* written in 1909. Dalton reserves some of his harshest language to describe this important text. In his "notorious blanket condemnation of modern civilization," says Dalton about this text, the "Simplistic categorization of Indian and Western civilizations respectively as 'moral' and 'immoral,' 'soul force' versus 'brute force,' presented a wholesale indictment of modernity, worse, a polarization into an attitude of 'us' and 'them' redolent of what Gandhi would later describe as 'violence of the spirit'." Dalton finds that Gandhi's argument is "grossly overstated, often misguided, and in some instances...lapses into pure fantasy." Dalton notes that Gandhi never retracted these remarks. But since he considers inclusivism the "hallmark" of Gandhi's "style," he interprets Gandhi's critique of modern civilization in *Hind Swarai* as the "high water mark of his exclusivist ideology...an uncompromising view of human experience [that] would later prove uncharacteristic of the Mahatma."

For subalternist historians such as Partha Chatteriee and Dipesh Chakravarty on the other hand, the critique of "modern civilization" in *Hind Swarai* is the part of Gandhi that animates his politics until the end. There is no evidence to suggest that there was a break between a youthful Gandhi and a mature Gandhi. It is this part of Gandhi that may explain why when the political battle against British colonial rule was almost won, Gandhi was alienated from the leadership of the Indian National Congress. Even though the modernizers who came to define India's anti-colonial nationalism may have been somewhat embarrassed by the anti-modernist Gandhi, there is no evidence that Gandhi himself gave up his critique of modernity.

Dalton's reading of *Hind Swarai* has implications for his analysis of Gandhian leadership. A major Gandhian moment in India's anti-colonial resistance was the Salt March of 1930. This and a second episode of Gandhian leadership—his fast in Calcutta to protest Hindu-Muslim violence in 1947—provide the foundation for Dalton's analysis of Gandhian leadership. Dalton discusses the remarkable "symbolism" of the salt tax issue. He cites Gandhi to the effect that "next to air and water, salt is perhaps the greatest necessity of life." Yet Dalton views Gandhi's decision to focus on the salt tax issue mainly as a masterful political stroke. Thus, he trivializes Gandhi's thinking on the subject describing one of his articles as Gandhi "waxing eloquent on some of his favorite themes," such as the destruction of the native salt industry. What "deserves to be underlined," writes Dalton, is "the symbolism of the issue," that "the image appears to be an outrageous injustice." But why is it only appearance? Why is it "symbolic" only in the nonconstitutive, shallow sense?

In my view the question of salt production touched the foundation of colonial rule in India.

Gandhi's attempt to build Indian political capacity by drawing attention to the persistence as well as the memory of pre-capitalist indigenous modes of production of salt outside the gaze of the modern state and of organized industry was not just smart politics. Here one meets the radical Gandhi who, unlike modernists of both the left and right variety, did not consider pre-capitalist formations to be simply a part of the "world we have lost," but unashamedly fought a relentless battle in their defense.

Dalton, incidentally, misreads an essay on Gandhi by subalternist historian Shahid Amin. Amin's essay "Gandhi as Mahatma" emphasizes how peasant perceptions of Gandhi in the Gorakhpur district were independent of the message that the congressional leadership wanted to bring to peasants. Peasant actions such as looting of shops, Amin points out, were often at variance with Gandhian ideas and methods. There were multiple readings of Gandhi, argues Amin. Yet Dalton reads this essay as evidence that Gandhi's message "had dug deeply into the popular consciousness"—precisely the view that Amin challenges.

To American readers the chapter "Mohandas, Malcolm and Martin" would be of special interest. Gandhi's influence on Martin Luther King, Jr., is well known. But Dalton makes an interesting connection between Gandhi and Malcolm X. Both struggled with "personal emancipation" and they wrote autobiographies that are about self-examination and inner growth. By contrast, Martin Luther King Jr.'s autobiographical *Stride Toward Freedom* "relates in impersonal tones the success of a method but without any journey of the self." Inclusivity, for Dalton, is the major theme in Gandhi. Swaraj, he says, is about "liberation from attitudes of political or social separateness that fosters ideologies of xenophobia and exclusivity." The book concludes on the note that Gandhi's life rested on the "premise of inclusivity, that we are all part of one another and violence retards that realization." In a world full of ethnic and racial conflicts, it may make sense to remember Gandhi's ability to transcend difference. But it is unfortunate that Dalton's emphasis on this theme had to be at the expense of obscuring Gandhi's critique of modernity in the colonies. After all, Gandhi and that other insider-critic of mainstream anti-colonial nationalism, Franz Fanon, had a lot to say about the false hopes of an emancipatory universal modernity coming to the colonies. To say that Gandhi was mainly about inclusivity is to miss his insights on what ails modern civilization especially in the capitalist periphery today.

If the Gandhian critique of modern civilization was sometimes "pure fantasy," as Dalton put it, that did not bother Gandhi. Indeed he relentlessly pursued that utopia, even if it meant that he had to stand "tragically alone" at the end.

Sanjib Baruah
Bard College

Jody S. Kraus. *The Limits of Hobbesian Contractarianism* (New York: Cambridge University Press, 1993), xii + 334; ISBN 0-521-42062-8 (cloth).

Predicting what great thinkers of the past would do in the present is a popular parlor and political science game. Many contemporary scholars believe they know what vocation Thomas Hobbes would have taken up had he lived during the late twentieth century. The Leviathan, they suggest, would have been a work of game theory and the social contract would have been conceptualized as a prisoner's dilemma. In *The Limits of Hobbesian Contractarianism*, Jody Kraus takes a skeptical look at contemporary neo-Hobbesians who use game theory to justify government. Although Kraus devotes some energy to elaborating the argument of the Leviathan, he is primarily concerned "with what can be said on Hobbes's behalf," and not with "what Hobbes said" (p. 36). To this end, his book studies in meticulous detail the work of three "'state-of-the-art, Hobbesian contractarian theori[sts]" (p. 37): Jean Hampton, Gregory Kavka, and David Gauthier.

Kraus clearly admires the work of the three theorists he discusses, but he does not believe that contemporary neo-Hobbesians have adequately overcome the problems that must be solved in order to provide an acceptable contractual justification for governmental authority. In particular, he identifies three problems with the works of Hampton, Kavka, and Gauthier. First, those theorists fail to solve the collective choice problem necessary to generate a set of authoritative rules out of the state of nature. Second, their theories tend to build their crucial conclusions into their description of the state of nature, thus begging the central questions that their work is supposed to resolve. Third, the solution to the prisoner's dilemma that neo-Hobbesian theorists reach would also justify states no one would want to live in. Indeed, this has always been the central problem of the Leviathan, that Hobbes provides as good a justification for obeying a liberal democratic legislature as for obeying a racist totalitarian dictator. More generally, Kraus points out, all contemporary Hobbesians have difficulty overcoming the naturalistic fallacy. At bottom, Hampton, Kavka, and Gauthier cannot deduce an "ought" from an "is," and they can reach "ought" only by sneaking that "ought" into their original presentation of the collective choice problem.

At first glance, *The Limits of Hobbesian Contractarianism* seemingly should appeal only to persons interested in game theoretic applications of Hobbes in general, and in the work of Hampton, Kavka, and Gauthier in particular. Such an impression, however is false. Kraus worked hard translating game-theory language into common English and for the most part he has succeeded admirably. As a result, any person interested in social contract theory will profit by reading his book. In particular, the opening chapter contains a wonderfully clear and thorough description of the three crucial elements of any social contract theory: the establishment of the original position; the way in which persons in the original position solve the collective choice problems necessary to form a social order; and the reason why actual persons ought to be bound by agreements reached by hypothetical persons in a fictional environment. This latter point is particularly important because, as Kraus points out, the more realistic the conditions of the original position and the inhabitants thereof, the more difficulty persons having solving the collective choice problems presented by the state of nature.

Kraus also does an excellent job detailing the various game theoretic problems presented by different versions of social contract theory. Political theorists unfamiliar with such problems as pure coordination games will have to read *The Limits of Hobbesian Contractarianism* slowly (there is much that experts will skim), but that reading will be rewarded. Unlike most works of the genre, Kraus writes for the reader who does not have any particular background in game theory. Before a particular problem in social contract theory is discussed, the work offers a detailed analysis of the various games that might be involved, an analysis that any intelligent student can follow. At no point will committed novices find themselves stranded without a guidebook in the land of formal theory jargon.

Of course, persons not very familiar with the writings of Hampton, Kavka, and Gauthier (i.e., this reviewer) may lack the grounding necessary to judge whether Kraus correctly states their arguments. Still, Kraus's arguments are clearly stated and quite intelligent. Even if the scholars critiqued may feel that their positions are not accurately stated, *The Limits of Hobbesian Contractarianism* does offer significant challenges for any theorist interested in devising a social choice justification for government. One does not have to be an expert on contemporary neo-Hobbesian theory to find thought provoking Kraus's insight that a prepolitical state of nature might differ substantially from a post-political state of nature (p. 68). This point is significant because, even if persons would prefer government to a prepolitical state of nature, conditions in a potentially milder post-political state of nature might prove more attractive to some rational persons than many governmental orders. Kraus's scholarly challenges to those who would reduce morality to rationality similarly requires no particular familiarity with the studies critiqued by his work.

That Kraus devotes virtually the entire body of his book to analyzing three prominent thinkers does, however, somewhat limit the appeal of his work. Readers less focused on Hampton, Kavka, and Gauthier will find the lengthy introduction to contract theory very stimulating, but are likely to be disappointed by the short ten-page summary of the general problems of Hobbesian contractarianism at the end of the book. More significantly, *The Limits of Hobbesian Contractarianism* is a work that always plays offense. We learn what is wrong with Hampton, Kavka, and Gauthier's efforts to take a Hobbesian approach to justifying government or morality, as well as something about the more general problems of Hobbesian contractarianism. Unfortunately, Kraus never plays defense and justifies a rival normative position of his own. This is important because no political theory may be able to stand up to the analytically withering attack that Kraus gives Hobbesian contractarianism. If this is the case, then the crucial question Kraus must explore is not whether there are limits to Hobbesian contractarianism, but whether those limits are more or less than the limits on other approaches to political justification. There is something, after all, to the quip that "democracy is the worst system except for all the rest."

These comments, however, are best understood as suggestions for future development than as serious critiques of Kraus's work. *The Limits of Hobbesian Contractarianism* is an excellent revised dissertation/first book. The author has mastered social contract theory, clearly demonstrated that mastery to the reader, and in a series of tightly reasoned arguments explains why previous arguments have failed to solve important political problems. All persons interested in social contract theory will benefit from reading this work. Like many first authors, Kraus plays it fairly close to the vest. Still, having demonstrated his scholarly skills, political theorists should look forward to future works that promise to be as scholarly, but hopefully a little more daring.

Mark A. Graber
University of Maryland

Henry J. Aaron, Thomas E. Mann, Timothy Taylor, eds. *Values and Public Policy* (Washington: The Brookings Institution, 1994), xiv + 216 pp.; ISBN 0-8157-0056-3 (cloth); 0-8157-0055-5 (paper).

For many decades the most influential policy science has been economics, and in their policy work economists have assumed that individuals' tastes and preferences are primary and stable and thus given. Although the core values and preferences have been assumed to be stable, policymakers could still affect behavior by changing incentives, especially economic incentives. Economists see that almost everyone prefers more money to less, so whatever their other preferences, people's behavior could be changed if the monetary costs and benefits of alternative courses of action were changed.

Since the end of World War II there has been no more prestigious home of policy economics than the Brookings Institution. One of the classics published there was Charles Schultze's *The Public Use of Private Interest*, which made the case for the incentive approach to public policy in an unusually powerful way. Schultze went so far as to assert that harnessing "the 'base' motive of material self-interest to promote the common good" was perhaps "*the* most important social invention mankind has yet achieved." Among the advantages of the incentive approach was the fact that it did not have to rely on "compassion, brotherly love and patriotism," which were in too short supply to be of much use.

Measures of this book's importance are its publication by Brookings and its questioning of the incentive approach to policy that has been so central to both economics and public policy analysis. The assumption from which the book starts is that the ordinary citizen who thinks that a better America will require changes in values, norms, and character is probably on to something. The book's contributors—political scientists, sociologists, and economists—all talk about and judge values, usually suggesting public policies that may change values deemed harmful and promote values considered desirable.

Jane Mansbridge's "Public Spirit in Political Systems" notes that patriotism or public spirit is not like other economic goods because its practice can create more public spirit in the public spirited themselves and in those who observe them. Without public spirit citizens would not vote and members of Congress would not "do their 'homework' in their areas of specialization." Since we need public spirit, political scientists should more often try to learn how to get more of it. For example, does serving on a jury promote public spirit, as Alexis de Tocqueville and John Stuart Mill thought? Mansbridge makes a case for perceived justice, political participation, and deliberation as causative forces.

Nathan Glazer's contribution on multiculturalism and education policy shows how hard it is to agree on a route to more patriotism and public spirit in a country where there is disagreement about whether Western thought and practice is the source of past glories or of present oppression. The teaching of history and social science is particularly difficult because conflicts cannot be solved by a simple rule such as "just tell the truth." Scholars differ about what is truth, or at least important truth, in history. In any case, social studies education has frequently, not just recently, shaded the truth in the service of national unity or civil harmony. While Glazer thinks the goal of civil harmony today overshadows truth and unity more than it should, he also thinks multiculturalism will not go away. He much prefers California's approach, which uses Martin Luther King to praise American ideals of equality and freedom, to New York's more divisive approach. Glazer sees the fears about multicultural schools as not unlike those about Catholic schools in an earlier era. Perhaps patriotism and national unity will emerge as easily from the current challenge because "[w]hatever the intentions of school curricula, American culture overwhelmingly leads to assimilation and homogenization."

Daniel Yankelovich's analysis of poll data suggests that there is still substantial American unity about many core values. For example, a substantial majority of Americans believe in freedom, equality before the law, equality of opportunity, fairness, democracy, the special moral status of America, and concern for the broader community. Americans respect the environment more than they used to and are far more accepting of blacks in their neighborhood and blacks or women in high office than they were several decades ago.

Other trends are more troubling. Whereas older Americans are much more likely to say that it is important to observe the rules over and above legal requirements, young Americans are much more likely to say that it is all right to look for ways to beat the system.

David Popenoe argues that Americans now value individualism, personal autonomy, and self-fulfillment so highly that social order is threatened. Popenoe's particular concern is the fate of the family, the institution that societies depend on to inculcate civic values such as honesty, trust, self-sacrifice, and personal responsibility. In the modern world Popenoe finds that "all available empirical evidence" shows the family structure that works best is the nuclear family with a male and a female living together and caring for the children. Children in single-parent families are far more likely to have emotional and behavioral problems. Divorce is a problem even if remarriage ensues since stepchildren are far more likely to suffer social deprivation than are children living with their biological parents. Popenoe thinks that less accommodating divorce laws for couples with children and better enforcement of divorced fathers' child support obligations would help. But he sees the heart of the problem as cultural. Married couples must increasingly come to believe that "they live in a society where marriage and marital permanence are valued."

James Q. Wilson's article on the underclass argues that changes in incentives cannot explain much of the increase in welfare dependency and crime in recent years. Criminality is strongly linked with weak impulse control and lack of empathy with others. Every society counts on the family to induce self-control and concern for others. The evidence suggests that families headed by never-married teenage mothers do not reliably perform this habituation function. We need better ways to socialize boys, and should experiment with "some combination of parent training programs, home visitations, preschool education, boarding schools, parental accountability laws, mother-child group homes, and criminal sanctions." Since some private organizations have had considerable success at changing underclass behavior and attitudes, Wilson thinks we should consider ways to direct public funds to such organizations.

Economists George Akerlof and Janet Yellen are convinced that community values are crucial to crime control in urban neighborhoods. Whereas in middle-class communities citizens usually report crime and criminals to the police, in low-income communities citizens frequently conceal information from the police. Akerlof and Yellen conclude their article with a brief mention of possible ways to generate stronger police cooperation norms in low-income communities, for example, strengthening churches and organizing citizen patrols. But returning to the Schultze approach, the article focuses on ways to affect crime-fighting norms indirectly, by changing incentives.

Low-income communities are less likely to side with the gangs than the police if the police less often chase and jail the wrong person. Fairer procedures and penalties will thus help strengthen tendencies to cooperate with police. So too will a more effective police force since the more likely the criminal is to end up in jail, the more likely witnesses are to risk retaliation by cooperating. Akerlof and Yellen also note that citizens in low-income communities may quite sensibly decide that success in defeating their local gang will just mean that a more violent gang in an adjoining neighborhood will move in. It would seem that a community's tendency to cooperate with police might thus be strengthened if the members of the most active and violent gangs were first brought to justice.

The collection of articles is of high quality. They were originally written for seminars involving commentary by major scholars—including some identified with the incentives approach to policy analysis (for example, Charles Schultze and Thomas Schelling). My only serious disappointment with the volume is that it does not include any summary of what must have been fascinating commentary and discussion.

Steven Rhoads
University of Virginia

Harold James and Marla Stone, eds. *When the Wall Came Down: Reactions to German Unification* (New York: Routledge, 1992), xviii + 351 pp.; ISBN 0-415-90589-3 (cloth); 0-415-90590-7 (paper).

The opening of the Berlin Wall on November 9, 1989, raised numerous questions. What would become of the two German states? Would they continue to maintain separate identities, even as they grew closer together, or would they merge into a single political entity? Of even greater urgency was the question of whether the two German states *should* be unified. What would be the consequences of unification not only for the Germans themselves but for Europe as a whole? Would it usher in a new period of instability and conflict? Or would unified Germany be a positive force for peace and economic development on a continent whose own division was only just being overcome?

Some of these questions have already been answered by subsequent events. The two German states were formally united on October 3, 1990, less than a year after the possibility had first presented itself that historic day in Berlin. Although unification occurred only after further dramatic developments and exhaustive negotiations, it appears in retrospect to have been all but inevitable. The lure of a better life in the West in combination with the moral bankruptcy of most East German political institutions left virtually no feasible alternative to a rapid merger almost entirely on West German terms.

Similarly, the normative issue of the desirability of unification quickly lost most of its original salience, if not its intrinsic interest. Germans on both sides of the former Iron Curtain today have much to complain about: higher taxes and recession in the West, severe unemployment and dislocation in the East. Yet there is no possibility of turning back the clock, and even some of those who had originally opposed a union later came to regard it as the correct outcome.

In contrast, the question of the implications of German unification for Europe and for international politics more generally remains highly relevant and continues to absorb the attention of numerous analysts. Some observers have detected an unsettling new tendency for unilateralism and assertiveness in German foreign policy, as evidenced by Germany's decision to recognize the break-away Yugoslav republics of Slovenia and Croatia in late 1991 and the Bundesbank's dogged insistence on autonomy in the realm of monetary policy, notwithstanding the stultifying effect of high German interest rates on economic growth throughout the region. Others, however, take heart in the German government's continued championing of the process of European integration, its steadfast support for NATO, and its leadership in efforts to promote political and economic reform in the East.

In the midst of this debate, *When the Wall Came Down* makes instructive reading. The book presents a wide range of reactions—more than 60 selections from 11 countries—first to the possibility and then to the reality of Germany unification. Covering the period from late 1989 through 1990, these views provide a valuable snapshot of opinion from that time of transition when so many of the old verities had been exploded and so much uncertainty about the shape of the future still existed.

Particularly refreshing are the selections that first appeared before it was clear that the opening of the Wall would lead to unification. At that juncture, several alternative outcomes seemed possible, or were viewed as desirable by various observers. While some of these selections, especially the advocacy of a "third way" between capitalism and authoritarianism, may reveal as much about the hopes of their authors as they do of the real possibilities inherent in the situation, others are remarkably prescient about how the unification process would unfold. And they all remind us of the important role that unforeseen conditions and events can play in shaping the outcome of even momentous political developments.

Of perhaps greatest relevance to contemporary debates, however, are the selections that address the question of Germany's likely future behavior on the international stage. At the risk of oversimplification, one might usefully divide these authors into two camps, the optimists and the pessimists, which in no way respected national boundaries. To the contrary, adherents of both groups could be found in the two German states, the United States, Britain, and elsewhere.

The optimists, on the one hand, saw little to worry about. Germany, in their view, had been fundamentally transformed following World War II. The sources of German expansionism and militant nationalism had been extirpated. In their place had taken root strong democratic institutions and values and a firm commitment to peaceful international cooperation among nations. Although a high degree of German economic influence might be expected throughout Europe, it would in fact be welcome in many countries.

The pessimists, on the other hand, found many reasons for concern. They questioned the resilience of German democracy, which had yet to be tested truly by economic adversity. Could these relatively young institutions withstand hard times? And what would be the impact of suddenly incorporating 17 million East Germans, who lacked any schooling in the finer points of democracy? They pointed to potential flaws in the German national character. Could one not discern in the period from 1871 to 1945 a certain predilection for authoritarianism? Some predicted a revival of German nationalism, resulting in a rejection of Western ties and perhaps even the rehabilitation of National Socialism and Hitler. Finally, the pessimists warned of the inherent danger of the concentration of so much national power in the heart of Europe. Would there not be a need for continuing external restraints? In short, German unification could easily have negative consequences for Europe.

Some of these concerns were probably without foundation, while others cannot be readily dismissed. Nevertheless, it is important to distinguish to the extent possible between the consequences of unification and those of the other profound changes that occurred in Europe concurrently. After all, Germany does not act in a vacuum but responds to the new opportunities and challenges presented by the decline of Soviet power and the reopening of Eastern Europe. As some of the contributors pointed out well before the breakup of the USSR, there was considerable potential for instability in the disintegration of the Soviet empire and the failure of political and economic reform in Moscow.

Taken together, these differing perspectives suggest the continuing need for careful analysis of the principle determinants of German behavior and the interactions among them. The selections indicate where some of these influences are likely to be found—in Germany's domestic political institutions, its political culture, and its external environment, for example—but they do not seek to evaluate them in any systematic way. Rather, much of the value of *When the Wall Came Down* lies in the spontaneous, unvarnished nature of many of the contributions, which help to capture the charged, yet confused atmosphere of the time. And although the selections are simply grouped by country of origin rather than being organized around central themes, they do successfully convey many of the hopes and fears that attended the unification process.

John S. Duffield
University of Virginia

Invitation to the Scholarly Community

The National Political Science Review (*NPSR*), a refereed publication of the National Conference of Black Political Scientists, is seeking to expand its contributor and subscriber base.

The *NPSR* was conceived with emphasis particularly on theoretical and empirical research on politics and policies that advantage or disadvantage groups by reason of race, ethnicity, or gender, or other such factors. However, as a journal designed to serve a broad audience of social scientists and humanities professionals, the *NPSR* welcomes contributions on any important problem or subject that has significant political dimensions.

The *NPSR* seeks to embrace the socio-political dimensions of all disciplines within the social sciences and humanities, broadly defined. Generally, the *NPSR* seeks to incorporate analysis of the full range of human activities which undergird and impinge upon political and social life and culture. Thus, in addition to contributions from political scientists, the *NPSR* seeks relevant contributions from historians, sociologists, anthropologists, theologians, economists, ethicists, and others. The *NPSR* strives to be at the forefront of lively scholarly discourse on domestic and global political life, particularly as disadvantaged groups are affected. While not meant to be exhaustive, the listing below is illustrative of the different areas of scholarly inquiry which the *NPSR* wishes to draw upon:

- Public policy (general)
- Health policy
- Social policy (general)
- Educational policy
- Science and technology policy
- Policy history
- Communications and media
- History
- Sociology
- Philosophy
- African studies
- Global studies
- Economics
- Criminology and criminal justice
- Race and ethnicity
- Gender politics and policy
- Anthropology and ethnography
- Public management
- Ethics
- Language and communication
- Religion and theology
- Law and legal studies

The *NPSR* welcomes conventional manuscripts as well as research notes on important issues. The *NPSR* is particularly interested in contributions that set forth research agendas in critical scholarly areas within the context of past scholarship and ongoing contemporary developments. In this regard, the editor encourages collaborative efforts by two or more contributors.

Manuscripts submitted for consideration for publication must not exceed thirty typewritten pages, double-spaced, inclusive of notes, and must be prepared according to guidelines that are available from the publisher. Four hard copies (with the author's name on one copy only) are required for the initial review. A 3.5" computer diskette is required for the final submission. Tables, figures, and graphs must be submitted in camera-ready condition upon acceptance for publication.

Correspondence and manuscripts should be sent to: Georgia A. Persons, Editor, *National Political Science Review*, School of Public Policy, Georgia Institute of Technology, Atlanta, GA 30332. Phone: (404) 894-6510. FAX (404) 894-0535.